The GOOD FOOD GUIDE

TO WASHINGTON AND OREGON

EDITED BY LANE MORGAN
INTRODUCTION BY MAUNY KASEBURG
PUBLISHED BY SASQUATCH BOOKS, SEATTLE

Printed in the United States of America

Cover design: Carol Davidson, TMA
Cover photographs: Barbara F. Gundle and Gregory J. Lawler/Small Planet Photography, Portland, Oregon
Interior design: Robert Dietz, TMA
Maps: Lisa Brower

Library of Congress Cataloging in Publication Data
The good food guide to Washington and Oregon: discover the finest, freshest foods grown and harvested in the Northwest/ edited by Lane Morgan; introduction by Mauny Kaseburg.
     p.   cm.
  Includes index.
  ISBN 0-912365-50-1 : $14.95
    1. Marketing (Home economics)—Washington (State)—Guidebooks.
2. Marketing (Home economics)—Oregon—Guidebooks. 3. Pick-your-own farms—Washington (State)—Guidebooks. 4. Pick-your-own farms—Oregon—Guidebooks.
5. Cookery. I. Morgan, Lane, 1949- .
TX356.G66 1992
630' .2094795–dc20   92-8504

Published by Sasquatch Books
1008 Western Avenue, Suite 300
Seattle, Washington 98104

CONTENTS

INTRODUCTION

When I teach a class, students frequently ask me if my mother was a good cook—is it from her that I developed my passion for good food? Like so many Baby Boomers of the 1950s, I experienced the age of frozen TV dinners, white bread, and peanut butter, and my earliest culinary memories are of Mom's everyday cooking: the tuna fish dish, macaroni and cheese, chicken and rice (cooked in a big, black iron pot that I now braise short ribs in). But here and there memories surface of the foods that grew around us in the Northwest and the special meals we enjoyed—pheasant cacciatore, Caesar salad with fresh romaine, cherry pie, salmon, and berries galore.

So, to help me sort memory from myth, I called "The Source": my mom, Blanche Carter. My mom and I reminisced about food and my youth. Unlike many children, I was not only allowed in the kitchen but given free rein to create. My mother was a good cook and she allowed free expression. But as we talked about her pies made with fruit from the old cherry tree in the backyard, which my sisters and I loved for its substantial climbing branches as much as for the luscious, translucent pie cherries it yielded, I realized that my family had never sought out regional foods; they were simply always there, a part of life itself.

My sisters and I grew up on a beach near Bremerton. All summer we'd make our way down the steep bank where huckleberry bushes thrived. In the fall, we'd be sent down with kitchen pans to fill with the deep purple berries, which Mom would turn into little jars of jelly, sealed with melted wax.

We dodged clam "geysers" as we walked around the mud flats, and found Pacific oysters as big as a woman's size 5 shoe—big not because of age, but because of all the nutrients in the bays. We threw these foot-sized bivalves on the barbecue or chopped them up for oyster stew. The oysters were really Daddy's domain. He'd use heavy gloves and a beige-handled oyster knife to wrestle with these mammoths.

Along the beach, blackberries and crabapple trees grew out over the sand. Mom remembers sitting on the beach with her three girls one summer day. Pretty soon, my little sister Margy and I toddled off. When Mom realized we were missing, she and my older sister, Marilyn, quickly set out to find us.

Mom found Margy and me up the beach, alternately stuffing our mouths and our pockets with beautifully ripe blackberries.

Then there was the requisite barbecued salmon stuffed with onions and sliced tomatoes whenever out-of-state visitors arrived. I'm sure we whined about not having hamburgers. Little did we know that people in more sophisticated places paid top dollar for fish we thought less worthy than ground beef. But now that I frequently pay the Parisian price of salmon, I have a newfound appreciation of those summer silvers that seemed as if they would never stop running.

After our family spent two-and-a-half years in Germany and experienced outdoor markets and an abundance of local specialties, Mom and Dad returned with a strengthened respect for Northwest foods. While some mothers nipped sherry, my mother now nipped Gai's French bread with fresh butter (in that margarine era), avocado, Roquefort, and garlic. This is probably what sustained her through days of taking care of three girls born close enough together to subject her to years of endless adolescent hair trauma!

It was after our years in Germany that I remember driving with Daddy to the site of a winery that had fallen victim to the early years of Prohibition. He'd pick up a station wagon full of Zinfandel grapes shipped up from California; at the time, eastern Washington's soil was still primarily devoted to apples and wheat. Soon, the smell of crushed grapes filled our basement, along with the inevitable plague of fruit flies, and bottle after bottle of the finished product was carefully stored in our bomb shelter-cum-wine cellar.

In late fall Mom and Dad would rendezvous with friends near Prosser, for a week of pheasant hunting in the sugar beet fields. The pheasants were brought back and plucked in the carport, the breasts boned and frozen, and the smaller feathers turned into beautiful Jackie Kennedy–type pillbox hats (my mother is very artistic).

It was not until I returned to La Varenne in 1977 that I came to appreciate the produce of the Northwest from the perspective of a professional cook and gourmand. And while I am saddened that the farms of my youth have been pushed farther and farther away from the urban areas and that the existence of all the good things I took for granted seems a little more fragile, I am thrilled with the ongoing popularity of regional foods. The cherry trees and the salmon and the farms are still here, and the Northwest remains one of the richest food-producing areas in the world. It is filled with superior things to eat and people who truly appreciate them. Let *The Good Food Guide to*

Washington and Oregon introduce you to them all. You'll remember how much better everything tastes when you discover it yourself. You may see an old hometown favorite celebrated here, or perhaps a tempting discovery you never realized was just a few minutes down Interstate 5. You may even take a fresh look at your own backyard.

Now, it's your turn to build memories and myths of your own.

Mauny Kaseburg
Seattle, Washington

ABOUT THIS BOOK

There are basically two kinds of farms in Oregon and Washington. The huge ones ship billions of dollars of products worldwide, making agriculture the biggest industry in the two states. But the fresh vegetables and berries, the pure honey, the milk and goat cheeses that make the Northwest famous for its food come from small operations that serve local markets. This book is a guide to the priceless bounty harvested on these small farms and a tribute to the men and women who devote their energy to working the fields and the sea.

Growing produce for the local market is hard, grimy, intermittently profitable work. It takes a daunting combination of skills: the ability to work, as the old-timers say, "from can't see to can't see"; to grow, gather in, and market a variety of crops; to forecast trends and charm customers; to repair a tractor and arrange a bouquet. I tried it and I didn't last long. But I haven't forgotten the allure or the challenge of the work.

Farmers get to work outdoors in beautiful settings, even if they seldom have a chance to stop and admire the view. They can set their own hours, even if those hours are endless. They have the privilege, increasingly rare, of producing something that is unequivocally useful. They can see a project all the way through, from planning to planting to sale.

Fisherfolk, oyster growers, and other food producers share the same privileges, and also face many of the same vulnerabilities. Growth and development aversely affect both sea and soil even as they increase the demand for local food. Those who fish our waters, for example, suffer the consequences of red tides, overfishing, and loss of marine habitats. Such vicissitudes, both natural and manmade, hurt the producer more than the consumer. If one year a Northwest apple crop fails, after all, we shoppers can buy our fruit from New Zealand. But in the long run we all suffer. Once an apple orchard is cut down and paved over, it is gone for good.

Successful regional food production must be a true partnership between producer and consumer. The producer must supply what people want, reliably and at a reasonable price, and consumers must appreciate—and pay for—freshness and quality. When you've been out in the dank October dawn to pull up leeks that have been taking room in the garden since April, rinsed off the clinging mud in icy water, trimmed, bunched, and boxed the leeks (and the shallots, and the cilantro, and the kale), driven 25 miles to market, set up your stand by 9am, and spent the day dispensing cooking advice and friendly smiles, you really don't want to hear that you should charge less than the discount supermarket because you're eliminating the middleman.

I remember listening to an urban visitor complain about a farmer who told her she could not pick a few pints of raspberries on a Labor Day weekend. Conditioned by imported treats year-round, she couldn't grasp the idea that a seasonal berry is only available in season. "You would think they'd want to make a sale," she kept saying.

Well, they do. Every sale made on the farm or at the farmers market is more than a financial transaction. It is a commitment on the part of both producer and customer to keep our farms thriving. It is an appreciation of our region's unique characteristics. This guide is designed to further the partnership, both for tourist and local. We hope you will travel our back roads, pick a row of blueberries, and sample cheese made from cows you can meet in the pasture. We hope local people will explore the food and farm economy at their doorsteps, both to eat well and to learn to treasure the bounty that surrounds us.

The book is divided into nine regions that roughly correspond to the distinct food-producing areas of the two states. Essays introduce the singular agricultural landscapes of the regions and profiles of producers help convey how our food is grown and harvested. Recipes encourage you to sample regional foods. At the end of each chapter you'll find county-by-county listings of local producers and farmers markets. These listings will lead you to great food and friendly people. (Remember: It's best to call the night before when arranging a farm visit. Farmers tend to be outdoors during the day.) If you have never eaten fresh strawberries bought from a grower on a cool Saturday morning in June, you may have missed a taste of the best of the Northwest.

This is only a sampling of the thousands of Northwest producers. Some asked not to be listed because they sell all they produce to longtime customers. Others we might have missed. We invite you to use the form at the back of the book to tell us about your favorite farm, fishmonger, market, or dairy.

Dozens of people helped gather the information here. Of all their labors, Emily Hall's were the most prodigious. This book would not exist without her research and her hundreds of phone calls. Sincere thanks also to Anne Depue at Sasquatch Books, whose patience and optimism are contagious, and to Sarah Beaumont who helped Emily with the phone calls. Farmers and their friends were generous with time and information. In particular I would like to thank Woody Deryckx, Gretchen Hoyt, Teri Pieper, John Doerper, Margaret Hollenbach, Joan Herman-Fencsak, Julie McFarlane, Sandi Fein, Camille Greb, Graham Vink, Jim Thompson, and Schuyler Ingle.

Lane Morgan
Sumas, Washington

NORTHWEST WASHINGTON AND THE SAN JUAN ISLANDS

In northwest Washington's corner, nearly every vista offers startling juxtapositions. Saturated hues of scarlet tulips and golden daffodils shimmer in geometric patches under the leaden skies of the Skagit Valley. Flamboyantly patterned Holstein cattle browse before a background of second-growth firs. Gnarled apple trees grow next to wind-bent madronas on the slopes of the San Juan Islands. Agriculture is the region's dominant industry, with more than 2,000 commercial farms and thousands more backyard enterprises, and its variety makes every road trip unpredictable. The view around the next corner could be the arched canes of raspberries, or a suburban yard covered with gill nets spread out for mending, or an ocean of yellow flowers, humming with the bees that turn blossoms into cabbage seed. The river valleys of the Snohomish, Stillaguamish, Skagit, and Nooksack support some large farms with international markets, and hundreds of smaller holdings are tucked into upland pockets in the Cascades and among the spreading mazes of storage buildings and housing developments.

Sculpted 10,000 years ago by the retreating Vashon Glacier, the region has been rearranged ever since by periodic flooding. The glacier left deposits of gravel, clay, and silt, and hundreds of landlocked lakes. As they slowly silted in and dried, the lakes created fertile natural prairies. The more porous, gravelly soils eventually supported forests of giant conifers. Rivers carved new westward routes from the Cascades through the glacial valleys to the swampy deltas at their mouths.

The first human settlers, probably immigrants from inland native cultures, followed closely behind the melting glaciers. They tended the prairies by periodically burning off grasses to favor bracken ferns, edible bulbs, and berries. When eighteenth-century Spanish traders arrived with potatoes—which they in turn had received from the Incas—Northwest natives raised them too.

But the most reliable sustenance came from the water. Warmed by the northerly sweep of the Japanese current, the coastal waters yielded tremendous catches. Low tides uncovered a banquet of shellfish, and salmon were so abundant during spawning season that later immigrants forked them from the creeks to fertilize their fields. By the turn of the century, giant salmon canneries processed the haul from local traps and gill nets. Although much depleted, the waters of northwest Washington still support important commercial fisheries in salmon, crab, herring roe, and less familiar catches, including sea urchins and sea cucumbers for export to Asia. Seafood farming of salmon and shellfish is also receiving more attention as wild stocks dwindle.

Commercial agriculture was slower to develop here. The real lures to settlement in most of northwest Washington were canneries, mines, and mills, and the first settlers grew only enough to feed themselves. By the early 1900s, coastal farmers could send their perishable produce to market on the Mosquito Fleet of small steamers that swarmed from port to port along Puget Sound and the northern waters, but inland growers had to wait for the coming of farm roads and highways before they could raise crops on a commercial scale.

Except for those who were able to buy or bully the Indians off the prairies, would-be farmers also had to log before they could plant. Many who reasoned that the soil that could grow a 200-foot cedar would produce gargantuan vegetables found themselves destitute on a plot of stumps. But luckier immigrants uncovered productive bottomland. The cultivation of river-bottom land began with prodigious labors of diking and filling, using teams of horses wearing wooden shoes the diameter of footstools to stay on top of the muck. Even after all the effort, the floodplains still flood.

Floods and dikes were nothing new for Dutch immigrants, however, and

beginning in the 1890s, Dutch families established northwest Washington as one of the premier dairy areas in the nation. With more than 300 dairies, Whatcom County is the largest milk producer in the state of Washington. Most local dairy farmers belong to the giant Darigold cooperative, but a few independents market their own milk and specialty cheeses. Both Pleasant Valley Goudas (see "Pleasant Valley Cheese") and Appel farmers cheese are produced on family farms near Ferndale.

Commercial berry production also began at around the turn of the century. Raspberries and strawberries are the major crops, followed by blueberries and less familiar varieties such as marionberries and loganberries. Raspberries in particular like rich soil, cold but not frigid winters, and warm but not blazing summers. Few places provide that combination so reliably as northwest Washington river valleys, producing fruit that is delicate but not mushy, sweet but not insipid. A fifth of the raspberries eaten in the United States come from Whatcom and Skagit counties, a statistic that presumably does not include the tonnage consumed by thousands of U-pickers who snack their way up and down the rows each summer. Most of the berries end up at the processors, where their special regional characteristics are lost, but incomparable fresh fruit is available from July through September. Beginning with strawberries in mid-June and continuing through raspberries, blueberries, sweet corn, and pumpkins, roadside stands pop up like mushrooms during the harvest season. Many operate on the honor system, staffed only by a price list and a coffee can.

Apple orchards were especially popular in the San Juan Islands, until they were forced out of business in the teens and twenties by the irrigated orchards east of the Cascades. In the last decade, however, westside apples have made a comeback. The cooler nights of northwest Washington alter the apple's balance of sugar and acid, producing fruit with a more complex flavor than that of the classic but often bland Red Delicious.

Chickens also thrive in mild weather. Draper Valley Farms, near Mount Vernon and Bellingham, produce some of the freshest fryers in the Northwest. Backyard egg flocks are common, and fresh eggs are sold along many rural roads. Alert travelers can also spot honey stands, flourishing blackberry patches, and even roadside patches of wild mushrooms. I once harvested a dinner's worth of morels from a planter strip in front of a Bellingham car wash.

Winters here are long, dark, and wet, and spring is completely unpredictable. The period from mid-July through October has the most reliable weather and the best selection of produce. Even during the intoxicating days of late summer, the season is dominated by the rains before and the rains to come. As crops race through the long northern days toward maturity, the moist breath of transpiring greenery cools the air beside the road. Sweating behind the dusty horses in an August hayfield, listening to the jingle of harness as the team shakes off flies, I can feel the dampness collecting just around the bend of the season.

Even as my haying partner tosses gold-green bales on the wagon, salmon are congregating at the river deltas, waiting for the downpour that will signal the beginning of their upriver journey. Mushroom spawn is twining through the duff under the firs, ready to erupt into chanterelles and boletus. In another couple of months, lowlanders will be pacing the dikes and ditches, wondering if their peas and pasture will return to swamp this year. Farmers cultivate the land here, but they will never truly control it.

Lane Morgan
Sumas, Washington

ALM HILL RASPBERRIES

Ben Craft and Mercéd Garcia are sorting raspberries by the cooling shed. Despite an unusually soggy spring and summer, the berries are big and firm. The men pour the berries gently across their hands, culling any that aren't perfect. As they work, more flats come down the hill from the six acres of berries above. One of the workers carries the boxes on his head in the style of his home village in Michoacán, Mexico. Within two hours of being picked, the berries will be in a forced-air cooler, and by next morning Alm Hill Gardens raspberries will be on sale at Pike Place Market and a few Seattle grocers.

Raspberries are an extremely perishable crop. Unlike strawberries and tomatoes, which can both be picked underripe and still look good enough to sell, the only harvestable raspberry is a ripe one. And once picked, they spoil fast. One moldy berry can ruin a box within a few unrefrigerated hours.

Raspberries grow biggest and best where summers are mild, but that same misty weather makes them vulnerable to rot. Partly for that reason, more than 90 percent of commercial raspberries in Washington State (which grows over half the national raspberry crop) end up at the processors. Most growers feel they can't take the risk of not selling their crop in the narrow window of time between ripe and rot.

But Ben and his wife and farming partner, Gretchen Hoyt, have taken another route. By growing locally adapted varieties (primarily Meekers and Chilliwacks), picking and sorting with extra care, and cooling promptly, they produce berries that will keep fresh and firm for four days, without the use of fungicides that are prevalent on most berry farms. Only their fall berries, which ripen as the days grow shorter and the morning dew is heaviest, need a fungicide to ripen properly. Ben and Gretchen keep their acreage small and pay their picking crews by the hour instead of by the pound so that they can concentrate on quality rather than quantity. Since their sandy hillside soil is not as fertile as the river-bottom farms where most raspberries are grown, they also pay particular attention to fertilizing.

Ben is a local boy, the son of a dairy farmer. After a tour in Vietnam, he returned to the 30 acres he had inherited outside of Everson, started building a house, and went to work for a local cannery. Soon he met Gretchen, who had grown up near the raspberry fields of the Puyallup Valley and wanted to farm.

Cannery prices for berries were good in the early 1970s, and Ben's boss told him raspberry growers were clearing $12,000 an acre annually. "Not being greedy or any-thing, I went home and put in two acres of berries," Ben said. "I figured to make $24,000 from a six-week season."

Ben and Gretchen mulched the new canes with seaweed, hauled in truckload by la-borious truckload from the coast 20 miles away. The next spring, 120 neighboring cows went through their fence, trampled the berries, and ate all the seaweed. "That's when I first began to suspect that it might not be so easy to make $12,000 an acre," Ben said, but they persevered.

By the early 1980s, Ben and Gretchen had settled into the grueling schedule of the truck farmer. Up at 5am to pack the car and get to Pike Place by 8, back home at 8pm, just in time to do chores before bed. The summer raspberry season is short, so they added spring peas, summer basil, fall pumpkins and potatoes, Christmas wreaths, and three seasons of flowers to their production. In 1985, they began selling berry vinegars in addition to fresh fruit.

Years of experiments in Gretchen's kitchen have resulted in recipes that make the most of the fruit flavor. Unlike many berry vinegars that have about as much berry as a dry martini has vermouth, hers are at least one-quarter juice. One proof is in the color of the vinegars. The raspberry vinegar is a deep port red, and the blackberry and blue-berry vinegars are nearly opaque. The juice is steam-extracted rather than boiled and strained. The steam process takes more time since batches are small, but the result-ing taste is fresher because the berries are not heated for long. Alm Hill vinegars have a distinctive fruity sweetness. Like balsamic vinegars, they are mild enough to use alone and flavorful enough to carry a dish.

Berry farms are going out of business throughout northwest Washington, pushed out by development, slumping cannery prices, and new regulations on labor and farm chem-icals, but Ben and Gretchen are looking to expand. Why are they thriving while others are not? Getting free of the canneries is one reason. And since they never used most of the roster of pesticides and fungicides many growers depend upon, they don't suf-fer at giving them up. Ben also credits their work crew. "We got lucky," he says, "and we go out of our way to make up in other ways for what we can't do financially." Friday night dinners with the crew are a ritual, with the entrée alternating between Mexican and Northwest recipes.

And being small has its own advantages. "Maybe it's not always bigger is better," said Ben. "We have total control and we can maneuver fast. When the market changes we can respond right away."

Lane Morgan

RASPBERRY SNAP PEAS

Fresh peas need little accompaniment. The trick is to get them in the pot as soon after harvesting as possible. Fortunately, snap peas don't need shelling.

½ pound snap peas, washed and ends with strings removed
3 to 5 tablespoons raspberry-wine vinegar
2 to 4 tablespoons sesame seeds, toasted

Steam snap peas until tender-crisp. Splash with raspberry-wine vinegar and toss until vinegar coats peas evenly, then sprinkle with sesame seeds.

Makes 2 to 4 servings.

Alm Hill Gardens
Everson, WA

Alm Hill Gardens
Ben Craft and Gretchen Hoyt
3550 Alm Road
Everson, WA 98247
(206) 966-4157

Mid-March–December: informal hours, call ahead.

Alm Hill Gardens berries are sold at Pike Place Market and in some Seattle QFC stores from June through September. The vinegars are available at the Market, by mail order in cases of 12, or by appointment at the farm.

Go east out of Bellingham on the Mount Baker Highway for about 15 miles, then take Highway 9 north for about 10 miles. Look for signs for Sumas, then Nooksack; they're on the first road to the right past Nooksack.

WHIDBEY FISH AND WHIDBEY PIES

Located in the small community of Greenbank on Whidbey Island, Whidbey Fish is a funky landmark of good fish and good food. Greenbank is a laid-back community on Highway 525, midway between Langley and Coupeville. Sweeping views of the Cascades to the east and the Olympics to the west are one benefit of its location on the narrowest portion of the island. There isn't much to Greenbank. Whidbeys Greenbank Loganberry Farm is to the north, and the Meerkerk Gardens are to the south. In between are the Greenbank General Store, the post office, and the real estate office on the west side of the highway. Sitting alongside them is Whidbey Fish.

Tom and Jan Gunn opened Whidbey Fish in the spring of 1986. As a child, Tom spent many summers on Whidbey Island, where he learned how to fish with his uncle at Dines Point. After a colorful career as a student and a memorable term as student body president at the University of Washington, Tom and his wife fled Seattle for a more peaceful, bucolic life on Whidbey Island. But the Gunns found one thing missing. Good fresh fish. They soon opened Whidbey Fish in an old mustard-colored cinder-block structure that Tom describes as "the ugliest building on Whidbey Island." Its former tenants included a laundromat, a welding shop, and, most recently, a tattoo parlor.

Whidbey Fish sells and serves a variety of local and international fish. For their halibut, salmon, ling cod, and crab, the Gunns deal with fishermen out of Whidbey, Blaine, Port Townsend, Neah Bay, and Aberdeen. Mussels are from nearby Penn Cove, and the oysters are raised by Erin and Walter Ruthensteiner's Neptune Sea Farms, located at Honeymoon Bay south of Greenbank. The Gunns dig their own clams for their chowder.

Along with the wide array of fish, specialty items at Whidbey Fish include chowder, crabcakes, smoked salmon, and loganberry pie. The Gunns have recently built a new smoker next to their house, inspired by Tom's journey to Scotland to study smoking techniques. Tom feels that smoking salmon is an art, not an industry, and is best done on a small scale. Jan's specialty is pies. She uses only organically grown berries, usually from Case Farms in Oak Harbor, which has been in business for three generations. Jan's loganberry pies can be purchased whole for $8 or by the slice for $3. Seattle shoppers can buy them frozen at Larry's Market.

Whidbey Fish sells fish and serves lunches and dinners Thursday through Monday in the summer, Friday through Monday in the winter. Hours can be variable, so it's wise to call first. "The ugliest building on Whidbey Island" has not been yuppified. The fish tanks are outdoors, the rest room is around the side, and the Gunns have yet to sell an espresso. Homegrown art and photographs line the walls. Expect to sit family style with people you don't know. Or pull up a chair at the bar, where you can talk to Tom or Jan as they prepare your food. There you can read customers' accolades, ranging from a thank-you letter from UW Husky football coach Don James to a postcard from author Calvin Trillin and his wife, Alice. There's even an original Gary Larson cartoon proclaiming, "I love the oysters at Whidbey Fish."

Don't miss the Monday Night Fish Feed. A recent sampling included prime silver salmon, halibut, Penn Cove mussels, Honeymoon Bay oysters, Dungeness crab, prawns, and seafood chowder. The menu varies from week to week, depending on availability.

Future plans for Whidbey Fish include a retail deli outlet in Langley by the spring of 1992, selling fish, chowder, smoked salmon, crabcakes, and pie. If you're not a fish lover, don't worry. One convincing comment scrawled by a customer on a napkin reads, "I'm not a fish lover, and I loved everything. I'm transformed."

Sue Frause

Whidbey Fish and Whidbey Pies
Tom and Jan Gunn
3078 State Highway 525, Greenbank
(206) 678-FISH

Year-round: Thursday–Monday (May through October); Friday–Monday (November–December, March–April); closed January–February; call ahead for hours.

Sixteen miles north of Clinton ferry on Highway 525, on the west side of the road.

QUINCE SAUCE FOR COD OR HALIBUT

Quince is a yellow, pear-shaped fruit that ripens in the autumn. It is most often used in jellies and preserves, but also makes a delicious complement to fish or poultry, as in this dish from the owner of Christina's on Orcas Island.

1 cup cooked, puréed quince, minus seed and peel
   (Christina puts it through a ricer)
1 cup apple cider
½ cup chopped mild onion or shallot
1 to 4 cloves garlic, crushed
2 thin slices fresh gingerroot
Sprig of thyme
1 cup spicy, not too dry white wine (such as gewürztraminer
   or Riesling)
½ pound cold unsalted butter
Honey
White pepper
Salt

Combine quince, cider, onion, garlic, gingerroot, and thyme in a nonaluminum saucepan. Reduce until almost dry. Add wine. Reduce again until almost dry. Cut butter into chunks and beat in gradually, keeping the sauce hot; do not let it break down. Remove from heat before the last butter chunk melts completely. Whisk. Add honey, pepper, and salt to taste. Strain. The flavor can vary, depending on how tart you want the sauce to be. Serve immediately with ling cod or halibut.

Makes about 2 cups.

Christina Reid
Orcas Island, Washington

PLEASANT VALLEY CHEESE

Verdant pastures throughout our region provide succulent, mineral-rich, and exceptionally nutritious forage for dairy cows. But there seems to be something unique about the meadows north of the Nooksack River where the fat soils (a highly productive amalgam of glacial and alluvial deposits and organic matter) grow—under the benign influence of our mild, moist climate—the kind of lush, savory grasses cows dote on. And those contented, well-fed cows do their best to turn the tasty greens into large volumes of superb milk.

In Ferndale, George and Delores Train have taken advantage of the quality of this milk to create several exquisite raw milk cheeses on their small Pleasant Valley Dairy farm. Raw milk cheeses, which depend on natural, milk, or airborne bacteria for their development, can be influenced by atmospheric conditions and, since the local climate reminded the Trains of the climate of southern Holland, where Gouda cheese is made, they decided to experiment with Gouda-style cheeses (instead of the Cheddars more commonly produced in the Northwest) when they began to make cheese for their own use. The results of their experiments were so gratifying that the Trains decided to go public with their product; they have made cheese commercially since December of 1980.

The Trains have about 35 dairy cows, and they do not plan to increase their herd, no matter how much demand for their cheese rises. They sell the milk from the evening's milking as fresh raw milk (it is packed into half-gallon cartons like homogenized and pasteurized milk), and they make cheese from the morning's milk—a maximum of about 270 pounds of cheese per week (it comes in two- to six-pound wheels).

To most consumers (unless they have spent much time on farms, or even helped milk cows, the way I did in my younger days—and what ornery beasts those cows were; they did *not* like being milked by hand, and more likely than not, you risked being kicked across the room for an inept stroke), milk is an ambiguous white liquid that sprouts up on supermarket cooler shelves in convenient cardboard cartons or plastic bottles. But whole milk is more than that. It is a complex mixture of water, protein, minerals, milk sugar, milk fat, and trace elements. Raw milk gives a firmer curd and tastier cheese than processed milk, but exceptional care must be taken to make sure that the cows are healthy and that the milk is free of pathogens. Raw milk also contains a beneficial natural flora, a number of active microorganisms which aid the cheese making (these have to be reintroduced when cheese is made from pasteurized milk). It is the action of these bacteria which causes raw milk to curdle if it is left to age. The cheese maker speeds up and controls the curdling process by adding rennet, an enzyme derived from a calf's stomach, to the milk. George Train prefers using a natural calf rennet for making his cheeses, because cheese made in this fashion will age better and have a nicer flavor; but he also makes a small number of cheeses with a microbial enzyme to meet the requirements of vegetarian customers.

George Train mixes the fresh milk from the morning's milking with the rennet and a special "Gouda" culture, which will give the cheese its special character. The milk is then heated to a temperature of 87° Fahrenheit and allowed to sit for a while to age. As the rennet curdles the protein part of the milk solids, the casein, the milk solidifies into a soft gel. Assistant cheese maker Ray Schultz checks on the progress of the curd by pressing down onto the custardlike mass with the back of his hand. When the curd comes away cleanly from the sides of the vat, it is ready to be cut.

Ray Schultz cuts the curd gently, with special instruments called cheese harps (he first uses one with horizontal wires, then one with vertical wires), into small pieces of fairly homogeneous size. As the curd is cut, the solids separate from the whey, a thin greenish liquid which contains most of the milk's sugar and water (the fat stays with the casein). The curds must be of a fairly uniform size because they will be firmed up through heating, and they will not achieve proper texture and consistency if "cooked" unevenly. But first the bulk of the whey is drained. As the liquid runs out, the curds are re-strained with the aid of a curd dam, a perforated sheet of stainless steel which is inserted into the vat, and with a sieve at the end of the drain pipe. Then hot water (100°F) is gradually added to the curds, and the cheese is allowed to heat and solidify gently for a couple of hours. This water/whey mixture is drained off when the curds are sufficiently firm—of about the consistency of a fresh cream cheese (at this point any spices, herbs, or seasonings are added for the flavored cheeses).

The fresh curds are carefully scooped from the vat into individual cheese molds (these had to be specially ordered from Holland) and pressed. The solid balls of cheese are next soaked in a heavy brine (strong enough to float a fresh egg). This is the only salting they will receive. Pleasant Valley cheeses are, fortunately, not as oversalted as most commercial cheeses. After the cheeses have been brined sufficiently—some 24 hours for small cheeses, two days for larger ones—they are transferred to aging shelves. For the first 30 days, they are turned almost daily to assure an even distribution of moisture as they dry. They are then covered with red wax and aged for an additional 30 days. By law, raw milk cheeses must be aged for a minimum time of 60 days before they may be sold (this assures that the fermentation process of the cheese has killed off any pathogens which might have been present in the raw milk), but most Pleasant Valley cheeses are much older when they are sold. Pleasant Valley "Goudas" are true "vintage" cheeses: Each is inscribed with the date of its manufacture.

Because these cheeses are completely natural, their taste will vary with the season. The best cheeses are made in May and in June when the new spring grasses have achieved their most luxurious growth, and then again in September, when the pastures which were seared by the summer's heat have been rejuvenated by fall rains and cool weather. But by October the grass loses its vigor, the days become short, and the weather turns cold. It is difficult to make natural cheeses in winter, when the weather is too chilly for the best development of beneficial bacteria and when the cows are fed on grass silage. Winter cheeses are gassier and have larger, more numerous eyes (this is when George Train makes a lot of "Swiss" cheese), but they are still delicious to eat. However, the Trains make most of their cheeses during the prime months and age them. I like the fresh, nutty taste of the 60-day-old cheeses as well as the old, pleasantly sharp wheels which may have grown to perfection for a year or more.

John Doerper
Eating Well: A Guide to the Foods of the Pacific Northwest

Pleasant Valley Dairy, Inc.
George and Dolores Train
6804 Kickerville, Ferndale
(206) 366-5398

June–December: Monday–Saturday, 9am–6pm; by appointment only the rest of the year.

North of Bellingham, close to Birch Bay; take I-5 north of Bellingham to exit 266 (the Birch Bay exit) and go west. The dairy is at the intersection of Kickerville and Grandview on the southeast corner.

APPLE PIE

This is the winning recipe from the 1991 Everson Fall Festival Apple Pie Contest, Men's Division. All entries to the contest were made with Whatcom County apples. Mr. Hagemeyer's apples came from his own King trees.

3 pounds apples (preferably King)
¾ cup sugar
1 teaspoon cinnamon
½ teaspoon nutmeg
½ teaspoon allspice
1½ tablespoons cornstarch
4 ounces aged Cheddar cheese, grated
½ teaspoon lemon extract

PASTRY

2 cups all-purpose flour
¼ teaspoon salt
¼ cup chilled butter
½ cup water
1 egg white, beaten
¼ cup half-and-half
Sugar, for sprinkling over crust

Preheat oven to 400°F.

Peel and slice apples and place in salted water to keep white until pie crust is ready.

Mix sugar together with the spices and cornstarch and set aside.

(continued on next page)

To make pastry, combine flour and salt and cut in half of the butter. Add water, a tablespoon at a time, mixing until dough pulls away from bowl. Roll out dough into a rectangle, and dot with half of the remaining butter. Fold dough up like a book, roll into a rectangle again, and dot with remaining butter. Fold, divide into two halves, and roll out one half to fit a 9-inch pie pan. Brush with beaten egg white.

Toss drained apples with spice mixture. Alternate layers of apples and grated cheese in the pie shell, ending with a layer of apples. Sprinkle lemon extract over top.

Roll remaining dough for top crust, place on pie, brush with half-and-half, and sprinkle with sugar. Cut vents in top and bake until done, about 40 minutes.

Makes one 9-inch pie.

Bill Hagemeyer
Everson, Washington

U-PICK FARMS AND ROADSIDE STANDS

U-Pick Guidelines: Call first, especially near the beginning and end of the season. Find out if your small children are welcome to help pick. Farms will supply picking containers, but you will need bags or boxes to transport your produce home. Pick carefully and conscientiously; a well-tended berry field or orchard represents years of knowledgeable labor. (Dogs should stay in the car.)

Harvests may vary greatly from year to year. A local chamber of commerce or county extension office can often supply up-to-date seasonal information. Also, many newspapers publish local farm maps in the late spring or summer.

ISLAND COUNTY, WASHINGTON

Neptune Sea Farms ☀ (206) 221-7783
Erin and Walter Ruthensteiner
4631 S Honeymoon Bay Road, Freeland

September–May (oysters may start later): call ahead.

The Ruthensteiners are mainly wholesalers, but if you'd like to pick up some of their Honeymoon Bay oysters or mussels, call ahead, and they'll harvest them right before your arrival. On Friday afternoons, in season, their son sells out of a truck in Bayview, across from Casey's Supermarket. The bivalves are also available at Pure Foods in the Pike Place Market, as well as other local stores.

Call for directions.

Whidbey Fish and Whidbey Pies ☀
(206) 678-FISH
Tom and Jan Gunn
3078 State Highway 525, Greenbank

Year-round: Thursday–Monday (May through October); Friday–Monday (November–December, March–April); closed January–February; call ahead for hours.

A selection of local and international fish and specialty foods including chowder, crabcakes, home-smoked salmon, and loganberry pie. The restaurant in "the ugliest building on Whidbey Island" is open for lunch and dinner.

Sixteen miles north of Clinton ferry on Highway 525, on the west side of the road.

Whidbeys Greenbank Farm ☀
(206) 678-7700
Wonn Road, Greenbank
Year-round: daily, 10am–5pm

Loganberry products, including liqueurs, preserves, toppings, and vinegars. Tasting room, gift shop, and picnic area. Loganberry Festival in July.

Off main highway just before Greenbank.

Rainbow Gardens ☀ (206) 221-3538
Lyman Legters and Marie Bird-Legters
5410 Maple Glen Road, Langley

Call ahead for appointment.

Herbs—several varieties of basil, chiles, arugula, cilantro, and other herbs and produce. Also sell at South Whidbey Farmers Market.

Off Highway 525 east of Freeland.

Case Farm ☀ (206) 675-1803
Michael and Sheila Case-Smith
98 W Case Road, Oak Harbor

July–September: call ahead.

Third-generation growers of crops including loganberries, marionberries, raspberries, beans, corn, pumpkins, winter squash, and gourds. Farm tours by appointment. U-pick (bring container) or call for advance orders. Suppliers to Whidbey Fish.

Two miles north of Oak Harbor, just off Highway 20 at milepost 34.

Dugualla Bay Farms ✶ (206) 679-1014
Bob and Carolyn Hulbert
3917 Highway 20, Oak Harbor
May–October: daily, 8am–6pm.

Strawberries, blueberries, raspberries, and local produce from other growers.

Three miles south of Deception Pass on Highway 20.

SAN JUAN COUNTY, WASHINGTON

Orcas Homegrown Store ✶
(206) 376-2009
Jeannie and Rick Doty
North Beach Road, Eastsound, Orcas Island
Year-round: daily, 8am–9pm (10pm on weekends).

Features local farmers' produce, fresh local seafood (including home-smoked salmon), and a deli.

Downtown Eastsound.

Dragonfly Farms ✶ (206) 378-2335
Louisa and Rob Rogers
4299 Roche Harbor Road, Friday Harbor, San Juan Island
In season: Saturday, 12:30pm–4pm.

The Rogers hold their own market Saturday mornings and are a popular source for specialty vegetables, including Asian veggies, all sorts of herbs and edible flowers, about a dozen varieties of lettuce, baby squash (with the blossoms still on), fennel, arugula, and sorrel. "There's just about nothing we don't grow," says Rob affably, "except carrots and onions." Their hybrid sweet corn goes fast—a record day saw 3,000 ears sold within 12 minutes. All produce is picked the morning it's sold.

At Pope's Lumber, at the top of Spring Street in Friday Harbor. Plenty of parking.

Giannangelo Farms ✶ (206) 378-4218
Frank and Vicky Giannangelo
5500 Limestone Point Road, Friday Harbor, San Juan Island

Year-round: Tuesday–Sunday, 11am–5pm.

Herbs, vegetables, and 7 varieties of garlic, all organically grown. Formal gardens for strolling. Herbed vinegars and herbal teas.

On San Juan Island, follow Roche Harbor Road 9 miles out of Friday Harbor. Turn right on Rouleau Road, go 1 mile, and turn right again on Limestone Point Road.

Island Green ✶ (206) 378-5775
Dale and Cyndi Piper
1121 Wold Road, Friday Harbor, San Juan Island
May–November: Wednesday–Sunday, noon–5pm.

Hydroponic varieties of tomatoes, peppers, lettuce, cucumbers, eggplant, and summer and winter squash, as well as some herbs. Also available at the Friday Harbor Farmers Market.

Five miles out of downtown Friday Harbor on San Juan Valley Road; take a left on Wold Road.

Westcott Bay Sea Farms ✶ (206) 378-2489
William Webb
4071 Westcott Drive, Friday Harbor, San Juan Island

Year-round: Monday–Friday, 8:30am–5pm; Saturday, 10:30am–5pm; Sunday, noon–5pm; closed Sundays in winter.

Westcott Bay and European Flat oysters.

On San Juan Island, take Roche Harbor Road to Westcott Drive on the north end of the island.

Rainwater Farm ✶ (206) 376-2458
Dennis George
Olga, Orcas Island

Dennis George varies his sales plan from year to year; sometimes he's at the Orcas Farmers Market, sometimes he just sets up a self-service flower and vegetable stand and leaves it at that. As of 1993, there are no on-farm sales. Rainwater Farm is where some of the island's top restaurants (including Rosario, Christina's, Cafe Olga, and Rose's) go for leaf lettuce, carrots, summer squash, and beans.

Island Farmcrafters

Steven and Linnea Bensel
Waldron Island, WA 98297

Mail-order source for wreaths, braids, and other decorative uses of garlic, shallots, herbs, and peppers from Nootka Rose Farm. The Farmcrafters catalog ($1) also features stationery, herbal products, and other craft items.

SKAGIT COUNTY, WASHINGTON

Specialty Seafoods ☀ (206) 293-4661 or (800)645-3474

605 30th Street, Anacortes, WA 98221

Year-round: Monday–Friday, 8:30am–5pm; Saturday–Sunday, 10am–5pm.

Retail store and mail order source for smoked seafood and chocolate decadence. Seasonings and gift packs also available.

At the corner of 30th Street and T Avenue.

Blau Oyster Company ☀ (206) 766-6171

E. E. Blau and Sons, Paul and John; manager Peter Nordlund
919 Blue Heron Road, Bow

Year-round: Monday–Saturday, 8am–5pm. Call ahead for selection. Orders placed 24 hours in advance get a 10% discount.

Blau is at the end of the road on Samish Island. It has been supplying locally caught seafood and shellfish since 1935. Live and fresh-shucked Pacific oysters, Manila clams, fish fillets, mussels, shrimp, and Dungeness crab.

Take Bow-Edison exit off I-5, continue west from Edison on Bayview-Edison Road and then on to Samish Island Road. Then follow the signs.

Taylor United Samish Bay Shellfish Farm ☀ (206) 766-6002

188 Chuckanut Drive, Bow

Year-round: Monday–Friday, 8am–5pm; Saturday, 10am–5pm; Sunday, 1pm–5pm.

Pacific Oysters. Formerly the Rock Point Oyster Company.

Take Chuckanut Drive exit off I-5. Driveway is next door to Oyster Creek Inn.

Potato Shed ☀ (206) 755-9319

Gerald Nelson
605 Avon Avenue, Burlington

Mid-September until potato supply runs out, usually around the end of the year (and sometimes into January). Before Thanksgiving: Monday–Saturday, 9am–5pm; after Thanksgiving: Monday–Friday, 9am–5pm; Saturday, 9am–1pm.

White, red, and Yellow Finn potatoes.

On Highway 20 east (Avon Avenue) at corner of N Pine.

Bentwood Farm ☀ (206) 826-3655

Woody Deryckx
3736 Cape Horn Road, Concrete

September–December. Call ahead.

Organic Liberty and Akane apples. Cider by the jug.

On Highway 20 east of Hamilton.

Cedardale Orchard ☀ (206) 445-5483

Larry Johnson and Gary Moulton
Conway Road, Conway

August–October: daily, daylight hours.

U-pick peaches (when available); apples — including Gravenstein, Summered, Akane, Jonamac, Gala, Spartan, Jonagold, and Melrose; Asian pears.

Take the South Mount Vernon exit off I-5, turn left on Conway Road. Farm is on the right; you can see it from the freeway.

Snow Goose Produce ☀ (206) 445-6908

2010 Fir Island Road, Conway
Call ahead.

Sells organic produce for a number of local growers. Fresh salmon, oysters, and clams.

On Fir Island Road near North Fork Bridge.

Annual Mount Vernon Rotary Strawberry and Raspberry Sale ☀ (800) 869-7107

P.O. Box 825
Mount Vernon, WA 98273

June and July.

Since 1971—fresh, unsugared local berries in 15-pound lots, cleaned and sliced and ready for jam. Order in advance and pick up at various locations around Skagit and Snohomish counties.

Appleberry Farm ✶ (206) 424-6574
Marvin Jarmin
Pulver Road, Mount Vernon

In season: Monday–Saturday, 8am–5pm.

Strawberries, raspberries, blueberries, and several varieties of apples, including Spartan and Melrose. Some U-pick (bring containers). Also sells at Pike Place Market.

Take the George Hopper Road exit off I-5 to Pulver Road.

Hedlin Farms ✶ (206) 466-3977
1027 Valley Road, Mount Vernon

Mid-June–mid-September: daily, 10am–6pm.

Strawberries, raspberries, blackberries, corn.

Stand is at corner of La Conner/Whitney and Chilberg roads, across from Pioneer Memorial.

Highlands Northwest ✶ (206) 757-4906
Roger E. Pederson
1032 Bay View Cemetery Road, Mount Vernon

Call ahead.

Grass-fed, organic beef from Scotch Highland cattle. Available frozen by the package, variety pack or halves. Food stamps accepted. Scotch Highlanders are shaggy, wide-horned cattle that produce good meat on scant forage. Their heavy coats substitute for an insulating layer of fat, making their meat leaner than that of most other breeds.

One-half mile north of Bayview State Park. Take exit 231 off I-5, just north of Burlington, and follow signs.

Hollybrook Farm and Llama Ranch ✶ (206) 445-5262
Cliff and Pat Skelton
2302 Legg Road, Mount Vernon

Call for schedule.

Rhubarb and llama wool. Some lamb pelts left over from sheep business.

One and a half miles south of Lake McMurray off Highway 9, east of Mount Vernon. Take the Conway exit off I-5.

Lange's Honey Skep ✶ (206) 424-9438
James and Ann Kahle
1875 Cedardale Road, Mount Vernon

Year-round: Monday–Saturday, 8am–dark.

Clover, fireweed, huckleberry, and wild blackberry honey. Creamed honey, honeycomb, beekeeping supplies.

This is the tantalizing place you see from I-5. Take exit 221 off I-5 north or 225 off I-5 south to Cedardale Road (E Frontage Road).

Merritt's Apples ✶ (206) 766-6224
896 Bayview-Edison Road, Mount Vernon

August–Thanksgiving: Tuesday–Saturday, 9am–5pm.

Gravenstein and Jonagold apples, juice, jams, honey, and gifts.

Exit 231 off I-5. Take Wilson Road 6 miles to the end. (Wilson Road is just west of the southbound freeway entrance, before the State Patrol building.) Turn right onto Bayview-Edison Road and go 2½ miles. Farm is on the left.

Mother Flight Farm ✶ (206) 445-5006
Glen and Charlotte Johnson
2052 Skagit City Road, Mount Vernon

Call ahead for bulk orders and hours.

Thirty varieties of organic produce, including chard, collards, and kale. Also sold at Snow Goose, local farmers markets, and Pike Place Market.

Call for directions.

Pleasance Garden Produce ✶ (206) 466-3009
Nona and Paul Avery
1183 Dodge Valley Road, Mount Vernon

June–September: Monday–Friday, 1pm–5pm; call for weekend appointments.

Tomatoes, tomato plants, black currants, herbs, vegetables—including garlic and shallots—pears, apples, and cut and dried flowers.

Call for directions.

Schuh Farms ✶ (206) 424-6982

Steve and Susan Schuh

1353 Memorial Highway, Mount Vernon

May–October: daily, 10:30am–6pm, or when sold out.

Rhubarb, strawberries, U-pick raspberries, some marionberries, a variety of vegetables, including U-pick pumpkins, winter squash, carrots, and Brussels sprouts.

Three and a half miles west of Mount Vernon on Memorial Highway. Take the Kincaid Street exit off I-5 in downtown Mount Vernon.

Secret Garden ✶ (206) 428-6788

Jerry and Doreen Schreuder

1343 Avon Allen Road, Mount Vernon

June–October: daily.

Full range of unsprayed vegetables, including sugar snap peas, sweet onions, kohlrabi, several varieties of garlic, and local Tarheel beans. Also sell at Skagit Valley Farmers Market.

From I-5, go west on Highway 20, turn left at light on Avon Allen Road. Farm is on left.

Swanson's Fruit and Veggie Stand ✶ (206) 466-3487

Swanson Brothers Farm

1650 Flats Road, Mount Vernon

July–August: daily, 10:30am–5pm; September–November: Saturday, 10am–4pm; call ahead.

Raspberries, tayberries, boysenberries, logan-berries, marionberries, Himalaya blackberries, vegetables, and apples, including Discovery, Gravenstein, Akane, Spartan, and Jonagold.

Go one mile north of La Conner on La Conner–Whidbey Road, and look for signs.

Cascadian Farm ✶ (206) 853-8629

Highway 20, Rockport

Spring–late summer: weekends and some week-days, 10am–dusk; call ahead.

One of the oldest and largest organic farms in western Washington. Roadside stand with fresh strawberries and raspberries, berry shortcakes, and a variety of preserves, pickles, potato chips, and juices.

One-half mile east of milepost 100 on Highway 20 between Rockport and Marblemount. Eleven miles east of Concrete.

Organic Garden Patch ✶ (206) 826-4378

Lucille Carnahan

1102 Cockreham Road, ~~Sedro~~ Woolley

May–October: ~~Monday–~~Friday, flexible hours.

Brown ~~eggs, str~~awberries, raspberries, salad gre~~ens, and~~ vegetables, all organic at reason-able, nonorganic prices. Farm is located on a scenic curve of a river.

Call for directions and large orders.

Perkins Variety Apples ✶ (206) 856-6986

Tom, Sue, and Jim Perkins

816 Sims Road, Sedro Woolley

August–December: Wednesday–Saturday, 10am–6pm; Sunday, 1pm–6pm.

Specialty apples, including Akane, Spartan, Mel-rose, and Jonagold; European and Asian pears; cider; and honey. The Perkinses raise more than 100 varieties of apples. Farm tours and samples by appointment. Sue says, "come hungry."

Three miles east of Sedro Woolley on Highway 20.

Tarheel Sausage ✶ (206) 855-0088

250 W Moore Street, Sedro Woolley

Invented by Bob Mahaffie and named in honor of the many North Carolina immigrants to the Skagit County hills. Wholesale only, but you can try this lean, all-pork sausage in the burgers at Daisy's, Concrete's best-known drive-in, or in the meat section of northwest Washington Thrifty Foods and Safeway stores.

SNOHOMISH COUNTY, WASHINGTON

Northwest Select ✶ (206) 435-8577

The Israel family

14724 184th Street NE

Arlington, WA 98223

Year-round: Monday–Saturday.

Salad mixture including wild and domestic greens and herbs, shipped to you; garlic braids; herbal wreaths; haricot vert beans. All certified organic. Annual garlic festival with live music and recipe contest held in August, and Christmas Festival with crafts and dried flowers.

Take exit 208 east from I-5. Follow Route 530 through Arlington and over bridge. Turn right on Arlington Heights Road and right again on Jordan Road and go 6 miles. Turn left on Mattson Road and drive to end of road.

The Blueberry Patch ✷ (206) 334-5524
Tom and Debbie Waters
10410 54th Street NE, Everett

Late July–mid-September: daily, 8am–dark.

U-pick or ready-picked blueberries.

Near Lake Cassidy; call for directions.

Laura and Bob Johnson ✷ (206) 252-3281
5211 52nd Street SE, Everett

In season: weekends, 10am–5pm.

Strawberries, raspberries, beans, cucumbers, corn, potatoes, squash, and pumpkins.

Three miles from Everett; take exit 194 off I-5, take first right, turn off trestle onto Home Acres Road. Follow for 2½ miles. Bear left at bridge, go down the lane to roadside stand.

Deer Mountain Jam ✷ (206) 691-7586
The Graham family
P.O. Box 257
Granite Falls, WA 98252

Year-round: daily, 9am–5pm.

Raspberry, blackberry, and strawberry jams made from their own fruit; gooseberry, loganberry, boysenberry, and blueberry jams made from locally bought fruit. Available by mail or from the plant.

Take Highway 2 exit off I-5 toward Lake Stevens, where you pick up Highway 9 to Arlington. In Arlington, take Highway 92. Just before Granite Falls, turn left on Jordan Road, go 3½ miles; farm is on the left.

Edgewood Hill Herb Farm ✷
(206) 691-7290
Nancy Fesl Craggs
8009 Robe Menzel Road, Granite Falls

Call for selection and hours.

U-pick herbs and flowers, all organically grown. Bedding plant sale each spring. "I'm a small herb farm but getting bigger by the minute."

Turn right (south) at 4-way stop in Granite Falls. Farm is 1½ miles on left. Look for the sign.

Biringer Farm ✷ (206) 259-0255
Mike and Dianna Biringer
4625 40th Place NE, Marysville

June–July: Monday–Friday, 8am–7pm; Saturday–Sunday, 8am–4pm; October–December: weekends, 9am–5pm.

Seasonal U-pick and farm market for strawberries, raspberries, cauliflower, and broccoli. Pumpkins in October and Christmas trees in December. The Biringers' daughter Melody sells the farm's product line—including their award-winning tayberry jam, raspberry vinegar, and other jams, syrups, and baking mixes—at her Pike Place Market store (1530 Post Alley, (206) 623-0890).

Off Highway 529 between Marysville and Everett. Take Marysville exit (199 going north, 195 going south) off I-5, turn right; at second light, turn right onto Highway 529, turn right after 100 feet, and go past second bridge to farm gate.

Dues Berry Farm ✷ (206) 659-3875
Clarence and Marge Due
14011 Old Highway 99, Marysville

Call ahead.

U-pick Shuksan and Rainier strawberries. Senior citizen discount.

Take 116th Street exit off I-5 north.

Kurt's Produce ✷ (206) 794-5940
Kurt Biderbost
SR 203, Monroe

June–November: daily, 8am–dark; self-serve set up when Kurt's not there.

U-pick and farm stand, seasonal produce.

From Highway 522 in Bothell take first Monroe exit, go right on Lewis Street, which turns into SR 203.

Old Cider Mill ☆ (206) 794-9335
Stan and Sylvia Vail
14821 High Bridge Ro~~ad~~, ~~Monr~~oe

~~CLOSED~~

Labor Day–Chri~~stmas~~: Wednesday–Sunday,
10am–6p~~m~~.

Cide~~r~~, honey, honeycomb, preserves,
syrups, Christmas trees.

From Highway 405, take exit for Highway 522
east; take Fales Road and follow signs.

Snow's Berry Farm
A Centennial Farm ☆ (206) 794-6312
Joan and Ron Snow
18401 Tualco Road, Monroe

Mid-June–mid-August: daily, 7am–7pm.

Strawberries and raspberries, U-pick and picked
to order.

From Monroe go south on Duvall Highway (SR
203) for 1 mile; turn right onto Tualco Road,
watch for sign.

Tualco Valley Bunny & Egg Farm ☆
(206) 794-6326
C. J. Peters
17910 SR #203, Monroe

Year-round: daily, daylight hours.

Sheep and goat meat, butchered on order;
brown- and blue-shelled fertile eggs; live rabbits,
pigeons, and poultry: "All our animals have always been well fed with natural grain and hay."

On Highway 203 at corner of Tualco Road, ½
mile south of Monroe (Lewis Street Bridge).

Craven Farm ☆ (206) 568-2601
Mark and Judy Craven
13817 Short School Road, Snohomish
In season: call ahead.

Strawberries, raspberries, marionberries (either
U-pick or ready-picked), jams, and syrups. Pumpkins in October.

Call ahead for directions; they're complicated.

Hagen Vegetables/Big B Store ☆
(206) 668-8588
or (206) 568-6945
Bryan Custer
11804 Springetti, Snohomish

June–October: Monday–Saturday, 9:30am–6pm;
Sunday, 11am–6pm; Big B is open year-round.

U-pick and ready-picked produce.

Farm stand is on Marshland Road between High-
way 9 and Larimer's Corner; Big B Store is a hay
and grain outlet.

Snoh-Fresh U-Pick ☆ (206) 568-7505
Earl and Joann Wilson
10707 Old Snohomish-M~~onroe R~~oad, Snohomish

July–October: d~~aily, h~~ours.

U-pick pr~~oduce; c~~all for availability.

Go s~~outh~~ out of Snohomish on Lincoln Street,
which turns into Old Snohomish-Monroe Road.
Farm is about 1 mile from town.

Stocker's "The Corn King" ☆
(206) 568-2338
Edwin and Edith Stocker
10622 Airport Way, Snohomish

Mid-June–early November: daily, 10am–dark.

Fresh produce: U-pick beans, cucumbers, pumpkins, and flowers. Local milk, eggs, honey.

One-half mile south of Harvey's Airport, near inter-
section of Highway 9 and Marshland Road.

Verdi's Farm-Fresh Produce ☆
(206) 568-0319
Mike and Susan Verdi
10325 Airport Way, Snohomish

Year-round: call ahead.

More than 100 kinds of vegetables, herbs, and
edible flowers; the Verdis also have a stand at
the Pike Place Market.

East of Harvey's Airfield in Snohomish.

Rent's Due Ranch ☆ (206) 629-4871
Joanie McIntyre and Michael Shriver
25708 90th Avenue NW, Stanwood

June–October: Sundays only.

Organic vegetable starts, produce, and flowers.

Six miles off the Stanwood-Camano Island exit off I-5. Look for the Exxon gas station and follow Legue Road all the way out.

Green's Acres Blueberry Farm ✭
(206) 793-1714
Tom and Dolly Green
32326 132nd SE, Sultan

Early July–early September: Monday–Saturday, 9am–2pm, evenings from 6pm–dark.

Five varieties of U-pick and ready-picked berries. Full-grown bushes for sale and "some knockout blueberry recipes."

One mile north of Sultan at corner of Sultan Basin Road and 132nd; look for signs.

WHATCOM COUNTY, WASHINGTON

Treehouse Deer Farm ✭
Jim Rich
2785 Valley Highway, Acme

Farm-raised venison. No retail sales, but sausage is available at Wright Smokehouse and at Everybody's Store in Van Zandt. Mail order through Norm Thompson catalog.

Cedarville Farm ✭ (206) 592-5594
Mike and Kim Finger
3081 Goshen Road, Bellingham

Call ahead.

U-pick organic raspberries; also available at Bellingham Farmers Market. The Fingers started a community-supported agriculture program in 1992. Call for information.

Take Mount Baker Highway east 7 miles from Bellingham to Sand Road. Turn left on Sand Road, right on Goshen Road. Farm is on right.

Clearian Farms ✭ (206) 592-5106
Carol Allison
5455 Allison Road, Bellingham

Mid-July–mid-August: daily, 7am–7pm.

Blueberries—U-pick and ready-picked.

Corner of Mount Baker Highway and Smith Road.

Fairhaven Cooperative Flour Mill ✭
(206) 734-9947
Bill Distler
1115 Railroad Avenue, Bellingham

Year-round: Monday–Thursday, 9am–4pm.

Bulk orders of fresh-milled, organically grown flours: wheat (fine, coarse, high-gluten, pastry, etc.), rye, buckwheat, garbanzo, and others.

Take the Lakeway exit off I-5 and turn right at the stop sign. Go 1 block to Lakeway and turn right. Go under the freeway and look for State Street. Turn left onto State, go 2 blocks, turn right on Maple Street, and go 1½ blocks. You'll cross Railroad Avenue, and ½ block later you'll see an alley; go right into the alley and go ½ block. Co-op is on the right.

Joe's Gardens ✭ (206) 671-7639
Carl Weston
3100 Taylor Street, Bellingham

Mid-May–mid-October: Monday–Friday, 9am–6pm; Saturday, 9am–5:30pm.

Famous local source for vegetable starts and produce. Joe's Special tomatoes are ubiquitous in Whatcom County gardens, where only the hardiest tomatoes win the race with time. Supplier to The Willows Inn.

Take Fairhaven/Valley Parkway exit west off I-5. Turn right on 24th Street and right again on Taylor.

Small's Gardens ✭ (206) 384-4637
Bob and Vivian Small
6451 Northwest Road, Ferndale
U-pick starts mid-June, stand is open mid-July–September: daily, 9am–6pm. Call ahead for availability.

In operation since 1960, the Smalls have U-pick pie cherries, strawberries, green and wax beans, plus sales of cauliflower, sweetmeat and acorn squash, and other produce.

Take the Northwest Road exit off I-5 just north of Bellingham. Head east (away from town). Farm is between Lattimore and Pole roads.

Twin Creek Orchard ✭ (206) 366-3351
Milo and Verna Voth
2425 Jess Road, Custer

Late September–end of apple season: call for hours.

Jonagolds by the box or bag. Great-tasting, homely looking culls available for 25 cents a pound. Mr. Voth is friendly and informative, and it's a nice drive.

Take the Birch Bay–Lynden exit (270) east off I-5 north of Ferndale. Go 2 miles to Delta Line Road and watch for signs.

Putnam Road Cherries ✸ (206) 592-2070
Jim and Marty Chapman
5738 Putnam Road, De~~ming~~

July: Monday–Sa~~turday,~~ 8am–7pm; Sunday, noon–7pm ~~call~~ead for availability.

U-pic~~k Mon~~morency pie cherries. Ladders and picking buckets provided. Bring your own containers.

Take the Mount Baker–Sunset Drive exit off I-5 in Bellingham. Continue east 8 miles to Nugent's Bridge. Putnam Road is ½ mile past the bridge on the left. Look for the big red-white-and-blue sign during cherry season.

Shumway's Berries ✸ (206) 592-2022
Ladd and Howard Shumway
3957 Mount Baker Highway, Deming

Mid-June–July: daily, 9am–6pm.

U-pick and ready-picked strawberries and raspberries.

Ten miles east of Bellingham on the Mount Baker Highway (Highway 542). Second location for raspberries only at 7867 Noon Road, Lynden (July only: 9am–6pm; (206) 354-5981).

Alm Hill Gardens ✸ (206) 966-4157
Ben Craft and Gretchen Hoyt
3550 Alm Road
Everson, WA 98247

Mid-March–December: informal hours, call ahead.

Alm Hill mostly markets off the farm (at area grocery stores and the Pike Place Market), but you can stop by for blueberries, strawberries, organic raspberries, some vegetables, flowers, and berry vinegars. The vinegars as well as Christmas wreaths and (beginning in spring of 1992) tulips are available by mail.

Go east out of Bellingham on the Mount Baker Highway for about 15 miles, then take Highway 9 north for about 10 miles. Look for signs for Sumas, then Nooksack; they're on the first road to the right past Nooksack.

Applewood Farm ✸ (206) 966-5183
Vernon and Karen Leibrant
3711 Cabrant Road, Everson

August–December: daily. Call ahead for availability.

Gravenstein, King, Jonagold, Spartan, and Melrose apples. Cider by the jug, or U-press by appointment. Winter squash and local honey.

Two houses north of Cloud Mountain Farm on corner of Goodwin and Cabrant roads.

Bosscher Lean ✸ (206) 966-7138
Dick Bengen and Ruby Bosscher
6300 Lawrence Road, Everson

Year-round: daily.

Dick and Ruby sell lean meat raised without hormones, antibiotics, or growth promoters. They quote lab tests on an untrimmed T-bone steak that yield a fat content 75% lower than a USDA choice T-bone and less than 1% higher than skinned chicken.

Take the Mount Baker Highway to Highway 9 north, go 3 miles to Lawrence Road.

Cloud Mountain Farm ✸ (206) 966-5859
Tom and Cheryl Thornton
6906 Goodwin Road
Everson, WA 98247

Mid-September–December: Thursday–Saturday, 10am–5pm.

Spartan, Elstar, Jonagold, Melrose, Mutsu, and Idared apples, by the box or by the bag. Local pears, cheese, and jams. Fresh cider. Pruning and orchard management workshops, fruit sampling, and other events. Nursery stock for sale in the spring. Write for catalog.

Take the Sunset–Mount Baker exit (255) off I-5 and turn right (east). Go 8 miles, across the Nooksack River, and turn left on Highway 9 north. Go 1 mile to Siper Road, turn right, and go 1½ miles, which puts you on Goodwin Road.

Robbins Hill Farm ☆ (206) 966-7123

Douglas Robbins

3653 Lindsay Road, Everson

Year-round: daily. Call ahead for availability

Certified organic raspberries, fresh in season (July), frozen in 28-pound lots otherwise.

Take the Lynden–Sumas exit off I-5 in Bellingham. Follow Guide Meridian to Badger Road, 2 miles north of Lynden. Turn right on Badger Road and continue straight 10 miles until the main road turns left. Leave main road and turn right onto Garrison Road. Take Garrison Road to Lindsay Road, and turn left; farm is on right.

Stoney Ridge Farm ☆ (206) 966-3919

2092 Van Dyk Road, Everson

September–early November: Wednesday–Saturday, 10am–5pm.

Ready-picked Jonagold, Melrose, Matsu, and Idared apples, cider, and dried apples.

Across from Everson Auction Barn.

Bode Farms ☆ (206) 366-3710

Lane and Donna Bode

2424 Zell Road, Ferndale

July–August: daily, sunup–sundown.

Raspberries and blueberries.

Five miles north of Ferndale off Enterprise. Look for signs.

Boxx Berry Farm ☆ (206) 384-4806

Bill and Charlene Boxx

6211 Northwest Road, Ferndale

Early June–October: Monday–Saturday, 9am–6pm.

U-pick strawberries, raspberries, blueberries, and beans. Bring containers. Other crops ready-picked: cucumbers, dill, garlic, broccoli, cauliflower, cabbage, potatoes, beets, corn, etc. The Boxxes are establishing a peach orchard, a rarity in northwest Washington.

Take the Northwest Road exit off I-5 just northwest of Bellingham. Head east (away from town). Farm is between Laurel and Piper roads.

Eagle Wings Farm ☆ (206) 366-5245

John and Nancy Kaye

3770 Aldergrove Road, Ferndale

Late August–November: Tuesday–Saturday; call ahead other times.

U-pick Akane, Jonagold, and Melrose apples. A few Elstars. Bring your own boxes. Call ahead for large-quantity pickings.

East of Arco refinery between North Star and Kickerville roads. Take the Ferndale exit from I-5 and head west to Kickerville Road, turn left and left again when you get to Aldergrove.

Eastview Farm ☆ (206) 384-3023

Tom and Joy Hughes

4983 Ferndale Road, Ferndale

Wholesale only.

Ready-picked blueberries.

Take exit 260 off I-5, and head west 3 miles to the intersection of Ferndale and Slater; turn right on Ferndale, and the farm is the first on the left.

Mary-B Farms ☆ (206) 384-1355

1498 Harksell Road, Ferndale

In season: Monday–Sa̶t̶u̶r̶d̶a̶y̶, 8am–5pm.

U-pick and re̶a̶d̶y̶-̶p̶i̶c̶k̶e̶d̶ blueberries.

East o̶f̶ ̶H̶a̶r̶k̶s̶e̶l̶l̶ Road.

Pleasant Valley Dairy ☆ (206) 366-5398

George and Dolores Train

6804 Kickerville, Ferndale

June–December: Monday–Saturday, 9am–6pm; Saturdays only the rest of the year.

Raw milk Gouda and farmstead (a Pleasant Valley creation with a texture a little bit like Cheddar) cheeses, in plain and herbed (caraway, cumin, and jalapeño. The cheese is hand-packed in small and large rounds.

North of Bellingham, close to Birch Bay; take I-5 north of Bellingham to exit 266 (the Birch Bay exit) and go west. The dairy is at the intersection of Kickerville and Grandview on the southeast corner.

Dale and Edith Reynolds Farm ✻
(206) 384-4580
5891 Olson Road, Ferndale
End of August–early September: daily,
8am–8am.

Sweet corn, Golden Jubilee.

One-quarter mile north of Mountain View Road.

Willey's Lake Cattle Company ✻
(206) 354-2401
The Wilsons
1289 Willey's Lake Road, Ferndale

Year-round: Thursday–Saturday.

USDA-inspected frozen buffalo meat—steaks, hump, roasts, hamburger, wieners, jerky, summer sausage, etc.—available by the piece, quarter or half, from the Wilsons' herd of 150. The herd bulls are kept near the shop, behind a very sturdy fence. The cows and calves graze in a pasture down the road. Buffalo meat tastes much like beef and is higher in protein (and in price) and lower in fat and cholesterol.

Take the Enterprise Road exit off I-5 north of Bellingham. Follow Enterprise Road as it zigzags north, and turn right on Willey's Lake Road. Farm is on the right.

Wright's Smokehouse ✻ (206) 384-0190
Don and Nancy Wright
5687 3rd, Ferndale
Year-round: Monday–Friday, 9am–5:30pm; Saturday, 9am–4:30pm.

Butchering, bacon, hams, and specialty sausage; venison sausage from commercially raised venison.

In downtown Ferndale. Take either Ferndale exit off I-5.

Blue Apple Farm ✻ (206) 758-2166
Earle and Anne Jewell
3805 Centerview Road, Lummi Island

September–October.

Nine varieties of grapes for juice or winemaking. Stemmer-crusher available if you just want to take home the juice.

Turn right from ferry dock and go ¼ mile.

Dick Bedlington Potatoes ✻
(206) 354-5264
8497 Guide Meridian, Lynden

Year-round: Monday–Friday, 9:30am–5pm; Saturday 9:30am–3pm; call for specialty orders.

Bedlington is a major seed potato grower and breeder. He sells several varieties by the pound from his plant, while they last. Call ahead for Yukon Golds, Purples, All-Reds, and other specialty varieties.

Take the Guide Meridian exit east off I-5 in north Bellingham and continue about 15 miles. Warehouse is on left.

Clark Berry Farm ✻ (206) 354-4551
Bender Road, Lynden

In season: Monday–Saturday, 8am–8pm.

Strawberries, U-pick or ready-picked, fresh or packed. This is a big operation.

Take the Lynden exit from I-5. Follow Guide Meridian north to E Badger Road and turn right, then right again on Bender, and follow signs.

Hardi Farm ✻ (206) 354-6699
1008 E Pole Road, Lynden

Call ahead.

Strawberries, raspberries, cauliflower, Brussels sprouts, zucchini, pumpkins. Roadside cart at Hannegan Corners nearby.

From Bellingham take Guide Meridian east to Pole Road. Turn right on Pole and look for roadside cart at Hannegan Road intersection, or continue a few hundred yards to farm, on left.

Jake Maberry Packing, Inc. ✻
(206) 354-2094
816 Loomis Trail Road, Lynden

Mid-June–mid-August: daily.

Strawberries, blueberries, and raspberries, fresh and packed.

Take Lynden-Sumas exit off I-5, take Guide Meridian to Lynden and head west on W Main. Main turns into Loomis Trail Road after about 3 miles.

McLean Farms ☆ **(206) 988-2002**
Fred Ricci
8883 North Pass Road
Sumas, WA 98295

Mail-order source for jams and preserves, made on the premises in open copper kettles. No on-farm sales, but dedicated customers can call if they're in the neighborhood. Suppliers of wonderful juice to local restaurants.

Holmquist Farm ☆ **(206) 988-9240**
Gerald and Lorrane Holmquist
9821 Holmquist Road
Sumas, WA 98264

Year-round: Monday–Saturday, 9am–5pm; open longer during the holiday season, but call ahead.

Producers of hazelnuts since 1928, specializing in the long, thin-shelled DuChilly variety rather than the more common Barcelona and Ennis types. Processing is done on the farm, and informal tours are likely. Gift shop sells baskets with local products, nuts in-shell or shelled, plain or roasted, chocolate covered or not. Also available by mail order.

The farm is right on the Canadian border. From Bellingham, take Guide Meridian exit off I-5, go 14 miles to E Badger Road, and turn right. Turn left on Northwood Road, right on Halverstick Road, and left on Holmquist Road.

Sonny's Orchard ☆ **(206) 988-5134**
Dick and Angie Braun
8883 North Pass Road
Sumas, WA 98295

Early August–December: Monday–Saturday, all day; Sunday, open at 2pm. Call ahead for availability.

European and Asian pears. Gravenstein, Jonagold, Mutsu, and Gala apples. Dried apples. Cider by the gallon, or press your own by appointment.

Take Guide Meridian east from Bellingham and follow signs to Sumas. Continue straight on Front Street for ¼ mile. Turn right onto Hovel Road and left onto North Pass Road. Roadside signs mark the way during harvest season.

FARMERS MARKETS

ISLAND COUNTY, WASHINGTON

Coupeville Farmers Market ☆
(206) 678-6757
Contact: Irene Thomas

April–September: Saturday, 10am–12pm.

Fifteen to twenty vendors come rain or shine, with spring and summer produce, bedding plants, honey, vinegars, and occasionally rabbits.

One block from Coupeville Courthouse on Main Street.

South Whidbey Farmers Market ☆
(206) 321-3062
Contact: Sally Pong

Mid-June–October: Saturday, 10am–2pm.

Mostly produce, with an organic emphasis; also honey, jams, seafood, and baked goods.

On Bayview Road between Langley and Freeland.

SAN JUAN COUNTY, WASHINGTON

Friday Harbor Farmers Market ✶
(206) 378-4218
Contact: Frank Giannangelo

May–October: Saturdays, 10am–1pm.

Produce, flowers, herbs, seafood, and gourmet foods from Island producers.

On Spring Street, across from the InterWest Savings Bank.

Orcas Farmers Market ✶ (206) 376-2458
Contact: Dennis George

April–October: Saturday, 10am–they're sold out.

At the Village Square on North Beach Road in Eastsound.

SKAGIT COUNTY, WASHINGTON

Anacortes Depot Market ✶
(206) 293-3663
Contact: Anacortes Arts Commission

May–mid-October: Saturday, 10am–4pm.

Fresh produce, baked goods, and crafts.

R Avenue and 7th Street; take R Avenue exit off Hwy 20 in Anacortes.

Burlington Farmers Market ✶
(206) 755-9382
Contact: Chamber of Commerce

Wednesday, 2:30–5:30pm

Cascade Mall, just south of main entrance.

Concrete Saturday Market ✶
(206) 853-8261
Contact: Mary Kollman

Mid-May–August: Saturday, 9am–4pm.

Local berries, produce, and crafts. Entertainment and free coffee.

Old Train Depot, Highway 20.

Skagit Valley Farmers Market, Mount Vernon ✶ (206) 428-8547
Contact: Chamber of Commerce

Mid-June–September: Saturday, 9:30am–1:30pm.

Berries, fruit, general and specialty produce, wild greens.

Take exit 226 off I-5 onto Kincaid. Turn right on 3rd and follow signs to Tulip Smokestack. In the parking lot next to the Tulip Smokestack.

SNOHOMISH COUNTY, WASHINGTON

Arlington Farmers Market ✶
(206) 659-7257
Contact: Grace Richards

July–September: Saturday, 9am–2pm.

An open-air market featuring organic vegetables, fruits, berries, and other produce; flowers— fresh and dried—and some crafts.

Across from the Olympic Theater, behind Legion Park in downtown Arlington.

Darrington Public Market ✶ (206) 436-1622
Contact: Leila Dempsey

June–September: 10am–5pm; held only on weekends when there are special events in Darrington.

Mainly a crafts market, but produce comes in late August and early September.

On Railroad Avenue.

WHATCOM COUNTY, WASHINGTON

Bellingham Farmers Market ✶
(206) 647-2060
Contact: Tere Moody

May–October: Saturday, 10am–3pm.

General and specialty produce, seafood, baked goods, espresso.

Corner of Railroad Avenue and Chestnut Street.

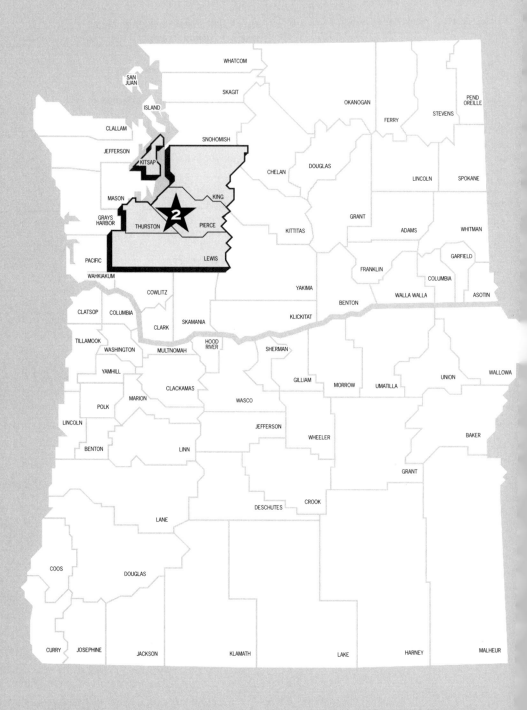

At the southern end of Puget Sound, fingers of salty water poke their way through foliage-covered land, creating inlets and charming coves, natural harbors, and unique microclimates. From these protected waters, some of the world's best oysters are harvested. In the nineteenth century, when oysters were abundant, about 50 small oysters would be discarded for every large one kept. Oystermen tossed thousands of bushels of young oysters on the beach, destroying them. In those days a two-bushel sack of oysters fetched about 70 cents when transported to Olympia. Nowadays, a bucketful of Olympia oysters, if you can find one, will cost about $25.

Fortunately, the days of wanton waste are gone, and Puget Sound still abounds with marine life, although not on such a lavish scale. Geoducks quietly grow to their enormous size, salmon are still running in the rivers and streams, and occasionally a stray whale or two is spotted in the southern inlets.

Just a few miles away from the smell of the sea, terrain and soil quickly change. Tucked among the shadows of mountains and forests are many bottomland farms, with rich silty or loamy soil. However, rolling hills, heavy forests, abrupt cliffs, and twisted valleys create a geography not exactly ideal for farming. Farms in southwest Washington tend to be of much smaller acreage than those east of the Cascades.

The weather here can be surprising. During the spring, dramatic cloud formations rush overhead so that a single day looks like a time-lapse video of a week's worth of weather. Brilliant sunbursts are punctuated by sudden hailstorms, torrential downpours, and fierce gusts of wind; the day can then end in a meek and mildly annoying gray drizzle. In the spring of 1991, our farm, which lies at the foot of the Black Hills, eight miles southwest of Olympia, received four hailstorms between mid-April and June. Fortunately, this being my third growing season, I was prepared. Everything growing in raised beds was tucked securely under cloches.

We farmers tolerate all this climatic madness because the soil beneath our feet is worth it. In my garden is evidence of the great upheavals that shook Washington State in the past (and can again at any time in the near future). According to the U.S. Geological Survey, Mount Rainier is no extinct volcano, but merely a sleeping beauty. Although massive eruptions usually occur only every 10,000 years or so, small-scale steam explosions can take place as often as once each century and perhaps as often as once each decade. Our Giles silt loam soil owes its richness to Mount Rainier ashes, which, in the words of the local soil conservation scientist, "is the kind of soil you could probably grow anything in" (weather permitting, of course). With a little modern technology, it's very easy to overcome the cool nights and fickle springs and summers. Our mild winters make it fairly easy to overwinter many crops and coax spring shoots off to a prosperous start.

Our farm has been carved out of reclaimed forestland. When we first started gardening, many cedar stumps remained from trees that had grown for hundreds of years in the same spot. Recently, we had a large bulldozer come in to clear another acre of tangled brush and old stumps. Watching the large steel teeth ripping through the ground made me think of the story our Realtor told us about a dairy farmer who owned one of first farms in the area. At about the turn of the century, he began clearing his land of the old-growth trees. He worked at it for some 10 years, and near the end of his arduous task, a giant fir tree fell the wrong way and killed him. We were able to accomplish in an hour what must have taken him months.

Unfortunately, as developers continue to gobble up land for housing, prime farming acreage is transformed into fenced backyards, paved roads, schoolgrounds, and convenience stores. King County has lost most of its farmland. The Green River Valley, which used to bill itself as the Head Lettuce Capital of the World, is down to three lettuce growers, and the urban expansion also threatens much of Pierce County as well. A little farther south, however, in Thurston County, farms seem to be holding their own against development. Here a large number of farmers (many of them certified as organic) have a viable market through both the popular Olympia farmers market and the Farmers Wholesale Cooperative, a broker dedicated to marketing organic produce with nationwide distribution.

Farmers markets are probably the best way to take full advantage of all the local produce without spending hours driving around looking for a farm stand. Small family farms have not all disappeared, but they have changed their marketing strategy. Most of the local organic growers I know are able to successfully farm small holdings of less than 100 acres (often as few as 10 acres) by carefully developing a few specialty crops and learning how to grow them very well. Some farms rely upon the combination of U-pick, wholesale selling, and the farmers markets. Another new approach is the concept of community-supported agriculture, in which a family or individual buys a share of the entire harvest and is assured a steady stream of fresh produce (and sometimes eggs or chicken) throughout the entire growing season. This form of cooperative buying helps to guarantee a stable market for the farmer, while often reducing costs for the consumer.

Pike Place Market is, of course, the ultimate farmers market. A serious food shopper should not be intimidated by the hordes of summer visitors at the Market; a number of top-quality local growers from farms scattered around Seattle come into the city, bringing their beautiful bounty with them. One day in early August, I was delighted to find packaged edible flowers, baby squash, yellow tomatoes, purple French beans, and lots of other garden delicacies attractively displayed. It is a feast for the eyes as well as the stomach.

Another great regional food adventure is fresh seafood. Salmon, you learn, comes in many different forms. There are coho, chum, sockeye and, of course, king (or chinook), and it comes fresh, frozen, filleted, cold-smoked, hot-smoked, and dried into jerky. Toward the end of summer, king salmon can be found for as low as $2 a pound, if you are willing to check the local newspapers for direct sources. I like to buy an enormous fish, whack off the head for my cats, trim away the fins, and slice the whole thing into thick steaks, which I toss into individual freezer bags for quick feasts. The free shoppers' guides from towns like Olympia or Shelton are my favorite sources for seafood bargains. One typical ad read "Fresh whole salmon. Smoked w/o preservatives. Authentic Indian jewelry. T-shirts and much more…"

Another strategy is to drive along Highway 101, around Hoodsport in Mason County. The drive is bordered by forestland and is extremely pretty, even when it's drizzling. Here you can buy salmon, geoducks, crabs, and oysters from a number of little stores along the shore. Some businesses are owned and operated by Native Americans, and during the autumn you can see families smoking fish as you drive by.

For the Indians around Puget Sound, fish are still central to the culture, providing subsistence, commerce, and spiritual significance. Many communities still hold first-salmon ceremonies to honor the first fish caught each season and to ensure the return of future runs. And since court decisions have given tribes power over fish habitat and management decisions, their age-old relationship with the salmon has translated into new political power.

The fertile land and productive waters that greeted the first Puget Sound people are still here, but we are learning their limits. Farmers, fishermen, and shoppers must work together to preserve the sources of this bounty.

Eunice Farmilant
Olympia, Washington

A DAY IN THE LIFE OF A DAY-STALL FAMILY

Sue Verdi doesn't mind giving price breaks to the people who come to her stand at the Pike Place Market with Market scrip. But she resents the well-heeled who come to bargain. "The other day a woman came to the stand specifically to buy these little tomatoes that we have. They are really good, and she knows that, because she has bought them before. I was selling them for two dollars a pound. 'Two dollars a pound,' she said, 'That's too much. How about half that?' I just don't understand how she can think two dollars a pound is too much for a specially good kind of food, yet she can be standing there with three or four glossy magazines under her arm which I know cost two or three dollars apiece."

Mike and Sue Verdi grow the vegetables, herbs, and flowers they sell at the Market. Mike's father and mother, Dominic and Pasqualina, started their stand in the mid-1950s. I've been buying vegetables there since 1964. One fall late in the harvest season, I asked if I could visit them, to learn more about what it takes to run a family farm.

It is difficult to succeed with a small farm, but I expected to find in Mike and Sue Verdi an example of that rare success. The Verdi stand is well-patronized by local restaurants as well as by individual customers. Until her death in 1991, Pasqualina was one of the Market's colorful personalities, a benevolent peasant grandma in a babushka. I expected, I think, to find the Verdis relaxed and prosperous.

What I found on the Sunday afternoon I visited was two very tired people. "I'm not moving very fast today," Sue explained with a grimace. "I've got cramps." Mike wasn't moving very fast, either—he had already loaded hundreds of pounds of pumpkins that morning and delivered them to a wholesaler. He was gathering his energy to begin loading 13,000 pounds more. A large, rumpled, dark-haired man in sweatshirt, jeans, and muddy boots, he smiled shyly, turned to attach an empty cart to a small tractor, climbed atop it, and drove off into the field.

Like Mike's parents before them, for about eight months out of the year—from early planting to late harvest—the Verdis get up before dawn to finish picking, cleaning, bundling, and loading the produce for the sale that day. Mike drops Sue and her vegetables off at the Market before 8am and returns to his day's work at the farm. She sets up the stand and deals, in her own inimitable way, with the public. Mike picks up Sue and the empty buckets and boxes at around 6pm. When they get home they head straight for the fields, where they harvest for the next day. Some of their crops have to be weeded at night because there are so many bees around during the day, and so Mike, Sue, and a hired hand strap on miner's lights at nightfall. "Whoever gets around to it first just throws together some supper. We eat a lot of vegetables and pasta, and that's about it," Sue said.

The family farm has a romantic image in American culture, but most of our food is actually raised by huge commercial enterprises. These capital-intensive farms are run by fewer and fewer people, who often do not live on the land they manage. Farmers make up only about 2 percent of the U.S. population; family farms, often at a competitive disadvantage in the national market, account for a third of the total number of farms. In local markets, family farms may find a niche by offering specialty products—unusual fruits or vegetables that are hand-raised or organically grown.

Conventional agriculture has flourished on the assumption that bigger is not only better but also more efficient—and efficiency, in commercial farming, is practically holy. Nonetheless, supposedly inefficient small farms, pronounced dead by conventional economics, have refused to disappear. The Verdis illustrate the remarkable commitment, possibly monomania, that it takes for small farmers to survive.

Mike and Sue Verdi's 50 acres sit squarely between Harvey Airfield in Snohomish and the Snohomish River. To get there, you take a gravel road off Highway 9, go up and over a railroad bed, and past a big orange "Pumpkins" sign. The road drops down over the tracks and continues on to the Verdis' farm and beyond it to the river. On the October afternoon of my visit, below the road and to the left stretched rows and rows of deep-red mums, as tall as ponies and as unruly. To the right, hundreds, maybe thousands, of pumpkins dappled a field that was pale green with fall weeds. Tasseled corn rose on the far side of the pumpkins, and beyond the corn a green embankment hid the river.

I asked Sue to put me to work, as I wanted to get a feeling for what they do. "Good," she sighed, storing her hands deep in the pockets of her coveralls. "I'm not used to talking.

Pike Place Market Rules

Farmers selling in Market low stalls must meet a stringent set of requirements. They must gross (or try to) at least $2,000 a year from their farm. They must grow or gather everything they sell, with the exception of a specific list of vegetables that they can buy for resale in the winter months only. They must process all jams, vinegars, and similar products themselves, and they must produce the main ingredient themselves. All farms are inspected, to ensure that the farmers really grow the crops they sell.

You can pick flowers." She pushed a huge homemade wheelbarrow out to the far end of a row of mums and told me to load its wooden platform about a foot and a half deep.

The flowers grew in thick clusters almost to my shoulders, with many deep-red blossoms on each stalk. They looked tossed about by the wind and rain, but there was only a light breeze that day, and the air was almost steamy. I fell into a routine of reaching down into a cluster and snapping off stalks with my right hand, cradling them in the crook of my left arm until a bunch had accumulated, and tenderly placing them in the wheelbarrow. After a while, it was hard to tell whether I was seeing so many red flowers or hallucinating them.

I picked for an hour, covered the platform with flowers, and began to pull the load back to the house. I could barely get my hands around the handles, which were pressure-treated 2-by-4s; the heavy cart lurched behind me, rolling from side to side. Sue stood on the hill by the house, laughing at me. After a deep breath or two and several forced stops, I got the cart into the carport and we were ready for the next step: pulling off the bottom leaves with a gloved hand, then binding the flowers into bunches and setting them in buckets of water. Sue gave me a pair of heavy work gloves, and we faced off across the cart.

As we cleaned and bunched the mums, Sue told me how she and Mike had found this land, Until 1989, they had raised all their produce on a few acres here and there in the South Park area of Seattle: Pasqualina had an acre, Mike had an acre, and they leased 10 or 20 acres wherever they could. This had meant moving equipment from place to place for irrigation and harvest. Every year or two they would have to find new land to lease, as owners would sell land or convert it to nonagricultural uses.

When they came to look at the farm in Snohomish, they were pleased that it came with a house, but their main interest was the soil. They toured the fields and looked at the soil, rolled it between their fingers, smelled it, dug down a few inches. The soil was dark, moist, and crumbly; it smelled good. There were plenty of worms. They knew they wanted the farm. And the farm's owner knew he wanted to sell it to them; they were the only prospective buyers who had looked at the soil.

Starting with good soil is crucial for the organic or sustainable-methods farmer. Intensive use of chemical fertilizers and pesticides breaks down the soil's natural structure, killing earthworms and beneficial microorganisms whose combined efforts make the soil loose and well-drained. Just a few years of conventional farming leaves the soil a compacted, almost sterile medium in which crops can grow only with the repeated addition of chemical nutrients. The antidote is remarkably simple: Seed the land with a nitrogen-fixing cover crop such as peas, alfalfa, or clover, let it be for a few years, and the whole biological community will come back. In those few years, however, the farmer may go out of business.

The Verdis knew what they were doing; they couldn't have started over on badly depleted and compacted soil, no matter how favorable the price or location, and still raise the crops they needed to keep their business going. Weeds can also pose an overwhelming problem, but they can be controlled mechanically if you start with fields in which weeds have not been allowed to go to seed. Thus another reason the Snohomish farm was so appealing was that it had been well-maintained, and the Verdis expected to have their few weed problems under control within a year.

Though they are not exclusively organic farmers, the Verdis keep their chemical inputs to a minimum. "We try not to use any pesticides," explains Sue. "A lot of insects can be controlled by companion growing. But if worse comes to worst, we'll spray something to save the crop. We don't do preventive spraying; if we use a chemical spray, it's in response to something that's happening."

To keep nutrients in the soil, they use crop rotation and "green manure"—legumes, rye, or other grasses, planted and then plowed under to rot and provide sustenance for new seeds. Both Mike and Sue learned these methods from growing up on family farms.

Like so many other farmers throughout the United States, the Verdis have to earn far more than what it would take to feed their family and pay themselves a wage; they have to make payments on land that is priced out of proportion to its agricultural value. Working 20 hours a day might not be enough; in the first year on new land, productivity is limited. They are still learning about the soil, finding out which crops do better where. And they have to install an irrigation system, a costly necessity.

"Well, why *do* you do it?" I asked Sue, along about 7pm that Sunday. We were working in semidarkness. Although Sue seemed to have gotten her second wind, my hands were cold, my legs were tired from standing on the cement floor, and I could no longer see the intense red of the flowers—all I saw were leaves and stems, stems and leaves, nothing but a lot more work to get done before they could clean the beets, onions, and Swiss chard and then go out into the dark to harvest corn and basil for tomorrow.

She looked at me as if I were a bit thick-headed. "Well, being out here today should give you some idea," she said with an air of finality, pulling the hood of her sweatshirt forward to cover her ears. I looked back, feeling cold and puzzled. "It's certainly beautiful out here, but is that enough?" "My husband is only happy when he's out in the fields working," Sue told me. "This is the only way we want to live."

Mike came into the light of the carport carrying a few ears of corn. "Dinner," he said. As we finished cleaning and bunching the last of the mums he told us his favorite story of the week. "It goes like this. We know a farmer down the road who won the lottery—a million dollars. He came right back here with all that money and went on farming. He said he'd keep on farming until it was all used up."

Margaret Hollenbach
Seattle Weekly

Verdi's Produce
Mike and Susan Verdi
10325 Airport Way, Snohomish
(206) 568-0319
Year-round: call ahead
East of Harvey's Airfield in Snohomish. The Verdis also have a stall at the Pike Place Market.

WHEN TO VISIT THE MARKET

Many people want to know the best time to visit Seattle's Pike Place Market, and I like to answer "any day," for the Market continually changes with the people who visit it, the farmers and craftspeople who attend, the season of the year, and the weather. No two days at the Market have ever, or could ever be alike, which is one of its ineffable charms. However, depending on what you want to buy, certain days of the week are better than others. For the total Market experience, Saturdays during any season of the year are the best overall day, when you'll encounter the biggest crowds and the most activity.

If you want to meet lots of farmers with the widest selection of fresh local produce, Wednesdays through Saturdays are your best bets. The farmers' spring crops include arugula, endive, spinach, lettuces, kale, cabbage, leeks, Chinese mustard greens, bok choy, and edible pea vines.

During the summer high season you'll find strawberries, raspberries, blackberries, blueberries, and many other kinds of berries; sugar snap, English shelling, and Chinese snow peas; Kentucky Wonder, Blue Lake, fava, Romano, and *haricots verts* beans; Walla Walla sweet onions; many varieties of corn; tomatoes; zucchini and squashes; and cucumbers on the farmers' tables.

Fall heralds the return of Golden Acorn, Sweet Dumpling, buttercup, butternut, Delicata, and spaghetti squashes; sugar pie, miniature, and full-size pumpkins; apples; gourds; Savoy cabbage; collard greens; kale; and Brussels sprouts.

The winter chill blows in fewer farmers, but those who do come to the Market bring potatoes, beets, chard, kale, turnips, parsnips, carrots, and evergreen wreaths, along with preserved products such as honeys, jams, and jellies.

During the winter months the sky can turn a thousand different shades of gray, the air is damp and chill, and a cool, gray light infused with yellow bathes the rain-slicked streets. The crowds are smaller and more local, the Market more solemn and reflective. During this quieter time of the year, the fishmongers, butchers, highstallers, and the few farmers who brave the Market can spend lots of time answering your questions. These can be trying times financially for owner-operated businesses, and by patronizing them during the tough winter months you'll quickly establish yourself as a much-appreciated regular customer.

The winter holidays are an especially beautiful time to visit the Market, when six-foot Noble firs festooned in white lights march across the tops of the tin roofs. With lists in hand, customers rush around in search of the freshest Dungeness crabs, crown roasts of beef, local chestnuts, fresh-killed turkeys, and sumptuous desserts for their holiday dinners, as well as that perfect present for Aunt Polly. Laden with sacks of gifts, food, and wine, they trudge through the Market as Thanksgiving, Chanukah, and Christmas draw near.

Regardless of the day or season of the year you decide to visit the Market, you don't have to get up too early to witness it arising, unlike farmers' markets elsewhere, which begin as early as 3am. Business along Pike Place starts at a more civilized hour. On a clear day, arrive at around 7am and watch the sun rise on the horizon and Mt. Rainier come out like a big blue cone in the distance. At this early hour the farmers unload their trucks and set out their produce in elaborate displays, while the fishmongers arrange their slippery charges over ice. The smell of coffee wafts through the air as the restaurants slowly come to life.

Later, around 9am, the craftspeople's roll call takes place at the end of the North Arcade. The craftspeople trundle their heavy, loaded carts over the worn brick street and set up shop in their stalls of the day. By 10am, thc Market is in full swing, its maze of farmers, craftspeople, and small-business owners set up and ready to serve you. Stroll at your leisure, stop to chat, buy a hand-crafted memento, nibble fresh cherries. Most important, soak up the Market's unique ambience as you partake of its endless bounty.

Braiden Rex-Johnson
Pike Place Market Cookbook

GEODUCKS

For generations of Puget Sound beachwalkers, the quest for the geoduck has had a mystique no other foraging can match. Huckleberries are almost too easy, and unearthing chanterelles is pure pleasure. But the continent's biggest clam has been almost as elusive as a Sasquatch, available only to those who were willing to seek out the year's lowest tides and then wallow in the mud.

Geoducks (pronounced "gooey-duck") are a sort of living Freudian slip. Commonly weighing in at about 6 pounds, they have been recorded at weights as high as 20 pounds. Their fragile, oblong shells are too small to contain their bodies, let alone the doubled siphon, which can extend two or three feet. Hazel Heckman of Anderson Island writes tactfully that the wrinkly tube "is remindful of an elephant's trunk." But she also recalls that years ago her freelance story on geoducks, with photos, was rejected by an East Coast editor as being "just too phallic for our nice family magazine."

There is also something primal about the hunt itself, taking place as it does at the times when the hidden is revealed. As Heckman explains in *Island in the Sound*:

> Daylight tides sufficiently low for geoduck digging occur so infrequently during any one year that they are known as "geoduck tides." A lesser ebb than minus three will rarely suffice. And, although he is unable to move his body (as does the razor clam) and can only extend and retract his siphon, the geoduck often wins the contest, which may well match the speed of the digger against the incoming tide.

> One factor in the geoduck's favor is that he is apt not to show at all until the tide has completed its slack and the flow has begun . . . The only visible part of the clam, when he does show, is the tip of his siphon, which may or may not protrude an inch or so above the sand, a roughish round knob, with an intake and a vent, through which he may (but probably won't) eject a fountain of water, thus betraying his position. If he fails to spout, it requires a sharp eye to find him among the seaweed and other debris left by the receding tide. Disturbed, he retracts his siphon quickly, leaving only a faint round depression to mark his withdrawal.

> Practiced diggers generally sink a tubular can, without ends, around the spot where the siphon disappeared, and dig inside the device to keep the

entire beach from caving into the excavation. The animal may not have retracted his siphon all at once, but may pull it in gradually, so that you might touch it occasionally. But don't try to pull him out by the siphon, even if you can get a grip on it, which is unlikely. He is probably too deeply and firmly embedded to remove in this manner, and the siphon is likely to break off in your hand.

A one-pound coffee tin, the wide kind, makes a good receptacle for dipping the sand and the water that comes flooding up into the cylinder. The cylinder itself, which should be provided with two handholds, can be pushed down as you go. When you can feel the shell, finally, embedded an arm's length or so beneath the surface, slip your hand underneath the animal and persuade him gently until you can work him loose from his resting place and bring him to light.

In my childhood summers at the Morgan family cabin on Hartstene Island, a bit farther south on the sound from Anderson Island, even the stovepipe was considered an affectation. Instead we used a crew of diggers: one to sprawl prone at the edge of the dripping hole and grope for the shell, the rest to make diversion ditches and bail out the tidewater. Usually the geoduck was saved by a cave-in and the designated groper got only an earful of muddy sand. But not always. Sometimes we marched back up the beach in triumph. In addition to the the the thrill of the hunt, the labor of digging a geoduck was

offset by the convenience of cleaning only one or two clams to get a potful of chowder.

Geoducks have two kinds of meat: the siphon and the belly. The siphon is the active part of the animal and it can be tough. After scalding it and peeling off the skin, either cook it very fast—no more than 30 seconds—at high heat or grind it for chowder or fritters. Thin, stir-fry strips can be cooked as is—they are wonderful with black bean sauce—or pounded and served as sashimi. Larger geoduck steaks should be pounded before cooking. The belly meat is more tender and has a stronger flavor.

In the past decade the state has granted licenses to commercial divers to take geoducks offshore. Their harvest shows up in restaurants and fish markets, so it is no longer necessary to dig your own. Most geoduck is sent to Japan or to Japanese restaurants out of state, but it is now available both fresh and frozen at Seattle-area markets. A geoduck should be alive when you buy it. The siphon should be short and plump, and it should move when you touch it. (If you can't bring yourself to touch it, how are you going to cook it?) If it doesn't move, don't buy it.

Geoducks are slow growing and not particularly prolific. The difficulty of getting them has long been their best defense. Commercial harvesting with power hoses and suction dredges is alarmingly efficient, but it also can be noisy and it takes place close to shore, so it is highly unpopular with waterfront property owners. These attributes—and state harvest limits—are likely to be the big clams' salvation. Despite their increasing popularity, it's likely that geoducks will survive to appall some squeamish editor of a future generation.

Hazel Heckman and Lane Morgan

JAPANESE GEODUCK SOUP

This is a simple, ethereally delicious soup that takes just minutes to prepare. It calls for kombu (sometimes spelled konbu), which is kelp, and readily available in most Asian grocery stores. In fact, the varieties of kombu available are a bit overwhelming—what you want for this recipe is just plain kelp, and not one of the many seasoned varieties. This soup makes an elegant first course.

½ pound geoduck siphon and breast meat (½ siphon and ½ geoduck breast)

1½ pounds spinach, washed, stems removed

4 cups loosely packed watercress, washed, stems removed

4 cups water

One 2-inch by 6-inch piece kombu (kelp), available in Asian grocery stores

1 dozen small mushrooms, trimmed, washed, and halved

1 tablespoon soy sauce

½ teaspoon grated fresh gingerroot

Juice of 1 lime

Salt to taste

3 green onions, finely chopped (for garnish)

Cut the geoduck siphon and breast meat into thin slices.

Blanch the spinach and the watercress separately in boiling, salted water. Drain, squeeze greens to extract as much water as possible, chop coarsely, and divide among 4 soup bowls.

Bring the 4 cups water to a boil with the kombu, add the geoduck, and let cook for 2 minutes or until the geoduck turns a light color. Remove geoduck from cooking liquid with a slotted spoon and divide it equally among the soup bowls. Discard the kombu. Add mushrooms and soy sauce to cooking liquid, bring to a boil, add ginger and lime juice, and cook an additional minute. Season to taste with salt, if necessary, then pour over the geoduck and chopped greens. Sprinkle with chopped green onions, if desired. Serve immediately.

Serves 4.

Susan Hermann Loomis

NETTLE SOUP

Revenge is one motive for eating nettles, but there are others. The stinging plant is one of the earliest greens up in the spring, and it is very nutritious. Chef Bruce Naftaly developed this recipe to make use of this plant, which is not commonly eaten in this country. Always wear gloves when gathering and cleaning nettles.

3 cups chicken stock
¼ pound Yellow Finn potatoes, peeled and cubed
½ pound stinging nettles
½ cup whipping cream
Salt, freshly ground white pepper, freshly ground nutmeg,
    and chervil, to taste
Fresh chervil, for garnish

In a non-aluminum saucepan, cook potatoes in the chicken stock until tender, about 10 minutes. Add nettles and gently boil about 5 minutes, until tender. Strain (reserve stock), purée nettles and potatoes, and return to pot with stock. Add cream to proper consistency and gently simmer 5 minutes. Season to taste. Garnish with fresh chervil.

Makes 4 cups.

Le Gourmand
Seattle, Washington

Nettles

Northwesterners were amazed when nettle soups began to appear at fancy prices in some Seattle restaurants. The ubiquitous stinging nettle is probably second only to the equally ubiquitous slug on the local hate list. However, cooking eliminates the sting, and nettles have a long and honorable history as a potherb. In his eighteenth-century tour of the Hebrides, Samuel Johnson reports sitting down to a bowl of nettle soup served on a cloth made of nettle fiber.

Because the stalks become very fibrous, nettles should be picked young, and only the leaves should be used in cooking. Use plants no more than six inches high for omelets. You have a little more leeway if you are making a purée.

Nettles are an early spring rather than a real winter plant. The late fall growth is too coarse to eat, and the first frost mows it down. But by late February in a mild year, the first new shoots can be found in city lots as well as rural woods. Keeping a patch trimmed will encourage tender new growth throughout the year, but they taste best in springtime. Wear rubber gloves for picking and cleaning.

Lane Morgan
Winter Harvest Cookbook

NORTHWEST CHESTNUTS

Omroa Bhagwandin, a biologist with a penchant for botany, first came to the Pacific Northwest in 1985 to see the temperate rain forests. What he did not expect to find were huge native American and European chestnut trees scattered throughout the western Cascades. Remnants of pioneer plantings had quietly grown to immense proportions, untouched by the blight that had wiped out billions of trees east of the Mississippi during the first four decades of this century.

Omroa concluded that chestnuts could be developed into a marketable crop in the Northwest, like hazelnuts, and he decided to turn his passion for these magnificent trees into a business. He moved his wife and family from southern Indiana to Morton, Washington, and started Northwest Chestnuts.

Omroa and his wife, Annie, are involved with every aspect of promoting and developing chestnuts. They have a nursery where they grow seedlings and rootstock. They harvest, process, and distribute nuts from established trees around the region and create other chestnut products. Currently, they offer both fresh and dried chestnuts, chestnut flour, and a real delicacy, Chestnut and Fig Conserve (based on a classic Italian recipe). The farm is certified organic. Their products are available on the farm, by mail order, and in some Northwest food stores.

Omroa spent a month in 1991 touring chestnut orchards in Italy. Some of the orchards—though not the individual trees—have been productive for more than a thousand years. Although there are technical problems to overcome, he believes Washington also could have a millenium of successful chestnut culture.

Omroa's main concern is with educating people about the uses and wonderful flavor of this almost forgotten food source. Compared with other nuts, chestnuts are much lower in fat and higher in protein, and they have a markedly sweet taste. (I am a big fan of roasted chestnuts and have fond memories of buying brown paper sacks full of burning hot nuts from Italian street vendors when I lived in Boston 20 years ago.)

Chestnut consumption is considerably higher in Europe than in the United States. This can be attributed in part to the lower quality of nuts exported to the United States from Europe and China. The chestnuts shipped here from Europe are not the classic French *marrons*, says Omroa, but rather a variety used in Europe for animal feed. Omroa says that regional chestnuts, although more expensive than the imported varieties, are well worth the investment. Not only are they sweet and fresh, but they are also free of the toxic fungicide that imported chestnuts are treated with to retard mold. (Fresh chestnuts should be kept in the crisper drawer of your refrigerator.)

Eunice Farmilant

Northwest Chestnuts
Omroa Bhagwandin and Annie Clark-Bhagwandin
183 Shady Grove
Onalaska, WA 98570
(206) 985-7033
January–April (for nursery stock only); call ahead. Also available at Pike Place Market, Seattle.
Call for directions.

Chestnut Torte

Chestnuts are perishable, so plan your purchases carefully. Look for firm, full nuts. Light weight and a blackened skin are signs of spoilage. Large nuts lessen the labor of peeling.

1¼ pounds chestnuts
½ cup light honey
½ cup butter, melted
1 egg, beaten
1 teaspoon vanilla extract
½ teaspoon ground cardamom
¼ teaspoon sea salt (optional)
2 egg whites

Preheat oven to 325°F.

To purée chestnuts, first slice them in half lengthwise (leave the shell on) and boil for 15 minutes. Drain and peel while still hot. Purée peeled chestnuts, and add honey, butter, egg, vanilla, cardamom, and salt. Blend until smooth. Beat egg whites until stiff, fold into batter, and pour into an oiled 9-inch springform pan. Bake 1 hour.

Serve with apple wedges and dessert wine.

Makes 1 torte.

Annie Clark-Bhagwandin
The Chestnut Cookbook

THE MAGIC OF MUSHROOMS

Autumn. The melancholy days are here again, the saddest of the year, days of the fall of leaf, reminder of one's mortality. So much for the poet. It is also the season of mists and mellow fruitfulness—the apple, the pear, the grape, the fig, and the mushroom.

Gathering wild mushrooms is a relatively new experience for many Americans, a phase of our coming of age gastronomically. We do not yet pursue it with the greed and zest and folkloristic superstitions that attended the hunt among the peasants of my native Italy. For them, the wild mushroom was not hunted to grace a steak or to raise the gastronomic level of a full dinner plate: they had neither. It was used to make stale, coarse bread more palatable, and to sell when pennies were needed to buy what could not be grown on the land.

Hence the avidity, the competition that attended the hunt, and the superstitious beliefs that were thought to assure its success. One had to go to the forest at the crack of dawn, make the sign of the cross before entering the mushroom patch, wear a garment inside out, and carry a probing stick that had acquired the virtue of a magic wand, and a tote bag, usually an old pillowcase, that had never been washed. The mushroom hunter then drank a glass of wine and began the hunt.

The proverbial sanction required it: *Non ti mettere in cammino se la bocca non sa di vino*—never venture forth on anything of consequence without the taste of wine in your mouth. And what could possibly be of more consequence than the search for mushrooms?

Success in the hunt was always attributed to these proverbial and superstitious preparations. When it failed, when there were telltale traces in the area that others had been there, the appropriate response was, *Ci sono bell' e stati!*—others have been happily here before us. Happily, because happiness is coming upon a host of mushrooms, especially what we call *Boletus edulis*—the King. Unfortunately for us, theirs was the happiness this time. Better luck for us next time. Such was the traditional, humane lament. Someone less humane might simply have uttered a curse: "Damn the ruffian who beat us to the patch!"

The patch, the grove, the limited area where one found mushrooms year after year, came to be regarded as one's own. Leading others to it, or even indicating in what general direction it lay, was simply out of the question. Such exclusive right to the patch, however, was invariably illusory, for sooner or later some roving hunter would find it.

How characteristically different is the American's orientation toward the mushroom hunt. No traditions, no superstitions, no avidity, no competition, no exclusive claim to the patch. Americans dress well for the woods, wicker basket in hand with a sandwich, a thermos of coffee, a mushroom book. If they find a patch, they share it with friends, and, inevitably, a mycological society is organized, officers elected, membership fees set, periodic meetings arranged. The mushroom hunt becomes a cooperative outing; it's the American, the democratic way, the way of people for whom the mushroom is not so much a food as a luxury.

Angelo Pellegrini
Vintage Pellegrini

FUNGI PERFECTI

As the popularity of mushrooms increases, the hunt for wild specimens is itself becoming a luxury. The common-law code of the amateur—walk lightly and harvest sparingly—is not enough to protect mushroom beds against the attentions of commercial pickers (most of whose harvest goes to Europe or Japan) and a growing population of enthusiasts.

This rush to the woods causes a number of problems besides the obvious danger of overharvest. One is trampling. The main part of a mushroom is not the fruiting body that we eat, but the masses of threadlike white mycelium underground. Mycelium favors rotting logs and spongy ground. It does not survive repeated stomping. Another concern is that repeated selective harvest of edible mushrooms may give an ecological advantage to the far more numerous inedible species, gradually causing a shift in the mushroom population.

One solution being pursued in various projects around Washington and Oregon is commercial cultivation of native species. These range from big corporate operations like Bonneville Foods, a Salt Lake City–based company that uses waste heat from a garbage incineration plant to run a wholesale shiitake operation in Whatcom County, to backyard growers with a few inoculated logs under tarps.

For the do-it-yourself producer, the most complete tools of the trade come from Fungi

Perfecti, run by Paul Stamets and his wife, Cruz, from their farm near Shelton. Stamets began by growing oyster mushrooms (genus *Pleurotus*), and has moved on to a big variety of offerings for backyard culturists and commercial growers.

"This is what we should be exporting," Stamets told Schuyler Ingle in an interview in 1986, "the oyster mushroom, fresh and dried, not wild mushrooms."

Stamets also grows shiitake mushrooms, which decompose hardwoods. He uses techniques first refined by the Japanese to inoculate alder logs with spawn, and his expertise, shared during his quarterly seminars, have spawned (forgive the expression) commercial shiitake projects throughout Washington and Oregon.

Backyard or even kitchen-table mycologists can order shiitake and *Pleurotus* logs, ready to produce. A large, mild variety of *Stropharia* will fruit for years in a pile of wood chips in the yard, and Stamets looks forward to a time when there is a fairy ring in every yard and a morel patch in every compost pile.

Lane Morgan

Fungi Perfecti
Paul Stamets
P.O. Box 7634
Olympia, WA 98507
(206) 426-9292
Catalog: $3.

RHUBARB BARBECUE SAUCE

This is a thick, spunky sauce of the hot, sweet-and-sour persuasion. Taste as you go; some people will prefer a sweeter version, and the number of hot peppers is equally personal.

2 oranges
4 cups rhubarb, sliced 1 inch thick
1 large white onion, coarsely chopped
¼ cup dried currants
1 cup brown sugar
¼ cup cider vinegar
3 dried Japanese red, hot peppers
4 cloves garlic
8 whole cardamom pods
1 tablespoon ground coriander
Sugar to taste

Grate orange rind, and juice oranges. Put the rhubarb, onion, and currants in a saucepan with the sugar, vinegar, orange juice, and hot peppers. Bring to a boil, reduce heat, and cook until thick, stirring frequently. When liquid is shiny and thick, press in the garlic, and add the spices and 1 tablespoon of the grated orange rind. Cook for another 5 minutes or so; then add sugar to taste. Remove and discard the peppers and the cardamom pods. Bottle the sauce or start brushing it on. It becomes even better after the flavors have melded overnight.

Makes 1½ to 2 cups.

Ann Lovejoy
Seattle Weekly

U-PICK FARMS AND ROADSIDE STANDS

U-pick Guidelines: Call first, especially near the beginning and end of the season. Find out if your small children are welcome to help pick. Farms will supply picking containers, but you will need bags or boxes to transport your produce home. Pick carefully and conscientiously; a well-tended berry field or orchard represents years of knowledgeable labor. (Dogs should stay in the car.)

Harvests may vary greatly from year to year. A local chamber of commerce or county extension office can often supply up-to-date seasonal information. Also, many newspapers publish local farm maps in the late spring or summer.

KING COUNTY, WASHINGTON

John Hamakami Strawberry Farm ☀ (206) 833-2081
John Hamakami
14733 SE Green Valley Road, Auburn
June–July: 7:30am–6pm.

U-pick or ready-picked strawberries. Bring containers.

Five miles east of Auburn on SE Green Valley Road.

Larosa and Sons Farm ☀ (206) 833-2103
14412 Green Valley Road SE, Auburn
June–October: daily, 8am–dark. (Closed 1993, open 1994.)

Fresh vegetables, picked daily. Will pick to order.

Two miles past Neely Mansion on Green Valley Road SE.

Rainier Natural Foods ☀ (206) 833-4369
Ray Huber
38629 Auburn-Enumclaw Highway
P.O. Box 280
Auburn, WA 98002
Year-round: Sunday–Thursday, 9am–6pm; Friday, 9am–3pm.

Whole-grain bakery makes 40 varieties of bread, including a celebrated sprouted grain and the Ezekiel 4:9 breads. Available by mail order or at the bakery.

On Highway 164, 2 miles south of Auburn city limits.

Canyon Park Orchard ☀ (206) 483-8654
Tom and Susan Berry
23305 39th Avenue SE, Bothell
End of August–mid-October: Wednesday–Sunday, 10am–5pm.

Thirty varieties of apples, including Paulared, Akane, Jonamac, Gala, Spartan, McIntosh, Melrose, Jonagold, King.

Call for directions.

Sunset Orchards ☀ (206) 481-0777
Gayle Logan
17425 Sunset Road, Bothell
Mid-September–mid-December: Thursday–Sunday, noon–5pm; call before visiting.

Only Red and Golden Delicious U-pick orchard in western Washington. McIntosh apples also available at the beginning of the season; cider pressing begins in mid-October. Herbs in the spring. Pumpkins, honey in the fall.

Take Mill Creek exit off I-5. Go east on 164th Street to Highway 527, turn left, and go to 180th. Turn left on 180th and you'll come to Sunset Road. Look for sign.

Game Haven Greenery ☀ (206) 333-4313
J. J. and Susan Schmoll
7110 310th Avenue NE, Carnation
Call ahead.

Vegetable plants, U-pick or ready-picked pumpkins.

Take the Carnation Farm Road one mile north of Carnation.

Game Haven Greenery ✶ (206) 333-4313
J. J. and Susan Schmoll
7119 310th Avenue NE, Carnation
Call ahead.

Vegetable plants, U-pick or ready-picked pumpkins, chemical-free beef.

Take the Carnation Farm Road one mile north of Carnation.

Harvold Berry Farm ✶ (206) 333-4185
Herman Harvold
32325 NE 55th, Carnation
Mid-June–mid-August: daily, 8am–8pm.

U-pick strawberries, raspberries.

Take the Carnation-Duvall Road (Highway 203) north of city limits to NE 55th.

Pfeiffer's Suffolk ✶ (206) 333-4934
Kay and Linda Pfeiffer
31439 W Commercial, Carnation
Open weekends, mostly; call ahead—let ring.

Naturally grown lamb and mutton; fleece and wool. Butcher will cut and wrap per your instructions; may be up to 1 month delay between order and pickup.

West Commercial is off Highway 203 between Duvall and Fall City; farm is 2 blocks west of the highway.

Remlinger Farms ✶
(206) 451-8740 or (206) 333-4135
Gary, Bonnie, and David Remlinger
NE 32nd Street, Carnation
April–December; call for "Ripe N Ready Report."

This is a great place to take the family for pony rides, pumpkins, and crafts at Christmas. An indoor market carries seasonal fruits and vegetables; U-pick also available.

One mile south of town off Highway 203.

Lydon's Blueberry Farm ✶ (206) 788-1395
Larry and Bette Lydon
14510 Kelly Road NE, Duvall
Mid-July–frost: Wednesday–Sunday, 9am–dusk.
Call ahead.

U-pick blueberries.

Six miles east of Duvall.

Sheepish Hollow ✶ (206) 825-2358
Tom and Dianne Smith
41724 254th Avenue SE, Enumclaw
Call ahead.

The Smiths sell their market lambs and, as an extra service, take them to the butcher so they're cut and wrapped. Order lambs early in the year, and they're ready in the fall, or even into next year (depending on how people like them). Sheepish Hollow lambs are Romneys (noted for their delicate flavor) and Border Leicesters, bred for wool as well as meat.

The Herbfarm ✶ (206) 784-2222
Ron Zimmerman and Carrie Van Dyck
32804 Issaquah–Fall City Road, Fall City
Year-round: daily, 9am–6pm.

Seventeen theme gardens (such as the Fragrance Garden, the Edible Flowers Garden) display over 600 kinds of herb plants. Tours, classes, potted herbs, and the gift shops attract all sorts of herb afficionados, as does the restaurant, whose innovative herbal meals take cooking beyond the everyday use of basil and oregano.

Take exit 22 off I-90. Go toward Fall City; after 3 miles, go left over green bridge.

Valley Growers ✶ (206) 392-2632 or -6559
Thomas Giberson
1675 Newport Way NW, Issaquah

Fresh produce and vegetable starts.

Take exit 15 from I-90; stand is ½ mile south.

Carpinto Bros. Farm Stand ✶
(206) 854-5692
Mike and Dan Carpinto
1148 N Central Avenue, Kent
Year-round (except November): daily, 9am–6pm.

Fresh produce and gardening store.

Take Highway 167 south to 84th Street–North Central exit. Go south on 84th; stand is on corner of 84th and North Central.

Cruz-Johnson Farms ✶ (206) 872-8017
Fred and Terry Johnson
22243 Frager Road, Kent
May–October: Monday–Saturday, 8am–6pm.

Ready-picked and U-pick rhubarb, pole beans, peas, strawberries, raspberries, beets, and carrots; other produce available at farm stand.

Take 188th Street exit off I-5, turn left into the Kent Valley.

D & D Farm ✿ (206) 872-8612
Dennis and Sylvia Fernando
21841 Frager Road, Kent
June–July: Monday–Saturday (closed Tuesday), 8:30am–6pm; Sunday, noon–6pm.

U-pick strawberries and raspberries.

One-half mile south of S 212th Street; entrance is on Frager Road.

Kent Berry Farm ✿
(206) 833-2016 or (206) 255-2428
Michi Chihara
2500 Frager Road, Kent
June–July: open 8am.

U-pick strawberries; bring containers.

Take the West Valley Highway ¼ mile south of Kent K-Mart.

T & M Berry Farm ✿
(206) 242-3370 or (206) 859-4193
Kent
Mid-June–July: 8am–dusk (to 6pm on weekends); call ahead.

U-pick raspberries.

Go south of Kent on 3rd about ½ mile, or north on 277th or 78th about ½ mile. Look for signs.

Bybee-Nims Farm ✿ (206) 888-0821
42930 SE 92nd Street, North Bend
Mid-July–mid-September: daily, 8am–8pm.

Blueberries—U-pick

Take exit 31 off I-90, turn right at signal, go 2 blocks to Ballarat Avenue N, turn north. Continue on arterial to 428th; at the T turn left, after the river go right and watch for signs. Farm is about 1¾ miles from town.

Con-Mid Old World Fruit Farm ✿
(206) 885-9441
Chayyau Chasengnou
13245 Woodinville-Redmond Road (Highway 202), Redmond
In season.

U-pick, farm stand, and call-in orders for raspberries, gooseberries, currants, pie cherries, and quince. Chinese vegetables. Also sells at Pike Place Market.

Take exit 20 (NE 124th) off I-405. Turn left on Highway 202. Farm is 1 mile on left.

Root Connection ✿ (206) 774-0451
Claire Thomas
13631 Woodinville-Redmond Road (Highway 202), Redmond
Call for days open.

Thomas is converting her customer-share garden into a roadside stand for her own and other local organic vegetables. Adding flowers and perennials.

One mile south of Ste. Michelle Winery in Woodinville on Highway 202.

Serres Farm ✿ (206) 868-3017
William and Nancy Serres
20306 NE 50th Street, Redmond
June–mid-July: daily, 8am–8pm.

U-pick strawberries.

From Redmond, drive east 3 miles on Redmond–Fall City Road (Highway 202) to the Gray Barn, then turn south on Sahalee Way, drive 1 block, turn west on 50th and go ¼ mile.

Kennydale Blueberry Farm ✿
(206) 228-9623
Darrel and Sue Kinzer
1733 NE 20th Street, Renton
Mid-July–late September: Monday–Saturday, 8am–7pm.

U-pick blueberries.

Take exit 6 off I-405 on the east side of the freeway. Follow the fence around the school, turn right on NW 28th, left on Jones Avenue, and left on NE 20th. Farm is third on the right.

Herban Renewal ✳ (206) 243-8821
Joe and Janice Peltier
10437 19th SW, Seattle
Open by appointment.

Organic fresh-cut and potted herbs.

White Center, north of intersection of SW 106th and 19th Avenue SW.

Augie's U-pick ✳ (206) 463-2735
Augie Takatsuka
11003 SW Bank Road, Vashon Island
Call ahead for hours.

Strawberries, raspberries, loganberries, cascadeberries, boysenberries, U-cut Christmas trees.

Three to four miles west of the Vashon Highway on 176th Street (Bank Road).

Country Store and Farm ✳
(206) 463-3655
Vi Beals
20211 Vashon Highway SW, Vashon Island
Year round: Monday–Saturday, 9am–6pm;
Sunday noon–5pm

Home-grown herbs, herb vinegars, mustard, and a specialty nursery. Also wholesales herbs and greens to a number of Seattle restaurants.

On the main Vashon highway, 7½ miles from either ferry landing.

Maury Island Farm ✳ (206) 463-5617
Peter and Judith Shepherd
P.O. Box L
Vashon Island, WA 98070
Call to arrange tours; 1-800-356-5880 for mail order.
Year-round: daily, 10am–5pm.

Fifteen kinds of jams, jellies, and marmalades, and 5 fruit toppings. Suppliers to several Seattle stores and restaurants.

Intersection of Vashon Highway and SW 204th Street.

Otsuka Berry Farm ✳ (206) 463-2406
T. Otsuka
16917 Vashon Highway SW, Vashon Island
Summer: daily, 7am–6pm.

U-pick strawberries (mid-June–July 4); U-pick raspberries (late June–mid-July); and sweet corn (mid-August–early September).

Located on main island highway between 168th and 171st streets, ½ mile north of town.

Sweet Woodroffe Herb Farm ✳
(206) 463-5871
Pam Woodroffe and Ivan Weiss
11222 SW 238th Street
Vashon Island, WA 98070

Mail-order gift packages of herbal teas, potpourri, and mulling spices. On-farm workshops are being planned; write for catalog and event schedules.

Wax Orchards ✳ (206) 463-9735
Betsy Wax Sestrap
Route 4, Box 320
Vashon Island, WA 98070
Year-round: Monday–Saturday, 9am–5pm;
Sunday, 11am–5pm.

The orchard, founded in 1920, now specializes in all-natural fruit syrups, condiments, and toppings, including low-calorie, fudge-sweet toppings made without fat, sugar, or additives. Also available by mail.

Ferries to Vashon leave from Fauntleroy in West Seattle and from Tacoma. From either ferry, take Island Highway (Route 99) to 204th Street. Turn west, go 3½ miles to 131st Street SW. Turn south, go ½ mile; the orchard is on the left.

Fred Zante Farm ✳ (206) 483-9676
13415 NE 170th Street, Woodinville
June–October: daily, 10am–7pm.

U-pick cucumbers and strawberries; other produce available at farm stand.

Take Woodinville exit off Highway 522 onto NE 175th. Go south to the end of 133rd.

KITSAP COUNTY, WASHINGTON

Coyote Farm ☆ (206) 842-0336
David Kotz
9203 Mandus Olsen Road, Bainbridge Island
Call ahead for hours.

Greens, root crops, tomatoes, squash, corn, brassica, wild mushrooms, berries, and herbs.

Take Highway 305 west to Madison Avenue, turn right onto New Brooklyn Road. Go about 1¼ miles to Mandus Olsen Road; Coyote Farm is second left.

Manzanita Organics ☆ (206) 842-1429
Karen Selvar
9229 Day Road NE, Bainbridge Island
In season: Wednesday–Sunday, 9am–4:30pm.

Organically grown vegetables and herbs.

From Highway 305, turn east at the Day Road traffic light; farm is on right side of the road.

Port Madison Farm ☆ (206) 842-4125
Stephen and Beverly Phillips
15015 Sunrise Drive, Bainbridge Island
Call ahead for hours and availability.

On-farm sales of organic vegetables and goat milk from their dairy.

From Highway 305, turn east on Day Road and left on Sunrise.

Sandy's Perennials ☆ (206) 842-7130
Sandra Noble
4205 Pleasant Beach, Bainbridge Island
March–September: Wednesday–Sunday, 10am–5pm.

Organic vegetable starts, perennials, and herbs.

Seven driveways south of Lynwood Center.

Suyematsu Farms ☆ (206) 842-4388
Akio Suyematsu
9229 NE Day Road, Bainbridge Island
In season: U-pick 8am–4:30pm; stand open 9am until sold out.

Strawberries, raspberries, Christmas trees.

From Highway 305, turn east at the Day Road traffic light; farm is on right side of the road (same location as Manzanita Organics).

Triad Fisheries ☆ (206) 842-1640
Bruce Gore
Bainbridge Island

Wholesales ultra-fresh salmon, flash-frozen and glazed against dehydration while still on the boat. Triad is known all over the U.S., and ships salmon to parts of Europe and Asia as well. In the Seattle area, notable restaurants such as Ray's Boathouse and Fullers cook with Gore's fish; it's sold uncooked at Larry's Markets.

White Goose and Gorse Farm ☆ (206) 842-6724
Irmgard Grabo
6840 New Brooklyn Road, Bainbridge Island
Call ahead for appointment and directions.

Goose eggs, herbs, flowers, and plants.

Clyde's Apiary ☆ (206) 377-7275
Clyde Allen
319 Sugar Pine Drive, Bremerton
Year-round: Monday–Saturday, 9am–6pm; also at the Bremerton Farmers Market. Call ahead.

Blueberry, raspberry, and fireweed honey. Maple honey in the spring. Brings an observation hive to the Bremerton Market.

Call for directions.

Silver Bay Herb Farm ☆ (206) 692-1340
Mary Preus
9151 Tracyton Boulevard, Bremerton
June to September: daily, 11am–5pm.

Herb plants, fresh-cut herbs, vinegars, and gift shop. Also offers classes and other events.

Take Bucklin Hill Road east from Silverdale, turn right on Tracyton Boulevard; driveway is ½ mile down, to the right.

Foulweather Farm ☆ (206) 638-1554
Maureen K. Vis
40444 Foulweather Bluff Road, Hansville
Monday–Friday, flexible hours. Call ahead.

Beans, beets, cabbages, carrots, chard, cucumbers, leeks, lettuce, fennel, pumpkin, and squash (both summer and winter).

Take Hansville Road to Hansville, then Twin Spits Road to Foulweather Bluff Road and look for sign.

Wood Family Farm and Nursery ✶
(206) 857-GROW
Jim and Carol Wood
12090 Olalla Valley Road, Olalla
Open for starts and bedding plants May–October;
call ahead before visiting.

Organically grown vegetables, naturally raised
free-run chickens, eggs, pumpkins, a variety of
farm animals (baby pigs, ducks, etc.).

*Take Southworth Ferry from West Seattle. Follow
signs to Highway 16. Turn left onto Sedgewick,
go 2 miles to Banner Road. Turn left onto Banner, right on Ollala Valley Road. Farm is 3 miles
down.*

Burley Cottage Naturals ✶ **(206) 857-
4372**
Barbara Wood
14970 Willow Road SE, Port Orchard
Year-round: call ahead.

Small, organic farm selling herbs: plants, fresh-
cut, and dried, as well as dried flowers. Wood
also makes berry preserves and apple butter.

In Burley, ½ mile from the Burley Store.

Minter Creek Farm ✶ **(206) 876-2803**
Rollo and Deanna Van Slyke
2236 SW Pine Road, Port Orchard
Year-round: call ahead before visiting.

Organically raised green beans, cucumbers, carrots, beets, chard, green onions, corn, tomatoes, apples, plums, pie cherries, summer and
winter squash, pumpkins, and eggs.

*South of Port Orchard Airport; west of intersec-
tion of Sidney and Pine roads. Look for sign.*

Harpis' Organic Acres ✶ **(206) 697-5377**
Jim and Donna Harpis
2095 NW Luoto Road, Poulsbo
In season: Tuesday–Sunday, 10am–5pm, and in
the evening by appointment. Call ahead.

Corn, potatoes, beets, spinach, peas, lettuce,
beans, carrots, zucchini, squash (butternut,
acorn, and pumpkin), tomatoes, broccoli,
cauliflower, and cabbage.

*Take Keyport exit from Highway 3 north, and
head toward Keyport. It's the first house on the
right after the exit.*

LEWIS COUNTY, WASHINGTON

Walkling Family Farm ✶ **(206) 736-8070**
William, Gene, and Karen Walkling
6641-210th Avenue SW, Centralia
June–August: call ahead for hours.

Beans, cabbage, cucumbers, dill, and potatoes.

*Take exit 88 west off I-5. Turn left at first stop-
light onto Old Highway 99 and go south for 1
mile. Turn right onto Old Highway 9 at sale barn
across from Junction Tavern, and then turn onto
210th Avenue. Follow to end of gravel road.
Farm is on left.*

Mt. Capra Cheese ✶ **(206) 748-4224**
Frank and Ann Stout
279 SW 9th St, Chehalis, WA 98532
Year-round at the cheese plant: call ahead. Sold
at food co-ops and specialty stores; available
through mail order.

Hand-made raw milk goat cheese in several
types. The Feta-type Olympic cheese is a stand-
out. In business since 1928.

Northwest Chestnuts ✶ **(206) 985-7033**
Omroa and Annie Bhagwandin
183 Shady Grove, Onalaska, WA 98570
January–April (for nursery stock only); call ahead.

The Bhagwandins harvest and distribute regional
chestnuts, including fresh and dried chestnuts,
and chestnut flour. On-farm sales are only for
nursery stock, but everything else is available by
mail order, or at the Pike Place Market during the
holiday season.

Call ahead for directions.

Aldrich Berry Farm and Nursery ✶
(206) 983-3138
Glen and Wisten Aldrich
190 Aldrich Road, Mossyrock
Seasonal: daily, 9am–6pm; call ahead.

Ready-picked blueberries.

*Twenty miles east of I-5 on Highway 12; turn
right at DeGeode Bulb Farm, go ½ mile, turn right
onto Aldrich Road.*

Grose's Farm ⭐ (206) 496-3358
Cyril Grose
156 Damron Road, Mossyrock
Call ahead for hours.

Ready-picked blueberries.

From I-5 go east on Highway 12, left at Mossy-rock blinking light. Turn right onto Damron Road, go one block; farm is on the left. (From the west on Highway 12, take the first road (Damron) on the right after the high bridge.)

Grouse Hills Farm ⭐
(206) 927-0187 or (206) 874-2872
Dick and Judy Battin
Napavine
Call ahead for hours.

On-farm sales of organic apples and Asian pears.

In Napavine area; take exit 72 off I-5. Call for further directions.

Burnt Ridge Orchards ⭐ (206) 985-2873
Mike and Carolyn Cerling-Dolan
432 Burnt Ridge Road
Onalaska, WA 98570
Open by appointment only.

Organic hazelnuts, chestnuts, English and black walnuts, and hickory nuts, available by mail order. The Dolans sell at the Olympia Farmers Market.

Cheney Family Farm ⭐ (206) 978-4358
Chris and Pam Cheney
717 Gish Road, Onalaska
In season: daily, open daylight hours; call ahead.

U-pick and ready-picked strawberries and sweet corn.

From I-5, go east on Highway 508 toward Onalaska. Drive 5 miles to Gish Road; farm is at milepost 3.

Orchard Home Farm ⭐ (206) 985-2316
Leonard Huntting
394 Huntting Road, Silver Creek
In season: daily, 8am–dark; call ahead.

Ready-picked raspberries.

From I-5, go east on Highway 12 to Silver Creek Road, turn right onto Huntting Road.

Latham Farms ⭐ (206) 848-1010
Mark and Tresa Latham
13514 McCutcheon Road, Orting
April–October: Wednesday–Sunday, 10am–6pm.

No longer producing food products. Mostly flowers and herbs.
Southeast of Puyallup.

Corwin Apple Orchard ⭐
(206) 845-1982 or (206) 747-3324
Fred Corwin
7523 Fruitland Avenue, Puyallup
End of August–October: daily, 10am to 5pm.

Fall apples, honey, prunes, and quince.

One and a half miles west of Puyallup; look for sign 200 yards south of Pioneer.

Puyallup Valley Jam Factory ⭐
(206) 845-0784
2615 Tacoma Road, Puyallup
Year round: Monday–Saturday, 9am–5pm.

Mail order and retail jams: marionberry, raspberry, strawberry, blueberry, boysenberry, and loganberry. Low-sugar varieties available. From June through August, fresh berries are available as well.

From I-5, take the Puyallup exit and head south on the Enchanted Parkway. After about 5 miles, the parkway becomes Meridian; in downtown Puyallup go right on Pioneer, and go about 1½ miles to the old Texaco station. Go right one mile to where the paved road ends; jam factory is on the right.

The Meat Shop ⭐ (206) 537-4490
Lee, Joe, and Bob Markholt
13419 Vickery Ave E, Tacoma
Year-round: Monday–Friday, 8am–6pm; Saturday, 10am–5pm

Fresh or frozen organic beef, chicken, pork, and lamb; hams, bacon, pastrami, corned beef, and other meats, cured without nitrates, nitrites, phosphates, sugar, or MSG. Custom cutting and wrapping available.

From I-5, go east on Highway 512. Exit at Portland Avenue and turn right. Turn left onto 112th Street and go 1½ miles to Vickery.

Y & Y Farms ☆ (206) 922-7577
Pete Yamamoto
2316 54th Avenue E, Tacoma
March–October: daily, 9am–7pm.

All kinds of produce, eggs, honey, and milk.

Take exit 137 off I-5, at Fife.

THURSTON COUNTY, WASHINGTON

Black Lake Organic Store ☆
(206) 786-0537
Gary Kline
4711 Black Lake Boulevard SW, Olympia
February–October: daily; evenings only in
September and October.

On-farm sales of organic snow peas, tomatoes, cucumbers, squash, and cabbage crops. Plants and organic fertilizer also available.

Turn right off Highway 101 at Capitol Mall.

Farmer's Own Organic Produce ☆
(206) 754-8989
P.O. Box 7446
Olympia, WA 98507

Growers and shippers of Washington-grown, certified organic produce.

Fungi Perfecti ☆ (206) 426-9292
Paul Stamets
P.O. Box 7634
Olympia, WA 98507

Mail order spawn and supplies for mushroom growers. Kits for producing oyster mushrooms and others inside, and several kinds of spawn for backyard growers. *Stropharia rugoso-annulata* is one of the largest and easiest to grow. Also organically grown shiitake mushrooms, fresh or dried. Send $3 for catalog.

Lattin's Country Cider Mill ☆
(206) 491-7328
Carolyn and Vic Lattin
9402 Rich Road SE, Olympia
Year-round: Monday–Saturday: 9am–6pm; daily from August–December.

Apples, dried fruits and nuts, honey, frozen berries, and six flavors of cider; fruits and vegetables in season. "Once you taste our cider or pies," says Carolyn, "You're addicted. There's no hope for you." Pies and freezer jam, too.

Take Air Industrial Park exit off I-5. Go left over the highway to the Old 99 Highway and go south. Go 3 miles on Old 99 to Rich Road, take a left, and go ½ mile. Often, you'll smell the apples before you get there.

Medicine Creek Farm ☆ (206) 491-9669
James and Elizabeth Myers
947 Old Pacific Highway SE, Olympia
Mid-August–end of October: daily, 10am–6pm.

U-pick pumpkins, apples, and corn.

Take exit 116 off I-5.

Annie Crothers ☆ (206) 446-7344
13224 Military Road SE, Rainier
Call for lambing schedule.

Order a whole or half lamb in advance. Lambing takes place in the spring (easier on Annie—and the ewes, who give birth outside), and the lambs are usually ready (depending on how old you want them) in the fall. Butchering takes place on the farm, and the meat is cut and wrapped for you. The sheep are a Lincoln-Romney cross; fleece and pelts are also available.

Three miles west of Rainier; take College Street out of town, which becomes Rainier Road, which is crossed by Military Road SE.

Helsing Farms ☆ (206) 273-8557
Pat Moore
12013 Independence Road, Rochester
June–November: 9am–5pm.

Helsing Farms operates as a community-supported agriculture program; a set price buys a share in the farm's production, which should feed a family of four for 26–30 weeks. This method of investment saves the farmer the work of borrowing money (as well paying interest), and gives shareholders plenty of food cheaply.

Heading south on Highway 12, go right on 185th Street and follow the main road until it becomes Independence Road. Farm is fifth on the left after the bridge.

Independence Valley Farm ✯ (206) 273-5882
Betsie DeWreede
13136 201st Avenue SW, Rochester
Call ahead.

On-farm and U-pick for a variety of organic produce, including carrots, Yellow Finn potatoes,

broccoli, peas, and organic strawberries, which are hard to find. Specializes in carrots and leeks. Also sells at Olympia Farmers Market.

Call for directions.

The Strawberry Patch ✯ (206) 273-9533
19246 Albany Road, Rochester
In season: daily, 8am–8pm; call ahead.

U-pick and ready-picked strawberries.

Take exit 88 west off I-5, go 5 miles to Rochester. Turn south at Rochester stoplight (Albany Road), and go 1 mile to the corner of Albany and James.

SPECIALTY STORES

Garvey's Enterprise (a.k.a Northwest Gourmet Foods) ✯ (206) 641-0232
15019 NE 14th Street, Bellevue, WA 98007

Mail order source for organic baking mixes (including Irish soda bread, brown bread, scones, and shortbread), honey, popcorn, soups, and teas. Available at Seattle-area Larry's Markets, Olson's, Exclusively Washington, and Williams-Sonoma.

Kitchen Kitchen ✯ (206) 451-9507
Bellevue Square, Bellevue
Monday–Saturday, 9:30am–9:30pm; Sunday, 11am–6pm.

Offers every kitchen gadget, houseware, and cooking class imaginable.

Bellevue Way and NE 8th Street.

Tokul Gold ✯ (206) 392-4794
Virginia Vadset
20121 SE 30th
Issaquah, WA 98027

Homemade caramels, with or without walnuts, conceived in the foothills of the Cascades. Available by mail and at local grocery stores.

Canterbury Cuisine ✯
(206) 881-2555 or (800) 733-6663
Lynn Kirwan and Leigh Zwicker
P.O. Box 2271
Redmond, WA 98073

Mail-order source for a variety of specialty foods, including quick-bread mixes (some requiring beer), cake mixes, and soup mixes. Also available at specialty and grocery stores.

Cossack Caviar ✴ (206) 435-6600
Gary Shaw
6900 191st Place NE, Arlington

Wholesaler of salmon caviar from Northwest roe. Available at University Seafood, Larry's Market, and fish vendors at the Pike Place Market.

Grand Central Mercantile ✴ (206) 623-8894
316 1st Avenue S, Seattle
Monday–Saturday, 10am–6pm; Sunday, 10am–5pm.

Imported kitchenware, including pottery, knives, and gadgets.

1st Avenue between Jackson and Main streets.

Larry's Market ✴ (206) 527-5333
10008 Aurora Avenue N, Seattle
Daily, open 24 hours.

Supermarket that stocks a wide variety of ethnic and specialty foods and local produce (ranging from the common to the exotic). Other stores are White Center, Totem Lake, Sea-Tac, and Bellevue.

East side of Aurora in Oak Tree Village between 100th and 103rd streets.

Made in Washington ✴ (206) 467-0788
Jack and Gillian Matthews
1530 Post Alley, Seattle
Monday–Saturday, 9am–6pm; Sunday, 10am–5pm.

Everything from soup to salmon to slug suckers, all locally produced, grown, baked, and smoked.

In the Pike Place Market. Other locations at Westlake Center and Northgate, and in Bellevue and Issaquah.

Mutual Fish ✴ (206) 322-4368
Dick Yoshimura
2335 Rainier Avenue S, Seattle
Monday–Saturday, 8:30am–5:30pm.

Specialty fresh (and live) seafood, smoked and processed salmon, seafood cakes.

Near the intersection of 23rd and Rainier.

The Pike Place Market Creamery ✴ (206) 622-5029
1514 Pike Place #3, Seattle
Monday–Saturday, 9am–6pm.

All sorts of dairy products, from raw cow and goat milk (raw milk has more calcium and is more easily digested than pasteurized), cottage cheese (with and without curds), rice pudding, butter, local sour cream and yogurt, and all kinds of eggs (white, brown, quail, duck, goose, etc.). Tofu and soy milk available as well.

In the Pike Place Market, behind Jack's Fish Spot.

Port Chatham Packing Company ✴ (206) 783-8200
632 NW 46th Street
Seattle, WA 98107
Monday–Friday, 8:30am–5:30pm; Saturday 9am–5pm.

Cold-smoked salmon, black cod, trout, oysters, and other seafood, canned and smoked. Gift packages and mail order.

Corner of 8th and 46th, south of Market Street in Ballard. Downtown store (1306 4th Ave, Seattle, (206) 623-4645) carries many of the same foods as the Ballard outlet.

Puget Consumers' Co-op ✴ (206) 525-1450
6504 20th Avenue NE, Seattle
Daily, 9am–9pm (hours vary in different branches).

Natural foods (grains, spices, pastas, legumes) sold in bulk as well as packaged. Chemical and additive-free meats and fish, healthy snacks, ethnic foods, organic produce, and delis (at some branches).

At NE 65th Street and 20th Avenue NE in Ravenna. Other branches are at Green Lake, View Ridge, West Seattle, and Seward Park in the Seattle area, as well as Kirkland and Everett.

Sur La Table ✱ **(206) 448-2244**
Pike Place Market, Seattle
Monday–Saturday, 9am–6pm; Sunday,
9:30am–6pm.

Kitchenware, cookbooks, linens, and cooking
classes. Everything imaginable.

*In the Pike Place Market, with entrances on both
Pine and Stewart streets.*

University Seafood and Poultry ✱
(206) 632-3900 or -3700
The Erikson family
1317 NE 47th Street, Seattle
Monday–Friday, 10am–6pm; Saturday,
9:30am–5:30pm.

Fresh fish, game birds and meats, eggs, wine.
Shipping available.

*Between University Way NE and Brooklyn
Avenue NE.*

The Wild Salmon ✱ **(206) 283-3366**
David F. Leong
Fisherman's Terminal
1735 W Thurman Street, Seattle
Monday–Saturday: 10am–6pm; Sunday,
11am–6pm.

Begun in the 1970s as a direct-marketing
cooperative for fishermen, the Wild Salmon is
now a private business but it still deals directly
with fishermen and sells only fresh wild fish—
not just salmon—and specialty canned fish
from local waters.

Off 15th Avenue NW at Fisherman's Terminal.

Uwajimaya ✱ **(206) 624-6248**
519 6th Avenue S, Seattle
Daily, 9am–8pm.

International District supermarket and department store featuring all manner of Asian foods,
including good fresh fish (and all the ingredients
for sushi) and produce.

*S Weller Street between 5th and 6th avenues;
second location at 15555 NE 24th Street in
Bellevue.*

FARMERS MARKETS

KING COUNTY, WASHINGTON

Issaquah Farmers Market
Contact: Dorothy Knitter, (206) 392-2229
April–November: Saturday, 9am–3pm.

*Gibson Park on Newport Boulevard, across from
hatchery.*

Kent Saturday Market
Contact: Nancy Woo, (206) 859-3369
May–mid-October: Saturday, 9am–4pm.

In operation since 1964, with up to 100 vendors.
A last stand for famous Green River Valley crops,
now mostly lost to development.

2nd and Smith in downtown Kent.

Pike Place Market, Seattle
Contact: Steve Evans, (206) 682-7453
Year round: Monday–Saturday, 9am–6pm;
Sunday, 11am–5pm.

In business since 1907, it's the oldest and
largest farmers market in the Northwest, drawing
vendors from around the state. More than 100
growers sell here, side by side with fish markets,
meat and cheese shops, bakeries, and ethnic
markets. Huge selection. Also, Northwest arts
and crafts.

1st Avenue and Pike Street.

Redmond Saturday Market

Contact: Bill Thurmond, (206) 821-4832
May–mid-October: Saturday, 8am–2pm.

7730 Leary Way in Redmond.

Vashon Market Association

Contact: Mary Steyh, (206) 463-3010
Year-round: Saturday, 10am–3pm.

In town, on the main highway.

KITSAP COUNTY, WASHINGTON

Bremerton Sunday Market

Contact: Don Atkinson, (206) 377-3041
May–October: Sunday, 10am–4pm.

At the Bremerton waterfront, on the new board-walk north of the ferry terminal.

Kingston Farmers Market

Contact: Marsha Adams, (206) 297-4485
May–October: Saturday, 9am–2pm.

Opened in 1990 and growing fast. Produce, flow-ers, seafood, honey, and eggs. Entertainment.

At the marina lawn area, Port of Kingston.

Kitsap Regional Market, Port Orchard

Contact: Carmen Davis, (206) 857-2657, or
Chamber of Commerce, (206) 876-3505
May–October: Saturday, 9am–3pm.

Produce, baked goods, and crafts: "Fourth largest outdoor market in the state." An indoor market is set up in December as well.

On the Port Orchard waterfront.

Kitsap Regional Market, Silverdale

Contact: Norma Hoem, (206) 692-2437
Mid-May–October: Saturday, 9am–1pm.

The Silverdale branch of the Kitsap Market.

At Waterfront Park in Silverdale's Old Town.

Winslow Farmers Market

Contact: Jeanne Wood, (206) 780-9003
May–September: Saturday, 8:30am–2pm.

An extension of the Kitsap Regional Market, with more emphasis on crafts. Holiday market, Satur-day in November and December.

At Winslow Green on Bainbridge Island.

PIERCE COUNTY, WASHINGTON

Eatonville Farmers Market

Contact: Dave Schactler, (206) 832-4345
May–September: Saturday, 10am–4pm.

309 Center Street E.

Gig Harbor Farmers Market

Contact: Roy Denton, (206) 851-4117
May–October: Friday, 9:30am–4pm.

Corner of Wollochet and Artondale Drive.

Puyallup Farmers Market

Contact: Chamber of Commerce,
(206) 845-6755
June–August: Saturday, 9am–2pm; September: Saturday, 8am–noon.

Local produce, crafts, and street food.

Pioneer Park, Meridian and Elm streets.

Tacoma Farmers Market

Contact: Chamber of Commerce,
(206) 627-2175
June–September: Thursday, 10am–3pm.

Antique Row, Broadway between 7th and 9th streets.

THURSTON COUNTY, WASHINGTON

Olympia Farmers Market

Contact: (206) 352-9096
April: Saturday; May: Friday–Sunday; June–Au-gust: Thursday–Sunday; September–October: Fri-day–Sunday; November–December: Saturday. 10am–3pm.

The second biggest farmers market in the state, with more than 100 vendors. Produce, meats, fish, baked and processed goods, and juried craft items.

Percival Landing, Waterfront Park.

THE OLYMPIC PENINSULA

The Olympic Peninsula, from the Strait of Juan de Fuca to the Columbia River, is primarily a vast forest of evergreens growing in shallow soil and fed by rains that can average as much as 200 inches a year. In summer, a traveler in this area might find lengthy periods of sunny weather and astonishing scenery. The road that meanders around the central core of mountains passes long-fingered bays, alpine lakes, Pacific beaches, Indian reservations, placid estuaries, and a national park the size of Rhode Island.

The land was formed five million years ago by undersea volcanic eruptions that pushed the sea bed east, where it collided with the American continent. Sedimentary rock and basalt were heaped up, and gradually, over millions of years, this ancient sea floor rose thousands of feet to form the Olympic Mountains. Then, through another geologic age, glaciers dug the contorted waterways, the lakes and gravel-bedded rivers.

The mountains have stood in their present configuration for about 10,000 years. Their crumbly base erodes easily; the soil that has built up is thin, and the heavy rainfall leaches out nutrients. But this unpromising combination provides a near-perfect environment for the growth of cedar, spruce, hemlock, and fir. The landscape is so dominated by forests that at first glance it seems that trees are the only natural resource. But the land has hidden riches, and the sea has provided humans with sustenance for thousands of years.

People of the Makah, Quileute, Ozette, Hoh, Quinault, Clallam, and Chimacum tribes had only to walk out at low tide to harvest shellfish, or station themselves in the rivers to catch the salmon during the fall runs. They hunted whale and halibut in dugout canoes and stalked deer and elk in the forests. The women gathered more than 30 varieties of berries and preserved almost everything by smoking or drying. These native tribes did not farm; they lived in congenial accord with nature.

Permanent white settlement of the peninsula began in the 1850s. The towns of Port Ludlow, Hadlock, Port Townsend, Port Discovery, and Port Angeles were all founded at this time. The rich valleys of the Dungeness and Chimacum were cleared and farmed. Most transportation to these settlements was by water. For years there were no proper roads, despite continued promises by governments and railroads. As a result, the settlers who went out to homestead around Lake Crescent, Lake Ozette, and along the northwest river valleys were completely isolated and barely managed to subsist by farming. The huge trees were hard to clear, the drainage was poor, and the damp weather often kept crops from ripening. Men were forced to move east to find seasonal work while their wives and children struggled to farm the wild, wet wilderness.

Today there are few signs of these early pioneers. The wet climate has rotted their wood buildings, and trees and blackberries cover their tools and gravestones. The rain, the forests, the lack of employment, and the isolation forced all but a very few to leave.

In the rain shadow of the Olympic Mountains, farming is much easier. For years the town of Sequim and its surrounding valley have been agricultural.

The valley land is rich, the rainfall averages only 17 inches a year, and there is plenty of water in the mountains for irrigation. Dairy farms once predominated, but today only a few are left. Enterprising farmers have turned to raising strawberries and raspberries or organic vegetables and herbs, but there is a mighty squeeze on the agricultural land in the Dungeness valley. In the past decade, Sequim's growing reputation as a "sunshine belt" has turned the sleepy farm town into a busy center for tourists and retirees. The elegant lines of the old grain elevator still offer a landmark, but the building now houses a Mexican restaurant. Many farmers have sold their pastures and fields to developers.

In the quiet Chimacum valley there are some large dairy farms and an occasional sheep ranch, but here too land prices are climbing and farming is precarious.

Change, of course, is inevitable. Perhaps because this river-laced land and its surrounding sea was one of the last areas to be settled, the changes seem more telescoped. It seems that only yesterday resources were unlimited.

When our cook called supper, a circle of happy faces gathered around a large Dutch oven filled of pigeon pie, fresh butter, trout in abundance, with many other good things that would make you hungry to hear mentioned, all cooked to the Queen's taste.

—Harry Fisher, Lake Cushman, July 5, 1890

In April of 1859, James Swan, a historian and anthropologist who traveled and wrote extensively about the peninsula, was invited on a fishing excursion by the chief of the Clallam tribe in Port Townsend. By the time the party, traveling by canoe, had arrived at Chimacum Creek, they had already been given dozens of fish by passing Indians. "The squaws, however, were not quite satisfied," writes Swan in *Almost Out of the World*, "but as the tide was out, they went ashore and soon dug two or three baskets of clams . . . Our dinner consisted of clams, roasted and broiled, broiled salmon, roasted trout, mussels, oyster, and barnacles, the last dish I never ate of before, but which I found delicious. The barnacle grows on the rocks around the bay to a great size, and is much esteemed by the Indians. After the barnacles, we were served up by way of dessert, with an immense skate roasted."

It is still possible to have such a feast, although not so easily. Swan probably ate littleneck clams, which are still burrowing in the sand of Port Townsend Bay, where clamming is restricted. Diving for the geoduck, the prime ingredient of great chowder around Puget Sound, is regulated. The razor clam that was once a mainstay of the Pacific coastal beaches is infected with a disease that does not affect humans but will, in time, probably wipe out the creatures. Diggers there are limited to 15 of these tasty bivalves at particular tides in the spring and fall. Thousands of people with clamming licenses dig furiously to retrieve their quota at these designated times.

Mussels still cling to rocks at the tide line in less traveled parts of the inland waters, and in Dabob Bay, not far from the site of Swan's repast, are oyster farms. In fact, the most productive and diverse oyster area in the United States is on the Pacific coast at Willapa Bay.

The shallow waters of this sprawling estuary have always been home to oysters, but the tiny native Olympia oysters were depleted by early fishermen who made fortunes supplying the booming city of San Francisco during its gold rush. The empty beds were seeded first from Chesapeake Bay and later from Japan. Today the oyster farmers of Willapa Bay grow the large Pacific oysters from Japan and harvest over 25,000 square acres, a crop worth more than $2 million a year.

The bay is also home to a healthy crab population, and in the hills to the east, the damp ground produces exotic mushrooms with such names as "wild turkey," "King Boletus," and "running hedgehog." At The Ark, a well-known local restaurant, sturgeon cooked with wild mushrooms is an autumn favorite.

Along with oysters, early settlers discovered wild cranberries growing in peat bogs to the east of Grays Harbor and Willapa Bay. In 1805 the Indians provided cranberry sauce along with wild geese, ducks, and deer for Lewis and Clark's Thanksgiving dinner in Chinookville. But the wild berries were too small for the Finnish settlers, who imported vines from Cape Cod in 1883. Today this cranberry area is one of the most productive in the country. In Ilwaco, the Cranberry Festival is held each October during the harvest.

For many years this corner of Washington grew rich from its timber, cranberries, and fisheries. The town of South Bend had high hopes of becoming the terminus of the Northern Pacific Railroad. In promotions, the town billed itself as the Baltimore of the West. In 1907, the Albee Hotel in South Bend issued its Christmas menu, a long list of culinary extravagances that are a fascinating blend of local harvest and stylish pretense. Here is a partial listing: "Stuart Point oysters on the half-shell, consomme pintanier royale, silver smelts, celery en branche, lobster a la Newburg, roast young turkey with oyster stuffing, cranberry sauce, entrecote of pork dauphinoise, New England mince pie, English plum pudding," and even "cafe noir." Interestingly, except for the oysters, this feast does not duplicate any of those foods that James Swan enjoyed so much with the Indians just 48 years earlier.

Salmon was not on the menu at all. Perhaps at the time it was considered too ordinary. Today, however, this delicious fish, although common, is increasingly threatened. Born in freshwater rivers and streams, salmon spend their lives at sea and return to the place of their birth to spawn and die. The vast watershed of the Olympic Peninsula, created and fed by glaciers and rains, and held together by forests, provides the Pacific salmon a relatively unhindered journey each year. But overfishing at sea, and logging and dams upriver, have reduced the salmon runs drastically. Throughout the Northwest, this legendary resource stands as a symbol of both the richness and the fragility of the region.

Ann Katzenbach
Port Townsend, Washington

DUNGENESS ORGANIC PRODUCE

In the 26 miles between its headwaters in the Olympic Mountains and the Strait of Juan de Fuca, the Dungeness River falls over 6,000 feet, making it one of the steepest rivers in the Pacific Northwest. With steepness comes velocity, with velocity erosion, and with erosion upstream, flooding and generous soil deposition downstream.

Over the centuries, the Dungeness has created deep, river-laid soils in the narrow band of lowland that separates the mountains from the sea. Since the town of Dungeness was founded in 1852, its river soil legacy has been celebrated widely. Produce and butter from Dungeness farms fed the growing cities of Victoria, British Columbia, and Seattle. Daily steamers docked at Dungeness to carry away the farm bounty that good soil and sunshine produced. But as highway transport replaced steamer traffic, Dungeness farmers lost out to more centrally located growers.

In 1978, Nash Huber began farming the lower Dungeness Valley organically, bucking the local trend of dying agriculture and conversion of agricultural lands to suburban development. His vegetable business began modestly, as garden plots on vacant lots in Dungeness. Gradually he moved to the edge of town, leasing dairy pasture and cultivating row crops in deep Dungeness soil that had never known sustained cultivation, herbicides, or chemical fertilizer. Today, the "farm" is a patchwork of scattered leased plots in and around Dungeness, worked by Huber and a crew that varies in size with seasonal demands.

Over the years, Huber's Dungeness Organic Produce has become known for what Huber calls his "hardware" varieties of produce—broccoli, cauliflower, carrots, sweet corn, celery, tomatoes, and potatoes. He markets locally, through limited grocery outlets, a food co-op, direct sales from his roadside stand, and at local farmers markets. Economic hard times on the Olympic Peninsula have forced him to compete directly with large food chains on price. "Port Angeles is a blue-collar town. My customers know the prices around town and I have to price for them." Given the competition, the principal advantages of Huber's organic produce are flavor, quality, and diversity that only a small operation can promise.

Huber has experimented over the years. "We produced a lot of edible flowers a few years back, but that seemed to pass," he said. Today, Dungeness Organic Produce grows kohlrabi, bulb fennel, radicchio, garlic, and basil for the small upscale segment of the local market—"people who know what to do because they read the magazines."

For the most part, however, Huber emphasizes the basics. "I come from a very conservative farming background and have seen a lot of people go out of business. You've got to concentrate on a local market and keep your ear to the ground." For him, the basics are "carrots that people kill for." Even potatoes can be surprising. In 1984, Huber produced huge Nooksack potatoes—five spuds to a 25-pound sack. ("It was a mistake, but it was lots of fun.") "I enjoy producing a nice patch of cauliflower. It looks good. I put it in a box, somebody eats it and it's gone." Huber estimates that only 20 percent of his sales are because his produce is organic. Most of his customers buy because of the quality of his product, loyalty to his business, and the fact that the price is right.

Huber sees tough times ahead for small organic producers. As more large California farms go organic, brokers and large grocery chains are buying California organic produce for the same reasons they have always bought California produce—consistency, ease, and price. "The economics of it are cruel," Huber says. "Some of those farms are bigger than all of the acreage being organically farmed in Washington put together." For Huber, the key to success is developing a loyal, educated market and sticking with the basics—knowing your soil, your climate, and your customers.

Bob Steelquist

Dungeness Organic Produce
Nash Huber
Sequim
(206) 683-7089
May–December: daily, daylight hours.
Farm stand is at the Dungeness Country Store, in downtown Dungeness.

CRANBERRY GOURMET

During fall harvest, Karen Snyder buys fresh-off-the-vine cranberries.

She knows most of the 29 cranberry growers on the soggy, peat-rich Long Beach Peninsula in southwest Washinton. For 11 years, she was one herself.

Now "I cook cranberry sauce. Wait—actually I'm an entrepreneur," Snyder says. She's not talking big, though her eyes twinkle like rapidly appreciating sapphires: In 1991 she sold $550,000 of her Anna Lena's Cranberry Products made from her neighbors' berries.

In October, when Snyder purchases a half-ton of peninsula berries, she cooks. Those 1,000 pounds yield 7,000 jars of such specialties as cranberry-citrus marmalade, cranberry port jelly, cranberry applesauce, and sweet-and-sour cranberry mustard.

When the sauces and syrups cool, Snyder's handful of workers wrap each jar with a red-and-white heart-and-cranberry label.

Anna Lena's label is as sweet and comforting as the good stuff inside the jars and bags. The products, the small print reads, "are made with the care and tradition of fine cooking passed down from my maternal great-grandmother, Anna Lena Berg."

Anna Lena Berg, Snyder's inspiration, settled in Washington's Pacific County after she left Sweden in 1886. She was single when she emigrated. "I liked that gumption," says Snyder, who has hung her great-grandmother's portrait in the showroom of her 4,500-square-foot warehouse and kitchen.

Snyder, 38, a fifth-generation peninsula native, appears to have inherited her ancestor's get-up-and-go. In four years, she has developed a line of 26 cranberry items, from cranberry catsup—without tomatoes—to cranberry curd. New products include cranola granola, crannies (dried cranberries, which make crunchy additions to cereals, baked goods, and salads), and bread stuffing with crannies and pine nuts. A sweet-hot cranberry mustard and a cranberry-citrus marmalade, flavored with hand-peeled oranges and grapefruits, draw the most orders, though Snyder has also had success selling packages of crannie-filled baked-good mixes.

Snyder experiments with family and heirloom recipes. But, she says, more than a talent for inventive cooking is required to sell specialty foods. You must turn out a consistent product.

Evidently her products are a cut above that. The Ark, the well-known destination restaurant 10 miles north of Long Beach in Nahcotta, sells three Anna Lena's private-label products: cranberry chutney, cranberry-garlic vinegar, and cranberry-raspberry jam.

Snyder believes she's stepped into a profitable niche ignored by gourmet-food producers. "I knew specialty foods were doing well when I started, but the only cranberry products I saw were jams and jellies."

She has yet to run across a competitor nationally or in the Northwest, though Cozette's, a Coos Bay, Oregon, business is producing similar products on a much smaller scale.

Moreover, Snyder has thrilled the Pacific County Economic Development Council with her local "value-added" products. Most Long Beach Peninsula raw materials, such as cranberries, mushrooms, fish, and oysters, leave the area. Snyder, on the other hand, creates new foods from the area's homegrown cranberry crop and sells them from the same place. "The council has always patted me on the back," she says.

Snyder also prides herself on the pure and natural way she prepares her products. She and her right-hand employee, Kristine Wirkkala, are Anna Lena's only cooks. They sweat over seven gas burners in the warehouse kitchen. They use 16-quart pans to simmer jams, jellies, and syrups. They spoon marmalade by hand into jars. Sometimes Snyder pours syrups from the saucepan into the jars with a 30-cup coffee pot.

Though she's adding a 30-gallon steamer, Snyder's methods are admittedly low-tech. "We do what you would if you were home-canning. I'm not a chemist."

Maybe not, but she knows how to combine compatible flavors. She sells a popular cranberry-raspberry jelly and cranberry-blueberry sauce, all made with Washington berries.

All but one of her products are free of preservatives, additives, and fine-print chemicals. The cranberry barbecue sauce, containing Worcestershire sauce, is the only exception.

Washington is small fry among the five cranberry-growing states and British Columbia. It produces about 5 percent of the nation's cranberries, and the Long Beach Peninsula crop accounts for about 1 percent. Washington berries, however, are known for their high color and tartness, attributes Snyder makes the most of in her good-looking, good-tasting foods. She buys other Washington-grown berries for her cranberry-raspberry jelly and cranberry-blueberry sauce, and she offers a sugarless cranberry-citrus relish for the cranberry-flavor purist.

Angela Allen

Anna Lena's Cranberry Products
Karen Snyder
P.O. Box 131
Long Beach, WA 98631
(206) 642-2184
Fax (206) 642-8948

Mail order products range in cost from $2.25 for a 5-ounce jar of jam to $5.25 for vinegars and chutneys. Gift packages range from $8.75 to $11 plus shipping. Anna Lena's goods are also available in stores throughout Washington, including Larry's and Olson's Markets.

APPLE-CRANBERRY BREAD WITH LEMON BRANDY SPREAD

The cardamom adds that special something to this honey-colored loaf with a mosaic of cranberries, apples, and walnuts. Created by Chef Nanci Main, it freezes well and goes well with coffee—the Swedish transfusion.

½ cup butter, softened
1 cup sugar
2 eggs
1 teaspoon vanilla extract
½ teaspoon almond extract
2 cups all-purpose flour
1 teaspoon baking soda
½ teaspoon salt
1 teaspoon ground cardamom
⅓ cup orange juice
1 cup apple, peeled, cored, and coarsely chopped
½ cup coarsely chopped walnuts
½ cup chopped cranberries

SPREAD

8 oz cream cheese
2 tablespoons powdered sugar
1 tablespoon grated lemon zest
1 tablespoon lemon juice
1 tablespoon brandy

Preheat oven to 350°F.

With an electric mixer, cream butter until light. Add sugar gradually. Add eggs, one at a time, scraping bowl after each addition. Add vanilla and almond extracts.

Sift together flour, baking soda, salt, and cardamom.

Add the dry ingredients to the creamed mixture alternately with orange juice.

Fold in apples, walnuts, and cranberries.

Spread the batter into a 9-by-5-inch loaf pan, lightly greased and lined on the bottom and along the sides with cooking parchment. Gently tap the pan on a counter to remove air pockets.

Bake 50 to 60 minutes, until a toothpick comes out clean. Cool in pan 10 minutes, then remove from pan to finish cooling.

To make spread, whip cream cheese using an electric mixer. Add powdered sugar, grated lemon zest, lemon juice, and brandy, scraping the bowl while mixing.

To serve, slice Apple Cranberry Bread. Using a pastry bag with a star tip, pipe cheese diagonally across each slice. Garnish with a walnut half.

Makes 1 loaf.

The Ark Restaurant
Nahcotta, Washington

CATCHING, CLEANING, COOKING SALMON

The best time to visit the Westport dock is late afternoon, or even just before dusk. You have to have something to go for, so you go for a fish. The rigging of the first troller can be seen coming around the sand spit, and a few minutes later the top riggings of other boats are to be seen throbbing in the racy turmoil that is the aftermath of the bar. Smart puffs of wind buffet the long dock. Now the first white troller breaks cover and comes into full sight, her trolling poles folded like up-turned wings, the tiny crossbar at the mast head reminiscent, somewhat, of the Crusades.

My vote for the Heroine of the Week: The woman who hurried into the post office to-day, a little breathless and with wisps of hair clinging to her damp forehead, and who ex-claimed, as she rolled down the sleeves of her gingham dress, "I've just canned two bears!"

—Kathy Hogan, October 30, 1943

There is something gallant about these little boats which put to sea each day in the proximity of coast defense, shore patrol, and hovering aircraft—like defenseless birds caught in a flight of eagles. The arrival of a loaded fishing boat makes everybody go to the edge of the dock and take a prideful look. The success of the fisherman is success for everyone, as is the symbol of one more conquest of man's archenemy, the sea. Once again we have walloped her, is the feeling.

The cargo is dumped on the floor of the fish-buying scows. A great heap of salmon slithers into the gloom of the lower deck; water drips from the slowly heaving scow, and ripples of reflected light shimmer on the fish buyer's face, and on the huge coal scuttle scales suspended on a chain. Set apart from the heap of salmon is a neat little row of oddments of the deep—a couple of sharks, a red snapper, and two or three ling cod, the usual dregs of the salmon catch.

You keep your eye open for an infant black-mouthed salmon, as you can't undertake the purchase of a really full-grown monster, and the selling rule is whole fish or none. This evening you are in luck. There are two small fish, allowing you the added pleasure of deciding between the two. For a dollar, you finally come up the gangplank with a 6-pound nugget of firm red meat under your arm.

Before you can eat this prize, there are two very special processes to be undergone, and the first of these is cleaning your catch. It is possible to bruise and mutilate a good salmon beyond recognition in the cleaning. In my case, it is not only possible, or even

Hubbard Squash

With the first touch of frost, I harvested my five Hubbard squash, which were re-markable for the fact that they were all of a flattened-out appearance and looked, one and all, as if they had been sat on, over a long period of time, by out-sized gnomes. I was distressed to find that my new book, The Joy of Cooking, hasn't got a recipe for squash pie. Could it be that there isn't any joy in a squash pie?

Kathy Hogan
November 18, 1944

probable, but inevitable. Turn me loose with a salmon to clean, and I will bring you, sooner or later, a fish with every bone in its body broken, and not one firm red flake clinging to another. So I don't clean them anymore. When I come off the dock with a fish, I turn my steps to the cottage of a Norwegian friend, Chris. Chris takes the fish, a batch of newspapers, a spotless carving board and departs for a hydrant in the backyard, stopping to grab from a drawer a gleaming machete-sized piece of steel, commonly called, in the family, a knife.

From the kitchen window, I watch the expert swish of the machete as the fish is scaled, scrubbed within an inch of its life, and then cut into thick slices—an inch and three quarters, to be exact.

Then, "You might as well let me cook it," says the wife of Chris. She claps one of those old-fashioned oval hotcake griddles on the stove, and ties on a starched apron. The heated griddle is brushed (and only brushed) with olive oil, and when it has reached the proper crackle, the salted and peppered fish is put on the griddle. When it is a ruddy brown on one side, and when a delicate test with a fork reveals that it is cooked exactly halfway through, the fish is turned. An epicurean aroma smites your nostrils.

In the meantime, the potatoes have been boiled, the tomatoes sliced, a lemon quartered, and the white luncheon cloth with the embroidered blue butterflies is put on the table. A fat aluminum percolator protesting on all four cylinders is removed from the fire and placed beside the cups and saucers, where it settles down with a final admonitory cluck, like a hen among chicks.

We sit down. There is a special plate for the bones. "Six bones to a piece," says Chris, and removes them deftly. I do likewise. After that there is no sound but the clink of cutlery, except from the open window where you can hear the north Pacific turning over on its side. After a while, Chris sits back with his last cup of coffee. "I remember one night off Destruction Island," he begins. "We were ten—Johnnie and Gus were there, and Arne, I remember, and we had anchored together for the night when..."

And so it goes. There isn't anything about fishing that I don't like.

Kathy Hogan
The Kitchen Critic: Cohassett Beach War Correspondent, July 18, 1942

MUSSELS

As they got to know each other, Emily and Charlie and Anne discovered that they all liked the water and the idea of being on the water, and of working on the water, and that they all liked making things grow. Living as they do, down at the southern tip of Puget Sound, so close to water, it was only a matter of time before their talk veered In the direction of aquaculture. The oyster pickers were In plain sight for ready inspiration, as were the clam diggers. But oyster pickers and clam diggers in the South Sound work clam beds and oyster grounds privately held for generations in close-knit families. Emily and Charlie and Anne figured that if they were going to be able to do anything of a waterborne nature it would have to be the growing of cultured mussels, something of a novel idea in 1981 when they set to work. Marine biologists familiar with bivalves, as well as the old-timers around Totten Inlet scoffed at the notion. They pointed out that South Sound mussels reach a certain size and a certain age, and then they die off. Some said the water warmed too much by the end of summer. Others said there was an overabundance of food in the water and the mussels ate themselves to death.

Nevertheless, the three friends pooled some minor resources, applied themselves to the requisite paperwork, and created Kamilche Sea Farms. They leased six acres of open water in Totten Inlet from the Department of Natural Resources.

That first year they built a small raft of Styrofoam and logs they cut from trees felled on Emily's nearby property, and they anchored it on their leaseholding. They lowered long lines from the raft into the cold water of Totten Inlet, capturing a fantastic set of mussels in spring when the black-shelled bivalves float free as near-microscopic larvae looking for an anchorage.

In spring and summer, algae blooms with abandon in Totten Inlet. Plankton and phytoplankton abound. The tides are substantial enough that the bay nearly empties at ebb tide, then fills at flood tide, all the while washing the young mussels with a slurry of nutrients. A healthy mussel siphons as much as three liters of water each hour, selecting out the most delectable morsels. As the mussels grew that first year, so too did the dollar signs in the partners' dewy eyes. The evidence, gaining weight right there in the water on the long lines hanging from the hundred-dollar raft, suggested that three pups in the world of aquaculture were about to accomplish what anyone with an opinion had said they couldn't do.

"We got right up to the fifth of September," recalled Charlie Stephens, who looks a little like Wally Cox. "That's when the scoters came back from Alaska." Surf scoters and white wing scoters are diving ducks. The males are black for the most part, though the white patches on the crown and nape of the surf scoter give credence to its nickname, "skunk-duck." Scoters will eat immature clams and oysters if given the chance, but they seem to be particularly fond of young mussels.

When Charlie Stephens boated out to check his lines in early September, he could see from a quarter mile away that the raft was floating high and appeared to be surrounded by a small congregation of black-shrouded morticians. The scoters took off at his approach, running like common thieves along the surface of the water before taking flight. "There wasn't a single mussel to be seen," Charlie said. "The scoters had wiped us out in one night."

After a disastrous attempt at protecting the mussels with a submerged net, the partners abandoned their hanging line technology for lantern nets that dangle from floating lines anchored at both ends to the bottom of the bay. Lantern nets had been used in some aquaculture operations to grow out oysters, but never mussels.

After eight years Kamilche Sea Farms finally started producing marketable mussels. But those old-timers and marine biologists had been on to something when they told Emily and Charlie and Anne that they were sure to fail. "We never did overcome the mortality problem with indigenous mussels," Emily allowed. "We would have a wonderful crop up until August, and then they would die off, just like everyone said they would." No matter what the partners tried, come August, the native mussels would siphon their last squirts of water and hand in their suits. Those mussels that made it to market under the Kamilche Sea Farms name had often been wild mussels harvested by the partners off clam and oyster beaches.

Finally, the partners started buying mussel seed from a specialist in Northern California who grows oyster, clam, and mussel seed under laboratory conditions. The seed arrives in a cooler on a Greyhound bus. The 1 million mussels that Kamilche Sea Farms buys for about $1,000 come wrapped in gauze and would fill a coffee cup. Around 10 percent of the seed survive the flatworms and the starfish and the silt and the other hazards to young mussels, but when the water warms and native mussels die, these California imports thrive.

The harvest of yearling mussels lasts from September to June. In spring and summer the partners concentrate on raising up the seed and thinning the populations as the mussels grow. From the consumer's point of view, December is a great month for mussels. Their flesh has firmed up and sweetened in the cold water. And they remain in prime condition much longer out of water, for up to a week if kept cold and moist. The majority of the Kamilche Sea Farms crop ends up in restaurant kitchens, although fishmongers like Harry Yoshimura at Mutual Fish in Seattle sell them during the season to home cooks, too.

Mussels have only recently gained any kind of meaningful audience in the Pacific Northwest. They have always been popular in various parts of Europe, predominantly in France, Belgium, Holland, Spain, and Italy. In the past, travelers returning to the Pacific Northwest from vacations in Europe have been the most likely candidates to harvest wild mussels off rocks and pilings. The first big step toward accepting mussels into a shellfish diet seems to be finding out just what to do with them. Once they are cooked, once their meat is swelling out of open shells in a broth laced with garlic and white wine and parsley, flavor takes over and convinces the most reluctant of diners of the culinary value of the black-shelled bivalve.

After removing the byssus and scrubbing the shells clean of any attached sea grasses and the like, Emily Garlich is one to steam mussels, like clams. Charlie Stephens admits to favoring a chowder that uses Snappy Tom tomato juice as a base. French cookbooks are always a good source for recipes. Italians have a way of involving mussels with tomatoes and pasta that reminds one in mid-winter of the joys of spring and summer.

It is a simple thing to clean the mussels (eliminating any that gape and refuse to close their shells when encouraged to do so), then put them in a covered pot with no more water than what clings to their shells. Over high heat they open and steam in their own juices in a matter of minutes. Care should be taken not to overcook these delicate morsels. Remove the cooked meat to a small bowl, discarding the shells and any mussels that failed to open. Then pour the nectar in the pot into a separate bowl, but through coffee filter paper or the like to catch any shell fragments or bits of sand. Pour good olive oil into a pan, add a large quantity of minced garlic, turn up the heat, enjoy the aroma, and just as the garlic turns color, heading from golden to tan, dump in a quart jar of canned tomatoes from the summer garden, or a drained can of Italian tomatoes. As the tomatoes begin to cook in the pan, stir and chop them a little, then add the mussel nectar. Raise the heat to boil off the nectar and it will leave its intensified flavor behind. Add a handful of finely chopped parsley and a sprinkling of red pepper flakes for a little snap. When the sauce has cooked long enough for the flavors to marry, taste for salt and add a little if need be. Stir in the mussel meat, then pour the whole out onto a platter of pasta cooked just to the point of turning tender. Marcella Hazan suggests a mussel dish much like this in one of her cookbooks.

By December, long-lasting high tides start early in the day in the South Sound. Scoters have been joined by northern grebes and ruddy ducks, and a few widgeons. Later in winter the canvasbacks will fly through, headed somewhere else. As Charlie and Emily motor out to their lantern nets they often find themselves crossing wakes in the morning with clam diggers and oyster pickers who have been out all night working by lantern light, taking advantage of the equally long-lasting low tides. Mussel grower, oyster picker, clam digger: When their crops are in prime condition they work in the dark in wind-driven, ice-edged downpours. Shellfish weather. No one else would bother. But there they are, out on the water, working on the water, making things grow.

Schuyler Ingle

Kamilche Sea Farms
Emily Garlich, Charlie Stephens, Anne Appleby
SE 2741 Bloomfield Road, Shelton
(206) 426-5276
Year-round: Monday–Friday, call ahead.
Between Shelton and Olympia on Totten Inlet; call for directions.

OYSTERS BAKED IN GARLIC CREAM SAUCE WITH GOAT CHEESE AND PESTO

Everyone has a favorite pesto sauce. Here is a delicious opportunity to use it with the Northwest's most delicate oyster.

24 to 36 Pacific oysters
Rock salt
¼ to ¾ cup clarified butter
3 to 4 tablespoons minced garlic
1 tablespoon minced shallot
¼ cup flour
1½ cups milk
Salt and pepper to taste
4 ounces mild goat cheese
Brandy (optional)
Pesto
Freshly grated Parmesan cheese

Shuck oysters. Set them in shells on a layer of rock salt in a baking pan, and set the pan aside.

Preheat oven to 425°F.

In a saucepan, heat butter and in it cook garlic and shallot until tender. Add flour and continue cooking 2 to 3 minutes, stirring frequently.

Add milk; reduce heat, being careful not to boil or scorch. Add a pinch of salt, and pepper to taste. Cook 5 to 6 minutes, or until sauce reaches a medium thickness. Remove from heat. Whisk in goat cheese. Set aside.

Lightly lace each oyster with brandy, if desired. Place 1 to 1½ tablespoons of the garlic sauce over each oyster and ⅛ teaspoon pesto in the center. Sprinkle with freshly grated Parmesan cheese.

Bake for 8 to 10 minutes.

Serves 10 to 12 as an appetizer.

The Ark Restaurant
Nahcotta, Washington

SMELT

Pacific Northwest fish lore is so dominated by salmon that other resources are often overlooked. Such is the case with smelt. Yet where these small fish congregate to spawn along shorelines, they create a sensation among locals, and continue a tradition that is as old as the salmon fishery.

Several smelt species—including surf smelt, night smelt, Columbia River smelt (also known as eulachon or "oolican"), and longfin smelt—range the North Pacific. European-American settlers heard the Native American term oolican as "hooligan," a name that still persists in some parts. Though they rarely exceed 9 inches in length, smelt make up for it in numbers. During their spawning runs into the rivers or onto the high beaches along the Pacific Coast, thousands churn in the shallows or rolling surf.

Abundant during the winter, smelt filled the gap when the Indians' salmon stores were depleted or beginning to spoil. Even more important was their rendered oil, which was used on everything from halibut to berries and was an important trade item. Because of their high oil content, eulachon were also called candlefish. By threading a strip of cedar bark lengthwise in a dried fish, Indians fashioned candles; the fish contained enough oil to stay lit.

The methods of taking smelt vary with species and location and are based on strong local traditions. On the Cowlitz River, eulachon are taken by dip net, often a large salmon-type boat net with a fine-mesh bag. On the outer coast, surf smelt are taken on high tides by dip nets with handmade wooden frames. In northern Puget Sound, smelt are snagged using jigs as large schools pass near the shore. Elsewhere in Puget Sound, smelt are caught with rakes. Throughout Washington, the daily personal catch limit is 20 pounds; the season is open year-round.

Smelt also are fished commercially. The 1989 commercial harvest of surf smelt was just under 100,000 pounds; more than 3 million pounds of eulachon were harvested from the Cowlitz River.

Once the smelt are caught, there remains one important and persistent question: Do you clean smelt before cooking them? The rule of thumb is: Purists and hungry people don't bother. The timid remove the heads and gut, cleaning the fish as though it were a small trout. The most common kitchen treatment is to dip them in egg and milk, dust them with seasoned breadcrumbs or flour, and fry quickly in a hot pan.

Bob Steelquist

SEAWEED AND OTHER SEA ODDITIES

More than 500 species of seaweed inhabit the marine waters of Oregon and Washington, forming the foundation of a rich and complex food web that sustains invertebrates, fish, seabirds, and mammals. As cultural and economic ties to other Pacific Rim countries have strengthened here, and as Asian-American populations have grown, Northwestern tastebuds have begun to be calibrated to the flavor subtleties of seaweed.

The most common edible seaweeds are kelps, including the eight species of *Laminaria*, which are used as a substitute for the Japanese "kombu" in stocks and for flavoring. *Porphyra*, which is sold as "nori" and is best known as the wrapping for sushi, is probably the most generally known. *Nereocystis*, or bull kelp, is used for pickles. The blades of the bull kelp also are used as a substitute for the Japanese "wakame" for flavoring and in soup stocks. All kelps are rich in vitamins, minerals, and protein.

Although seaweeds are abundant in both Oregon and Washington, coastal environments and human populations differ greatly. The Oregon coast consists of exposed beaches and rocky headlands, making large-scale seaweed gathering impractical. Sheltered estuary habitat—where seaweed could be grown commercially—is limited because of space and water quality.

The Washington coast includes almost 2,000 miles of protected shoreline around Puget Sound, as well as two major coastal estuaries, Grays Harbor and Willapa Bay. During the 1970s, Puget Sound was viewed as a sea garden of the future, where intensive aquaculture would enhance natural systems and boost the sound's capacity to feed its burgeoning human population. Technology refined over hundreds of years in Japan was imported, first for mussel and other shellfish production and then for fish and seaweed. But the "Blue Revolution" never materialized. Local interests—particularly shoreline property owners—often approved of aquaculture in principle, but they did not want to see it from their windows. Fragmented regulatory authority made it difficult to create workable policies for licensing and regulating new ventures. Once-enthusiastic investors withdrew their dollars in the face of mounting delays and opposition.

While the development of commercial stocks of seaweed hasn't materialized, demand for wild seaweed has soared, due to the growth of Asian immigrant populations in the Puget Sound region. Wild seaweed stocks, along with moonsnails and other less-familiar mollusks, are heavily harvested for personal consumption. Personal-use harvests of seaweed have been so heavy in recent years that public beaches in state parks and other readily accessible areas are showing signs of overuse. Relatively little seaweed is harvested for personal use in Oregon because of the low population density in the coastal region, but some seaweed experts there are nonetheless concerned about overharvest. Language and cultural barriers only exacerbate the difficulties resource managers and Asian-American communities face in resolving the issues together.

Unless the disputes over siting and funding seaweed culture are resolved, the seaweeds used in adventurous Northwest kitchens will most likely be imported from Asian countries where large-scale growing operations are accepted. On the other hand, Asian consumers of two other forms of sea life—sea urchins and sea cucumbers—are increasingly likely to get them from Washington State. Sea cucumber divers work from the lower sound to the San Juan Islands, rotating through four districts over a four-year period. The sea cukes, which more closely emulate slugs in their sliminess and protean shape, are trucked to Tacoma for processing and shipment. Most of the crop ends up in China, but some will return, dried or pickled, to Asian markets in the Northwest. They are used primarily in soups and stir-fries, where their soft texture and mild taste fills somewhat the same role as tofu.

Sea urchins are a bigger industry—5.2 million pounds were taken in 1990, a value of about $2.5 million. Washington has five sea urchin districts, and each is harvested by hand once every three years by divers. Sea urchins are valued for their fragile orange gonads, called "uni" in Japan. Really fresh uni has an almost fruity flavor. It is most commonly served on sushi, but it is also good by itself. At Sooke Harbour House on Vancouver Island, Sinclair Philip serves the roe simply rinsed in dry pear cider for about 15 seconds and then spooned into an empty sea urchin shell. It takes the gonads of four urchins to fill one shell.

Most uni is flown to Japan the day after harvest, but there is a small local market in the Northwest. To get it fresh, try Mutual Fish or Pike Place Market in Seattle. Less perishable (though also less desirable) salted uni is available in Asian markets.

Bob Steelquist

BLACKBERRY SCALLOP CEVICHE

This ceviche brings together some of the best of our regional bounty—delicate scallops and sun-ripened blackberries—for a fine blending of subtle flavor and texture.

1½ cups olive oil
1 cup blackberry juice
1 cup orange juice
¾ cup lemon juice
¾ cup lime juice
1 red onion, julienned
4 shallots, minced
1 teaspoon minced garlic
1 ounce fresh anise hyssop, chopped
½ teaspoon salt
½ teaspoon pepper
½ teaspoon cayenne pepper
3 pounds fresh scallops
2 cups Blackberry Marinated Onions (see page 90)
1 cup Blackberry Ketchup, for garnish (see page 91)

Combine all the ingredients except the scallops, Blackberry Marinated Onions, and Blackberry Ketchup. When well mixed, add the scallops and marinate in the refrigerator for 8 hours or overnight. Prepare Blackberry Marinated Onions and Blackberry Ketchup and chill.

When ready to serve, make nests on each plate with Blackberry Marinated Onions. Arrange some scallops in the center and spoon the marinade over the top. Garnish with Blackberry Ketchup and fresh anise hyssop or slices of lemon, lime, or orange.

Serves 6 as an entrée, or 8 to 12 as an appetizer.

BLACKBERRY MARINATED ONIONS

4 red onions
2 cups blackberry vinegar (or raspberry vinegar)
½ cup honey

Peel the onions and slice them as thinly as possible. Mix together the vinegar and honey. Add the onions and marinate overnight at room temperature—they will turn a vibrant pink.

Refrigerate. Onions will keep for 2 weeks.

Makes 4 cups.

BLACKBERRY KETCHUP

8 cups blackberries
2 shallots, minced
1 yellow onion, chopped
2 teaspoons dried tarragon
2 teaspoons dried marjoram
1 teaspoon dried rosemary
Juice and grated zest of 1 lemon
¾ cup balsamic vinegar
½ cup sugar
1 teaspoon salt
½ teaspoon pepper

Combine all ingredients except the salt and pepper in a large saucepan. Cover and bring to a boil. Reduce heat and simmer for 10 minutes.

Cool slightly, then purée the ketchup in a blender and strain it through a medium sieve into a clean saucepan, pressing it to retrieve as much purée as possible.

Add the salt and pepper and reduce over low heat to 4 cups. Chill.

Makes 4 cups.

Note: Use this ketchup as you would tomato ketchup. It is great with poultry and meats, and will hold in the refrigerator for at least six months.

Shoalwater Restaurant
Seaview, Washington

U-PICK FARMS AND ROADSIDE STANDS

U-Pick Guidelines: Call first, especially near the beginning and end of the season. Find out if your small children are welcome to help pick. Farms will supply picking containers, but you will need bags or boxes to transport your produce home. Pick carefully and conscientiously; a well-tended berry field or orchard represents years of knowledgeable labor. (Dogs should stay in the car.)

Harvests may vary greatly from year to year. A local chamber of commerce or county extension office can often supply up-to-date seasonal information. Also, many newspapers publish local farm maps in the late spring or summer.

CLALLAM COUNTY, WASHINGTON

Slather's Smokehouse Salmon ☆
(206) 374-6258
R.R.1, Box 5050
Forks, WA 98331
October–May: Monday–Thursday, 11am–9pm; Friday, 11am–10pm; weekends, 4pm–9pm. Summer: Sunday–Thursday, 11am–10pm; Friday–Saturday, 11am–11pm.

Alderwood-smoked salmon available by mail and at the restaurant in Forks.

The Smokehouse Restaurant is on Highway 101, 1 mile north of Forks.

Cedarbrook Herb Farm ☆ **(206) 683-7733**
Terry and Toni Anderson
986 Sequim Avenue S, Sequim
March–late December: daily, 9am–5pm.

Plants, fresh-cut herbs in season, herb vinegars, dried herbs and flowers, several varieties of garlic.

Heading west on Highway 101, go south at the first stoplight in Sequim, and drive 1 mile toward the mountain.

Dungeness Organic Produce ☆
(206) 683-7089
Nash Huber
Sequim
May–December: daily, daylight hours.

Mixed vegetables, at the Dungeness Country Store and at Port Angeles Farmers Market.

Farm stand is at the Dungeness Country Store, in downtown Dungeness.

GRAYS HARBOR COUNTY, WASHINGTON

Karin's Lingonberry Farm ☆
(206) 482-3691
Karin and Ralph Koal
P.O. Box 760
Elma, WA 98541

The Koals are the only lingonberry farmers in the country, and are dedicated to the propagation of this small, tart red berry from Scandinavia. They'll sell you an almost-mature lingonberry plant (so you can harvest within a year) as well as lingonberry jam, lingonberry cake, and other products including hazelnut honey. Mail order, specialty stores, and grocery stores.

JEFFERSON COUNTY, WASHINGTON

Triton Cove Oyster Farms ☆
(206) 796-4360
Ron and Henrietta Powell
39521 Highway 101, Brinnon
Year-round, but not open as much in spring and summer. Call ahead.

Pacific and Manila oysters (bottom culture).

Eight miles south of Brinnon.

Spring Hill Farms ☆ **(206) 732-4856**
Margaret and Gary Walters
5370 Beaver Valley Road, Port Ludlow
Call ahead.

Since by law they'll only sell live lamb, you can order in advance and pick up the meat at your local butcher, cut and wrapped (the butchering is actually done at the farm). Spring Hill lambs are born earlier than other farms, in January and February, since they sell a lot of breeding stock and show at local fairs; hence, lamb is ready around May. You can also visit the farm and browse the other products: sheepskins, wool comforters and yarn.

Take Highway 104 over the Hood Canal Bridge (towards the Olympic Peninsula) and go 5 miles to Beaver Valley Road. Turn right and go 3.6 miles more.

MASON COUNTY, WASHINGTON

Stretch Island Fruit ☆ (206) 275-6050
E 16371 Highway 3, Allyn
Year-round: Monday–Friday, 8am–4:30pm.

Stretch Island Fruit Leathers are available in regular and organic flavors.

South of Allyn on Highway 3.

Davis Farm ☆ (206) 275-2032
Marilyn Davis
NE 170 Davis Farm Road, Belfair
July–October: daily, 10am–6pm. Call ahead before visiting.

Beans, broccoli, beets, cabbage, corn, cucumbers (fresh and pickled), greens, peas, potatoes, peppers, tomatoes, herbs, squash, pumpkins, and blackberries.

Opposite Belfair Firehall; take the Old Belfair Highway ¾ mile north of Belfair.

Sea-Fresh Seafood Company ☆ (206) 877-5177
23490 Highway 101, Hoodsport
June–September: am–9pm.

Fresh salmon, steamer clams, and smoked salmon; oysters or fish and chips available to eat at picnic tables outside.

Right outside Hoodsport, on the water side.

Hama Hama Seafood ☆ (206) 877-5811
Barbara and Al Jaske
35846 Highway 101, Lilliwaup
Year-round: Monday–Saturday, 8:30am–5:30pm; Sunday, 10am–5pm.

Pacific oysters (bottom culture); smoked oysters and scallops (all smoking done on the premises); more unusual foods, such as squid steaks; fresh shellfish and fin fish; and a cooking section with cookbooks and travel books, sauces, and spices.

Seven miles north of Lilliwaup, next to the Hama Hama River.

Kamilche Sea Farms ☆ (206) 426-5276
Emily Garlich, Charlie Stephens, Anne Appleby
SE 2741 Bloomfield Road, Shelton
Year-round: Monday–Friday, call ahead.

Mussels.

Between Shelton and Olympia on Totten Inlet; call for directions.

Olympia Oyster Company ☆ (206) 426-3354
SE 1042 Bloomfield Road, Shelton
Year-round: Monday–Friday, 8am–2pm (and sometimes until 4pm).

Olympia oysters are on the ropes again, hit by two cold winters in a row. Weather permitting, they should be back in commercial production in a few years. Pacifics are available for 25 cents apiece.

On Oyster Bay between Olympia and Shelton. On Highway 101 watch for milepost 356. Look for signs.

Hunter Farms ☆ (206) 898-2222
E 1921 Highway 106, Union
Year-round: daily, 9am–6pm.

Sweet corn, cucumbers, beans, fruit, cider, U-pick pumpkins, oysters, smoked salmon, clams.

From Gorst take Highway 3 to Belfair, turn right on Highway 106 toward Union. The farm is on the right 3 miles past Union.

PACIFIC COUNTY, WASHINGTON

Ekone Oyster Company ☆ (206) 875-5494
Joanne and Nick Jambor
192 Bay Center Road, Bay Center
Monday–Friday, 7:30am–4pm.

Pacifics (long-line and off-bottom culture); smoked Willapa Bay oysters. The Jambors are on the cutting edge of oyster technology, and

Willapa Bay is one of the cleanest oyster-growing waters in the country. Buy fresh oysters by the dozen or by the sack. Shucked and alder-smoked oysters also available; suppliers to the Shoalwater and other restaurants. Also available by mail from Star Route, Box 465, South Bend, WA 98586. Ekone is Chinook for "Good Spirit."

On the east side of Willapa Bay. From Highway 101, go north toward Bay Center. At the KOA campground, turn left, go 3 miles. At the corner of Rhodesia Beach Road and Bay Center Road.

Anna Lena's Cranberry Products ☆ (206) 642-2184
Karen Snyder
P.O. Box 131
Long Beach, WA 98631

Anna Lena's goods are available in stores throughout Washington, including Larry's and Olson's Markets. Some mail order as well; call for a catalogue. Mouth-watering products include cranberry sauce, cranberry-citrus marmalade, cranberry port jelly, cranberry applesauce, sweet and sour cranberry mustard, cranberry ketchup, cranola granola, crannies (dried cranberries), crannie-filled baked good mixes, cranberry vinegar, cran-raspberry jam, and cranberry barbecue sauce.

The Crab Pot ☆ (206) 642-2524
1917 Pacific Highway, Long Beach
Closed winter (when there's no crabbing); daily otherwise, 11am–9pm.

The restaurant serves mainly deep-fried seafood, but the market up front sells live and cooked crab, as well as other seafood.

On the main drag in Long Beach.

East Point Seafoods ☆ (206) 665-4158
P.O. Box 340, Ocean Park
Monday–Saturday, 10am–5pm; closed December and January.

Oysters and a variety of smoked and canned fish.

Sandridge and 273rd on Nahcotta Dock in Nahcotta. You can't miss it.

Jolly Roger Oyster Company ☆ (206) 665-4111
P.O. Box 309, Ocean Park
Year-round: Saturday 8am–4pm; Sunday 10am–3pm.

Oysters (bottom culture) and sometimes shrimp.

On Nahcotta Dock in Nahcotta. You can't miss it.

FARMERS MARKETS

CLALLAM COUNTY, WASHINGTON

Forks Farmers Market ☆
(206) 374-6623
Contact: Joanne McReynolds
May–September: Saturday, 10am–2pm.

This is mainly a crafts market, but local gardeners do bring in their surplus. It's under cover, which is a big issue in the rain forest.

In the Thrifty Mart parking lot.

Port Angeles Farmers Market ☆
(206) 928-3659
Contact: Gertrud Rohrbach
Year-round: Saturday, 9am–5pm.

Gertrud Rohrbach farmed 100 acres in New York, and when she moved to Port Angeles to be near her children, she found retirement boring. So in 1978 she founded the Port Angeles Farmers Market, which supplies bedding plants, vegetable starts, fresh and dried flowers, and produce.

8th and Chase; 8th is the main throroughfare through Port Angeles.

GRAYS HARBOR COUNTY, WASHINGTON

Grays Harbor Farmers Market, Aberdeen
☆ **(206) 533-7637**
Contact: Nancy Lachel
Year-round: Saturdays, 9am–4pm.

On Riverside Drive in Hoquiam.

JEFFERSON COUNTY, WASHINGTON

Port Townsend Farmers Market ☆
(206) 385-2135
Contact: Steve Habersetzer or Kerry Bourke
May–October: Saturday, 9am–12pm.

Up from the Quincy Street Dock.

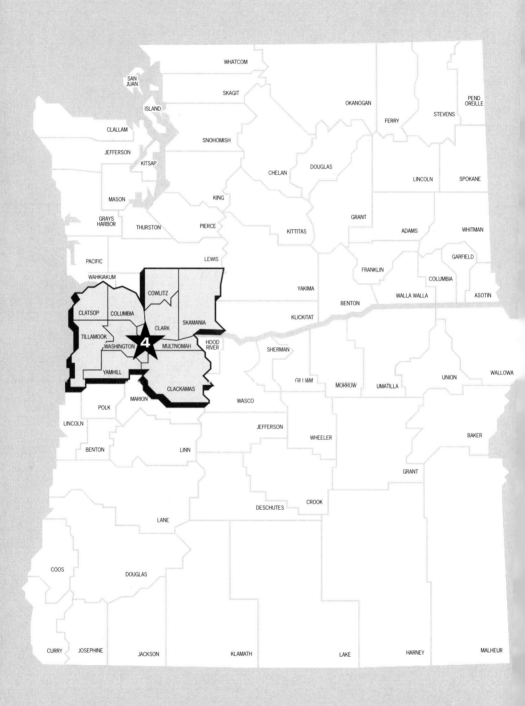

Sit on the banks of the Columbia River, watching tugboats push gigantic barges toward the sea and fishermen reeling in salmon, and it's easy to see how this river has always been the lifeblood of the region.

Now quieted by many dams, the Columbia was once a torrent that sustained an entire civilization. For thousands of years, the people living here didn't need to farm at all. Most of the tribes living in the region believed in the demigod Coyote, who created the world and in whose belly lived three wise sisters, who were huckleberries. Coyote was a greedy eater, and he was in the right place: Nearby forests gave mushrooms, berries, and fiddlehead ferns.

Prairies were covered with the blue flowers of camas, and marshes provided wapatoo, the Indian potato. Venison, game birds, and elk were plentiful, and the river teemed with steelhead and sturgeon. And from the sea came crab, shrimp, oysters, scallops, clams, and smelt.

Europeans first heard of the Columbia about 400 years ago, and hoped it might be the fabled Northwest Passage, a water route from the Atlantic to the Pacific. Businessmen eager to trade with China fervently wished for such a waterway. Despite the economic incentive, it took awhile to find the mouth of the Columbia amidst the fogs and breakers of the Pacific Coast. The Spanish explorer Bruno Heceta located it in 1775, but his crew was too weak from scurvy to cross the bar.

Two years later, Captain Cook, of Hawaiian Islands fame, went looking for the river and passed it by one stormy night without realizing it. Then George Vancouver, surveying the coast, passed by the mouth in 1791. He didn't believe the myths about the great river, so despite seeing swarms of feeding gulls, brown water, and drifting logs, he denied the evidence of his senses and went on. His omission gave the young United States claim to "the great river of the West" when Captain Robert Gray crossed the bar on May 11, 1792, in the schooner *Columbia Rediviva*. Things were never the same.

Thirteen years later, Lewis and Clark arrived from the east, traveling down the Columbia. Fur trappers and mountain men tramped through the forests, and the white civilization follwed quickly thereafter. John Jacob Astor landed in present-day Astoria in 1811, and by 1825, John McLoughlin, chief factor for the Hudson's Bay Company, had set up shop at Fort Vancouver. He imported livestock and feed and started farms, for local consumption and trade with the Russians. He also built lumbermills. Fort Vancouver became the industrial, commercial, social, and political center of the Northwest.

The Columbia River tribes were already accomplished traders, and many welcomed the new markets for their fish, furs, and horses. But the arrival of the whites turned out to be a disaster. By 1830, smallpox and other diseases had wiped out between 75 and 90 percent of the Native Americans, and in another 30 years the survivors had been divested of nearly all their land.

Immigrants swarmed west to take advantage of the free land thus acquired. A man and his wife could claim a full square mile of farmland simply by paying a fee and living on the property. By mid-century, farms had shifted from subsistence to market agriculture.

Today, market agriculture continues to dominate the landscape. Despite urban sprawl, with suburban malls and housing developments covering more and more farmland, the area around Portland and north in Washington State and west to the ocean still supports about 150 cash crops. And although urbanization pushes out farms, it also provides markets for high-quality fresh food. The *Tri-County Produce Guide* for Oregon's Clackamas, Multnomah, and Washington counties lists a tremendous variety of produce for sale: berries of all types, apples, melons, cherries, peaches, and other fruit; and sweet corn, squash, tomatoes, cucumbers, green beans, and asparagus, to name only a few.

The valleys support wineries that turn out prize-winning vintages from such Oregon favorites as Tualatin Vineyards, Ponzi Vineyards, Sokol Blosser

Vineyards, Veritas Vineyards, and Elk Cove Vineyards. Ranchers bring to market spring lamb, rabbits, chicken, and beef. Creameries such as Tillamook offer golden cheeses and rich butter.

From this bounty comes the emerging Northwest cuisine, based on the freshest locally grown food, teamed with the best wine. In backyard cookouts, this Northwest cuisine is translated into a gregarious, relaxed style, where the sweet barbecue smells of alder smoke and grilled salmon drift through the summer air. Chefs at area restaurants find the bounty a fresh inspiration, producing everything from informal, bistro-style food, simply prepared and not pretentious, to fancy dishes in fancy restaurants, including such creations as Dungeness Crab with Columbia River Caviar, Pickled Sturgeon with Toasted Garlic Paste, Alder-Smoked Sausage Sauté, and Smoked Duck Confit with Blackberry Sauce.

Now, let's deal with the issue I've avoided so far. Yes, it rains here. But, as the politicians say, let's look at the context: The Portland area is in the Willamette Valley, between the coastal mountains and the Cascades. Most of the rain falls on the coast before it gets to the valley. And the Cascades prevent most of the continental air masses from the east from entering the valley. As a result, Portland's weather is milder than that in most of the country.

Extremely high winds—reaching 80 miles per hour on occasion—sometimes scream down the Columbia River Gorge, which acts as a wind tunnel through the mountains. But winters are generally mild, cool, and rainy, with little snow, and summers are warm and dry. The average rainfall in Portland is 37.4 inches. What the rain lacks in volume, however, it makes up for in duration. Clouds hide the sun 72 percent of the time. William Clark summed up the effect of the winter climate when he noted, on January 23, 1805, "When the sun is said to shine, or the weather to be fair, it is to be understood that the sun barely casts a shadow, and that the atmosphere is hazy, of a milky white color."

But the weather doesn't bother most people. Locals often don't even carry umbrellas for that stuff they call mist—the lazy kind of rain that falls from late fall to about June. That's because rain and clouds are part of the bounty. They make this land so rich and plentiful, so green and renewing.

James Mayer
Portland, Oregon

POSEY'S MARKET

By most standards, Mike Posey is not a rich man.

Weekends, Posey sells arugula to citified cooks, outdoors, in downtown Vancouver. His usual Saturday T-shirt, with its Vancouver Farmers Market logo, is ripped and sneaking up on his belly. But that doesn't bother a big guy like Posey.

Because Posey, in some ways, is as rich as Columbia River Valley soil.

He owns 2¼ acres of farmland dead center in Clark County. This part of southwest Washington, to Posey's dismay, is gradually selling out its rural soil to suburban developers.

For one thing, the value of Posey's land jumped by $20,000 between 1990 and 1991, from $74,000 to $94,000. Posey thinks he might have to move his gardens deeper into the country. Up north, land is cheaper and taxes lower.

Wherever he lives, Posey will farm. It's in his blood.

His grandfather, Byron Posey, coaxed corn and barley, potatoes and beans out of bone-dry Idaho soil a half-century ago. He raised ladybugs, gallons of them, and let them feast on pests crawling his square-mile spread.

He farmed, 60 years back, without a chemical.

So does Mike Posey. Moreover, he *sells* ladybugs at the Farmers Market. "It's a matter of conscience. I can't put poison on something and say `eat this.' "

"My grandfather would laugh at me here," Posey says from behind his booth's bunches of herbs and plastic containers of edible flowers. "But at the same time, he'd probably be proud of me."

He might also be a bit jealous, considering how much his grandson makes off a shoebox of basil. With inflation taken into account, Byron Posey earned the same from a truckload of corn.

Mike Posey's specialty produce (fresh herbs, gourmet lettuces, baby vegetables, and edible flowers such as pansies and dianthus) reaps a much higher per-acre profit than barley or corn. And much of Posey's produce thrives right up through the warm part of the winter in the mild climate west of the Cascades. This extended harvest also extends his income.

Besides, Posey Patch produce caters to a niche: people who like to eat fresh and to know where their food comes from. They shop at farmers markets. And it's a good thing, too.

Posey Patch would wash out with the fall rains if it weren't for such open-air outlets as the Vancouver Farmers Market and the farmers markets on the Oregon side of the Columbia River. "There's no way I could survive on a small farm without farmers markets. I can't sell enough to restaurants to make it," Posey says.

It was Posey who came up with the idea to start the Vancouver Farmers' Market in 1990. The Saturday market has breathed some life into a dead-quiet downtown and given an outlet for dahlia peddlers and vegetable growers from southwest Washington.

From his position as president of the Washington State Farmers Market Association, Posey is watching the number of farmers markets increase right along with his land's value.

In 1990, Washington had 23 member markets. A year later, 33 were going as strong as chives in a wet spring, and other informal markets are cropping up in community halls and parking lots.

Farmers markets offer the consumer good deals. Shop at the supermarkets and you get California peaches. Shop at your farmers market, and you buy from your neighbor who picked the Redhavens the same morning.

Short of yanking the produce out of your own backyard, the food is as close to picked-to-order, fresh-from-the-garden as you may find.

Moreover, farmers markets are places for talking, connecting, rubbing shoulders, and exchanging recipes, it's no surprise that centuries ago, farmers markets sprang up on the same plot of land as city halls.

Mike Posey likes what that life means, though his 15-hour days and hopelessly dirty fingernails get him down every so often. It takes patience, and time, even to turn a profit on a small farm, and the profit is small. "I juggle bills every month," he says, though five years into his business, he's seeing a glimmer of financial gain.

While many growers get into the game and get out, Posey plans to stick around. His blood-red radicchio and oily oregano always will settle their roots somewhere near the Columbia River basin, he promises. He's right: "How could you quit with a name like Posey Patch?"

Angela Allen

HONEY

Jim Weimer backed a wooden trailer into the pink-blossomed peach orchard and began unloading a platform with 16 beehives. He worked inches from one buzzing gray box. The bees boiled out of the hive, swarmed around Weimer's uncovered face, and then flew off. Not a one stung the 73-year-old Vancouver beekeeper.

"That one's a little on the pecky side this morning," Weimer said. The beekeeper continued working, smiling widely, his blue-gray eyes the color of the foggy morning sky. "They was warning me," he added. "But they didn't sting."

Once Weimer had the hives in place, he pulled the trailer away with his half-ton Chevy pickup and headed home. As he drove, he talked of how he and thousands of other small beekeepers are an essential part of Pacific Northwest agriculture. Oregon and Washington have 140,000 commercial hives that produce about 7 million pounds of honey a year. Moreover, these busy bees pollinate virtually every orchard and berry bush in the region. If it weren't for the bees, Northwest fruit production would fall by more than half.

As the road wound its way through orchards in bloom, Weimer explained how each crop produces a different type of honey. Bees go to the closest source of nectar, a trait that allows a diligent keeper to produce pure strains of honey. The color and flavor differ depending on the blossoms. Honeys range from nearly colorless to dark brown, and their flavor varies from mild to distinctly bold, almost like molasses. Some, such as carrot and mint honeys, are too strong for human palates, but the bees don't mind. These are the honeys keepers leave in the hive to sustain the colony over the winter.

In the summer, after the agricultural fruits have finished blooming in the valleys, beekeepers move their hives into the forests. There, bees capture the light taste of fireweed, the pink-flowered colonizer of clearcuts and burned ground. Once summer turns to fall, the bees make thick, dark honey from the forest's pearly everlasting blossoms. Other Northwest honeys include blackberry, salal, huckleberry, alfalfa, and buckwheat. The common designation "wildflower" is a catchall term for honey made from a variety of blooms. Since it takes the nectar from about two million flowers to make a pound of honey, beekeepers need to watch closely in order to produce pure flavors.

To sample the distinctive tastes of these Northwest favorites, visit a farmers market or a greengrocer. Look for local honey that has a specific crop listed on the label. Big producers may take their hives as far as North Dakota or Alberta to get enough flowers. Beekeepers like Weimer, with a couple hundred hives or fewer, tend to work close to home. Next, look for nonfiltered, nonheated honey, which is the finest tasting, most full-bodied honey you can buy. Commercial producers often filter and heat honey to give it a longer shelf life and to keep it from crystallizing, but this destroys the subtle flavors and makes it thinner. It's a simple matter to put crystallized honey in a pot of hot water to reliquefy it.

Once you've tasted pure honey, you've sampled a true taste of the Northwest.

NancyAnn Mayer

Weimer's Honey Farm
3403 NE 86th Avenue, Vancouver
(206) 256-1659
Year-round: Monday–Saturday, 11am–dark.
Honey, bee pollen, royal jelly, and beekeeping supplies
Southeast of Vancouver. Take Fourth Plain Road to Andresen to NE 86th Street and turn south. There are some small signs on Fourth Plain Road.

FRANZ POPPERL'S APRICOT DUMPLINGS

Local apricots have a short summmer season, from mid-June to early August. Buy them fully ripe, as they do not continue to ripen after harvesting.

1 pound starchy (such as russets) potatoes (3 medium)
1½ tablespoons butter
¾ cup all-purpose flour
4 tablespoons semolina
Salt
1 egg yolk
10 apricots
10 sugar cubes
½ cup butter (1 cube)
½ cup dry bread crumbs (see note)

Boil potatoes with skin in salt water. Peel while hot and work through a sieve. Let cool.

Mix together butter, flour, semolina, egg yolk, and salt and add to cooled potatoes. Mix well until it forms a nice dry loaf. Let dough rest for ½ hour.

Remove the pit of each apricot, leaving fruit whole, and replace with a sugar cube. Divide the dough into 20 equal pieces. Place apricot in the center of a piece of potato dough, top with another piece, and form to a well-closed snowball. Place the dumplings into a pot of boiling, salted water. Stir so that they rise to the top and don't stick to the bottom of the pan. Simmer 10 minutes.

Remove dumplings with a slotted spoon and roll them in the bread crumbs. Place on plate and dust with powdered sugar.

Makes 10 servings.

Note: To make bread crumbs, cut one slice bread into cubes. Place on baking sheet and cook in 300°F oven for 8 to 10 minutes, until lightly browned and dry. Then crush in food processor or blender. Melt butter in sauté pan and roast the dry bread crumbs until golden brown.

Franz Popperl
Portland, Oregon

WILLAMETTE VALLEY BERRIES

Doubtless, God could have made a better berry
[than the strawberry], but doubtless, God never did.
—William Butler, 1535–1618

Sweetly delicious red strawberries conjure up visions of freshly cranked ice cream on the back porch. Luscious ruby raspberries and dark, delectable black raspberries bring to mind desserts that are praised by the most discriminating palate. Toothsome plump blueberries? What else would do for those All-American pancakes and muffins? The taste of home-baked is in those pies piled high with marion, boysen, or loganberries. Would Thanksgiving be the same without cranberries on the side? All the more appetizing because of their elusiveness are the tangy huckleberries and wild blackberries found high in the Cascades. Along every backroad byway and many highways, forbidding tangles of blackberry bushes, their fruit larger and seedier than their mountain counterparts, beckon the picker brave enough to take on thorny stickers and the yellow jackets that hover protectively over every bush.

Oh, yes. To the berry devotee, summer in the Willamette Valley is a season that is most avidly awaited and most sadly mourned when past.

Strawberries are the most prolific of valley berries. A smaller wild version of today's strawberries was prized by the Native Americans and pioneers hungry for the taste of fruit. Commercial cultivation began around the turn of the century. Valley old-timers love to reminisce fondly about a strawberry strain popular in the 1930s to the 1950s.

"Marshall strawberries, from high in Silverton Hills, were the best strawberries ever grown," said one who mourned their passing. "The best ever grown" may be arguable in other parts of the world, but you'll never get an Oregonian over 50 to admit that.

So what happened to the beloved Marshall berry? Bob Conroy, now with Kerr Concentrates in Salem, has spent most of his adult life working with Willamette Valley berries. He says Marshalls produced only about three tons to an acre (compared with more than four tons per acre for newer varieties), and eventually the strain was allowed to run out. Hard on the heels of the Marshalls came the Northwest variety, an excellent berry for ice cream, said Conroy. In the 1960s, the Hood berries came into prominence. Hood berries had a brilliant red color and would hold that color under glass (for preserves) for five months.

Today, 70 to 80 percent of the strawberries grown in Oregon are Totems, which originated in British Columbia. They have a good texture and look good under glass for four to five months.

Why does Oregon produce such quality berries? Conroy sums it up in one concise phrase: "Warm days, cool nights." Of course, if pressed he can and will elaborate scientifically on just why the warmth of the day and the coolness of the nights make for a perfect sweet, firm berry. And, of course, he also might tell you how the taste of a California strawberry can't compete with an Oregon berry. But he generally says with a slow smile, "Let's don't go into that."

Strawberries, with 50 million pounds grown on 60,000 acres in 1990, lead the state's berry market. Raspberries accounted for 20 million pounds in 1990 and blueberries, 6 million pounds. Cranberries, grown in bogs in the coastal county of Coos, have much smaller harvests.

Lesser known cultivated berries dear to the hearts of Oregonians include:

Marionberry: A type of blackberry prized for their sweet pulpy goodness—fewer seeds make it so—the hybrid marionberry is used for eating, pies, and jams. It is a Marion County original, a cross between the Olalli and the Chehalem berries, now rarely grown in Oregon. There were 20 million pounds of marionberries grown in 1990.

Loganberries: A cross between the blackberry and raspberry, the logan, developed in California, began to gain in popularity when a thornless variety was developed. Like raspberries, logans are best eaten fresh without cooking. Oregon produced 700,000 pounds in 1990.

Boysenberries: Developed in California and popular at Knott's Berry Farm near Los Angeles, the boysenberry is a large, purple-black berry with a distinctive taste. Boysenberries are good for eating, freezing, jams, jellies, pies, and tarts. Three million pounds were grown in 1990.

Evergreen blackberries: Ten million pounds of evergreen blackberries were grown in 1990. A tad seedy, they are good in pies, jams, and jellies.

Most berries grown in the Willamette Valley are still hand-harvested because the human hand is gentle and the human eye is the best judge of ripeness. Ninety-five percent of Oregon's commercially grown berries end up in ice cream and yogurt. Why? Their sweet firmness holds its own in the freezing process.

Huckleberries are rarely cultivated and can be found mostly in higher elevations in the Cascades. A favorite with visitors, though not always with landowners because they grow profusely on empty lots, pastures, and roadsides, are the wild Himalayan and evergreen blackberries.

Take care with berries; they are very perishable. For best results, they should be chilled as soon as picked, and you should pick only as much as you are able to process or eat within 24 hours. If you are picking your own, take an ice-filled cooler to the fields. Arrange the berries in shallow layers between paper towels.

Eat and enjoy! Summer in the Willamette Valley is the berries!

Gloria Bledsoe Goodman

BLUEBERRY-RASPBERRY UPSIDE-DOWN CAKE

Janie Hibler bakes this wonderfully moist cake in a 9-inch cast-iron frying pan—the heavy pan keeps the butter from burning and the handle makes it easy to flip the cake upside down when it is done. It can be served warm from the oven for dessert or as a coffee cake for a brunch, but once it has cooled, the cake needs to be tightly wrapped in plastic wrap—it will get more moist the longer it sits.

7 tablespoons butter, divided
1 cup brown sugar
2 eggs
1 cup sugar
½ cup milk
¼ teaspoon salt
1 cup all-purpose flour
1 teaspoon baking powder
1 pint fresh raspberries

1 pint fresh blueberries
2 cups whipping cream
¼ cup powdered sugar
1 teaspoon vanilla extract

Preheat the oven to 375°F.

Melt 5 tablespoons butter in a heavy skillet and stir in the brown sugar. Cook over medium heat until the sugar dissolves. Keep warm over low heat.

Beat the eggs and sugar together until they are light, about 4 minutes.

Melt the remaining 2 tablespoons butter in the milk over low heat or in the microwave, on High, for 1 minute.

Sift together the salt, flour, and baking powder. Add the dry ingredients and the warm milk to the beaten eggs and sugar.

Stir the brown sugar and butter mixture in a cast-iron skillet and sprinkle the raspberries and blueberries over it. Pour the batter over the berries and bake the cake for 45 minutes, or until a toothpick stuck in the center of the cake comes out clean.

As soon as it is done, carefully turn the cake upside down onto a large platter with a lip, to catch the juices.

Whip the cream with the powdered sugar and vanilla. Serve the cake warm with a dollop of whipped cream.

Serves 8.

Janie Hibler
Dungeness Crabs and Blackberry Cobblers

TILLAMOOK AND BANDON CHEESE

As soon as European immigrants reached Oregon's Pacific shore, their cows found grass heaven and promptly produced some of the sweetest milk in the world. And their owners quickly began making cheese to rival any on the West Coast. Cheese-making plants sprouted at most major intersections, and cows soon outnumbered people.

That lush, abundant grass still makes the difference. Fed by frequent rains and clear creeks, it's grazed almost year-round by coastal cows. Nowadays, few dairy cattle range so freely; most are penned and fed much of the year on hay and fermented silage. And many dairies and cheese plants have disappeared.

That's not the case in two coastal valleys, near Tillamook and Bandon, where cheese-makers perfect their craft. There, visitors savor the results of the cows-plus-grass-plus-cheesemaker chemistry.

On the north coast they head for the Tillamook County Creamery Association's state-of-the-art processing plant and visitors center, which is Oregon's third most popular tourist attraction. Folks go there to watch the cheesemaking process, see historical cheese-making equipment, pick up recipes, and buy high-quality gifts and cow kitsch.

But more, they come to eat: free samples of fresh cheese curds and Tillamook's renowned Cheddars, full-sized scoops of Tillamook ice cream, ample cheese sand-wiches, and omelets and espresso from the deli, and fudge from the sweets counter. And for picnickers there are all the fixings: alder-smoked salmon, Oregon's finest jams, mustards, nuts, wines, and more, all to accompany Tillamook cheese. For those who can't visit the center, Tillamook cheeses are sold throughout the West and by mail order.

On the southern coast, the English art of hand cheddaring endures at Bandon Foods. Most cheesemakers, including those at Tillamook, have switched to computer-assisted processes overseen by a head cheesemaker. This ensures high product consistency but loses some of the old aura. Bandon is one of a very few plants to continue the old ways. If visitors hit it right in the two-days-on, one-day-off schedule, they'll watch cheese-makers hand-turn the mats of fresh cheese to expel the whey and compress the curds into Cheddar. At all times, a video explains the process.

Locals know to watch for the "Cheese Curds Today" sign out in front of the plant's store. That means it's a cheesemaking day and the bite-sized, squeaky curds are right-now fresh.

The Bandon plant is smaller and the store is more intimate than the ones at Tillamook. Of course, there are samples: curds, jalapeño and aged Cheddars. Plus there's Umpqua ice cream, smoked salmon sticks, jerkies, Oregon wines, and other gourmet treats. Bandon's cheeses also are available in retail stores in Oregon and southern Washington, and by mail.

Marnie McPhee

Tillamook County Creamery Association
4175 Highway 101 N, Tillamook
(503) 842-4481
Year round: daily, 8am–8pm (summer); 8am–6pm (winter).

Three miles north of Tillamook on Highway 101. Also available by mail order from P.O. Box 313, Tillamook, OR 97141.

Bandon Cheese
680 E 2nd, Bandon
(503) 347-2456
Year-round: daily, 8:30am–5:30pm.

Downtown Bandon on Highway 101. Also available by mail order at P.O. Box 1668, Bandon, OR 97411.

SEEING AND EATING THE ARTICHOKE

The globe artichoke was first cultivated in southern Italy, then spread to other areas in the Mediterranean basin. It was brought to the United States early in the nineteenth century and is now extensively grown in the central coast counties of California. The plant, *Cynara scolymus*, is an herbaceous perennial of thistle ancestry that thrives in a climate where the summers are sunny, but cool and moist, and the winters are mild. Where the temperature falls to 28°F, the growth above ground will be destroyed; but the unaffected root system, deep and woody, will produce new shoots in the spring. If, however, the temperature falls to the low twenties or below, the entire plant will be killed, a loss that can be avoided by such protective measures as mulching and covering it with black plastic. In 40 years' experience with this delectable vegetable, I have lost all my plants only once, years ago in November when the temperature dropped to 12°F.

To cultivate the plant properly and use its produce to best advantage in the kitchen, it is well to know its morphology. A mature root crown, three or more years old, will produce several seasonal shoots, in the spring and the fall. These will grow to a height of 3 feet and a round spread of 4 or 5 feet. The fruit-bearing stem, an inch or more in diameter, rises from the center of the leaf cluster, bearing the developing artichoke at its tip end. As the stem elongates, it produces several lateral branches, each with fruit somewhat smaller than the one on the parent stem. Thus a single shoot from the root crown will produce at least four artichokes. When these have been harvested, the bearing stem is cut at ground level. Soon thereafter, new shoots will rise from the root crown, and one or more will bear fruit. Since the plant is perennial, this fruiting process goes on indefinitely twice a year, in midspring and late fall.

Their marketable portion, the so-called bud, is actually the immature flower head, composed of numerous closely overlaid bracts or scales. The edible portion consists of the tender bases of the bracts, the young flowers, and the receptacle or fleshy base on which the flowers are borne. If the bud, the artichoke, is not removed, it will develop into a purple-centered, thistlelike flower with a head 6 to 8 inches in diameter. At the base of the flower, in the receptacle, will be hundreds of seeds, about the size and shape of sunflower seeds. The artichoke is best for the table when it is about the size of a large lemon and its bracts are tightly closed at the top. As they open and spread, the plant's energy goes to the production of the replicating seeds and the bud becomes tough, bitter, and less edible. The so-called "jumbo" artichoke, with its bracts opening at the top, and its receptacle a mass of developing seeds, has little but its size to recommend it.

To prepare the artichoke for cooking, cut off the thorny tip end (about half an inch) using a very sharp knife, since the bracts are tough. Then cut away the upper part of the outer bracts to the inner ones that are tender and edible. When this is properly done, you will have a pared artichoke, the whole of which is edible, including an inch or so of the stem. Cut in halves or quarters longitudinally, and cook it in one of the following ways. Boiled in a small quantity of salted water until tender but firm, artichokes may be served with hollandaise sauce or a sauce of olive oil, lemon juice, a dash of Tabasco, salt, and pepper. Or the halves can be sautéed in olive oil, butter, a dash of lemon juice, garlic, and parsley, then combined with sautéed chicken for an elegant main course. Combined here means stirred in with the chicken during its final minutes of cooking. For fried artichokes, cut the halves into three or four slices lengthwise, dredge in a light batter of egg and flour, and lightly brown on both sides in enough olive or other oil to cover the bottom of a nonstick skillet. Drain them on absorbent paper, sprinkle with salt, pepper, and lemon juice, and they will elicit the praise of whoever eats them.

Angelo Pellegrini
Vintage Pellegrini

Bear Creek Artichokes
Bill and Cindy Miles
1604 Fifth Street, Tillamook
(503) 398-5411
February–November: weekends until mid-March, then daily; 10am–5pm in spring; 9am–7pm in summer; 10am–5pm in fall.

The Mileses are pioneer Northwest artichoke growers, with 15 years of experience. Bill's premium artichoke harvest season is late September through early October, after the summer heat and before the heavy frosts. "Any time the temperature gets over 75, the quality starts to suffer," he says. Their produce stand is one of the few along the northern Oregon coast, their pumpkin patch draws scores of kids every Halloween season, and their expanding nursery business now produces 500 to 600 varieties of perennials.

Roadside stand is 11 miles south of Tillamook on the east side of Highway 101.

BOTTOM FISH

If beauty is truly in the eyes of the beholder, only a bottom fish's mother could say, "What a little darling!" However, when the homely bug-eyed, fat-mouthed bottom fish is filleted and prepared for table, it becomes the darling of many as more and more people turn to the sea for healthy eating. And although salmon may remain the gourmand's fish of fish, it is the delicately-flavored bottom fish that is more compatible with a variety of preparations and seasonings.

Actually, bottom fish is a generic catch-all term encompassing all edible fish which live nearer the ocean floor. Caught either commercially or for sport, Northwest bottom fish categories include rockfish, flatfish, ling cod, sculpin, and bass.

The rockfish family is the most prolific with more than 60 species. Their size can range from six inches to three feet. With their compressed bodies, large mouths, and spiny head, rockfish can be a colorful addition to the day's catch. Although predominantly red or brown, they also can emerge in such lively colors as pinkish red, orange red, black and blue, orange and gray, yellow and black, or olive green and yellow. A particularly lovely fellow is the copper rockfish, which sports two copper-colored bars radiating back from its head. More than 30 million metric tons of rockfish were caught off the Pacific coast in 1989.

Flatfish, given that name because both eyes are on the same side of the body, lie around on the bottom of the ocean and often bury themselves in the bottom with just their eyes exposed. Flatfish groups include halibut, sole, flounder, and turbot. The adults vary in size from about 6 inches to 10 feet. Halibut caught off the Oregon coast can weigh more than 100 pounds and can be exhausting to land. One sports writer compares catching a huge halibut to "pulling a refrigerator off the ocean floor."

Culinary classics in the flatfish grouping are the petrale and Dover sole. During 1989, four million metric tons of sole were brought in to Oregon's fish processing plants.

Handsomest of the bottom fish clan (which isn't saying much) is the ling cod, which is highly prized among both commercial and sports fishermen. Although the raw flesh is not good to look upon—young specimens are green—the ling cod cooks up tastily white and firm. A versatile and delicious catch, ling cod can be fried, baked, sautéed, broiled, or poached, and works happily with most seasonings. In 1989, more than 2½ million metric tons of ling cod were taken off the Oregon coast.

Although the bass-like snapper doesn't adapt as easily to all recipes as does the ling cod or the sole, the darker-fleshed red snapper is a favorite among cooks, especially the cost conscious ones. It works up well with heartier seasonings. An up-and-coming bottom fish among trendy diners is the cabazon, a member of the sculpin family. The flesh is good eating, but sports fishermen should remember that the eggs are poisonous. Like that of the ling cod, the cabazon's flesh can be greenish, but turns white when cooked.

Hundreds of commercial fishermen set out year-round from the primary port cities of Astoria, Newport, Charleston, and Brookings. They stay out anywhere from one to five or more days, plying the sea in trawlers which drag nets behind them. (Trawlers' nets are not to be confused with illegal drift nets which are used by some foreign countries and which wreak havoc with sea life in the open ocean.)

These fishermen ice their fish immediately after catching. When the boat's limit is reached, the catch is quickly brought in to one of the many fish processing plants. With today's technology, fresh bottom fish is available year-round.

Are these waters in danger of being fished out? Definitely not, said Jerry Butler, marine biologist for Oregon Fish and Wildlife. Butler added that state and federal agencies work constantly and vigilantly to keep both sport and commercial catch as high as possible without endangering the long-term stability of the species.

Gloria Bledsoe Goodman

U-PICK FARMS AND ROADSIDE STANDS

The Tri-County Farm Fresh Produce Guide for Oregon's Clackamas, Multnomah, and Washington counties runs a Ripe and Ready Hotline with weekly updates from May to October, (503) 226-2112.

U-Pick Guidelines: Call first, especially near the beginning and end of the season. Find out if your small children are welcome to help pick. Farms will supply picking containers, but you will need bags or boxes to transport your produce home. Pick carefully and conscientiously; a well-tended berry field or orchard represents years of knowledgeable labor. (Dogs should stay in the car.)

Harvests may vary greatly from year to year. A local chamber of commerce or county extension office can often supply up-to-date seasonal information. Also, many newspapers publish local farm maps in the late spring or summer.

CLACKAMAS COUNTY, OREGON

Joe Casale and Son
Joe and Jennie Casale
13116 NE Denbrook Road, Aurora
June–October: Monday–Saturday, 9am–6pm.

U-pick and ready-picked produce.

On I-5 going south take exit 282B (Charbonneau); going north take exit 282 (Canby).

Fir Point Farms ☆ **(503) 678-2455**
Ed and Judy Strizke
14600 Arndt Road, Aurora
April–December: daily, 9am–6pm.

U-pick and ready-picked produce and flowers.

Take I-5 south to Canby exit. Turn left on Arndt Road, look for signs.

Riley & Sons Oregon Blueberries ☆
(503) 678-5852 or -5761
Rick and Marie Riley
26022 NE Butteville Road, Aurora
Early July–August 14: Monday–Saturday,
8am–7pm; Sunday, 10am–7pm.

U-pick and picked to order blueberries. Bring containers.

Seven-tenths of a mile from I-5; look for signs from I-5.

Sonnen Farm ☆ **(503) 982-9570**
Rick and Jan Sonnen
8644 Broadacres Road NE, Aurora

June–October: Monday–Friday, 8am–6pm;
Saturday, 8am–5pm; Sunday, 9am–5pm.

Produce, U-pick, ready-picked, and picked to order.

Take the Woodburn exit off I-5. Farm is 4½ miles northwest of Woodburn at Broadacres Road.

Bithell Farms ☆ **(503) 663-6182**
Bob and Mary Bithell
28355 SE Kelso Road, Boring
June–August: daily, 8am–6pm.

U-pick only: raspberries, marionberries, blueberries, loganberries, boysenberries, blackberries, gooseberries, red currants, and pie cherries. Bring containers.

East on Highway 26, turn right onto SE Kelso Road. You'll see berry signs, 2½ miles on the right.

Kelso Blueberries ☆ **(503) 663-6830**
Diane Kelso
28951 SE Church Road, Boring
July–September: daily, 8am–8pm.

U-pick blueberries, boysenberries, raspberries, and Suncrest peaches.

Call for directions.

Thomson Farms ☆ **(503) 667-9138 or
(503) 658-4640**
Larry and Betty Thompson
24727 SE Bohna Park Road, Boring
June–August: daily, 8am–6pm.

U-pick strawberries, red raspberries, marion-berries, and boysenberries.

Also operate a farm produce stand located 5 miles south of Gresham on 242nd or 1 mile north of Highway 212 on 242nd.

John's Peach Orchard ✱ (503) 266-9466
Bertram John Fawver
7335 S Fawver Road, Canby
Mid-June–October: Monday–Saturday, 8am–7pm; Sunday, 1pm–5pm.

Homegrown produce, flowers, herbs. Raspberries, strawberries, 4 varieties of peaches. U-pick or picked to order.

From I-5 take exit 282A. Go to the light and turn left, keep left when the road makes a Y. Turn left on South Barlow Road and follow signs.

Three Rivers Farm ✱ (503) 266-2432
Kurt and Martha Schrader
2525 N Baker Drive, Canby
February–March 15 (spring lambing): Saturdays, noon–5pm.
June–October: Tuesday–Saturday, 9am–5pm. Membership farm; call ahead.

Organically raised produce, fruit, and livestock available to members. Also eggs, honey, and organic coffee beans. Membership $30/year, due before May 15 (somewhat flexible).

Call for directions.

Tutti Frutti Farms ✱ (503) 266-3379
Bill and Eileen Osmer
718 SE Township Road
Canby, OR 97013
July–January 1: Monday–Saturday, 9am–6pm.

Mail-order source for homegrown popcorn for 80 cents a pound or $10 for a gift package of three 3-pound burlap bagsful, plus shipping. Sweet corn sold on the farm. Bill has brought his Kansas corn know-how to northern Oregon. Other fruits and vegetables in season.

From Highway 99E, head toward Molalla; after 4 blocks in this direction, turn on Township Road and follow signs ¼ mile.

H.-I. Bar Farm ✱ (503) 630-5639
Mike Chittick
25271 S Springwater Road, Estacada
Mid-July–mid-September: daily. Call ahead.

Organic blueberries and marionberries, U-pick or picked to order.

South of Estacada on Highway 211; take 211 just under 5 miles. When it becomes Tucker Road, turn right, go 100 feet, and turn left onto S Springwater; go ⅛ mile to the farm.

Gloria Sample & Company ✱ (503) 636-3520
425 2nd Street Alley, Lake Oswego
Year-round: Monday–Friday, 9am–5pm.

Fruit preserves (marrying flavors such as cantaloupe, peach, and marionberry tinged with apricot liqueur), conserves, fruit vinegars, cranberry sauce, catsups (both savory and sweet), and fruitcake available by mail from 199 "E" Avenue, Lake Oswego, OR 97034, or at the retail shop.

Between A and B avenues in Lake Oswego.

Parsons Farm Greengrocer ✱ (503) 635-4533
Jack and Melissa Parsons
15964 SW Boones Ferry Road, Lake Oswego
Year-round: Monday–Saturday, 7am–7pm; Sunday, 5pm.
Fresh produce, bakery, deli, and dining room.

From I-5 take Route 217 exit. Turn left (east) off ramp; road ends in a T. Turn right on Boones Ferry Road; farm is 6 blocks along.

Hartnell Farms ✱ (503) 655-1297
Larry and Jeff Hartnell
15000 SE Johnson Road, Milwaukie
May–September: Monday–Saturday, 8am–6pm.

U-pick and ready-picked strawberries, raspberries, blueberries, pole beans, cucumbers, and tomatoes. Other produce also available.

A half mile south of Milwaukie on Johnston Road; look for the K-Mart for the intersection of Highway 224 and Johnston Road.

Jake's Famous Products ✷ (800) 777-7179
4252 SE International Way
Milwaukie, OR 97222

Mail-order source for smoked seafood, seafood sauces, clam chowder, and chocolate truffle cake. Jake's sells to McCormick and Schmick's and McCormick's Fish House in Seattle, and Jake's in Portland.

Moore Natural Foods ✷ (503) 654-3215
Bob Moore
5209 SE International Way
Milwaukie, OR 97222
Year-round: Monday–Saturday, 9am–5pm.

Stone-ground, whole-grain flours, grits, rice, cereals, pastas, dried fruit, nuts, and couscous. No preservatives or chemical additives. His extensive catalog is also available for mail order.

From I-205 take exit for Highway 224 west and go 2 miles west.

Albeke Farms ✷ (503) 632-3989
Doug and Becky Albeke
16107 S Wilson Road, Oregon City
June–October: Monday–Friday, 9am–7pm; Saturday, 9am–5pm; Sunday, noon–5pm. Call ahead for availability.

U-pick and ready-picked fruit and vegetables.

Take Park Place exit off I-205 onto Highway 213 and drive to Beavercreek Road. Turn left and follow signs.

Pavlinac Farms ✷ (503) 656-8833
Randall and Jessie Pavlinac
19629 S Meyers Road, Oregon City
June–October: Monday–Friday, 8am–8pm; Saturday–Sunday, 8am–5pm.

U-pick strawberries, red raspberries, Waldo blackberries, Jubilee and white sweet corn, and pumpkins.

Take I-205 to Highway 213, go 3 miles, and turn right at the Community College junction. Turn left at Gaffney Lane, turn left at next stop sign and right at Meyers Road; farm is second house on the left.

Dennis' Organic Farm ✷ (503) 638-4211
Dale and Margaret Dennis
25006 SW Gage Road, Wilsonville
May–December: Tuesday–Saturday, 9am–6pm.

Certified organic produce includes basil, shallots, garlic, and grapes.

Take I-5 to Stafford exit, go east 1 mile on Elligsen Road and follow signs.

McKnight's Blueberry Farm ✷ (503) 638-4989
John and Linda McKnight
24275 SW Nodaway Lane, Wilsonville
July–August: Wednesday–Saturday, 8am–6pm; Sunday, 11am–6pm.

U-pick or ready-picked blueberries (3 varieties).

Take Stafford exit off Highway 205 and go south to Newland Road. Follow signs for 1½ miles.

CLATSOP COUNTY, OREGON

The Community Store ✷ (503) 325-0027
1389 Duane Street, Astoria
Monday–Saturday, 10am–6pm.

Cooperative store (open to the public) featuring Clatsop and Pacific County produce when available.

One block off Commercial (Astoria's main drive).

Hauke's Sentry Market ✷ (503) 325-1931
Skip and Audrey Hauke
3300 Leif Erikson Drive, Astoria
Year-round: daily, 7am–10pm.

"The best purveyor of truly fresh fish in Astoria, at reasonable prices," says local food writer Joan Herman Fencsak. Fresh-caught fish daily, plus a deli and bakery with seating area.

On Highway 30 on the east end of town.

Josephson's Smokehouse ✷ (503) 325-2190
Linda and Mike Josephson
106 Marine Drive, Astoria
Year-round: Monday–Friday, 8am–6pm; Saturday–Sunday, 9am–5:30pm.

Cured, smoked, canned, or pickled salmon (and salmon jerky), as well as sturgeon, Dungeness crab meat, tuna, scallops, oysters, black cod, and fresh clam chowder. Also available by mail from P.O. Box 412, Astoria, OR 97103.

On the main drive in Astoria.

Bell Buoy Crab Company ☆ (503) 738-6354
Highway 101, Seaside
Year-round: daily; 8am–6:30pm in winter; 8am–9pm in summer.

Crabs, razor clams, and other seafood.

At the south end of Seaside on Highway 101.

Pacific Seafood Company ☆ (503) 738-7226
S Highway 101 and Avenue M, Seaside
Summer: Monday–Thursday, 10am–6pm; Friday–Sunday, 10am–7pm. Call for winter hours.

Fresh, smoked, and frozen fish and shellfish.

On Highway 101 in Seaside.

Warrenton Deep Sea Crab and Fish Market ☆ (503) 861-3911
A. F. Charlston
45 NE Harbor Place, Warrenton
Summer: Monday–Saturday, 9am–5:30pm; Sunday, 10am–4pm; winter hours vary.

Dungeness crab is the specialty here—fresh and hand-packed. A full line of other fish is available as well.

On the Skipanon River in Warrenton.

COLUMBIA COUNTY, OREGON

Bonaventura ☆ (503) 556-2126
John Ullman and Marilyn Kenn
P.O. Box 763
Rainier, OR 9704

CLOSED

Italian-style (both hazelnut and orange flavo raspberry conserve, all made with an emphasis on Northwest ingredients. Mail order only.

MULTNOMAH COUNTY, OREGON

Larson Farm ☆ (503) 695-5882
Clair Klock
Christensen Road, Corbett
Early July–late August: Monday–Saturday, 8am–8pm; Sunday, 10am–6pm.

U-pick and picked to order: raspberries, marion-berries, blueberries, boysenberries, early apples; also blueberry plants.

Five miles southeast of Troutdale. Take Columbia River Highway to Springdale to Northway Road South, go 1½ miles.

Schwartz's Farm ☆ (503) 695-5428
Henry and Marie Schwartz
34926 E Crown Point Highway, Corbett
June–September: daily, 11am–7pm.

U-pick and ready-picked raspberries and blue-berries. Homemade jams and syrups.

One-quarter mile west of Corbett.

The Berry Basket ☆ (503) 621-3155
David and Vickie Egger
15318 NW Sauvie Island Road, Portland
June–September: Monday–Saturday, 9am–7pm; call ahead.

Farm stand features raspberries, strawberries, marionberries, blueberries, peaches, and other produce and canning supplies. U-pick at Sauvie Island Farms (see entry).

Located ¼ mile from bridge on Sauvie Island Road.

Cascade Mushrooms ☆ (503) 294-1550
530 NW 112th Avenue, Portland

Mail-order source for wild mushrooms in season and dried mushrooms year-round. Winter mush-rooms include hedgehog, yellowfoot, and black trumpet; spring brings morels, and chanterelles appear in the summer.

Giusto Farms ☆ (503) 253-0271
Augie and Dominic Giusto
3518 NE 162nd Avenue, Portland
August 1–January 30: Monday–Saturday, 10am–6pm.

Summer and winter produce available at this farm stand includes fennel, leeks, shallots, 5 varieties of winter squash, lots of red potatoes, parsnips, chestnuts, eggplant, bok choy, cucumbers, peppers, beets, broccoli, cauliflower, French carrots, garlic, and parsley.

One and a half blocks south of Sandy Boulevard.

Pumpkin Patch Vegetables ☆ (503) 621-3874
16511 NW Gillihan, Portland
June–November: daily, 9am–6pm; open again in December on weekends for Christmas trees.

U-pick and ready-picked produce.

Take Highway 30 to the Sauvie Island Bridge. Cross the bridge, turn left under it, and go 2 miles.

Rossi Farms ☆ (503) 253-5571
3839 NE 122nd Avenue, Portland
August–January: Monday–Saturday, 9am–5pm.

Ready-picked farm produce.

West side of NE 122nd Avenue between Sandy Boulevard and the Banfield (I-84) Highway.

Sauvie Island Blueberry Farm ☆ (503) 621-3332
Anne K. Jones
15140 NW Burlington Court, Portland
July–mid-August: daily, 8am–6pm.

U-pick and ready-picked blueberries.

On Sauvie Island. Take Sauvie Island Road to Reeder Road, and follow the signs. Farm is 2½ miles from bridge.

Sauvie Island Farms ☆ (503) 621-3768 or -3988
Gerald and Carol Egger
19730 NW Sauvie Island Road, Portland
June–September: Monday–Saturday, 8am–7pm.

U-pick strawberries, raspberries, marionberries, peaches, and blueberries. Farm stand at The Berry Basket (see entry).

Three and a half miles from the bridge on Sauvie Island Road.

Sauvie Island Market ☆ (503) 621-3489
Denny and Nancy Grande
13743 NW Charleton Road, Portland
June–October: daily, 9am–7pm.

U-pick and farm stand.

One and a half miles north of Sauvie Island Bridge.

Spada U-Pick Farm ☆ (503) 253-2313 or -7846
Ron Spada
4939 NE 158th Avenue, Portland
May–November: 8am–6pm on Saturday; 9am–5pm on Sunday.

A large variety of U-pick and ready-picked produce includes European, Asian, and Middle Eastern vegetables.

Between Sandy Blvd and Marine Drive on 158th Avenue.

Trapold Farms (The Barn) ☆ (503) 253-5103
The Trapold family
5211 NE 148th Avenue, Portland
June–December: Monday–Saturday, 9am–6pm.

U-pick and ready-picked produce; Christmas trees.

From I-205 take Airport Way E exit. Head east on Airport Way to 148th. Take a left on 148th. Farm is on the left.

Van Buren Farms ☆ (503) 253-7459 or (503) 252-7102
3001 NE 148th Avenue, Portland
June–end of the season.

U-pick strawberries, raspberries, boysenberries, loganberries, cascadeberries, and marionberries.

Other U-pick fields located at 6300 SE 190th Drive and 17344 NE Halsey Street, and at NE 147th and Sandy Boulevard.

For more Portland listings, see the Washington County section.

TILLAMOOK COUNTY, OREGON

Hayes Oysters ☆ (503) 377-2210
Sam Hayes
Bay City
Summer: daily, 8~~~~~~~~~~~~~~~, weekends primarily in winter.

Paci~~~~~~~ Kumamoto oysters.

On Highway 101 between Tillamook and Garibaldi. Look for the pile of oyster shells on the highway.

Smith's Pacific Shrimp Company ☆ (503) 322-3316
Bill Schrieber
608 Commercial Drive, Garibaldi
Call ahead.

Pacific pink shrimp cannery; fish flash-frozen for better flavor and texture.

In the boat basin in Garibaldi.

Karla's Krabs 'n Quiche Delight ☆ (503) 355-2362
Karla Steinhauser and Amelia Lanier
2010 Highway 101 North, Rockaway Beach
Summer: Monday–Saturday, 7am–6pm.
Winter: Monday–Saturday, 7am–4pm.

From the back of her shop, Karla produces mouthwatering alderwood-smoked chinook salmon, tuna, black cod, trout, and a variety of shellfish. Fresh and canned fish also sold. Smoked and canned fish available by mail from P.O. Box 537, Rockaway Beach, OR 97136. The restaurant features home-smoked seafood, bouillabaisse, and fish'n'chips.

Seventeen miles north of Tillamook on Highway 101.

Bear Creek Artichokes ☆ (503) 398-5411
Bill and Cindy Miles
1604 Fifth Street, Tillamook
February–November: weekends until mid-March, then daily; 10am–5pm in spring; 9am–7pm in summer; 10am–5pm in fall.

The Mileses are pioneer Northwest artichoke growers, with 15 years of experience. Bill's premium artichoke harvest season is late September through early October, after the summer heat and before the heavy frosts. "Any time the temperature gets over 75°, the quality starts to suffer," he says. Their produce stand is one of the few along the northern Oregon coast, their pumpkin patch draws scores of kids every Halloween season, and their expanding nursery business produces 500 to 600 varieties of perennials.

Eleven miles south of Tillamook on Highway 101.

Tillamook County Creamery Association ☆ (503) 842-4481
4175 Highway 101 N, Tillamook
Year-round: daily, 8am–8pm (summer);
8am–6pm (winter).

Oregon's third most popular tourist attraction is the creamery association's processing plant and visitors center, where you can watch the cheese-making process, see historical cheesemaking equipment, pick up recipes, and sample curds and Cheddars and Tillamook ice cream. A deli sells all sorts of picnic supplies. Also available by mail order from PO Box 313, Tillamook, OR 97141.

Three miles north of Tillamook on Highway 101.

WASHINGTON COUNTY, OREGON

Gordon's Acres ☆ (503) 324-9831
Doug and Barthene Gordon
48360 NW Narup Road, Banks
June–October: daily, 8am–dark.

U-pick and ready-picked strawberries, raspberries, blueberries, tomatoes, peppers, cucumbers, picklers, squash, and pumpkins.

Three miles west of Banks; take Highway 6 to milepost 46, turn north on Cedar Canyon and follow signs.

The Frank Lolich Farm ☆ (503) 628-1436
Frank Lolich
18th on Scholls Ferry Road, Beaverton
June–early September and all of October: daily, 8:30am–dusk.

U-pick blueberries, ready-picked marionberries, boysenberries, pumpkins. Frank is an ex–New York Met who says that blueberries need long cool summers—the best are to be found in mid-August to September.

Five miles west of Washington Square on Scholls Ferry Road (Highway 210).

Rosedale Orchards ✿ (503) 649-7354
Ray and Millie Vandegrift
23100 SW Rosedale Road, Beaverton
July 15–December: Monday–Friday, 8am–dark; Saturday–Sunday, noon–6pm.

Garden produce, cider, honey, pumpkins, squash.

Corner of Rosedale Road and 229th, between Tualatin Valley Highway and Farmington Road.

Duyck's Peachy-Pig Farm ✿
(503) 357-3570
Gary and Sally Duyck
Johnson School Road, Cornelius
Year-round: daily, 8am–dark.

U-pick and custom harvest of fruit, vegetables, and nuts. Gourmet foods, freezer hogs. Tours can be arranged; children welcome to see and touch animals.

Four miles south of Hillsboro on Highway 219, turn right on Simpson Road and go 3 miles. Turn left at golf course, then right on Johnson School Road and go 1 mile.

Lakeview Farms ✿ (503) 647-2336
Mike and Sue Cropp
31345 NW North Avenue, Cornelius
July–September: Monday–Friday, 9am–7pm; Saturday, 9am–5pm; Sunday, noon–5pm; limited hours from October–December.

Produce, including fresh-picked corn, tomatoes, and a variety of berries.

Take Sunset Highway (Highway 26) to the North Plains exit, go north, follow signs 1 mile.

Pruitt's Farm ✿ (503) 357-6981
George Pruitt
39470 SW Geiger Road, Cornelius
April–November: Monday–Saturday, 8am–7pm; Sunday, 12:30pm–7pm.

U-pick tomatoes and other ready-picked produce.

Go 1 mile south of Forest Grove on Fern Hill Road. Turn left onto Geiger Road.

Sunshower Orchard ✿ (503) 357-6423
Ted and Beth Schlapfer
5010 SW Hergert Road, Cornelius
August–December: call for hours.

U-pick or ready-picked organic apples (12 varieties).

From Cornelius go south on 10th Avenue to Blooming Fernhill Road, turn right to blinker, left on Hergert Road and go 2,000 yards.

Barb's Dutchmill Herbfarm ✿
(503) 357-0924
Barbara and Larry Remington
6640 NW Marsh Road, Forest Grove
March–December: Wednesday–Saturday, noon–6pm or by appointment.

Fourth-generation herb farm features herb plants, fresh basil, herb wreaths, living succulent wreaths, and other gift items. Largest selection of lavender on the west coast.

Take Tualatin Valley Highway (Highway 8) from Portland. In Forest Grove, turn right (north) at the second light (Quince Street). Go 4 miles; the road dead-ends, and farm is last house on the right.

Giles Farm ✿ (503) 357-3944
or (503) 771-8320
Ken and Lora Giles
Shearer Road, Forest Grove
July–October: call for hours.

U-pick and ready-picked pie cherries, Redhaven peaches, Brooks prunes, and hazelnuts.

From Banks, go 5 miles west on Highway 6 (Wilson River Highway), turn left onto Timmerman Road, turn left onto Shearer Road, and go ½ mile.

Jiminez Farm ✿ (503) 357-7990
Pablo Jiminez
1628 Douglas Street, Forest Grove
June–July: Monday–Saturday, 5am–2pm and 4pm–6pm.

Certified organic strawberries, U-pick and ready-picked. Bring containers.

Call for directions.

Normandin and Sons ✲ (503) 357-2351 or -7000
50520 NW Clapshaw Hill Road, Forest Grove
August–September, 8am–7pm.

U-pick pears and peaches. Bring containers.

Take Highway 8 to Gales Creek. Turn right on Clapshaw Hill Road.

Orca Farm ✲ (503) 357-9116
Fred and Harlene Lloyd
46719 NW Clapshaw Hill Road, Forest Grove
July–September, 7am–dark.

U-pick and ready-picked produce. Bring containers.

From Highway 26 take Banks exit. Follow signs for Tualatin Valley Winery.

Oregon Prune Exchange ✲ (503) 357-6800
1840 B Street
Forest Grove, OR 97116
Year-round: Monday–Friday, 8am–4:30pm.

A cooperatively owned farm selling peaches, dried fruit (pears, apricots, and apples), honey, walnuts, hazelnuts, syrups, and jams. Mail order also available from the above address.

From Main Street in Forest Grove, turn onto B Street.

Orchard Dale Produce and Nursery ✲ (503) 357-0578
Peter B. Day
Highway 8, Gales Creek
In season: daily, call for hours.

Cabbages, corn, cucumbers, lettuce, mustard greens, pumpkins, scallions, spinach, tomatoes, winter squash.

Six miles west of Forest Grove on Highway 8; 30 miles west of Portland: take Highway 26 west to Highway 6, take Highway 6 west to Highway 8. Go left on Highway 8 and continue 2 miles east.

Baby Gotter's Pumpkin Patch ✲ (503) 628-1366
Stan and Jane Gotter
24375 SW Scholls Ferry Road, Hillsboro
October: daily, 9am–6pm.

Pumpkins, sweet corn, winter and turban squash, cider, walnuts, gourds, and Indian corn.

Nine miles west of Washington Square on Scholls Ferry Road (Highway 210).

B. F. Carson and Sons ✲ (503) 640-5469
Ben, Helen, Jerry, and Dennis Carson
7100 SW Straughn Road, Hillsboro
June–December: 8am–dark; call ahead.

Blueberries (June and July), hazelnuts, walnuts, kiwi fruit and plants; visitors are welcome to talk kiwi fruit culture anytime. Bring containers. Kiwi plants available all year long.

South of Hillsboro. Take Rood Bridge Road to Larson Road to Straughn Road.

Currant Ideas ✲ (503) 647-5948
Ken and Bev Stewart
21949 NW West Union Road, Hillsboro
June–July.

Red and black currants.

Call for directions.

Golden Orchard ✲ (503) 647-5769
Pat and John Golden
15253 NW Mason Hill Road, Hillsboro
Late July/early August–mid-September: 9am–6pm; call ahead for availability.

Peaches: Vivids and Veterans. U-pick (bring containers) or picked to order. Peach marmalade, peach butter, peach conserve, berry preserves, fruited cream honeys, gift packs.

From Sunset Highway (26), turn north on Jackson Road, go 2½ miles to second stop, turn left on NW Mason Hill Road. Go 2 miles. Orchard is on left.

Tom Gregg Farm ✲ (503) 681-9584
Tom and Donna Gregg
31660 Hornecker Road, Hillsboro
June–September: 9am–7pm.

U-pick or ready-picked peaches, Redhaven, Veteran, and Elberta; bring containers.

One and a half miles northwest of Hillsboro at Hornecker and Leisy roads.

Dave Jossi and Son ✶ **(503) 647-2158**
Dave and Joanie Jossi
10315 NW Alphorn Lane, Hillsboro
June: Monday–Saturday, 9am–7pm.

U-pick Shuksan strawberries; bring containers.

Take the Helvetia Road exit from Sunset Highway (Highway 26), go north 2½ miles to Bodertscher Road, watch for signs.

Jossy Farms ✶ **(503) 647-2136 or -5668**
Bob and Don Jossy
31965 NW Beach Road, Hillsboro
July–November: call for hours and availability.

Peaches, pears, apples, hazelnuts, and walnuts, U-pick, ready-picked, or picked to order.

Take Sunset Highway (Highway 26) to North Plains exit. Go south ⅛ mile, and turn west on Beach Road.

Loughridge Farm ✶ **(503) 628-1286**
Shawn Loughridge
13300 SW River Road, Hillsboro
July–December: Tuesday–Saturday, 10am–dusk.

Elephant and Italian garlic, basil, honey, walnuts, hazelnuts, apples, and gifts.

Nine miles west of Washington Square.

Mason Hill Farm ✶ **(503) 647-5669**
Mark and Pat Susbauer
13145 NW Mason Hill Road, Hillsboro
Mid-August–October: Wednesday–Sunday, 9am–6pm.

Picked to order apples (Gravenstein, Jonagold, Mutsu, Melrose, Criterion) are sold at the farm stand, but the Susbauer's line of gourmet foods is gradually becoming the real business. Their apple butter, apple cider jelly, rhubarb blueberry jam, and pumpkin butter ("like pumpkin pie in a jar," says Pat) are available all over the Northwest, including in Made in Oregon stores, Nordstrom and Larry's Market in the Seattle area, and throughout eastern Washington.

From Sunset Highway (26), turn north onto Jackson Road, go 2½ miles, turn right onto Mason Hill Road, go 1,000 feet to second house on the left.

Meyers Produce ✶ **(503) 648-5251**
George and Theora Meyers
2305 SW 325th Avenue, Hillsboro
July–November: Monday–Saturday, call for hours.

U-pick and ready-picked produce.

One and a half miles off Tualatin Valley Highway. Look for signs.

Oregon Heritage Farms ✶ **(503) 628-3353**
22801 Scholls Ferry Road, Hillsboro
Mid-August–mid-December: Wednesday–Sunday, 10am–5pm.

Apples, cider, and local produce.

Seven miles west of Washington Square on Scholls Ferry Road.

Peterson Farms Apple Country ✶ **(503) 640-5649**
Frank and Pat Peterson
4800 NW Glencoe Road, Hillsboro
July–December: Wednesday–Sunday, 10am–dusk.

Country store and orchard, featuring 45 varieties of apples.

Midway between Sunset Highway (Highway 26) and Hillsboro on Glencoe Road.

Sara's Blueberries ✶ **(503) 649-6000**
Sara Ackerman
24375 SW Drake Lane, Hillsboro
July–mid-August: 8:30am–dark.

U-pick and ready-picked blueberries (4 varieties). Bring containers.

East of Hillsboro, turn north from Tualatin Valley Highway at 239th and follow the yellow signs for 1 mile.

Simantel's Farm and Nursery ✶ **(503) 648-0925**
Marcus and Marilyn Simantel
31665 NW Scotch Church Road, Hillsboro
March–December: Monday–Friday, 9am–6pm; Saturday, 9am–5pm; Sunday, noon–5pm.

U-pick strawberries (call for hours) and other crops; ready-picked also available.

One mile south of Sunset Highway (Highway 26), take the North Plains exit.

Smith Berry Barn ☆ (503) 628-2172
Ralph and Sue Smith
24500 SW Scholls Ferry Road, Hillsboro
Mid-June–mid-December: call for hours.

U-pick, ready-picked, and produce stand.

Ten miles southwest of Washington Square on Scholls Ferry Road.

Susie's Peaches ☆ (503) 628-1353
Susan D. Snead
17500 SW Hillsboro Highway, Hillsboro
Mid-July–Labor Day: peaches.
October–November: walnuts.

Ready-picked only. Call ahead for walnut orders.

One mile west of Scholls; look for the gazebo.

West Union Gardens ☆ (503) 645-1592
Cheryl and Jeff Boden
7775 NW Cornelius Pass Road, Hillsboro
June–Halloween: Monday–Friday, 8am–8pm; Saturday, 8am–5pm.

U-pick, picked to order, and produce stand.

Take the W Union exit from Sunset Highway (Highway 26), turn north on Cornelius Pass Road, and go 1.7 miles.

Chehalem Mt. Fruit and Nut Company ☆ (503) 628-0181
Doug and Judy Olsen
20125 SW Hillsboro Highway, Newberg
June–October: Friday–Monday, 9am–5:30pm.

Cherries, pie cherries, herb plants, beans, tomatoes, peppers, prunes, corn, and hazelnuts.

On Highway 219, 13 miles south of Hillsboro, 9 miles north of Newberg.

Jaquith Family Farm ☆ (503) 628-1640
Kenneth and Gertrude Jaquith
23135 SW Jaquith Road, Newberg
June: Monday–Saturday, 8am–8pm.

U-pick and ready-picked strawberries, Hood and other varieties. Bring containers.

Two and a half miles south of Scholls; Jacquith Road is off Highway 219.

Bonny Slope Blueberries ☆ (503) 645-1252
Joan Gunness
3565 NW South Road, Portland
July–August: daily, 9am–6pm.

U-pick and ready-picked blueberries; bring containers.

Near Beaverton; follow signs along W Union Road, NW Skyline Road, or Cornell Road in Cedar Mill to Thompson Road; follow signs to South Road.

Kennedy Farm ☆ (503) 645-1416
Jim and Donna Kennedy
17035 NW Brugger Ro____ ___and
June–December: ____ availability.

Raspberri__ ___erries, and dried walnuts.

Off ___ ___ser Road, between Germantown and Springville roads.

CLOSED

Lukas Blueberries ☆ (503) 245-2116
Les Lukas
9495 SW Moss Street, Portland
July–September: Monday–Saturday, 9am–dusk; call for U-pick appointment.

Blueberries and honey.

Off SW Scholls Ferry Road and 92nd.

Taylor's Blueberries ☆ (503) 645-1643
Don and Lois Taylor
13325 NW Thompson Road, Portland
Early July–August: 8am–6pm; call ahead.

U-pick blueberries and corn. Bring containers.

Take Murray Road exit off Sunset Highway (Highway 26), turn left onto Cornell Road, right onto 143rd, and right onto Thompson Road.

For more Portland listings, see the Multnomah County section.

Blueberry Hill Farm ☆ (503) 590-1525
16997 SW Beef Bend Road, Sherwood
July: Monday–Thursday, 8am–8pm; Friday–Saturday, 8am–5pm; Sunday, 10am–5pm. Call ahead.

U-pick and ready-picked blueberries.

Go west on Scholls Ferry Road for 4 miles, turn left on Beef Bend Road; farm is ¼ mile down on the left.

Gramma's Place ☆ (503) 625-7104
Don and Margaret Wachlin
21235 SW Pacific Highway, Sherwood
May–frost: 10am–5pm.

Fresh seasonal produce.

On Highway 99 in Sherwood.

Nichols Orchards ☆ (503) 538-2386
Bob and Ruth Nichols
26085 SW Chehalem Station Road, Sherwood
August–December (closed last week in September): Sunday–Friday, 10am–6:30pm.

U-pick prunes (bring containers); ready-picked apples, peaches, pears, hazelnuts, and walnuts.

Three miles west of Sherwood on Highway 99W.

Oliphant Orchard ☆ (503) 625-7705
Richard and Patricia Oliphant
23995 SW Pacific Highway, Sherwood
July–October: daily, call ahead.

U-pick cherries, sweet and pie. The Oliphants will run your pie cherry harvest through their commercial pitter. Apples, peaches, plums, prunes, pears, pumpkins, cider, and flowers.

Halfway between Tigard and Newburg, on Highway 99W.

Lee Berry and Tree Farms ☆
(503) 692-0275 or (503) 638-1869
Larry and Joyce Lee
6050 SW Borland Road, Tualatin
May–Christmas: daily, 8am–6pm.

U-pick and ready-picked produce, fresh and dried flowers, nuts, honey, jam, Christmas trees. Pony and hay rides in season. Call ahead.

From I-5, take the Tualatin exit (289). Turn left at the light, follow the road ½ mile. Turn left at the top of the hill onto Borland Road.

Wilhelm Farms ☆ (503) 638-5387
6001 SW Meridian Way, Tua...
April–January: Monday...8am–7:30pm;
Saturday, 8am–5...day, 9am–5pm.

U-pick stra...s, raspberries, loganberries,
boys...s, marionberries, blueberries,
be...cucumbers, tomatoes, pumpkins. Farmer-owned produce stand; jams, syrup, and apple

butter made on farm.

From I-5 take the Tualatin exit; turn left, go 3 miles, follow signs.

YAMHILL COUNTY, OREGON

The Arterberry Ciderworks ☆
(503) 472-1587
Fred Arterberry
905 E 10th Street...nville

Dry, low-al...rbonated cider and other
gourm...wines. Available at pubs throughout P...land, including McMenamin's.

Willamette Valley Walnuts ☆
(503) 472-6722
Don Heigerken
475 E 17th Street, McMinnville
October–March: Monday–Friday, 8am–5pm.

Walnuts.

Take 99W into McMinnville.

Hurst's Berry Farm ☆ (503) 843-3185
23301 SW McKibben Road, Sheridan
July–August: call ahead for hours.

Gooseberries, raspberries, and blueberries. Mainly wholesale, but he'll retail if you're in the neighborhood.

500 yards east of the Dairy Queen on Highway 18.

CLARK COUNTY, WASHINGTON

Mary Baur ☆ (206) 573-0868
4316 NW 169th Street, Ridgefield
Late August–early October: Monday–Saturday, 9am–5pm.

U-pick or ready-picked pears (Bartlett, d'Anjou, Bosc, Packham, Comice).

Take exit 9 off I-5, go west on 179th NW, turn left onto 41st Avenue NW, go ½ mile, then turn right onto 169th.

Kunze Farms ☆ (206) 693-5238
6109 NE 53rd Street, Vancouver
Year-round: Monday–Saturday; 9am–5pm in winter; 9am–6pm in summer.

Grows and packs hazelnuts and fruit.

One mile west of Vancouver and one mile north of Highway 500, which connects I-5 with I-205.

Weimer's Honey Farm ☆ (206) 256-1659
Jim Weimer
3403 NE 86th Avenue, Vancouver
Year-round: Monday–Saturday, 12pm–8pm.

Honey, bee pollen, royal jelly, beekeeping supplies.

Southeast of Vancouver. Take Fourth Plain Road to Andresen to NE 86th Street and turn south. There are some small signs on Fourth Plain Road.

SPECIALTY STORES

The Brigattine Monks Gourmet Confections ☆ (503) 835-8080
23300 Walker Lane
Amity, OR 97101

Mail-order fudge in four flavors (chocolate with and without nuts, chocolate amaretto, and pecan praline) and from October–May hand-dipped truffles are available.

Cook's Corner ☆ (503) 644-0100
Beaverton Town Square, Beaverton
Daily, 10am–9pm.

Exotic and practcial kitchenware, from porcelains to gadgets.

Across from the Fred Meyer parking lot.

Our Lady of Guadalupe ☆ (503) 852-7174 or (503) 627-9547 (November–February)
Trappist Abbey
P.O. Box 97
Lafayette, OR 97127
Year-round: daily, during the day.

Dense, fruit-laden fruitcakes and date cakes. The fruit and date cakes are soaked in brandy and aged for 2 months. Available by mail or at the porter's lodge at the monastery.

From downtown Lafayette, take the paved road across from Bill's Market, and follow signs 3 miles to the abbey.

Comella & Son & Daughter ☆ (503) 245-5033
Steve Comella
3839 SW Multnomah Blvd., Portland
Daily, 8:30am–7pm

Produce, deli meats, flowers.

Multnomah Boulevard turns into Garden Home Road at the 69th Street crossroads.

Gartner's Country Meat Market ☆ (503) 252-7801
7450 NE Killingsworth Street, Portland
Tuesday–Saturday, 8am–6pm.

A variety of meats—roasts, filets, steaks, chops, hams, and bacon (the latter two are smoked on the premises).

At the intersection of NE 5th and Killingsworth.

Green's Seafood Inc. ☆ (503) 246-8245
6767 SW Macadam Avenue, P̶o̶r̶t̶l̶a̶n̶d̶
Monday–Friday, 9am–6̶p̶m̶;̶ ̶S̶a̶t̶u̶r̶day,
10am–4pm.

Supplies m̶a̶n̶y̶ ̶o̶f̶ ̶P̶ortland's restaurants with fres̶h̶ ̶f̶o̶o̶d̶; has a fine retail business as well.

One-half mile from the Water Tower, across the street from Willamette Park.

Kruger's Specialty Produce ⭐
(503) 288-4236
1200 NE Broadway (Holladay's Market), Portland
Monday–Friday, 8am–9pm; Saturday, 8am–8pm;
Sunday, 8am–7pm.

High-quality organic and non-organic produce, including some more exotic items, gourmet and bulk natural foods.

At Broadway and NE 13th Street in Holladay's Market; another branch is at NW 21st and Johnson in the City Market.

Made in Oregon ⭐ **(503) 273-8354**
34 NW 1st, Portland
Daily, 10am–5pm.

Oregon-produced specialty foods and gift items include jams, preserves, breads, chocolates, and jerky. Eleven outlets throughout Oregon.

This branch of the pan-Oregon store is in Portland's Old Town, next to the Saturday Market; another one is at the Galleria. Other stores are in malls throughout the state.

Nature's Fresh Northwest ⭐
(503) 288-3414
3449 NE 24th Avenue, Portland
Daily, 9am–9pm.

Health and specialty foods, organic produce, hormone- and nitrate-free meats, wines, and deli food. Other branches in Beaverton, Lake Oswego, and on SW Corbett Street in Portland.

On the corner of NE 24th and Fremont.

Newman's Fish Company ⭐ **(503) 284-4537**
1200 NE Broadway, Portland
Monday–Saturday, 10am–7pm;
Sunday, 11am–6pm.

Local seafood.

In Holladay's Market at NE 12th and Broadway.

Strohecker's ⭐ **(503) 223-7391**
2855 SW Patton Road, Portland
Daily, 9am–8pm.

Specialty foods and wines, meat and seafood, Oregon products.

Take SW Broadway past Portland State University, bear right on Broadway Drive, which turns into Patton Road.

FARMERS MARKETS

MULTNOMAH COUNTY, OREGON

Gresham Farmers Market
Contact: Maggie Lang, (503) 665-1131
Mid-May–October: Saturday, 8am–2pm.

Gresham City Hall parking lot at Division and Eastman.

People's Inner-City Organically Grown Farmers Market, Portland
Contact: (503) 232-9051
June–harvest: first Sunday of every month, 10am–2pm.

Certified organic produce only, sponsored by People's Food Store.

3029 SE 21st Street, 1 block north of Powell.

Portland Saturday Market
Contact: (503) 222-6072
March–Christmas Eve: Saturday, 10am–5pm;
Sunday, 11am–4:30pm; plus extra Christmas days, 11am–5pm.

Primarily a craft market, with live music and food stands.

Under the Burnside Bridge.

WASHINGTON COUNTY, OREGON

Beaverton Farmers Market
Contact: Laurie McEachern, (503) 643-5345
June–October: Saturday, 8am–1:30pm.

Strictly a farmers market—all locally grown plants, produce, and cut flowers; no crafts. Wide variety of produce and several organic growers.

Hall Boulevard between 3rd Street and 5th Street.

Hillsboro Saturday Farmers Market
Contact: Merrill Ludlam, (503) 357-3518
June–mid-October: Saturday, 8am–noon.

On the corner of Main and Second streets in Hillsboro.

YAMHILL COUNTY, OREGON

McMinnville Farmers Market
Contact: West Valley Farmers, (503) 472-6154
Last Saturday in August, first 3 Saturdays in September: 8am–1pm.

In the West Valley Farmers parking lot on Highway 99 at the north end of town. Across from the K-Mart.

CLARK COUNTY, WASHINGTON

Vancouver Farmers Market ✷
(206) 737-8298
Mid-May–October: Saturday, 9am–3pm.

5th Street between Main and Broadway.

COWLITZ COUNTY, WASHINGTON

Cowlitz County Farmers Market, Longview
Contact: Terry Miracle, (206) 425-1297
May–October: Tuesday and Saturday, 8am–1pm.

A well-established, friendly market, "where people sell to their neighbors."

Cowlitz County Fairgrounds, 5th and Washington Way in Longview.

LEWIS COUNTY, WASHINGTON

Lewis County Farmers Market, Centralia and Chehalis
Contact: Mary Lewis, (206) 785-3101
May–October: Friday (in Centralia) and Saturday (in Chehalis), 9:30am–1pm.

Founded by Emil and Bernice Rosselli, the market is 15 years old and growing fast. In addition to fresh produce and bedding plants, it sells baked goods, homemade pasta, tortillas and salsa, and crafts. The market opens with the traditional bell rung at 9:30am.

In Centralia, at Pine Street between Tower and Depot roads. From Main Street, turn left onto Tower and go 1 block. In Chehalis, across from the Lewis County Depot Museum in the city parking lot, at the corner of National and Market streets.

5

THE WILLAMETTE VALLEY AND CENTRAL OREGON COAST

If you asked a native to describe the terrain of the Willamette Valley and central coast regions of Oregon, he or she just might burst into song, something like, "From the mountains, to the prairies, to the ocean, white with foam…" One could add to that well-known refrain that the trio—the mountains, the prairies, and the ocean—of and adjoining the Willamette Valley provide a bounty of edible riches that rivals any growing spot on this planet.

It didn't seem so bountiful to Jason Lee and his little band of Methodist pilgrims who, after an arduous journey, arrived in the valley of the Willamette in the cold winter of 1834. Food was not uppermost in their minds, however. These missionaries were willing to suffer in order to begin their experiment in applied Christianity on the local Indians. While working at converting the Calapooya Indians, a tribe much reduced by illness several years previously, they spent a weary winter subsisting on unleavened bread from their meager stores of wheat, whatever venison their Indian converts brought in, and some pork and peas acquired from the British settlement at Vancouver.

By 1841, things in the food department were looking up. Lieutenant Charles Wilkes, sailor and explorer, commented on a dinner served at Jason Lee's home in what would become Salem, Oregon's capital city.

"We dined à la Methodist on salmon, potted cheese, pork, vegetables, and strawberries," the explorer wrote in his diary. Not a meager board, even by today's standards.

During the next few decades, thousands of families braved the dangers of 2,000 miles on the Oregon Trail. Unlike the Forty-niners in California, these homesteaders were seeking agricultural treasure, and already the fertility of the Willamette Valley was legendary. "An immigrant will come in during the autumn," wrote a mid-nineteenth-century pioneer, "put himself up in a log house with mud and stick chimney, split boards and shingles. His wife has a few cooking utensils, few chairs... You call upon him the next year and he will have a fine field ripe for sickle. There will be a patch of corn, another of potatoes, and another of garden vegetables. His cattle and horses and dogs will be on the prairie, thriving and increasing."

Many traces of these pioneers still can be found in the Willamette Valley. Jason Lee's home—where Wilkes dined "à la Methodist"—is carefully preserved at the Mission Hill complex in Salem. And if today's travelers look carefully, they can still see the ruts worn by the wagons along the Oregon Trail. In the back country, gnarled old fruit trees and tangled Rose of Sharon vines mark the sites of early homesteads. Throughout the valley, Oregon Century Farm signs, seen on farms now boasting the most advanced farm machinery, inform the passerby that on this spot a pioneer family made its mark more than a hundred years ago.

Geologically, the Willamette Valley is the result of erosion by the Willamette River and its tributaries. The floor of the valley is largely covered with gravel, but laid upon that gravel is the river sand and silt that forms the region's famous topsoil. The southern part of the valley is a relatively level plain 5 to 25 miles wide and more than 100 miles long, interrupted here and there by low, rolling hills.

Roughly comprising Benton, Marion, Lane, Polk, and, to some extent, Yamhill and Douglas counties, the Willamette Valley contains the majority of the state's 34,000-plus farms. Douglas is the largest county, with 5,044 square miles, and Lane is next with 4,563. Both of these counties reach from the Cascades on the east, to the Pacific Ocean.

The region's rich harvest of food begins above the valley, in the Cascades. On the now-forested slopes of ancient volcanoes, tiny wild blackberries and huckleberries are available to those patient and thick-skinned enough to search for the prizes. Mushroom hunters also comb the Cascades for fall chanterelle and spring morel mushrooms.

The Cascades roll down into the foothills, which have, in the last two decades, begun to blossom with vineyards. Many wineries are open to the

public, and during the year their owners sponsor a variety of festivals designed to present their wines. Each year, Willamette Valley wines gain more respect from wine experts around the world.

Scattered amidst the rolling hills are prairies where Native Americans once hunted for plentiful game. Now the prairies offer some of the richest farming land in the world.

Each summer, Howell Prairie, some 20 miles from Salem and the Willamette River, produces a vast array of fruits and vegetables. Broccoli, cucumbers, and berries are still harvested by hand, while beans and corn are gathered by machine. Golden Jubilee corn, prized by food processors, is a prime crop in the valley, with more than 25,000 acres in cultivation. Bush beans, descendants of the high-quality Blue Lake pole bean that yielded four or five pickings a season, occupy more than 20,000 acres of valley soil. Both hills and flatlands in the region produce fine-quality peaches, cherries, hazelnuts, and prunes. In the summer months near Turner and Aumsville, the fragrance of a nearby peppermint field perfumes the air, and in early autumn, pumpkin fields glow under gray October skies.

Each year, more and more family-owned fruit and vegetable stands make their appearance on valley roadsides as farm families supplement their incomes by selling fresh-from-the-field produce.

Bordering the valley on the west is the Coast Range. From the Coast Range, the land descends to coastal plains and the ocean, which offers up its own harvest of salmon, bass, and bottom fish as well as shellfish.

Newport, in southern Lincoln County, is touted as the Dungeness Crab Capital of the World, while Coos Bay in Coos County is the most important saltwater shipping port between Seattle and San Francisco.

Although agriculture, fishing, and logging are still the region's prime industries, others have begun to take hold, and new residents have arrived to work in them. The Willamette Valley and central coast regions are fast becoming a melting pot. Each year, more and more Asians and Hispanics join the earlier arrivals who came from the East Coast and the Midwest, from Germany and Scandinavia. Latter-day pioneers are the Russian Old Believers group, religious colonists who began arriving from China and South America in the 1960s. Hard-working and colorfully clad, the Old Believers keep mainly to themselves, although each year sees more and more of their young people breaking from the tradition.

If you ask an Oregonian how he or she feels about the culturally and agriculturally rich Willamette Valley, you will get a variety of answers—some glowing, some proud. You may even be sung a phrase from "God Bless America." Or you may get the answer one tourist got:

"What's the Willamette Valley like? Well, it's just like the Garden of Eden, only colder and rainier!"

Gloria Bledsoe Goodman
Salem, Oregon

GATHERING TOGETHER FARM

Gathering Together Farm in Philomath is what its name implies. It's run by a group of farmers committed equally to growing high-quality produce in as environmentally positive a way as possible and to maintaining a strong commitment to one another.

The farm evolved from co-owner John Eveland's love of gardening and a ready demand for fresh organically grown foods at Nearly Normal's, a vegetarian restaurant in nearby Corvallis that he runs with family and friends.

Today, Eveland, Sally Brewer, Joe Hanson, and other friends farm about 19 acres in small plots bordering the Marys River. Eveland notes that each plot has a dynamite swimming hole. They don't quite grow every kind of temperate-climate vegetable, but almost. Thanks to a microclimate that adds a month to their growing season, and because of their use of greenhouses and cold frames, they harvest produce 365 days a year.

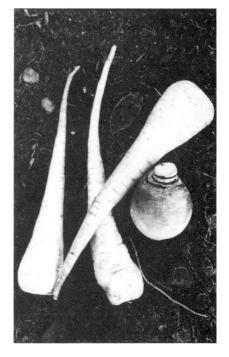

Each year they raise the tried-and-true crops, but Eveland says that every year they try crops they don't know, "to keep things interesting." Standbys include potatoes, lettuce, winter squash, sweet corn, kale, tomatoes, cucumbers, and cabbage. To that they add parsnips, burdock root, melons, eggplant, beets, carrots, onions, tomatillos, chard, salad greens, and a few herbs. And usually garlic, though "it wasn't in the cards for 1991," according to Eveland.

Nearly Normal's uses a chunk of the bounty and soon will use more as the restaurant begins marketing salsa, pasta sauce, salad dressings, and baba ganouj, an eggplant-based dip.

But increasingly, Gathering Together's growers tilt toward direct marketing through farmers markets in Corvallis, Beaverton, and Newport. Their lush displays of perfectly ripe produce have won a steady clientele. Occasionally they sell on the farm, especially when the seasonal surplus hits from mid-August through frost. The rest is wholesaled through an organic produce cooperative.

As dedicated farmers (Brewer's a fifth-generation farmer who's "had dirt under her fingernails since she was a pipsqueak." according to Eveland, and he grew up on a typical Iowa grain and livestock farm), the folks at Gathering Together do what they can to sustain small farm-based communities. He's just ended a term as president of the local chapter of Oregon Tilth, a statewide organization that certifies that growers' practices merit the "Oregon Tilth Certified Organically Grown" label. And she's served on the state's organic advisory board and is involved with a grant to research healthy organic family farms.

That's what Gathering Together Farm is: growers who work 60-hour weeks year-round and share the results with their satisfied customers.

Marnie McPhee

Gathering Together Farm
John Eveland and Sally Brewer
25159 Grange Hall Road, Philomath
(503) 929-4289
May–October: daily, 11am–6pm.

Three-quarter mile south of the intersection of 13th and Highway 20/34. Go ¾ mile over Marys River and turn right 100 feet after the bridge; farm is ¼ mile down the road.

Folk Art Labels

"I've created folk art? That's news to me. I just wanted to make the labels on my canned fruit interesting and appealing," said Mark Gehlar of Salem. "Actually, my father, Max Gehlar, came up with the idea of chatty labels. He may well have had the first descriptive fruit labels. I just enlarged his concept," said Gehlar, who went into the Willamette Valley canning business with his father in 1935. An attorney by profession and a Marion County administrator by election, the elder Gehlar most enjoyed working in his prune orchards in the West Salem Hills.

"We were a big hit during the Depression," Gehlar said. "We offered fruit for a dime a can." During those days, he typed out the copy for the labels on an old typewriter.

With just a few changes since the Depression, the Oregon Fruit Products cans, sporting glossy black labels highlighted with full-color photos or drawings of the fruit within, fairly jump off the shelves with visual appeal. In addition to the vivid coloration, each label offers little homilies about the fruit inside or gives recipes for preparation.

One of the first labels, for the company's strawberries, bore the information: "Fruit Quality: Our Finest; Fruit Size: Large; Flavor: Sun Ripe; Sweetening: Heavy Syrup, and Approved For: Guest Table Use."

Although Oregon Fruit Products' apple cubes never really caught on with consumers, the copy remains one of Gehlar's favorites. The label depicts a drawing of an apple overlaid by a graphic cube. Then there is a drawing of Mount Hood, where the apples were grown. The label tips consumers to "eat em, salad em, bake em." But alas, the apple cubes were not winners. Neither were the thinly sliced pears, a consumer mystery Gehlar says he still doesn't understand.

For every loser, however, Oregon Fruit Products has produced more than enough winners. The dark sweet cherries are excellent, as are the pie cherries, raspberries, strawberries, and spiced green grapes.

Oregonians traveling abroad often pack cans of Oregon Fruit Products for gifts. When a Salem delegation made an official visit to Kawagoe, its sister city in Japan, a large container of OFP went with them. The gifts were greeted with cries of delight from the Japanese host families. As popular as the fruits are, the labels are even more popular. Gehlar has many letters from people who enjoy the labels and regard them as collector's items. Older labels now sell for as much as $20 apiece, and there is an Oregon Fruit Products Labels Collectors Club.

"Some art critics say our labels are, well, too busy," said Gehlar. "But I sort of like them that way."

Take the can of blueberries, one of the firm's biggest sellers. A jolly blueberry face wearing a crown is shown, the happy face grinning toward a blue-bordered barrel-shaped

white space. Under a "Burgeoning Blueberries" headline, the space contains a philosophical description of plant breeders as "an idealistic, patient lot." Information is given on crossing blueberry strains, followed by a tidbit on how and why blueberries are processed all year round. Then follows a tantalizing recipe for Spicy Blueberry Cobbler. A cheery "Thanks for buying this can" completes the copy.

Busy? Well, maybe, if minimalism is your art of choice, but to many consumers, Oregon Fruit Products labels are cozy and inviting. Gehlar has his own theory for the popularity of his labels:

"People are really lonesome, and a label that talks to them—well, I think it lets them know that somebody is out there."

Now 75, Gehlar has handed over the artistic reins to an advertising agency, but when it comes time to yea or nay a label, the master of the descriptive label is right there. He doesn't want anyone to be lonely.

Gloria Bledsoe Goodman

A CORNER FOR HAZELNUTS

It's the official state nut, declared so by the Oregon Legislature. A thousand growers tend more than three and a half million trees in the state and provide 99 percent of the crop to the rest of the country. In the northwest corner of the United States, Oregon corners the hazelnut market.

Cultivated hazelnuts—also known as filberts—got their start in Oregon in 1858 when a retired sailor from the Hudson's Bay Company by the name of Sam Strictland planted the first tree in Scottsburg. Eighteen years later a Frenchman named David Gernot made the first significant planting when he dug a home for 50 trees along a fence row in the Willamette Valley.

It is not surprising that they thrived. A smaller native variety already flourished throughout the maritime Northwest, and the mild winters, wet springs, and dry summers of the Willamette Valley region are especially hazelnut-friendly.

Today three hazelnut varieties—Barcelona, Ennis, and Daviana—cover 28,460 acres in Oregon. The trees are commonly grown in neatly rowed orchards. Old limbs are pruned all winter long to promote new branches, as the bushy trees produce nuts on fresh growth. Fertilizing comes in April, and the ground beneath the trees is mowed monthly during the summer to maintain a smooth bed for nut harvesting. The harvest itself comes in October, when the farmer cruises a mechanical rake beneath the trees and scoops up the smooth, round hazelnuts.

Hazelnuts are high in protein, vitamins A and E, and minerals, although it's also true that their luscious flavor derives in part from a high percentage of fat. Properly dried, they will keep for at least a year. Nuts bought fresh from the farm should be hung to dry in a warm place until the meat darkens to a creamy color. A fresh, uncured nut is lighter in color and noticeably moist when eaten. They can be substituted freely for walnuts and almonds in recipes calling for nuts.

The local uses for hazelnuts have expanded greatly since the first tree was planted in Oregon. Today you're likely to see hazelnut paste, hazelnut flour, hazelnut candies, hazelnut butter, hazelnut oil, and a host of other hazelnut-related products when you enter specialty food stores, gift shops, or food markets in Oregon and around the country.

Crabtree and Crabtree Ltd. of Eugene is just one Oregon company that offers proof of the hazelnut's many uses. A family home business started in 1986 by Dale Crabtree and his son Dave, Crabtree and Crabtree specializes in chocolate hazelnut spread, hazelnut waffle mix, hazelnut chocolate clusters, hazelnut truffles, and hazelnut oil.

Dale explains that he and his son were looking for a food product drawn from the abundance of the Northwest, and the hazelnut fit the bill. Versatile and virtually omnipresent in the Willamette Valley, hazelnuts inspired the Crabtrees' first product, chocolate hazelnut spread. The father and son bought the hazelnuts wholesale and spent 18 months experimenting with combinations of milk chocolate and hazelnut butter, cooking it in a large kettle gleaned from an old Portland jam factory. The Crabtrees finally perfected their product. "Our friends in the community sampled it until we got it right," Dale notes.

One hazelnut product led to the next. The oil extracted from the nuts while cooking the spread is now marketed separately (Dale says that a chef from Seattle's Union Bay Cafe calls often to keep tabs on availability of the high-quality oil). The spread is used as the center for the truffles. The flour, when ground at an Oregon mill, leaves a sediment of coarse nut pieces used in the clusters.

The garage of Dale Crabtree's home, in a quiet neighborhood in north Eugene, is crowded these days. Boxes of hazelnuts fill every corner. A utility/production room holds the large hot-water-heated jam kettle, ready for the next batch of milk chocolate and hazelnut butter.

The elder Crabtree passed the business on to his sons Dave and Jack a year ago. Both sons are pursuing doctorates at the University of Oregon, and Jack says they're unsure if they'll stick with their burgeoning business or sell it.

But one thing, at least, is sure: If they do choose to keep Crabtree and Crabtree Ltd. going, there'll always be a local supply of hazelnuts.

Michael Page-English

Crabtree and Crabtree Ltd.
The Crabtree Family
89618 Armitage Road, Eugene
(503) 687-6575

Products are available at specialty stores throughout the Northwest, including Larry's Markets, Made in Oregon, and Williams-Sonoma.

SHARING THE FARM

"I want to get kids and people out here so they can link up with the 10,000 generations of farmers who came before us." John Sundquist is walking between the rows of his 33-acre Rivers Turn Farm in Coburg, Oregon, indulging in what he calls "tractor-seat philosophy." A stocky man sporting overalls, a bandana around his neck, glasses, and a tight, curly beard that frames his balding crown, Sundquist looks like Oregon author Ken Kesey gone organic.

Sundquist was a founding member in the early 1970s of the Hoe Dads, an Oregon reforestation cooperative of hippie idealists that's still going today. He and his wife, Marsha, bought Rivers Turn Farm in 1983 to be involved in the "basics of society." In recent years, he's used the farm as a place to experiment with sustainable organic farming. His eclectic approach includes recycled materials—ash from a steam-generated electricity plant, rock dust from a local quarry for soil fertility—and educational tours for children. Long rows of apple and pear trees, grapes, strawberries, and a fair-sized hazelnut orchard are interspersed among rows of vegetables. Weeds are tolerated. Patches of bare soil at Rivers Turn are rare. The farm is alive.

Sundquist has also implemented "The Garden Club," a cooperative program that allows city-dwellers from nearby Eugene to become members of the farm. The Garden Club is simple and works like this: Members pay a $25 annual fee at the beginning of the growing season, when they place a roughly estimated order for the type and amount of produce they want. Throughout the year members can then buy organic U-pick produce direct from the farm at 65 percent or less of retail prices.

Sundquist believes that both the farmer and the member benefit. He saves on picking and labor costs, develops a built-in market, and reduces packaging and shipping.

Members get fresh organic produce at a cheaper price, along with a direct relationship to the farm—some real country dirt on those city shoes.

Membership farms similar to Sundquist's Garden Club are cropping up in both Oregon and Washington. Muslin Creek Farm in Cottage Grove, Oregon; Three Rivers Farm in Canby, Oregon; Hannavan Creek Farm in Veneta, Oregon; and Latham Farms in Puyallup, Washington, are all beginning to experiment with the idea of member-supported farming.

Sundquist grows crops that will appeal to members. The aforementioned fruits, watermelons, corn, carrots, onions, garlic, broccoli, tomatoes, potatoes, sugar peas, squash, and pumpkins are just a few of the foods he plants. Greens all year long, seasonal flowers, culinary and medicinal herbs, and specialty crops—from artichokes to zinnias—are all available.

One crop that Sundquist specializes in is pole beans. While many Northwest farms have turned to bush beans for the ease of harvesting and processing (Oregon processes a fifth of the nation's beans, mostly bush beans grown in the Willamette Valley), the membership U-pickers at Rivers Turn Farm make pole beans a viable crop. "I can grow 16 tons of pole beans an acre," Sundquist boasts, motioning down a long row of fence posts and wire covered with bean plants. "That's a lot of protein, and it's four times what I could grow with bush beans." Beans that aren't harvested fresh are left to dry on the pole, for the seed market and for soup beans.

"We're moving along here," Sundquist says, gazing over his acreage at Rivers Turn Farm. "It's a process, but we're getting a better handle on it."

Michael Page-English

Rivers Turn Farm
John and Marsha Sundquist
31139 Lanes Turn Road, Eugene
(503) 683-1905
Year-round (for members): June–October, Wednesday–Sunday, 9am–5pm; November–May, call ahead.
Twelve miles north of Eugene, west off the Coburg-Harrisburg Road.

FRESH-SHIPPED CRAB

If you love fresh crab but can't get to the Oregon coast to taste it, Rick Goché has a business proposition.

Goché, owner of a small dock in Charleston, Oregon, will ship two live, premium Dungeness crabs to your doorstep, anywhere in the continental United States, for $32 plus the cost of Federal Express shipping.

Why would a crab eater pay this premium price when most seafood markets sell live crab?

"You don't know how long the crab has been in the tank," said Goché, who has worked the sea since he was 14 and now buys seafood from 35 boats working off the Oregon coast. "Unless the person operating the live tank at your store knows what he's doing, the crab gets a musty, ammonia taste to it."

Here's how it works: Call Goché's company, Aquatic Resources, at (503) 888-3185 and leave your order 48 hours before you want it to arrive. When the crabs reach the dock, workers grade them and select two of their finest. The crabs are given an extra dose of oxygen and shipped in an environmentally controlled box, whose design is Goché's trade secret. He says you can't get a healthier live crab—unless you catch it yourself. Crab is harvested from the Pacific about 10 months of the year, but the best time to buy big, healthy specimens is during the peak of the season—December through March.

Charleston, one of Oregon's oldest fishing ports, is at the mouth of Coos Bay. Here, fishermen and brokers like Goché build their lives around the rhythms of the sea. Compared to other buyers in the area, Goché is a small fish. Oregon fishermen harvested about 11 million pounds of crab in 1990, and his share was 400,000 pounds. But he compensates by stressing quality. Buyers throughout the United States and Japan order from Aquatic Resources for their restaurants and retail markets.

Goché begins building his reputation out at sea. All fishermen selling to Aquatic Resources must go through training in special crab-handling techniques. In addition, he designed the holding tanks that each boat uses to keep the crabs in their native waters all the way to the dock.

If you want the fresh, rugged taste of Oregon and love fresh crab, pull out the candles, dim the lights, and grab the phone. The Oregon coast is only a phone call away.

NancyAnn Mayer

BRAISED RABBIT WITH WILD MUSHROOMS, FRESH FENNEL, AND TOMATO

Serve this dish with vegetables of the season, especially steamed and buttered green beans, and pasta.

2½ to 3 pounds rabbit
Several sprigs fresh thyme
4 shallots, chopped
½ cup Madeira, divided
2 cups fresh wild mushrooms (see note)
2 tablespoons light olive oil
1 tablespoon chopped fresh parsley
1 tablespoon chopped fresh thyme
4 cloves garlic, minced
¼ cup dry white wine
1 teaspoon black peppercorns
1½ cups diced tomato, divided (peel and remove
    seeds first)
2 fresh fennel bulbs, stemmed, cored, and sliced
    lengthwise
Poultry stock, if needed
Dry white wine, if needed
Salt and pepper to taste
1 or 2 tablespoons butter (optional)

Preheat oven to 325° F.

Portion the rabbit by removing the saddle and quartering the body, or cut into smaller pieces if you prefer.

Combine the fresh thyme sprigs, chopped shallots, and ¼ cup of the Madeira and marinate the rabbit in this mixture for a couple of hours.

Clean the mushrooms. Slice the larger ones and leave the smaller ones whole.

Reserving the saddle, brown the rabbit in the olive oil. (The saddle does not need to be braised.) Drain off the excess fat, and place rabbit in a baking dish with the chopped parsley and thyme, garlic, white wine, remaining ¼ cup of Madeira, and peppercorns. Add half of the chopped tomatoes and all of the fennel. Cover tightly and braise in the oven at 325°F for approximately 1½ hours.

When done, the rabbit should be tender but firm. Remove the rabbit and the fennel from the braising liquid with a slotted spoon and arrange on a serving platter.

The braising liquid becomes the base for the sauce. You may not need all of it, or you may need to augment it with poultry stock. Pour the braising liquid into a sauté pan, adding the mushrooms, remaining tomatoes, and white wine, if needed. Add the saddle now—it will cook as the sauce reduces—or cook the saddle on a grill instead. Reduce the sauce until thickened. Add more stock if necessary. Adjust the seasoning.

Remove the saddle from the sauce or grill, slice, and arrange on the serving platter, fanning the slices on the plate. Finish the sauce by whisking in a tablespoon or two of butter for a richer, more velvety texture.

Serves 4.

A note on wild mushrooms: In the fall, there are many varieties to choose from and the availability of vine-ripened tomatoes makes this dish especially appealing then. Chanterelles—white, amber, or black—are good for this dish as well as milder mushrooms. Experiment with boletus, hedgehog, and chicken of the woods. In the spring you may find morels.

Cafe Central
Eugene, Oregon

WILTED BASIL TOPPING FOR SALMON

This topping, devised by Chef William Purdy, is excellent on fresh troll-caught chinook salmon fillets that have been grilled over a flame, or baked in Chardonnay.

¼ cup olive oil
½ cup diced fresh tomato
1 tablespoon minced fresh garlic
½ teaspoon salt
1 cup coarsely chopped fresh basil
2 tablespoons white wine
1 tablespoon balsamic vinegar

This goes together very quickly, so prepare all ingredients in advance and have them at hand. Have the salmon ready to serve.

Heat a sauté pan over high heat. Heat olive oil in pan until just ready to smoke. Carefully add tomato, garlic, and salt to pan and cook for 30 seconds, tossing to avoid scorching the tomatoes or garlic. Toss in fresh basil and add the wine and vinegar, tossing until basil wilts (10 to 20 seconds.) Spoon over salmon and serve immediately.

Makes about 1 cup.

Bay House
Lincoln City, Oregon

U-PICK FARMS AND ROADSIDE STANDS

The Linn-Benton Women for Agriculture began placing crop identification signs in Linn County in 1974 to spread the word about Oregon's agricultural diversity. The project is now statewide. A descriptive brochure of major crops is available from the Agri-Business Council of Oregon, 8364 SW Nimbus Avenue, Beaverton, OR 97005; (503) 627-0860.

U-Pick Guidelines: Call first, especially near the beginning and end of the season. Find out if your small children are welcome to help pick. Farms will supply picking containers, but you will need bags or boxes to transport your produce home. Pick carefully and conscientiously; a well-tended berry field or orchard represents years of knowledgeable labor. (Dogs should stay in the car.)

Harvests may vary greatly from year to year. A local chamber of commerce or county extension office can often supply up-to-date seasonal information. Also, many newspapers publish local farm maps in the late spring or summer.

BENTON COUNTY, OREGON

Gathering Together Farm ✻
(503) 929-4289
John Eveland and Sally Brewer
25159 Grange Hall Road, Philomath
May–October: daily, 11am–6pm.

Standard, tried-and-true crops (potatoes, lettuce, kale, sweet corn) may be accompanied by more exotic items like parsnips, burdock root, and tomatillos. Gathering Together supplies Nearly Normals, a vegetarian restaurant run by Eveland in nearby Corvallis.

Three-quarter mile south of the intersection of 13th and Highway 20/34. Go ¾ mile over Marys River and turn right 100 feet after the bridge; farm is ¼ mile down the road.

COOS COUNTY, OREGON

Bandon Fisheries Retail Market ✻
(503) 347-4454
250 SW 1st Street, Bandon
Year-round: Monday–Saturday, 9:30am–5pm (winter); daily, 9am–6pm (summer).

Processing plant for shrimp, salmon, and Dungeness crab. Viewing windows allow customers to watch the catch being processed. Gift packs of salmon and tuna, smoked and not. All fish are listed as "dolphin safe."

On the riverfront in downtown Bandon. Look for a big blue building.

Bandon Fishmarket ✻ (503) 347-4282
249 1st Street, Bandon
Year-round: daily, 10am–6pm.

Fresh, locally caught fish, fish and chips, chowder.

Off Highway 101 in Old Town Bandon, at the corner of Chicago and 1st.

Bandon Foods ✻ (503) 347-2456
680 E 2nd, Bandon
Year-round: daily, 8:30am–5:30pm

Cheeses, including Monterey Jack, Cheddar, and other smoked and seasoned cheeses, jams, and jellies.

In downtown Bandon on Highway 101. Also available by mail order at P.O. Box 1668, Bandon, OR 97411.

Cranberry Sweets Company ✻
(503) 347-9475
Cliff and Margaret Shaw
Chicago and 1st, Bandon
Year-round: Monday–Saturday, 9am–5:30pm; Sunday, 9am–5pm.

All-natural chewy, jellied Cranberry Sweets—and about 25 other kinds of candy, cranberry and otherwise. Also available by mail at P.O. Box 501, Bandon, OR 97411.

Factory, seconds store, tours, and coffee shop located at 1005 Newmark Street in Coos Bay, (503) 888-9824.

Misty Meadows ☆ (503) 347-2575
Mike and Martha Keller
Route 1, Box 1730
Bandon, OR 97411
Year-round: daily; call ahead for hours.

Jams, jellies, and syrups, available by mail order or at the farm. The Kellers grow their own blueberries, which they also sell fresh in season, and they use only Bandon-grown cranberries in their preserves. Other flavors include wild huckleberry, black raspberry, and sugar-free blackberry. "No coloring agents, preservatives, corn syrup, or other fillers."

Five miles south of Bandon on Highway 101; look for signs.

Aquatic Resources ☆ (503) 888-3185
Rick Goché
Charleston

Call and leave your order for fresh crab delivered within 48 hours.

Cozette's Gourmet Foods ☆ (503) 888-3012
Joann Coughlin-Sundbaum
757 Newmark Street, Coos Bay
No retail hours; call ahead to see if anyone's around.

A variety of cranberry products, including cranberries in port wine, cranberry ketchup, cranberry citrus mustard, and brandied cranberry syrup. Everything is made on the premises; products are retailed through stores on the coast and all over Oregon (House of Myrtlewood in Coos Bay, Bandon Foods in Bandon, Stroehecker's in Portland, Oasis Foods in Eugene, and Made in Oregon stores throughout the state), but if you're in town they'll sell you anything you like from the factory and give you a tour if possible.

Off Highway 101 between North Bend and Coos Bay. Go west on Newmark Street for just over 3 miles.

Qualman Oyster Company ☆
(503) 888-3145
Larry and John Qualman
4898 Crown Point Road
Coos Bay, OR 97420
Year-round: September–May, Monday–Saturday, 8am–5pm; June–August, daily, 8am–5pm.

Pacific oysters and a few Kumamotos. They'll ship their oysters all over the country during the cooler months.

Qualman Oyster Company is actually in Charleston, toward the ocean beaches from Coos Bay. If you go to the Charleston Bridge and make a U-turn, you'll see signs.

DOUGLAS COUNTY, OREGON

Sunray Orchards ☆ (503) 839-4116
John and Peggy Black
2320 Gazley Road, Canyonville
Call ahead for hours.

Italian, Brooks, and Moyer prunes, unpitted to preserve the flavor of the fruit, with no additives. Also available by mail at P.O. Box 348, Canyonville, OR 97417.

Take Gazley Road exit off I-5 near Myrtle Creek. Drive 2 miles east and look for yellow mailbox.

Elkton Asian Pears ☆ (503) 584-2636
Sherry Breed
1590 Longview Drive, Elkton
Mid-August–December: Monday–Friday, 10am–6pm.

Certified organic Asian pears.

Five miles southeast of Elkton.

Umpqua Aquaculture ☆ (503) 271-5684
723 Ork Rock Road, Winchester Bay
Year-round: closed Tuesday and Thursday, call ahead for hours.

Pacific and Umpqua flats oysters; mussels.

At the end of the center spit in the Winchester Bay boat basin.

LANE COUNTY, OREGON

Eden Valley Farm ✳ (503) 942-2216
Jerry and Laura Berden
77699 Mosby Creek Road, Cottage Grove
Late May–September/October: call ahead for
days and hours.

Blueberries, marionberries, strawberries, and
vegetables.

*Take Dorena Lake exit off I-5. Head east on Roe
River Road about 1 mile. When you see the weigh
station on the left, on the right is Roe River con-
nector road—a very short road. Turn right, then
left onto Mosby Creek Road; farm is 2½ miles
down on the right.*

Muslin Creek Farm ✳ (503) 942-0805
Tal Carmi and Leslie Rubinstein
79296 Repsleter Road, Cottage Grove
Mid-May–December; call ahead.

Subscription farming: members pay $350 for the
season; in return they get an average of twelve
pounds of produce every week for 28 weeks.
U-pick is sometimes available to the public.

*Four miles out of Cottage Grove on the Cottage
Grove-Lorane Highway.*

Patton's Produce ✳ (503) 942-7672
Donna Patton
80432 Delight Valley School Road N,
Cottage Grove
Call ahead.

U-pick vegetables and flowers; roadside stand
offers produce as well.

*One mile off I-5 from exit 176. Go 1 block west
and then north 1 mile; farm is on west side of the
road and is well-marked.*

Sweetwater Nursery ✳ (503) 895-3431
83036 Weiss Road
Creswell, OR 97426

Wholesaler, but will retail by mail (only). Edible
flowers, culinary herbs, salad greens, oyster
mushrooms.

Hannavan Creek Farm ✳ (503) 935-2322
Eliza Erskine and Ted Drummond
Elmira

Membership farm only; no on-farm sales. A full
share buys enough produce for a family on a regular basis, delivered to the member's home.
They're fully subscribed for the 1992 season.
"We grow what people expect," says Drummond,
"corn, tomatoes, and lettuce."

Adkins Farms ✳ (503) 741-0373
or (503) 342-2829
85995 Gossler Road, Eugene
Year-round; call ahead for availability.

U-pick and ready-picked marionberries, blueberries, raspberries, strawberries, sweet cherries,
apples, peaches, pears, pumpkins, and Christmas trees.

*Take 30th Street exit off I-5 and cross freeway.
Go down to Franklin Street and from there to
Seavey Loop and look for signs.*

Crabtree and Crabtree Ltd. ✳
(503) 344-0257
1243 Woodside Drive, Eugene

Wholesaler of hazelnut-based products, including
chocolate hazelnut spread, hazelnut waffle mix,
and hazelnut oil. Available at specialty stores
throughout the Northwest, including Williams-
Sonoma, Larry's Markets, and Made in Oregon.

Delta Farm ✳ (503) 485-2992
3925 N Delta Highway, Eugene
In season: Monday–Saturday, 9am–6pm; Sunday,
noon–6pm.

Organic beans, peppers, pumpkins, squash,
tomatoes, garlic, herbs, blueberries, and raspberries. Vegetable plants also available.

*Take Beltline exit off I-5 to Delta interchange and
go 1 mile north.*

Euphoria Chocolate Company ✳
(503) 343-9223
Bob Bury, Jr.
6 W 17th Avenue
Eugene, OR 97401
Eugene: Monday–Friday, 10am–6pm; Saturday,
11am–5pm.
Salem: Monday–Friday, 10am–9pm; Saturday,
9am–9pm; Sunday, 11am–7pm.

Hand-dipped truffles (shipped only in winter months) in several flavors; a gorp mix of chocolate-covered raisins, peanuts, and pistachios; and milk and dark chocolate bars. Some seconds available. Visit the store (or outlets all over Washington and Oregon), or order by mail.

The Eugene store is located at the corner of Willamette Avenue and W 17th Street. In Salem, 401 Center Street (in the Salem Centre); (503) 362-5451.

Foothill Farm ☆ (503) 344-4877
90901 Coburg Road, Eugene
Mid-June–mid-July: 8am–7pm.

Certified organic raspberries and honey.

Take Coburg exit off I-5 and go south ¼ mile.

Green-Hill-Aire Blueberry Farm ☆ (503) 688-8276
Stan Hunsdon
28794 Hillaire Road, Eugene
August–September: daily, 8am–8pm; call ahead.

U-pick organic blueberries.

From Highway 126 turn on Green Hill Road. Turn west onto Royal Avenue and right on Hillaire Road. Farm is ¼ mile on the left.

Johnson Vegetable Farms ☆ (503) 343-9594
Walt, Sandy, and Doris Johnson
89733 Armitage Road, Eugene
June–November: hours vary with season.

Raspberries, strawberries, and boysenberries in June and July (U-pick strawberries only), corn and other produce through November.

Take Springield exit off I-5, which puts you on the Beltline. Take first left; farm is 1 mile down on the right.

Lester's Farm ☆ (503) 747-0728
Lester Stoner
33450 Cherry Hill Lane, Eugene
July–October: 8am–7pm.

On-farm sales and U-pick organic produce, including broccoli, cauliflower, green beans, potatoes, peas, peppers, tomatoes, summer and winter squash, snow peas, berries, and a new orchard for peaches, apricots, plums, apples, and pears.

The orchard fruits, according to Lester, are "sized down for more flavor and more sugar."

Two and a half miles south of Goshen off old Highway 99, or ¾ mile from I-5 between Goshen and Creswell. Take Dillard Road west for ¾ mile, look for a sign on the left.

Me & Moore Farms ☆ (503) 741-4790
Scott Moore
34137 Seavey Loop Road, Eugene
End of June–end of October.

Apples, beans, corn, cucumbers, hazelnuts, honey, peaches, pears, pumpkins, sweet cherries, and tomatoes.

Two miles east of I-5.

"R" Harvest Farms ☆ (503) 343-8523 or (503) 688-1846
3835 W 11th, Eugene
In season: Monday–Saturday, 9am–6pm.

Many fruits and vegetables, including rhubarb, blackberries (boysenberries, marionberries, and loganberries), quince, hot peppers, herbs, garlic, honey, and nuts.

Four blocks west of Fred Meyer on the right side of W 11th.

River Road Harvest ☆ (503) 688-7895 or -1846
3825 River Road, Eugene
In season: daily, 9am–6pm.

Roadside stand with a variety of produce, herbs, and honey.

One and a half miles north of Beltline on River Road.

Rivers Turn Farm ☆ (503) 683-1905
John and Marsha Sundquist
31139 Lanes Turn Road, Eugene
Year-round (for members): June–October, Wednesday–Sunday, 9am–5pm; November–May, call ahead.

The farm's "Garden Club" allows others (mainly city-dwellers from Eugene) to become members of the farm. With their annual fee, members estimate what and how much fresh, organic produce they'll want that year, which they can then buy at 65% (or less) of retail prices. Crops include apples, pears, grapes, strawberries, filberts, watermelons, corn, carrots, onions, garlic, broccoli, tomatoes, potatoes, sugar peas, squash, pole beans, and pumpkins, among others (as well as flowers, herbs, and specialty crops).

Twelve miles north of Eugene, west off the Coburg-Harrisburg Road.

Spring Creek Blueberry Farm ☆ (503) 688-2962
101 Spring Creek Drive, Eugene
In season: Monday–Saturday, 7am–6pm.

U-pick blueberries.

Two and a half miles north of Beltline off River Road.

Thompson's Fruit and Produce ☆ (503) 688-0725
3910 River Road, Eugene
July–January: Monday–Saturday, 8am–6pm.

U-pick and ready-picked fruits and vegetables.

Take Beltline to River Road and go 2 miles north.

Nielsen's Berry Patch ☆ (503) 937-3042
Tom Nielsen
39843 Place Road, Fall Creek
End of June–November: daily, 8am–7pm; call ahead.

U-pick blueberries and grapes; loganberries and raspberries also available.

Twenty miles southeast of I-5; 3 miles north of Highway 58.

Bush's Fern View Farms ☆ (503) 935-4083 or (503) 998-6805
Dwayne Bush
90536 Territorial Road, Junction City
End of June–September: daily, 8am–7pm, unless picked out.

U-pick peaches, raspberries, and strawberries; roadside stand also offers apples, vegetables, dill, basil, hazelnuts, and walnuts.

From I-5 take Beltline Road west to W 11th Avenue. Turn right and go 10 miles to Veneta. Turn right at the light and go 5 miles north on Territorial Road. Farm is on the left.

Harwood Farms ☆ (503) 688-1846
91984 River Road, Junction City
In season: daily, 9am–6pm. Call ahead.

Apples and cider, berries, vegetables, hot peppers, honey, and nuts.

Four miles north of Santa Clara on left side of River Road.

Hentzes ☆ (503) 998-8944
30000 Hentze Lane, Junction City
June–November: daily, 9am–6pm. Call ahead.

U-pick cherries, marionberries, strawberries, raspberries, walnuts, and beans. A slew of other vegetables are available at their roadside stand.

Take Highway 99 1½ miles outside Junction City.

Lone Pine Farms ☆ (503) 688-4389
91909 River Road, Junction City
June–November: daily, 9am–7pm.

Roadside stand includes vegetables, fruit, herbs, honey, and nuts.

Four and a half miles north of Beltline on River Road; look for signs.

Henrietta Sogaard ☆ (503) 998-8579
29262 E 18th Avenue, Junction City
In season: Monday–Saturday, 9am–5pm.

U-pick sweet cherries.

CLOSED

Turn east on 18th from Highway 99E at the Y in Junction City. Farm is the second driveway on the east side of 18th after you cross the railroad tracks.

Watts Berry Farm ☆ (503) 998-8842
92355 River Road, Junction City
In season: Monday–Thursday, 8am–5pm; Friday–Saturday, 8am–4pm. Bring containers.

U-pick and ready-picked.

On River Road, 5 miles north of Santa Clara.

Tucker's ✲ **(503) 688-5844**
2755 Echo Lane, Santa Clara
June–October: Monday–Saturday, 7am–dark.

Raspberries.

Off Hunsaker.

Herrick Farms ✲ **(503) 741-1046**
88088 Millican Road, Springfield
In season: Monday–Saturday, 9am–6pm.

U-pick strawberries and pumpkins in season; other ready-picked produce available.

Four miles out of Springfield on Highway 126.

Little Pine Orchard ✲ **(503) 726-8861**
Lois Puustinen
3560 Hayden Bridge Road, Springfield
June–October: daily, 8am–8pm.

Walnuts, blueberries, cherries, grapes, raspberries available U-pick and ready-picked. Also available: apples, boysenberries, marionberries, hazelnuts, herbs, pears, and quince.

Call for directions.

Smith's Blueberries ✲ **(503) 747-7779**
Willis B. Smith
37256 Camp Creek Road, Springfield
Mid-July to Labor Day: daily, 9am–6pm.

U-pick and ready-picked blueberries.

Four and three-tenths miles east of Hayden Bridge in Springfield.

Wicklund Farms ✲ **(503) 747-5998**
Dorcas and Eric Wicklund
3959 Maple Island Farm Road
Springfield, OR 97477

Pickled, spiced green beans (Blue Lake variety) made with vinegar, garlic, dill, and other spices. The beans are hand picked and hand packed. Available through mail order by the case. Also sold by the jar in Made in Oregon stores and in Safeway stores throughout Washington and Oregon.

No visits.

LINN COUNTY, OREGON

Nichols Garden Nursery ✲ **(503) 928-9280**
Rose Marie Nichols McGee
1190 North Pacific Highway
Albany, OR 97321-4598
Year round: Monday–Saturday, 9am–5pm.

Nichols is not only a mail order seed company and herb nursery, but also a good source for a range of seed tubers. From their selection of three to five varieties, you might grow Yellow Finnish Binje potatoes, Yellow Finns, or Yukon Golds. Rose Marie's father was given a head of big, sweet garlic decades ago by a Czechoslovakian farmer; the result is elephant garlic as we know it. All sorts of seeds, "an eclectic, slightly eccentric collection," says Rose Marie.

Retail shop at the north end of Albany.

Detering Orchards ✲ **(503) 995-6341**
30946 Wyatt Drive, Harrisburg
July–January: 8am–dusk.

U-pick: apples, blueberries, cherries, peaches, pears, plums, rhubarb, and vegetables. Roadside stand: various vegetables and fruit.

Fifteen miles west of Eugene toward Harrisburg on Coburg Road.

Glory C Ranch ✲ **(503) 258-5496**
Ron and Carolyn Garris
41100 Oupor Drive, Scio
Year-round: call ahead for hours.

Certified organic beef.

Fifteen miles east of Albany.

Queener Fruit Farm ✲ **(503) 769-7570**
40385 Queener Drive, Scio
Mid-July–October: Monday–Saturday, 8am–6pm; Sunday, 1pm–5pm.

Peaches (Harkins, Suncrest, Veteran), apples, corn, beans, tomatoes. U-pick, ready-picked, or picked to order.

Go through Stayton on Stayton-Scio Road to Cole School Road. Turn left, and left again on Queener. Farm is first on the left.

MARION COUNTY, OREGON

Bauman Farms ✳ (503) 792-3524
Clyde, Margaret, Rick, and Barbara Bauman
12989 Howell Prairie Road NE, Gervais
Winter: Tuesday–Saturday, 1pm–6pm. Summer: Monday–Saturday, 10am–6pm.

Fresh produce, ready-picked and some U-pick/picked to order.

Take Highway 99E (Portland Road) 1 mile south of Woodburn to Howell Prairie Road, stand is ½ mile down. Follow signs.

D. A. Nusom Orchards ✳ (503) 393-6980
Donald A. Nusom and Donald A. Nusom, Jr.
13501 River Road NE, Gervais
June–November: hours vary; call ahead; bring containers.

Cherries, peaches, apples, pears, berries, and other produce. U-pick, ready-picked, and picked to order.

Eight miles north of Keizer on River Road NE.

White's Produce ✳ (503) 393-0753
11392 Wheatland Road, Gervais
July–November: daily, 8am–7pm; bring containers.

U-pick or ready-picked. Berries, fruit, vegetables, and nuts. They have just about everything. Call for availability.

One and a half miles north of intersection of Keizer Road N and Chemewa. Turn left on Wheatland Road, go 4 miles to White's sign. Angle left onto Mission Bottom and go 2½ miles. Stand is on right.

Bountiful Farms ✳ (503) 982-0831 or (503) 981-7494
Jay, Julia, Brent, and Cheryl Nelson
19931 Folbert Road, Hubbard
End of July–August: Monday–Saturday, 8am–5pm.

U-pick or picked to order peaches (Redhaven, Sun Crest, Veteran, Elberta).

Corner of Folbert Road and Highway 99E.

Kraemers Corner Crops ✳ (503) 845-2860
13318 Dominic Road NE, Mount Angel
June–September: Monday–Saturday, 9am–6pm; Sunday, 11am–6pm.

Fresh produce.

One mile north of Mount Angel on the corner of Highway 214 and Dominic Road NE.

Bahnsen's Orchard ✳ (503) 393-3533
1620 Clear Lake Road NE, Salem
June–November: Monday–Saturday, 9am–6pm; Sunday, 1pm–5pm; bring containers.

U-pick, ready-picked, and picked to order: apricots, cherries, pie cherries, apples, peaches, pears, walnuts, and honey.

Go north on River Road, left on Clear Lake Road. Stand is ½ mile down on the left.

Blue Heron Farm ✳ (503) 838-0495
7496 S River Road, Salem
Mid-June–early August: Monday–Saturday, 10am–6pm; Sunday, 1pm–4pm.

U-pick red raspberries, marionberries, and Waldo blackberries. Also available: blackcaps, boysenberries, blueberries, and kotata berries.

Two miles east of Independence Bridge or 8 miles from Salem's Commercial Street on S River Road.

Daum's Produce ✳ (503) 362-7246
Gary and Kathy Daum
8801 Wallace Road NW, Salem
June–November: Monday–Saturday, 9am–7pm (until dark in late fall). Sunday, 11am–6pm.

U-pick, ready-picked or picked to order: strawberries, raspberries, marionberries, boysenberries, peaches, apples, plums, grapes, green beans, and other produce and flowers. Cider, pears, and honey sold at roadside stand.

Nine miles north of Marion Street Bridge on Wallace Road NW (Highway 221).

Foster Farms Fruit Stand and Cider Mill ☆ (503) 393-2932
4993 Hazel Green Road NE, Salem
Year-round: hours vary seasonally.

Fresh produce, U-pick, ready-picked, and picked to order.

One mile east of Portland Road (Highway 99E) on Hazel Green Road NE.

Lindbeck's Fruit Farm ☆ (503) 581-1855
1417 Orchard Heights Road NW, Salem
June–October: hours vary.

Fresh produce includes plums, quince, berries, and currants. U-pick walnuts and grapes.

Three quarters of a mile from Wallace Road on Orchard Heights Road NW. Farm is first on the right after the park.

Olson Peaches ☆ (503) 362-5942
6925 Joseph Street SE, Salem
July–September: Monday–Friday, 9am–8pm; Saturday, 9am–7pm; Sunday, 11am–7pm; call ahead.

Peaches, apples, pears, Italian prunes, plums, cherries, and other produce. U-pick, ready-picked, and picked to order.

Five miles east of Salem on Highway 22 (use Joseph Street exit).

Willamette Apples ☆ (503) 393-9507
C.C. Chambers
11250 Portland Road NE, Salem
Mid-September–April: Tuesday–Saturday, 10am–5pm.

Twenty varieties of apples, cider in season, apple jams and jellies.

Six miles south of Woodburn or 1 mile north of Brooks on Highway 99E.

Christine and Rob's ☆ (503) 769-2993
Christine and Rob Bartell
41103 Stayton-Scio Road
Stayton, OR 97383

Mail-order-only source for thick-cut, old-fashioned oatmeal, as well as oatmeal cookie mix, pancake mix, biscuit mix, and a variety of berry preserves and syrups.

POLK COUNTY, OREGON

The Prune Tree ☆ (503) 623-3779
Larry and Deann Green
12393 Smithfield Road
Dallas, OR 97338
October–December: Monday–Saturday, 10am–5pm; January–September: by appointment or by chance.

CLOSED

Parson Sweet prunes, hazelnuts, and walnuts; also fruit and nut mixes, available on the farm or by mail order.

Thirteen miles west of Salem via Highway 22. Turn north on Smithfield Road and go ¼ mile.

Green Villa Farms ☆ (503) 838-3702
Joost, Charlotte, Ginger, and Samantha Vanderhave
Independence

Golden Jubilee corn, peas, strawberries, and "designer" potatoes are sold at Ginger and Samantha's stand during harvest.

Take Highway 22 west out of Salem four miles, turn left on Highway 51 and go three miles; the stand is on the left side of the road.

The Strawberry Patch ☆ (503) 879-5552 or -5377
Lyle Buswell
26860 Salmon River Highway, Willamina
Summer: daily, 8am–8pm; late October–Christmas: daily, 8am–6pm.

"Good local produce, gifts, best peanut brittle in the world" (made across the road). During summer months, a stand adjacent serves "the best strawberry, boysenberry, or peach shortcakes in the entire universe," says a fan.

Twenty miles inland of Lincoln City on Highway 18 west.

FARMERS MARKETS

BENTON COUNTY, OREGON

Corvallis Farmers Market
Contact: Larry Landis, (503) 752-1510
May–October: Saturday, 9am–1pm.

Madison Avenue between 1st and 2nd streets.

Mid-Willamette Growers Association Market, Corvallis
Contact: Jack Lawrence, (503) 847-5641
May–Thanksgiving: Wednesday, 9am–1pm.

Benton County Fairgrounds, on 53rd Street.

LANE COUNTY, OREGON

Lane County Farmers Market, Eugene
Contact: David Amorose, (503) 342-5856
April–November: Saturday, 9am–5pm.

Produce, crafts, street food, and entertainment.

East 8th and Oak streets; from I-5, take exit 194-B to I-105. Then take Exit 1 to Eugene City Center Mall. Cross the Willamette River and take the 8th Avenue exit. Free parking in Parkade or City lots.

June–October: Tuesday and Thursday, 10am–6pm.

Eighth and Willamette at the downtown mall.

LINCOLN COUNTY, OREGON

Lincoln County Small Farmers Market, Newport
Contact: Sally Jennings, (503) 444-2687 or Cooperative Extension, (503) 265-6611 x207
May–October: Saturday, 10am–noon.

Eggs, shiitake mushrooms, and baked goods as well as produce.

Lincoln County Fairgrounds, off Highway 101 just south of Newport.

LINN COUNTY, OREGON

Mid-Willamette Growers Association Market, Albany
Contact: Jack Lawrence, (503) 847-5641
May–Saturday before Thanksgiving: Saturday, 9am–noon.

Corner of Broadalbin and Water streets.

MARION COUNTY, OREGON

Salem Public Market
Contact: Donna Heilman, (503) 393-3758
Year-round: Saturday, 8:30am–noon.

The Salem Public Market has been in operation since 1942, and some of its vendors have been there most of that time. It is small—around 17 vendors—and very local. Don't expect a lot of tourist hoopla. Rose Michalek has been coming for 32 years. She sells vegetables "until my garden eases up, and then I bake."

1240 Rural Street SE, between 12th and 13th streets.

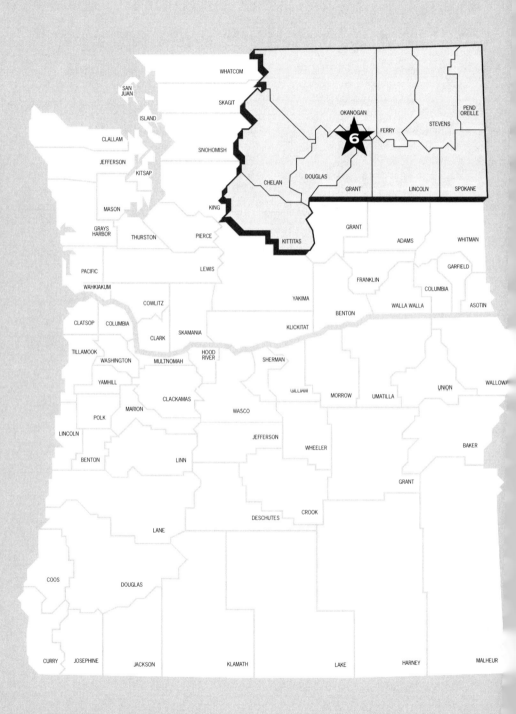

NORTHERN WASHINGTON

To understand how water behaves in the soils of the eastern slope of Washington's Cascades, imagine arriving home with a basketful of garden-fresh fruits and vegetables from, say, the Methow Valley Farmers Market in Twisp. Strawberries, carrots, green onions, rhubarb, potatoes. You want to get the last bit of Methow grit off the potatoes, so you tumble them into the sink. If your sink is equipped with a nozzle sprayer, use it. Let it rain. Squirt until you've washed the spuds bright and clean, then let go of the nozzle and listen. Hear the water trickle down the drain? Now dig to the bottom of your sink. Any water standing around? Or are there just puddles and rivulets fast disappearing down the drain?

That's how water falling from the sky acts when it hits east-slope soil: It dives right to the bottom, washing the rocks and sands and fossils the way you nozzle-hosed your potatoes. It drips and splashes through the buried mix of glacial debris and ancient seabed rubble until it hits bedrock as slick as porcelain, and then it runs downhill, lickety-split, until it's gone. It's not like westside double-fudge chocolate cake soil, which slurps and sucks up water and holds it in soggy black layers.

This unstable landscape began 60 million years ago as a flat, mud sea floor that buckled on the rising shoulders of molten rock when inner earth lurched to its knees and stood. Magma poured from rents in the earth's crust, piled on itself, and spread eastward, to be smothered by volcanic ash and by ice sheets thousands of feet thick that crawled down from the Arctic and nested as far south as Yakima, leaving coarse gravel, earth dams, and ice-borne boulders when they retreated north. The result is the backbone and muscle of central Washington—the mountains and eastern foothills, plateaus, and river valleys of Kittitas, Douglas, Chelan, and Okanogan counties.

There is more water at any moment than you might imagine, looking across the brown, rocky hills. Farmers and ranchers in these four northern tier counties use an estimated 1.5 billion gallons every year to irrigate their ground. Every year enough water falls in these mountains, froths down these rivers, skitters and pools unseen along bedrock to fill two Kingdomes.

Knowing how water acts when it hits the east slope helps you to understand the constant, sometimes grim and heroic efforts of the region's farmers and ranchers. From Okanogan County's border with Canada to Kittitas's Manastash Ridge, from the Pacific Crest Trail to the Columbia River, this territory spans almost 8 million acres, a hybrid zone of food-growing that offers mountain beef, valley fruits, and prairie grains to world and neighborhood markets alike.

Driving across the state from west to east, you'll travel Interstate 90 from the mountains down through the upper Yakima River Valley in Kittitas County. East of Cle Elum the road flattens among emerging basalt cliffs—reminiscent of picturesque canyonlands in John Ford westerns—then rolls into high prairie. You'll pass dense stands of fir and pine forests and broad swells of grassland, while the horizon rolls back twenty, thirty miles. This is the gateway to the mountain prairies of America. The sun is relentless here;

by midsummer the still-wild hills are as dry and brown as a hemp carpet. Wherever water surfaces, green growth is rampant: Cottonwood, aspen, and willow flash silver leaves in the wind along every stream. The valley soil is coarse gravel deposited by ancient rivers and the catastrophic flood of ancient Lake Missoula 25,000 years ago, when 6.3 cubic miles of water per minute— ten times the combined flows of all the rivers in the world today—rushed across this central basin.

Twenty-seven percent of Kittitas County—403,338 acres—is farmland. The first irrigation canal you'll see as you drive across the county meets the road east of Elk Heights (the cleft in the earth to your left is the bed of the Yakima River). The water descends in rivers and streams and from the lakes in the mountains behind you. This is the Kittitas Reclamation District ditch, which helps irrigate more than 77,000 acres of wheat, oats, barley, sweet corn, potatoes, pears, apples, and hay for beef cattle and dairy cows raised in the Yakima Valley—food valued at more than $54 million in 1990.

Within half a mile after you cross the Columbia River, on the Douglas County side, farmers raise apples, cherries, peaches, and prunes in a strip running from Rock Island to Bridgeport. To the east is desert plateau, rolling sagebrush hills that climb to 2,400 feet above sea level, bordered by the Columbia River on the north and west and the Grand Coulee on the east and south. The coulee is a former course of the Columbia River, a thousand-foot-deep, mile-wide detour the river carved when the lobe of a polar glacier blocked the Columbia's present route along the Big Bend to the southwest. Dry Falls near Coulee City is the site of an ancient cascade. To comprehend the immensity of the great river, visitors are advised to stand at an overlook a mile away: The half-flooded bowls the size of moon craters that you see at the base of the basalt cliffs in the distance are the old river's plunge pools, where the torrent scooped out volcanic rock at the base of the falls.

Of Douglas County's 1,178,240 acres of land, 987,000 acres are farmed, producing more than $82 million in wheat every year. Recent record crops have filled grain elevators and spilled the excess in nearby mounds that are larger than New England ski hills.

Until about 10,000 years ago, central Washington was a geologic three-ring circus, with magma welling up into basalt bulwarks, the gigantic Columbia swaggering wherever it pleased, ash hailing from Cascade volcanoes, glaciers scouring and scooping out the countryside, floods of water measured in hundreds of cubic miles, and prehistoric rivers cutting channels through rock. The valleys thus created are complex compositions of gravel and loam, granite and shale at elevations ranging from 600 to 3,000 feet. Here, on the eastern slope of the Cascades, conditions are excellent for cultivating tree fruit: Hot summer days and cool nights, fertile ground, and enough water flowing past to irrigate, if only it can be diverted from its pell-mell race downhill.

The Columbia River and Interstate 90, intersecting at roughly the center of the state, are the cross hairs of industry and nature, production and distribution. While the fruits, beef, and grains of central Washington travel I-90 and the railroad to the rest of the world, the Columbia River drainage system delivers the water that transforms this arid territory into a thriving garden.

Billed on license plates and brochures as the Apple-Growing Capital of the World, Wenatchee is the clearinghouse for fruit growers from Douglas, Chelan, and Okanogan counties (Yakima handles fruit from the southern districts). Orchardists in these three counties will contribute more than a million tons of apples to local, regional, and world markets this year. Once the province of Red Delicious apples, north central Washington orchards have diversified since the late 1980s. While Reds still dominate, apple growers have planted new varieties—Granny Smiths, Galas, Fujis, and Braeburns—alongside Red and Golden Delicious trees. The new fruits are crisp, tangy, and full flavored, well suited for lunchbox and dessert plate. Besides planting new types, orchardists also are trying new techniques, such as higher-density planting of dwarfing rootstocks that bear fruit in half the time and occupy a third as much space as nondwarf varieties. These practices promise a more consistent supply and a quicker rotation of varieties. Farmers here also annually produce tons of apricots, sweet cherries, peaches, and prunes. Pears are a major future crop: Production of Bartlett, d'Anjou, and Bosc varieties totaled 164,000 tons in 1989.

To the north, the Methow and Okanogan valleys and the Pateros, Brewster, and Bridgeport area along the Columbia produce the majority of north central Washington's apples. These districts also produce peaches, pears, and cherries for worldwide markets, as well as a growing garlic crop.

Above the Okanogan and Methow valleys' orchards, ranches produce beef that feeds the nation. Of the 3.2 million acres in Okanogan County, 2 million acres support cattle. This is where beef is born, literally. Okanogan's strength is in starting the calves that mature in Nebraska, Iowa, California, and Oregon—25,000 calves, or 13,750,000 pounds of young beef every year. The mountains provide the perfect backdrop for ranching. Cattlemen start the newborns on spring grasses in the foothills; then, as summer comes on, the herds gradually move into the Cascades, feeding on fresh wild grasses until fall roundup, when single- and double-trailer cattle trucks haul the young beeves out of the valleys and south to Ellensburg and the Columbia Basin, for their journey east along I-90 to the rest of the world.

John Bonica
Methow Valley, Washington

FRESH WILD HUCKLEBERRY PIE

Wild huckleberries grow in the upper elevations of the Cascade Range. Their season usually runs from mid-August through September. Margaret Sage, who created this recipe for Mineral Springs Resort, buys her huckleberries by the bucketful from a local woman who loves to pick them. This pie is a real winner in the Northwest. Sage says that when huckleberries are in season, people call from Seattle to reserve a piece of this pie!

4 cups fresh, uncooked huckleberries
9-inch pie shell, baked
Whipped cream or nondairy topping

JUICE
1 cup huckleberries
1 cup water

GLAZE
½ cup sugar
3 tablespoons cornstarch
1 tablespoon unflavored gelatin
1 cup huckleberry juice

Wash and drain the huckleberries. To make the juice, cover and bring 1 cup huckleberries and 1 cup water to a boil in saucepan. Remove from heat and strain through a sieve, reserving huckleberry juice.

To make the glaze, mix together thoroughly sugar, cornstarch, and unflavored gelatin. Stir mixture into the huckleberry juice. Cook until thickened, stirring constantly. Remove from heat and cool. Pour a little glaze into a *baked* 9-inch pie shell. Arrange half of the berries on the bottom of the pie shell. Cover with a small amount of glaze. Add the rest of the berries. Cover with remaining glaze. Chill until firm.

Serve garnished with whipped cream or nondairy topping.

Makes one 9-inch pie.

Mineral Springs Resort
Blewett Pass, Washington

APPLES IN STEHEKIN

Harry was something else. And oddly enough, you'd have to call him the valley's achiever. He had the one real commercial farm in the valley, apples, acres and acres of apple trees. He had come into the valley to help his uncle, Henry Buckner—the one whose name is tacked onto Buckner Mountain, the peak with the two glaciers you see as you look up the valley from Stehekin—and they had cleared land with a team of horses and a stump puller. That's hard work, really hard work; but they managed to get a big clearing that they put into orchard, and there was a fine view across to Rainbow Falls, which you could hear from the house at the opposite edge of the orchard.

And there was McGregor standing up at the far end of the ridge, sharp-pointed and for most of the year white-faced to the ragged edges of its cliffs.

Harry and his uncle built a barn and later Harry built a big packing shed with a cement floor that was great for square dancing and Harry learned to be a fine caller for the dances. The house had a fireplace Harry had built and there was a spot outdoors with a table and a fireplace with chairs and all, and you could sit out there in the evening swapping stories with Harry and the others and watching the light on McGregor and listening to the falls in the background and it was just about the finest spot you had ever been in. Everybody liked it and everybody turned up there, people from the valley and downlakers as well, always a crowd.

Harry was the one man in the valley the downlakers couldn't cut. He was doing something useful, growing apples, like they were. Sure they would go out into his orchard and make remarks about this or that, but you could see that this was simple envy for what Harry had managed for himself and his family. And he got some cash income out of the orchard. That made him a good man, even if the money wasn't all that big by downlake standards. The thing was that he had to pay those big freight charges on the barge to

get his apples to market. This hurt, but he had an advantage the downlakers had lost long ago. The orchardists at the other end of the lake had long been obliged to spray their trees with a big array of poisons; one kind for this bug, another for that, and then still another and another. This of course took a lot of money, and since these bugs had not yet found their way uplake, Harry could still sell his apples and ship them out at a modest profit. His apples were better because they were not loaded with all those poisons, but in the marketing they were mixed up with the others, so he never got the extra price he should have. However, he did have the satisfaction of providing apples to several downlake orchardists for their own use; they knew what was good, as well as safe.

So Harry had the best of both worlds. He had a handsome place; things were maybe cobbled up in a lot of places, but even the unpainted boards on his house had taken on a deep rich color from the weather and it was really fine looking. And he had a fine family with his wife and three daughters. So he was a man of substance, dealing with the downlake marketers and doing something serious, raising apples. Only really he was just letting the trees grow the apples and he spent a lot of his time fishing in the river where it bordered his place and going to the dock. Of course, most of the people from downlake who came to his place didn't know all this; they just thought he was a sound man.

Maybe there's some law of nature that says such things can't go on. Whether or not this is true, there were some lesser laws of nature that brought it to an end. First of all, the girls grew up. All three of them were handsome and they all got married and left the valley. They had been the backbone of Harry's labor force during those times when the orchard did take a lot of work, thinning, picking and sorting. The next thing was that the bugs at last found the valley. I don't mean that Stehekin didn't have bugs of its own—it did, lots of them. But these were things like mosquitoes, yellow jackets, and blackflies that can make humans miserable. What was new was the sort of bugs that specialize in apples programmed for New York. So it was up to Harry to begin spraying the orchard. It was just for the one kind of bug, I suppose, but Harry knew that this would be just the beginning. So he didn't spray. There was a small crop or two that could be sent downlake after that, but the trees were old now and Harry stopped pruning and the apples just fell to the ground. Anyone was welcome to come and help himself. People had always done that, but it wasn't the same. There wasn't a party in the packing shed for making cider and so on and, in fact, the packing shed collapsed one winter. So, when Beryl quit as postmaster, Harry took the job; and then he really had to go to the dock every day.

Grant McConnell
Stehekin, A Valley in Time

Apples—Heirlooms and Newcomers

Akane: A Japanese apple, also known as the Tokyo Rose. Beautiful bright red and nice crisp texture. The perfect lunchbox apple, it ripens just in time for the start of school. It's also especially good for pies. (Sources listed for Regions 1 and 2)

Discovery: Very early, crisp, red-and-yellow apple. An English variety, best for fresh eating. (Region 1)

Elstar: A Dutch cross between a Golden Delicious and an Ingrid Marie. Similar to Jonagolds in appearance, but not as sweet. Good for salads and appetizer trays because the cut flesh is slow to discolor, and great for pies. Flavor mellows in storage. (Region 1)

Gala: A medium-sized yellow apple with red flushes and flecks, developed in New Zealand. Crisp, juicy, very sweet and aromatic. Ripens in October and keeps until Christmas. (Regions 1, 2, 6, 7, and 8)

Gravenstein: An old favorite and the best early apple, ripening in late August. It is good for eating and great for applesauce and cider, but not so good for pies, because the tender flesh breaks down easily. Keep refrigerated. Northern California is the real Gravenstein country, but some Northwest orchards grow them. (Regions 1, 2, 4, 5, 6, and 7)

Idared: Looks a lot like a Spartan. Keeps longer, and its sweet, slightly winy flavor improves in storage. (Regions 1 and 6)

Jonagold: A cross between a Jonathon and a Golden Delicious and better than either. A fine cooking apple as well as being delicious fresh. Locally grown Jonagolds taste better than the New Zealand imports found in the stores. (Regions 1, 2, 4, 6, and 8)

King/Tompkins King: Another classic backyard apple, developed in New York in the early 1800s. Not seen in stores. Large green apples with red stripes and mottling. Sweet and aromatic. Flavor remains good in storage, but the skin gets a greasy feel. (Regions 1, 2, and 4)

Liberty: A recent variety. Elongated, dark red, intensely flavored. Ripens in late fall and stores well, but it tastes best right off the tree. Also good for cooking and cider. (Regions 1 and 4)

Melrose: A crisp, medium-sized, red-and-green apple that develops its full fragrance and flavor after Christmas and keeps until spring. (Regions 1, 2, and 4)

Mutsu/Crispin: Big, yellow-green apples that show their Golden Delicious ancestry in their looks and sweet flavor. Mutsus stay crisper than Golden Delicious without controlled atmosphere storage. They were developed in Japan. (Regions 1 and 4)

Northern Spy: A slow-growing, erratically bearing, great-tasting cooking and eating apple originally from upstate New York. The Northern Spy traveled west with American expansion, but it does not have the characteristics of a big shipping-and-selling apple, so it has remained a backyard treasure. Ripens late in October and keeps until spring. (Region 5)

Pippin: Wonderful tasting, generally homely apples, of various types. Pippin is a generic nineteenth-century English synonym for delicious. Many of them have a russeted, brownish cast. Cox's Orange Pippin and Newtown Pippin are probably the best known in the United States. Don't miss a chance to try these. (Regions 4 and 7)

Spartan: A purplish red, tender, tasty apple that ripens in October and keeps past Christmas. Developed in British Columbia in the 1920s, Spartans are beginning to appear in some supermarkets. (Regions 1, 2, 4, 6, and 7)

Apples for Cider: The best cider comes from a mix of fruit. Most people get their mix by a thoroughly unscientific process of scavenging hither and yon and dumping the fruit by bagfuls into the washing tub. Each batch tastes different from the next, depending on the chance of the mixture. But the renaissance in heirloom apples makes it possible to buy or grow a planned cider mix. In general, the best cider comes from a blend of — in descending order — sweet, bitter, tart, and aromatic apples. Some apples, like Akanes and Spartans, can play more than one part in an orchestrated cider.

Sweets: Spartan, Jonagold, Akane, Russet, and other dessert apples.

Bitters: Kingston Black, Michelin, Dabinett. These English cider varieties are beginning to show up in nurseries such as Cloud Mountain and Raintree.

Tarts: Discovery, Gravenstein, Liberty, Idared, Cox.

Aromatics: Gravenstein, Akane, Spartan, Melrose, Cox, Jonagold.

GARLIC

Diversity can lead to chaos, and garlic is strong medicine. These are just a couple of the truths Bob Elk has learned along his road to becoming one of the preeminent organic garlic growers in eastern Washington.

The road braids backward in time, along furrows of sandy loam in the Yakima Valley and through the orchards of Toppenish near Rattlesnake Hills, back to a farmer named McDonald.

Clark McDonald was an old man when he introduced methods of organic gardening to a young Bob Elk in the 1970s. Those were the early days of modern organic farming, when back-to-the-landers tried to change the world, beginning with a plot of earth and a cultivating fork. Bob was part of a cooperative in the orchard country near Yakima, growing plums, watermelons, tomatoes, and more. The more the better. Co-op members believed diversity—both in crops and personal experience—was a key to health and livelihood; yet to be learned was the lesson that pursuing too many tangents can breed chaos, leaving the practitioner spent and mostly empty-handed.

One day old Mr. McDonald held up a satin-skinned, voluptuous, purple-veined bulb. It was a garlic called Greek Blue. McDonald's uncle had handed him *his* first Blue in Portland, Oregon, in 1939. The uncle had brought the juicy, aromatic cousin of a lily west from the family's New York garden in the last century. The bulb that McDonald handed to the young hippie was the foundation of Spanish Roja (roy-yah), a variety that Bob Elk has introduced throughout north-central Washington in the intervening years.

Since then, Okanogan County has gained a reputation across the state for its Spanish Roja crop. The bulb thrives in the sandy loam (mostly sand and clay) soil typical of north-central Washington and does well in a climate that swings from 20[degrees] F or colder in winter to the high nineties in the summer. The cold temperatures harden the plants; the dry climate drives roots deep for water, where they tap more minerals. The result is a garlic both flavorful and hardy.

One of Roja's strengths is its big cloves that are easy to peel. Its flavor begins subtly and builds to mildly hot without a bitter tinge. The Roja is characteristic of superior garlic, Elk says: large and firm with a papery sheath, consistent in shape and flavor. Another local variety is Chet's Italian Red from Tonasket, a bulb with a red blush that yields slightly more and stores longer than the Roja, but perhaps without the same delivery to the palate. A clove of Okanogan organic garlic rolled on the tongue then tucked in the

Roasted Garlic

To roast garlic, cut the tips off a whole head of garlic, but do not peel or separate. Wrap each head in foil and bake at 350°F until the cloves are soft and pulpy. Squeeze the mush onto crackers, toast, or good fresh bread.

cheek will check a cold in its nascent stages, Bob says, but be careful: Garlic is powerful medicine. More than a couple of raw cloves in succession will make something happen; Elk doesn't say what, exactly. Perhaps something to do with feverish blood, perspiration, and giddiness.

Elk and his partner, Ed Welch, at Mountain Meadows Farm near Twisp, plant an acre and a half of garlic in the fall and harvest it in July. They water sparingly, cultivate the ground carefully with a minimum of internal combustion machines, then pull and shake five tons of garlic from the warm summer ground. A crew of five to ten people work the garlic—digging, cleaning, trimming, sorting, and peeling for powder, all by hand. They ship raw bulbs, decorative and useful braids, and shakable ground garlic to Virginia, Michigan, New York, California, and places in between. Bob connects with customers and distributors through what he calls a "friendship market"—friends of friends of friends "who support working toward a better world."

The farmers at Mountain Meadows began small and remain small; they work mostly by hand. They cultivate one crop, and they do it well, and so they have built a business by the organic method, delivering a product that is at once compact and powerful. Thus they have narrowed their choices and reduced the chaos to produce a flower for seasoning and health.

John Bonica

Mountain Meadows Farm
Bob Elk
P.O. Box 863
Twisp, WA 98856
(509) 997-2680

IN THE SHADOW
OF GRAND COULEE

The Columbia River enters the United States in northeast Washington near the small community of Northport in Stevens County. This majestic 1,200-mile river has dominated the land for thousands of years. For centuries its huge salmon runs provided Native Americans with food and fish for trade, and both natives and settlers used the river for transportation.

The Columbia has designed the geography of the region, cutting deep coulees in the landscape as it flowed through and then changed courses. The dry falls near Coulee City are an example of the awesome power and size of the river.

The headwaters of the Columbia are in the Canadian Rockies south of Banff. Tributaries flowing into the river come from the American Rockies, Cascades, and smaller ranges such as the Kettle Range in northeast Washington. With limited precipitation, the region's farmers depend on the river's watershed to replenish aquifers or to provide direct irrigation.

The first concentrated commercial agricultural endeavors in the inland part of Washington were begun in the 1820s near Marcus, just north of Kettle Falls. The Hudson's Bay Company established Fort Colville to supply food and goods to other Hudson's Bay posts in the interior. Hudson's Bay employees raised livestock, including beef cattle and hogs for meat, sheep for wool, and dairy cattle for cheese and butter. They planted orchards and gardens and built a grist mill to grind the settlement's wheat.

Food and supplies were shipped downriver to Fort Vancouver and then north by ship and overland by packers to the inland areas of Canada and Alaska. A thriving community, the biggest non-Indian settlement between the Rocky Mountains and the Cascades, Fort Colville was maintained even after 1846, when the present border between the United States and Canada was established. In 1871, however, the company moved north into British territory.

By the turn of the century, a thriving orchard industry had sprung up along the river from Northport to Hunters, 40 miles downriver. Large packing houses were built in Kettle Falls, and trainloads of apples were shipped out of the area each fall. Three packing houses from this period are still standing. One is still used as a packing house, mostly selling locally. One is a community theater with apartments on the top floor, and the third was a farm supply business until the late 1980s.

Irrigation ditches and water flumes were built to provide water to the orchards, but the industry began to decline after the departure of the Hudson's Bay Company. World War I led to the loss of German capital for irrigation development, an additional blow. Major east-west highways and railways were developed in areas where the terrain was less rugged, adding to the isolation of region. The construction of Grand Coulee Dam in 1939 and the resulting creation of 130-mile-long Roosevelt Lake eliminated towns, fisheries, barge traffic, and farms along that stretch of the river. In late winter and early spring when the lake is lowered to accommodate snow runoff, rows of tree stumps can still be seen in the river bottom, along with remnants of flumes that watered the now-drowned orchards.

Stevens, Ferry, and Pend Oreille counties are mountainous, with vast stands of pines. Today, nestled in the valleys of the Columbia, Kettle, Colville, and Pend Oreille rivers are small orchards, dairies, and subsistence farms, along with industry— primarily wood products and mining.

As you move away from the rivers and into the higher elevations, dryland wheat and beef ranching begin to predominate, with much of the area providing open range for livestock. Be careful as you drive and watch for Open Range signs.

Stevens County is one of the larger wheat producing counties in the state, even though most of the county is mountainous. The ranches are located at the ends of unimproved roads, and unless you are an adventurous soul, you won't see them.

As you travel south toward Spokane and out of the mountains, the land flattens and the pine forests become scattered. Fields of wheat and alfalfa stretch along the horizon. Within minutes of Spokane's city center is the Green Bluff area on the Little Spokane River. The giant aquifer beneath this area provides water for orchards rich with cherries, peaches, apricots, and apples. Bringing home boxes of fresh fruit or vegetables to process at home is still a large part of local tradition. Festivals held in conjunction with cherry harvest in July and apple harvest in September add to the holiday atmosphere. You will also find trucks parked at intersections in Spokane, full of peaches, corn, or tomatoes. Despite this bounty, however, the standard of agriculture here is still wheat and alfalfa.

As you travel west from Spokane into Lincoln County, the dryland wheat ranches are beautiful to behold, from the green shoots early in the spring to the ripe golden fields

in the fall. Some farmers have drilled artesian wells to provide water for huge circles of corn, but most farm without irrigation, since the systems from the Columbia River haven't yet reached this section of the state.

In Grant County the full effect of the Grand Coulee Dam becomes apparent. Water pumped from Roosevelt Lake into Banks Lake, which was also created as party of the dam project, waters thousands of acres. Driving along a country road, you will often see off in the distance a clump of trees. On getting closer you will discover the remnant of an old homestead with parts of buildings and possibly the frame of a windmill. If you have ever farmed you can feel the heartbreak of the family that built the home during the good years when it rained and starved out in the bad years when it didn't. Irrigation has now made it possible to hang on through the dry years. Unfortunately, the dam also spelled the end to upriver salmon runs that once provided native people with over a million pounds of fish a year.

Since I was born the year Grand Coulee was built, I have watched the transformation of this land in my lifetime. The water from the Columbia and human ingenuity have turned a desert into a virtual cornucopia. Irrigation ditches crisscross the water table and form seep lakes throughout the area. The addition of water to the rich volcanic soil and the hot summer weather have made the region a farmer's delight. Semi trucks full of corn leave for places west for fresh market or processing. The average consumer would be amazed to discover how many Idaho potatoes are grown here. Thousands of acres of orchards are being planted. A drive in the country takes you past fields of tomatoes, peas, beans, and cabbage, as well as vineyards. Sleepy towns like Mattawa have doubled in size since the latest irrigation projects started.

Seasons in northeast Washington are as varied as the landscape. Spring is that wonderful season that sometimes comes hard, with temperatures of 80 degrees one day and snow the next. Summer is hot enough that they talk about hearing the corn grow, which is really true. Autumn comes as a relief with cooler nights and frost on the pumpkins. Winter is cold and crisp with snow, frozen lakes, and an occasional blizzard, which makes spring all the more welcome.

Through all the year we pray for snow in the mountains because the deeper the snowpack, the more water we have in the Columbia. It is the river that moderates our valleys in the north and provides water for irrigation and recreation in the south. Ample water makes it possible to protect the remaining spawning salmon below Grand Coulee without sacrificing crops. When we have enough water, we can provide for everyone.

Alice Sullivan
Kettle Falls, Washington

CURRIED RED LENTIL AND TOMATO SOUP

Red lentils are wonderful legumes. They look as good as they taste, which is something of a feat for a member of the legume family. This is a fine supper soup. From start to finish it takes just over an hour to prepare—and for most of that time it simmers quietly on its own. For extra protein, top each serving with a dollop of yogurt or sour cream.

2 tablespoons unsalted butter
2 large onions, chopped
4 cloves garlic, minced
1½ teaspoons garam masala, or to taste
1 teaspoon ground coriander
3 jalapeño chili peppers, halved, cored, seeded, and
    minced
1 pound red lentils, rinsed and checked for extraneous
    material
1 can (28 oz) diced tomatoes with juice (or 3 cups of
    peeled, diced fresh tomatoes in season)
8 cups homemade chicken stock
6 tablespoons lemon juice
Coarse salt
Freshly ground black pepper
Yogurt or sour cream (optional)

In a soup pot, melt the butter and cook the onion until softened but not browned. Add the garlic, garam masala, coriander, and chili peppers, and cook gently for another minute or two.

Add the lentils, tomatoes, and stock. Stir and bring to a simmer. Simmer slowly, partially covered, for about 30 minutes, stirring occasionally, until the lentils are tender but not falling apart.

Add the lemon juice and season to taste with salt and pepper.

Garnish servings with yogurt or sour cream, if desired.

Serves 8 to 10.

Susan Bradley
Pacific Northwest Palate

Potato Varieties

With more than 100 varieties of potato available to Northwest growers, there's no telling what will turn up at your local farmers market. The essential culinary difference between potatoes is in the amount of starch. Potatoes high in starch mash into fluffy mounds and make light potato pancakes and hash browns, as well as the classic baked potato. Less starchy potatoes are the waxy types best for boiling and potato salads. All potatoes become starchier the longer they stay in storage.

The many variations in color and shape are primarily of cosmetic interest, although some, like Yellow Finns, do have distinctive flavors. Small, round Dutch varieties are the right size for boiling and steaming, especially if you don't have to peel them.

Blue Martin, All-Blue, Purple Peruvian: Blue-skinned, blue-fleshed potatoes that keep their color when cooked. Good for baking, mashing, and amazing the uninitiated. Some are round or oblong; others are small "fingerling" types.

Desiree: Red-skinned, yellow-fleshed Dutch boiling potato. Increasingly popular as a farmers market variety.

Red Gold: A red potato with waxy gold flesh.

Norkota, Nooksack Russet, Russet Burbank: Big, brown-skinned, white-fleshed bakers. The standard meat-and-potatoes potatoes. Nooksacks were developed in the Nooksack Valley of Whatcom County, Washington. Russet Burbanks make up the bulk of the Northwest's immense potato crop.

Red Pontiac, Norland Red: Round, red "new" potatoes. Great for boiling and, after some time in storage, for mashed potatoes.

White Rose: A thin-skinned, pale, new potato. Has a delicate flavor and does not store well. Best for boiling or steaming. Doesn't hold up in a potato salad as well as a Yellow Finn.

Yellow Finn: A handsome, wax-type potato with an outstanding, almost nutty flavor. Smaller and not as productive as Yukon Gold, but worth seeking out for superior potato salad.

Yukon Gold: A yellow-fleshed, versatile potato with gold-buff skin and pink "eyes." Good-sized and keeps well.

FARM-RAISED RABBIT

Rabbit is often compared to chicken, which isn't fair to the integrity of either animal. Each has its own distinct flavor. Cooks approaching rabbit for the first time with a chicken model in mind will find themselves confused, as will dinner guests trying to tackle meat on the plate. The body of a rabbit and the body of a chicken have nothing in common. The big meat pieces on a rabbit are found on the haunches, the hind legs, which can be cut away from the carcass without too much trouble. Dinner guests will no doubt appreciate a cook who bones the thigh, leaving the shank intact. The thigh bone can then be used in a rabbit stock. The forelegs are as inconsequential as chicken wings and often serve a better purpose in a stock pot along with any other pieces of the carcass not intended for the plate.

The center of the body is the loin, which should be long and thick in a well-bred meat rabbit. This is the most delicate meat on the animal, and the most easily overcooked. There is next to no fat on a rabbit, and the cook who fails to appreciate this fact will forever produce dry, tough results. The rib cage can be cut away from the loin without much ado. The flaps on either side of the loin that on a steer would be called flank steak are easily trimmed away and reserved. They can be cut into strips and added to stews. The loin can be boned, which requires a little practice, or simply cut crosswise into pieces.

Most recipes for rabbit ask that the meat be browned, then finished in several ways. A boned loin can be browned in a matter of minutes in a hot skillet, then finished in a 350° F oven in 5 to 8 minutes. No more. The meat should be bright white fading to pink at the very center. Cut the boned loin crosswise into small, elegant medallions, arrange them on a warm plate, and nap with a reduced rabbit stock, perhaps with huckleberries added. Or include the warm loin medallions with a salad of well-chosen greens and use the juices in the pan with balsamic vinegar to create a warm salad dressing.

Karl Beckley, former chef/owner of the Greenlake Grill in Seattle, grew up in northeastern Washington, in Colville. He credits his mother's farm kitchen with giving him a leg up as a cook. Beckley uses the boned haunches and loins of two rabbits for a roast rabbit dish he prepares with garlic and roasted red peppers.

He quickly browns the pieces of rabbit in olive oil in a large sauté pan, then removes them to a small roasting pan. He browns the peeled, whole cloves of an entire head of garlic in the sauté pan, then deglazes the pan with a cup of dry vermouth, bringing it to a boil. He adds a cup and a half of rabbit stock (which can be made ahead from the carcasses of the two rabbits) to the pan and reduces the liquid to ⅓ cup. Right at the end he adds two red peppers that have been roasted, peeled, and sliced into half-inch strips.

While the sauce reduces, he places the rabbit in a 350° F oven for no more than 8 minutes. When the sauce has reduced, he removes it from the heat and whisks in a stick of unsalted butter, a piece at a time. Chef Beckley arranges the rabbit on warm plates, serving a leg and a piece of loin to each of four guests, and pours the sauce over.

Fresh rabbit raised and packed in Washington is available in the larger urban centers throughout the state. Look for the "Washington grown" sticker. The meat should have a pink blush and a clean, fresh appearance. It is often possible to find a rabbit raiser willing to sell home-processed rabbits, in which case it is up to the consumer to decide whether a credible level of hygiene has been maintained. Rabbit in the market can cost upwards of $3 a pound, a far cry from the chicken to which it is so often compared.

Much of that price difference is in the labor. Chicken fryers don't come from hens, they come from egg incubators. There's no lifting of chickens and moving them from cage to cage. Rabbits can't be put on automatic feeding systems. It is all done by hand, once a day. Most rabbitries are family hobbies, sidelines to a pension or a regular job. And most of them got started by accident. Ask any rabbit raiser and you are likely to hear the same story: A friend gave me some rabbits, they say, looking up from their feeding, and watering, and cleaning, and butchering. A friend.

Schuyler Ingle

POT ROAST WITH HAZELNUT BARLEY

A version of this hearty dinner was the winner in a Washington State contest for beef recipes. One food writer at the time sniffed that it wasn't very nouvelle, but the proof is in the eating. Tender meat, a tangy sauce, and a chewy barley-nut mixture make a good meal with a minimum of fuss.

1 tablespoon olive oil
3- to 4-pound boneless chuck or other lean roast
2 medium onions, chopped fine
2 cloves garlic, chopped
2 tablespoons Dijon mustard
1 teaspoon fresh tarragon or ½ teaspoon dried tarragon
2 canned tomatoes, drained and chopped
Salt and pepper
2 tablespoons butter
½ cup finely chopped hazelnuts
3 cups water
1 teaspoon salt
1 teaspoon Worcestershire sauce
1½ cups pearl barley

Heat olive oil in a heavy pan. Brown roast over medium heat. Add onion and garlic and cook until they begin to soften. Add mustard, tarragon, tomatoes, salt, and pepper. Cover pan, lower heat, and simmer until roast is tender, 1½ to 2 hours. You don't need any other liquid.

During the last 40 minutes of cooking, melt butter in a heavy saucepan. Add hazelnuts and cook over medium-high heat until they are crisp and brown. Add water, salt, Worcestershire sauce, and barley. Cover and steam over low heat until water is absorbed, about 30 minutes.

Remove meat, slice, and serve with barley and pan juices.

Serves 4.

Lane Morgan
Winter Harvest Cookbook

A SALMON MEMOIR

My earliest memory of salmon isn't so much of the fish as of the long, wood-slatted box in which it had arrived in Colville from the coast, packed in shaved ice. My grandfather collected the fish at the bus depot in town, or maybe the train office. Or maybe he drove into Spokane and picked it up at the train station there. I don't recall what became of that salmon, how it was prepared for the table, or who came in from all corners of northeastern Washington to eat it, or what it tasted like. If it was a special occasion, it must have been of greater meaning to an adult than a little boy. All I remember is salvaging that shipping crate and carrying it from the kitchen to the backyard of the Ingle place where a small creek gurgled its way on into town. I remember dumping a small pile of blood-colored ice onto the grass, then floating the crate in the creek, pushing it free of the watercress with a stick.

My parents' first contact with salmon was much different. They remember the Colville Indian camps at nearby Kettle Falls, the salmon leaping in the river, the Indians working day in and day out for the duration of the run, netting salmon at the end of long poles, then splitting the fish and drying them in the sun and wind on racks erected along the shore. My parents remember the powerful smell of drying fish. I never witnessed the spectacle of the Indians at the Falls. My own child, when I point to the place in the river where Kettle Falls once existed, will simply look at me and blink at the recounting of what will be for him such ancient history. I hope he is able to find wild salmon in rivers, and not just in the dog-eared pages of books. I hope he eats a Columbia River chinook that tastes like it has ranged through cold ocean water for four years, laying down thick layers of fat against the day it turns its nose toward fresh water. He already loves the sauce.

I call it my mother's sauce, but she is the last person to claim it as her own. She found it years ago in the newspaper and it has been part of the family oeuvre ever since. Pacific Northwest fish and shellfish expert Jon Rowley tells me that he has encountered versions of this sauce from Alaska to Northern California. He often finds brown sugar included among the ingredients. I'll have to try that one of these days. Maybe on a piece of chinook grilled over hot coals. It just may be the best piece of salmon I will have ever eaten.

Schuyler Ingle

JOYCE INGLE'S SALMON SAUCE

1 clove garlic, minced
¼ cup ketchup
¼ cup soy sauce
2 tablespoons prepared mustard
1 tablespoon Worcestershire sauce
1 tablespoon fresh lemon juice
Freshly cracked pepper
½ pound butter, in small pieces

Mix all the ingredients in a small pan except the butter and warm over low heat, allowing the flavors to combine. Then, off heat, whisk in the butter a piece at a time to complete the sauce. Keep warm. This sauce has a tendency to separate if it gets too hot, but it still tastes great.

Makes 1¾ cups sauce.

Schuyler Ingle

PASTA À LA NORMA

This Sicilian eggplant dish is named for Vincenzo Bellini, who wrote the opera *Norma*. It is made with salted ricotta, which is firm enough to be grated, from Quillisascut Cheese Company of Rice, Washington.

2 medium eggplants
Salt
1 to 2 cups vegetable oil
Salt and freshly ground black pepper, to taste
1 pound fettuccine
2 cups tomato sauce
1 cup grated salted ricotta

Wash eggplants and dry them with a paper towel. Slice ½-inch thick. Sprinkle with salt. Layer the slices in a colander. Put a plate over the slices of eggplant, put something heavy on the plate, and let drain for about 1 hour. Rinse well, drain, pat dry, and then fry eggplant slices in hot oil until golden brown on both sides. Drain on paper towels. Season to taste with salt and pepper.

Bring 4 quarts of cold water to a boil in a large pot. Add a small handful of salt when water begins to boil. Add pasta and cook until al dente. Drain the pasta. Toss pasta in a bowl with the heated tomato sauce and half of the ricotta. Put the fried eggplant on top and sprinkle with the rest of the ricotta. Serve immediately.

Serves 4.

Cafe Lago
Seattle, Washington

U-PICK FARMS AND ROADSIDE STANDS

U-Pick Guidelines: Call first, especially near the beginning and end of the season. Find out if your small children are welcome to help pick. Farms will supply picking containers, but you will need bags or boxes to transport your produce home. Pick carefully and conscientiously; a well-tended berry field or orchard represents years of knowledgeable labor. (Dogs should stay in the car.)

Harvests may vary greatly from year to year. A local chamber of commerce or county extension office can often supply up-to-date seasonal information. Also, many newspapers publish local farm maps in the late spring or summer. For more information on local produce, call (800) 57-APPLE.

CHELAN COUNTY, WASHINGTON

Bob's Apple Barrel ☆ (509) 782-3341
Bob Spanjer
Highway 2, Cashmere
Mid-March–mid-November: daily, 8am–7pm; weekends only rest of the year.

All local produce in season; apple and cherry cider, and jam all year long.

Just off Highway 2 in Cashmere.

Rosemary's Kitchen ☆ 782-2498
603 Cottage Avenue,
Call for hours.

Apple but sauce, jams, jellies, pie and stru gs.

Call for directions.

Cox Fruit ☆ (509) 782-1508
Ed and Shirley Cox
3081 Fairview Canyon Road, Monitor
July–end of December: Monday–Friday, 9am–5pm.

Cherries, U-pick peaches and nectarines, apricots, apples and fresh cider, Asian and Red Bartlett pears. Also vegetables, sold at local farmers markets. Customers "can come and pick their fruit on Friday, leave it in the cold storage and enjoy the weekend camping and touring the area or visiting relatives. When they are ready to go home, they can come pick up their fruit and go." Dried fruit and apple juice also available.

Call for directions.

Smallwood's Harvest ☆ (509) 548-4196
Mike Smallwood
10461 State Highway 2, Peshastin
April–November: daily, hours vary.

All Washington produce: asparagus (fresh and pickled), jams, cakes, dried apples; also antiques.

On Highway 2, 2½ miles east of Leavenworth.

The Apple Shoppe ☆ (509) 662-2690
22 N Wenatchee Avenue, Wenatchee, WA 98801
Year-round: Monday–Friday, 8:30am–5:30.

"Snappy" (dried) apples and apple butter (as well as other crafts and food), made by developmentally challenged people, sold to benefit the United Cerebral Palsy fund as part of the Wenatchee Challenge 2000. Mail order also at the above address.

In downtown Wenatchee.

Skookum Inc. ☆ (509) 662-5783
9th and Railroad Crossing, Wenatchee
Year-round: Monday–Saturday, 8am–5pm.

Several varieties of apples and other seasonal produce.

In downtown Wenatchee.

DOUGLAS COUNTY, WASHINGTON

Pipitone Farms ☆ (509) 884-0653
Jerry and Andrea Pipitone
5250 Pennsylvania, Rock Island
June–October: daily, daylight hours.

Certified organic apricots (fresh and dried), peaches, and garlic. Also sells at the Wenatchee Farmers Market.

Eight miles southeast of East Wenatchee.

GRANT COUNTY, WASHINGTON

Robb and Shirley Richmond ✮
(509) 787-3681
2894 Road 2 NW
Moses Lake, WA 98837
September–December: call ahead.

Several varieties of apples—including Braeburn, Gala, and Fuji—and 20th-Century, Hosui, and Shinseiki Asian pears. Available by the pound or in gift packs; UPS shipping available. Also sold at the Columbia Basin Farmers Market in Moses Lake.

Call for directions.

Walker's Wondermelons ✮
(509) 765-8378
Lee and Wendy Walker
6349 Road K.5 SE, Moses Lake
Mid-August–September: call ahead.

Watermelons and cantaloupes. Also sold at the Columbia Basin Farmers Market in Moses Lake.

Call for directions.

Homestead Organic Produce ✮
(509) 787-2248
Bill Weiss
20034 Road 7 NW, Quincy
Mid-summer–fall.

Apples: Red and Golden Delicious and Red Fuji; Quincy Sweet onions, Korean garlic.

Three miles south and 3 miles west of Quincy at the corner of 7th and T.

P & P Farms ✮ (509) 346-9474
(produce stand) or (509) 346-9383 (home)
Alice and Ivan Parker
8582 Road K SW, Royal City
Late June–mid-October: daily, call ahead for selection.

Broccoli, green beans, a variety of peppers and tomatoes, winter squash. The Parkers are also expanding their plantings of black-eyed peas and okra. "Once we took them to the farmers markets, we found out how many Southerners there are around here," said Alice.

One mile east of Adams Road on Highway 9 SW (5 miles north of Highway 26 and 10 miles south of I-90). Produce also sold at Spokane and Columbia Basin (in Moses Lake) farmers markets.

Royal Organic ✮ (509) 346-2428
Peat Eriksen
Star Route 1, Royal City
Call for an appointment.

Certified organic; on-farm sales of grain, beans, and apples.

Call for directions.

LINCOLN COUNTY, WASHINGTON

Lean Edge Meats ✮ (509) 982-2581
Jaime and Staci Kissler
Odessa
Call ahead to see if anyone's around.

All kinds of meats, from their own recipes for German sausages and pepperoni to custom orders.

Between Odessa and Moses Lake; call for directions.

OKANOGAN COUNTY, WASHINGTON

Van Doren Ranch ✮ (509) 689-2701
Monse, Brewster
July–September: daily, 7am–7pm.

U-pick optional. Varieties of apples, peaches, plums, apricots, nectarines, peppers, and tomatoes. "We are a family orchard business. My husband and I do most of the work, hiring just during harvest and pruning and thinning times."

Fruit stand at Old Monse General Store, 7 miles north of Brewster on Highway 97 at Monse.

Filaree Farm ✮ (509) 422-6940
Ron and Watershine Engeland
Rt. 2, Box 162
Okanogan, WA 98840

Mail-order source for dozens of varieties of garlic from all over the world, all certified organic. Their catalog is an encyclopedia of garlic description and classification. Spanish Roja, a gourmet variety that came west with Greek immigrants in the nineteenth century, and Chet's Italian Red, salvaged in the 1960s from an abandoned garden in Tonasket, are two of their top sellers. The Engelands also raise apples, peaches, and vegetables, which are sold within the county.

Sage Ridge Farm ✬ (509) 826-0189
Barnett and Elizabeth Hagell
Grimm Road, Omak
May–October: Thursday–Friday, Monday–Tuesday, daylight hours.

Certified organic. U-pick optional: peas, beans, corn, tomatoes, peppers, peaches. Sells at Twisp and Okanogan farmers markets.

Go north out of Omak on Robinson Canyon Road towards the airport; go right on Grimm road about ¼ mile, and look for signs on the south side of the road.

Hidden Meadows ✬ (509) 486-4058
Randy and Patti Brown
94 Frosty Creek Road, Tonasket
Call ahead.

Organic pork and beef, finished on farm-grown grain. Supplies organic grain to Fairhaven Cooperative Flour Mill in Bellingham.

Call for directions.

Mountain Meadows Farm ✬ (509) 997-2680
Bob Elk
P.O. Box 863
Twisp, WA 98856

Sells a variety of garlic (including Greek Blue and Spanish Roja) to farmers markets in the Northwest.

Sunny Pine Farm ✬ (509) 997-4811
Ed Welch
Twisp
July–October (potatoes and garlic through March): call ahead for hours.

Garlic, potatoes, and vegetables. Certified organic. Sells at Twisp Farmers Market. He's beginning sales of quinoa and other grains.

Ten miles west of Twisp on Twisp River Road.

Sally Jackson Cheeses ✬
Sally Jackson
Oroville

Goat, cow, and sheep cheese. Mostly hard cheeses. The cheeses, served by many Northwest restaurants (including Le Gourmand and McCormick and Schmick's), are available in Seattle, Tacoma, and Bellevue, in stores such as Larry's Markets, The Wedge, Vinotique, and Quality Cheese in the Pike Place Market. The aged sheep's milk cheese is highly recommended.

PEND OREILLE COUNTY, WASHINGTON

Newport Naturals/Spruce Corners ✬ (509) 447-2552
Robert and Linda Karr
N 205 Craig, Newport
Mid-June–mid-October: daily.

Hot peppers and other produce, including 120 varieties of herbs on their 1¼-acre garden in Newport. They will sell at the farm by appointment and they also deliver produce baskets once a week to customers in Spokane. All produce is organic. The Karrs prefer retail to wholesale selling because they want their produce to be eaten the day it's picked.

Two blocks north of the city park in Newport.

SPOKANE COUNTY, WASHINGTON

Bowker's Orchard and Cider ✬ (509) 238-6971
Gary and Carolyn Bowker
8814 E Green Bluff Road, Colbert
July–September/October: open most days; call ahead for hours.

U-pick and ready-picked cherries, apricots, peaches, pears, apples, and cider.

Just off Newport Highway (Highway 2); look for signs.

Gibson's Orchard and Cider Mill ★
(509) 238-4874
Bill and Rosie Gibson
N 19405 Sands Road, Colbert
Late June–October: daily, 8am–6pm.

U-pick and ready-picked strawberries, cherries, peaches, plums, apples, and vegetables. Honey and cider available as well.

Six miles off Highway 2.

McGlade's Treemendous Fruit ★
(509) 467-8340
Jerry and Roberta McGlade
E 4301 Day–Mt. Spokane Road, Colbert
May–Christmas: Monday–Saturday, 9am–6pm.

U-pick pumpkins, strawberries, raspberries, blueberries, cherries, huckleberries, apricots, peaches, pears, apples, cider, honey, apple butter, and garden products.

Five miles north of Spokane; take Green Bluff exit off Newport Highway (Highway 2).

Mel and Bonny Walker ★ **(509) 238-6762**
N 17512 Green Bluff Road, Colbert
June–Thanksgiving: daily; call ahead for availability.

Strawberries, apples, peaches, pears, cherries, beets, cabbage, carrots, cucumbers, dill, parsnips, potatoes, pumpkins, and squash.

North of Spokane, off Newport Highway (Highway 2) on Green Bluff Road.

Timberland Orchards ★ **(509) 276-8173**
John Seagreaves
5206 Burroughs-Casberg Road, Deer Park
October–November: call ahead.

Apples (Empire, Spartan, and Red and Golden Delicious).

Eight miles west of Deer Park; call for directions.

Anderson's Acres ★ **(509) 238-6760**
Louie and Barb Anderson
North 17715 Day–Mt. Spokane Road, Mead
July and September–October: daily, 9am–dark.

U-pick cherries (Bing, Rainier, Van, Lambert) and U-pick/picked to order apples (Transparent, Gravenstein, Gala, Delicious, Jonathan, Rome). Squash and pumpkins in season.

Northeast of Spokane; ½ mile south of the Green Bluff store on Day–Mt. Spokane Road.

Dick Laws Fruit Farm ★ **(509) 238-6237**
Dick and Helen Laws
N 17308 Day–Mt. Spokane Road, Mead
July–January: daily, 7am–7pm (U-pick); 8am–6pm otherwise.

U-pick or ready-picked strawberries, apricots, cherries, and peaches; pears and apples ready-picked; dried fruit, walnuts, honey, and jellies.

In Green Bluff, 7 miles northeast of Mead, 4 miles east of Highway 2. Look for signs on highway.

Granny's Orchard ★ **(509) 238-4991**
Dianne and Jim Baird
N 18207 Sands Road, Mead
Mid-July–October: daily, 8am–8pm.

Cherries, apricots, peaches, and apples—U-pick or ready-picked.

In Green Bluff, ½ mile east and ½ mile south of Green Bluff Store on Sands Road.

Hidden Acres ★ **(509) 238-4031**
Terry and Karene Simchuck
16802 Applewood Lane, Mead
Year-round: daily, 8:30am–4:30pm during summer and harvest; call ahead otherwise.

Produce from their diversified orchard includes raspberries, cherries, peaches, apricots, plums, pears, 15 varieties of apples, and dried flowers. Their retail store also sells homemade jams, butters, preserves, and syrups. No fresh fruit from January to June.

Located in Green Bluff, north of Spokane. Take Highway 2 north 7 miles and turn right on Day–Mt. Spokane Road. Go 4 miles to Dunn Road; farm is on the left side of Dunn.

Lobe's 3L Acres ★ **(509) 238-6478**
Larry and Jackie Lobe
E 10707 Day–Mt. Spokane Road, Mead
Mid-June/July–August: Monday–Saturday, 8am–6pm.

Perfection Rival apricots, U-pick and ready-picked, and garden vegetables.

One-half mile east of Green Bluff Store on Day–Mt. Spokane Road.

Siemers Pick and Pack ✳ (509) 238-4893
Donna and Byron Siemers
E 11125 Day–Mt. Spokane Road, Mead
Mid-June–September: daily, 7am–7pm; October–Thanksgiving: daily, 9am–6pm.

Strawberries, cherries, apricots, peaches, apples, potatoes, carrots, squash, pumpkins, cabbage, cider, honey, and jam. Huckleberry milkshakes in summer; stuffed potatoes in the fall.

In Green Bluff, 8 miles north of Newport Highway (Highway 2).

Thorson's Perfection Fruit ✳ (509) 238-6438
Lloyd and Janet Thorson
N 17007 Sands Road, Mead
Mid-July–mid-November: Monday–Saturday, 8am–6pm; Sunday, 1pm–5pm.

U-pick and ready-picked cherries, apricots, peaches, pears, apples, and grapes.

In Green Bluff, 16 miles NE of Spokane.

Walter's Fruit Ranch ✳ (509) 238-4709
Tracy and Leta Walters
E 9807 Day Road, Mead
July–end of December: daily, 9am–5pm.

U-pick cherries, peaches, and apples; honey, apple butter, and other produce in season. Gift boxes and the "Fruit Loop Express," a train tour through the orchard.

Thirteen miles northeast of Spokane. Take Day–Mt. Spokane Road exit from Newport Highway (Highway 2) and go 4 miles. Look for signs.

Wellens' Luscious Fruit and Antiques ✳ (509) 238-6978
Warren and Anne Wellens
16420 Sands Road, Mead
July–October: Monday–Saturday, 8am–8pm.

U-pick or picked to order strawberries, plums, cherries, apricots, peaches, pears, apples (10 varieties); also fresh uncooked jam, and baked goods.

In Green Bluff, 15 miles north of Spokane off Highway 2.

Yaryan's Orchards ✳ (509) 238-6261
John Yaryan
10229 Day–Mt. Spokane Road, Mead
August–October: call for availability.

U-pick or picked to order: cherries, apricots, peaches, and apples.

One-half mile east of Green Bluff Store.

Carver Farms ✳ (509) 226-3602
N 9105 Idaho Road, Newman Lake
June–October: daily, 7am–dark.

U-pick and ready-picked fruit and vegetables including raspberries, squash, cabbage, sweet peppers, beans, garlic, and pumpkins.

One-half mile north of Trent on Idaho Road.

Bart's Berry Patch ✳ (509) 466-5134
Lynn and Kathie Bartholomew
W 14010 Lincoln Road, Spokane
Mid-June–mid-July: call ahead for hours.

Strawberries — mostly U-pick.

Northwest of Spokane in the Seven Mile area.

BJ's Riverside Gardens ✳ (509) 482-0867
Matt Collin
E 6303 Upriver Drive, Spokane
Mid-May–mid-October: Monday–Saturday, 7am–5pm.

Cabbage, herbs, sweet corn, beets, carrots, squash, green beans, pickling cucumbers, strawberries, and raspberries.

One mile east of Upriver Dam.

Buckeye Beans ✳ (509) 926-9963
Jill Smith
P.O. Box 28201
Spokane, WA 99228-8201

Mail-order beans, peas, lentils, bread mixes, and pastas with herb seasonings.

Dan Freas ✳ (509) 924-0584
10502 Morrison Road, Spokane
June–November: weekends, call for hours.

U-pick and ready-picked grapes, apples, plums, peaches, cherries, rhubarb, and apricots.

In Northeast Spokane, off Sullivan Road.

Peasant's Place ☆ (509) 466-6066

Walt and Marge Steinke
N 8611 Orchard Prairie Road, Spokane
July 4th–mid-August: daily, anytime.

U-pick raspberries and blueberries.

Three miles northeast of intersection of Frances and Market streets. Right off Bigelow Road.

Tate Honey Farm ☆ (509) 924-6669

Wes and Jerry Tate
E 8900 Maringo Drive, Spokane
Year-round: Monday–Friday, 8am–noon;
Saturday, 9am–noon.

Clover and alfalfa honey, bee packages and bee-keeping supplies. Tours available by appointment.

North of the Spokane River from Millwood.

Wilds of Idaho ☆ (509) 327-3385

Louise Sevier
3012 W Fairview
Spokane, WA 99??

Wild huckl??? ?roducts: whole-fruit jam, top-pings ??? ?ssert filling. Mail order only.

CLOSED

VanHees Orchards ☆ (509) 926-3700

Scott VanHees
E 14025 12th Avenue, Veradale
Year-round: Monday–Saturday, 9am–5pm;
open until 6pm from June–September.

Tomatoes, broccoli, cauliflower, apples. During growing season, local produce is available; the rest of the year, VanHees draws on other sources.

Ten miles east of Spokane on I-90. Take the Pines exit, and go south to 12th Avenue.

STEVENS COUNTY, WASHINGTON

China Bend Vineyards ☆ (509) 732-6123

Victory and Loyalty Israel Alexander
3596 Northport-Flatcreek Road, Kettle Falls
Call ahead for an appointment.

Members of the Love Israel family, a longtime communal group and spiritual family, the Alexanders have on-farm sales of certified organic tree fruits, raspberries, grapes, tomatoes, peppers, and vegetables. They also have a cannery for organic produce from local farmers and from

Northwest Select, the Love family farm in Arlington, Washington. Processed goods include tomatoes, salsa, tomato paste, sauces, jellies, jams, and fruit butters.

On the road to Northport on the west side of Roosevelt Lake. Call for directions.

Cliffside Orchard ☆ (509) 738-6165

Jeff and Jeanette Herman
Kettle Falls
In season: daily.

Peaches, apricots, cherrries, pears, apples—all certified organic.

Ten miles south of Kettle Falls on Highway 25. Call for directions.

Rattlesnake Ranch ☆ (509) 732-6163

Hilary Ohm and Steve Campbell
P.O. Box 630 Northport, WA 99157

Mail-order source for certified organic Spanish Red garlic, available loose, bagged, or in braids. Spanish Red (or Spanish Roja), is a gourmet variety with large cloves and exceptional flavor.

They'll sell from the farm if you call ahead for directions and hours.

Quillisascut Cheese Company ☆ (509) 738-2011

Rick and Lora Lea Misterly
2409 Pleasant Valley Road, Rice
Call ahead for hours.

Second-generation cheesemakers, the Misterlys use a Spanish Manchego recipe for goat cheeses that are sweet when young, assertive when aged. Some are flavored with lavender and fennel, others with pink peppercorns and dill. They also produce a feta, a grape-leaf-wrapped chèvre aged in olive oil, and a maceres potted cheese with garlic chives and rosemary. Farmstead cows-milk cheeses are flavored with black pepper and garlic, or rosemary and savory. Suppliers to The Shoalwater Inn, The Cactus, Fullers, Ray's Boathouse, Rover's, and The Hunt Club. Sold retail at DeLaurenti (in the Pike Place Market), Larry's Markets, Brie and Bordeaux, Lakewood Natural Foods, Brusseau's, Vinotique, and Puget Consumer Co-ops.

Call for directions.

FARMERS MARKETS

CHELAN COUNTY, WASHINGTON

Wenatchee Farmers Market, Wentachee, East Wenatchee, and Cashmere
Contact: Mariah Cornwoman, (509) 662-1609
June–October.

Wenatchee: Riverfront Park, at the foot of 5th Street, Wednesday and Saturday, 8am–1pm. East Wenatchee: the old Speidel's parking lot at the corner of Rock Island Avenue and Grant Road, Sunday, noon–2pm. Cashmere: Location to be announced, Tuesday, 8am–1pm.

GRANT COUNTY, WASHINGTON

Columbia Basin Farmers Market, Moses Lake
Contact: Allen Burritt, (509) 762-9794, or Teri Pieper, (509) 766-0101
June–mid-October: Saturday, 8am–1pm.

As many as 55 vendors, with produce, fruit, honey, baked goods, and crafts. Two Hutterite colonies participate with eggs, bread, and pies. Weekly drawings for free items.

Dogwood Park, 3rd and Dogwood, in Moses Lake.

OKANOGAN COUNTY, WASHINGTON

Twisp Farmers Market
Contact: David Sabold, (509) 996-2368, or the Community Center, (509) 997-2926
Mid-April–October: Saturday, 9am–noon.

Fifteen to thirty vendors with produce, bedding plants, baked goods, and fruit, plus a separate crafts market.

In the parking lot of the Methow Valley Community Center, on Highway 20.

PEND OREILLE COUNTY, WASHINGTON

Pend Oreille Valley Earth Market, Newport
Contact: Robert Karr, (509) 447-2552
May–mid-October or first snowfall: Saturday, 9am–1pm.

The market has been going since 1979. It is small, usually about a dozen vendors, but Karr reports that more than a hundred customers are typically lined up and waiting when business starts. Featured crops are cool-weather vegetables, garlic, honey, herbs, and herbal vinegars. All the produce is grown in the Pend Oreille Valley or just across the border in Idaho. It is nearly all organic, "but not certified organic," says Karr. "Up here we don't like government, even good government."

300 N Washington (Newport's main street).

SPOKANE COUNTY, WASHINGTON

Spokane Marketplace
Contact: (509) 482-2627
July–October: Wednesday and Saturday, 10am–6pm.

E 20 Riverside Avenue.

STEVENS COUNTY, WASHINGTON

Northeast Washington Farmers Market, Colville
Contact: Alice Sullivan, (509) 738-2547
Last Saturday in June–October: Saturday, 9am–noon.

Main Street and Tiger Highway.

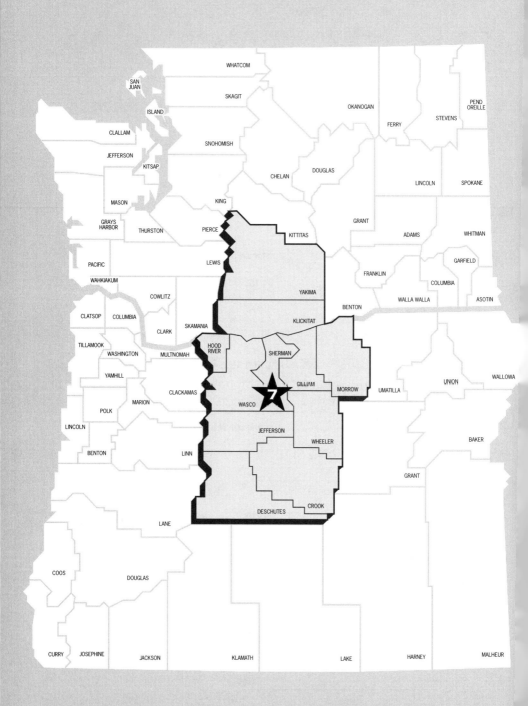

If flexibility is the key to success, then Yakima and Hood River valley farmers should be among the most successful in the world. On the 100-acre hillside where I live near Yakima, the past decade has seen the cherries, which always seemed to ripen and split in the week of heavy rain around the Fourth of July, be replaced with wine grapes. The Bartlett pears have been re-placed with trellised Jonagold apples. The Rome apples have been pulled and that acreage now supports a flourishing orchard of juicy, golden Nashi pear-apples from Japan. Even the hallmark Red Delicious apples have been replaced with trellised Fujis, the sweetest and crunchiest apples the orchardists have found. The old Concord grapes are now shoulder to shoulder with vinifera grapes as Washington and Oregon wines receive international recognition. In 1978, when we planted our small vineyard, there were four wineries in Washington; today there are more than forty. In addition to the traditional processing markets, fruit crops are being used for specialty wines—alcoholic and nonalcoholic—sparkling juices, concentrates, and fruit sweeteners. The world's main suppliers of mint and hops, located on both sides of the Columbia, see their market increasing, as do the several award-winning microbreweries.

The same changes are taking place in the Hood River Valley of Oregon, where wine grapes, Asian pears, and other new crops flourish in the volcanic soil. Farther south across the high desert plateau of the Deschutes River in Oregon, dryland wheat and grass farming has given way in places to cattle, pasture, potatoes, and world-class wine grapes, watered by sprinklers in circles so huge they are visible to the astronauts. Barley and rape (a cabbage-family plant that is the source of canola oil) also cover the interior highlands.

From the air, the east side of the Cascades is a patchwork quilt that starts with fringes of orchards and gardens in the pine-covered foothills. The forests are left at higher altitudes, and the orchards fill the river basins and climb the plateaus in ever larger expanses planted with fruits, grapes, hops, corn, mint, and finally grains, maintained in gigantic plots by agricultural equipment unknown two decades ago.

When I was growing up in western Washington, we would visit Yakima in the spring to pick asparagus along the ditch banks in the heady fragrance of blooming orchards. We would return to the Yakima Valley in September, always to a glorious Indian summer, to load the station wagon with boxes of apples, pears, tomatoes, potatoes, and onions for the canning season. Our gray, rainy winter was brightened by memories of the dry heat and the jars of sunshine from the east side. Today, people from "the coast" (anyplace west of the Cascade crest) still come to fill their white buckets with a variety and abundance of produce.

The Yakima and Hood River valleys are separated by the Columbia River, which not only provides a water highway for the transport of inland crops to western ports but also serves as a climatic equalizer. The gales that make the gorge so popular with windsurfers in their neon garb are the result of equalizing air pressures between the moist west and the drier east. The vistas are dramatic: Waterfalls drop hundreds of feet from highland plateaus to the Columbia, while a patchwork of crops stitched together with irrigation channels covers the country on each side. The geology that formed the landscape is equally dramatic. The deep gorge testifies to the power of the ancient Spokane Floods, and the basalt cliffs on each side were built up by millenia of volcanic eruptions. The volcanic ash also enriched the soil of the Yakima and Hood River valleys.

Sitting on what was once the western coast of the North American continent, the Columbia Basin was formed between 13 million and 16 million years ago. Lava flows erupted through fissures from a very large volcano in the area we now call Grande Ronde, located in northeast Oregon and southeast Washington. Over and over, these fissures spread nearly level flows of molten basalt north to the Okanogan, west to the Cascades, and east to the Rockies. Lava flows glazed the huge basins every thousand years or so, with pools hundreds of feet deep in places and extending over 2,000 square miles at a time. The flows stacked up in layers that are easily visible in river canyons today.

Native tribes along the Columbia used the river as a highway for food gathering and commerce, and the first European-American settlers took the same route. Arriving with 10 children and 700 fruit scions, Henderson Luelling began his orchards in Oregon in 1847. Japanese workers cleared the forests around Hood River, and the first apple trees were planted there by the Coe family and other pioneers. The first boxcar load of apples from the Pacific Northwest arrived in New York City in 1900.

Those who made their new homes in the Columbia, Yakima, Deschutes, and Hood River valleys found the soil and climate very suitable for productive orchards. In the vast drylands, horses, cattle, and sheep grazed across lush 4-foot-high stands of prairie grass. This ranching subsided along with the grass, and a need for water brought irrigation to the eastern slopes, where more than 200,000 acres in the Yakima Valley alone were irrigated before 1910. Today irrigation helps produce over a billion dollars a year in crops.

While some Native Americans along the river still struggle to eke an existence from fishing, the docks and barges along the dammed rivers carry a new commerce from the industry and harvest of the land now irrigated, planted, and reaped by some of the world's largest and most productive agricultural corporations.

East and West have met culturally here also, with European-Americans settlers relying on workers from the Pacific Rim to clear the forests, help build the transportation and irrigation systems, and work the land. The itinerant workers were and still are an indispensable part of the life of the land, and Hawaiian, Japanese, Filipino, and now Southeast Asians have joined the Native Americans, Hispanics, and many other nationalities to establish a land rich in traditions as well as harvests.

A day's outing could take you to stands run by fourth-generation Filipino-Americans, whose fields hold ten varieties of squash, five types of tomatoes, the sweetest onions, and peppers of every size and color. A half mile away, at a stand managed by a young boy and his grandfather, who came from Japan as a boy, you may find every vegetable needed for an oriental dinner. Across the road may be a fruit stand with 20 varieties of apples, pears, cherries, and peaches from a controlled-atmosphere warehouse. And don't forget the fresh-picked Golden Jubilee and white corn. Huckleberries picked by Native Americans on the slopes of Mount Adams are iced and ready for pies. After a stop at a winery, you can go on to a tortilla factory with a restaurant and a Mexican herb shop. An old-time mercantile store on the way home provides a choice of a sarsaparilla ice cream float, a glass of apple cider squeezed while you wait, or a fresh peach sundae to be enjoyed at the picnic tables in the owner's orchard of antique apple trees.

A friend, a scholar in urbanization, bites into a Nashi and muses about the communities that will be built here when we are gone. He envisions huge, domed, climatically controlled cities that will feed and employ millions. I'm glad I'm here now.

Julie McFarlane
Yakima, Washington

CHUKAR CHERRIES

The bright and cozy tasting room is filled with wonderful smells from local foods. Crafts, gifts, and picnic items are all on display, but the centerpiece is a large table spread with the cherry and berry products conceived by Guy and Pam Auld. Platters of pitted and dried Bing, Rainier, and Montmorency cherries burst with the flavor of July even in the winter. More dried cherries are encased in chocolate, and blueberries and cranberries come with a white chocolate coating. An array of sauces, preserves, and condiments—from Cherry Jubilees to the Cherry Poultry and Game Sauce that won first place at the Atlanta National Food Show—are ready to be spread on crackers and tasted. Other specialties include Bing Cherry Scone Mix and Tart Cherry Waffle Mix.

Cherries

Bing: *Developed in the Hood River Valley and named after a Chinese orchard manager. The most common market cherry and one of the world's most luscious tastes. (Regions 6 and 7)*

Lambert: *Bing-like cherry, grows on the hillsides and ripens a bit later than Bings. Look for green stems and dark cherry color. It has just a bit more acid than the Bings. (Regions 6 and 7)*

Rainier: *Developed in Washington and planted since the mid-1960s. Large, pale, sweet cherry with the golden blush coloration of a peach. Rainiers are soft and very perishable. Buy them at the farm if you can. (Mark P. LaPierre, Region 7)*

Royal Ann: *Predecessor to Rainier. Reese Orchards, near Milton-Freewater, Oregon (Region 6), is one place that carries this nice old variety.*

Van: *Similar to Bings and Lamberts. Often found in westside orchards, where it resists cracking better than Bings. (Regions 6 and 7)*

Pie cherries: *Usually Montmorency, though occasionally you will see Olivette and North Star cherries. High-acid, flavorful pie cherries are very perishable and are seldom seen in stores. They are great for canning. Several orchards in the Green Bluff area outside Spokane and Upper Lake Roosevelt area around Kettle Falls (both Region 6) sell them. Also, Regions 1, 2, 4, and 8.*

Processors in the Yakima Valley have come up with a myriad of high-tech fruit products in the past decade—from fried cinnamon apple chips to fruit concentrates for sale to Japan. But a whole new specialty market has been opened through the innovative processing and selling techniques developed by the Aulds.

Guy Auld was raised on a farm in Yankton, South Dakota. He was living in the Southwest and working for the YMCA when he and his wife, Pam, went to visit her parents in the Yakima Valley. Guy's college degree in biology and his childhood on the land enticed him to buy a 13-year-old cherry orchard in 1983.

The Aulds still grow their cherries for the lucrative fresh market, but cherries are the most vulnerable of tree fruits. One unseasonable rain can ruin the year for a fresh market crop. The Aulds talked to friends who dried rain-cracked and too-small cherries for home use. Through much research, Guy and Pam developed a large-volume dryer that retains the robust cherry flavor and color without the use of preservatives or coloring. Soon their seasonal fresh fruit business was supplemented by the year-round market for Chukar Cherries.

They now have 35 brokers distributing their cherries to all 50 states as well as Japan and Canada. Their success is a boon to other cherry and fruit growers, who now have a quality alternative to the fresh market.

The Aulds named their product after the chukar, a species of quail found in the Yakima Valley. "Its image reflects the similar characteristics of our Northwest cherries and berries ... tempting and sweet, fleeting in season, challenging to capture." Working with their three daughters—Vivian and twins Wynne and Alexandra—they have captured a new market in the challenging fruit industry.

Julie McFarlane

Chukar Cherries
Guy and Pamela Auld
306 Wine Country Road, Prosser
(509) 786-2055

From I-82, take exit 80 (Gap Road) south toward Prosser 1 mile. Shop is at the corner of the airport, just before the Yakima River bridge.

RIVER BEND COUNTRY STORE

Glacial meltwater from Mount Hood's northern slopes feeds the Hood River, which then waters the apple and pear orchards covering the volcanic soils of the Hood River Valley.

On its tumbling course north to the Columbia River Gorge, the river passes a sunny flat surrounded by forested glades. That's where you'll find River Bend Country Store.

Outside, there's a one-acre garden where you can pick your own flowers, herbs, vegetables, and berries, while discussing how to grow baby's breath or basil organically with master gardener Betty Aslin.

Inside the store, aromas of baking apple pies and huckleberry cobblers mix with those of the dried flowers and herbs that hang from the beams. Historic photos depict the site's past as the center of Tucker, Oregon, an old sawmill town.

Visitors can eat their way through the store and out into the garden, sampling cheese torta flavored with pesto and sun-dried tomatoes, garlicky mustards, marionberry preserves, local pears and apples, and fresh cider served iced in summer and hot and spiced in winter.

Fresh specialty produce fills a cooler and bushel baskets: tender greens, red and golden tomatoes, squashes, herbs, slim green beans, and apples and pears. Some of it is grown on the farm's 31 acres and is certified as meeting Oregon's high standards for organic produce. The rest is raised at area farms, many of which are also organic.

Antique cases display bright dried flower arrangements and wreaths, River Bend Country Kitchen's made-on-the-premises products such as spiced peaches, peach chutney, and ketchup, plus blueberry syrup, salad dressings, and other high-quality foods from other small Northwest farms.

River Bend's products are available off the farm too. Chefs at the Columbia Gorge Hotel rely on the farm for spinach and baby lettuces for their award-winning salads. In addition, River Bend's owners, Bob and Kaye White, sell their products at the Farmers in the Park farmers market in downtown Hood River. The firm also offers organic fruit gift packs by mail order. Their catalog includes dried pear slices covered with Belgian chocolate, raspberry-pear butter, hand-tied herb wreaths, and their popular Holiday Sampler, a selection of 12 varieties of apples and pears.

Marnie McPhee

River Bend Country Store
Bob and Kaye White
2363 Tucker Road
Hood River, OR 97031
(503) 386-8766
March–December: daily, 10am–5pm.
Located about five miles south of Hood River. Take Oak Street west to 13th Street and turn south. Follow the signs toward the town of Odell.

HOOD RIVER FRUIT LADY

When she started, back in the early 1970s, all Ann Franklin meant to do was harvest berries at the U-pick farms down near Portland, then sell her goods out of the trunk of her car in The Dalles at the Saturday market.

After a few years Ann discovered she could buy fruit wholesale, though she liked the idea of picking her own. "I'm a country girl," Ann says, harking back to a hardworking childhood on a Sacramento Valley farm in the 1930s and '40s. Her berry business grew beyond the capacity of her car and settled into her garage in The Dalles. Farm wives would drive from as far away as Grass Valley, out in the high desert wheatland, to buy their canning and jam fruit from Ann. After a while, they convinced her to start driving out to them. And when she did, and word spread, people in one town after another asked Ann if she wouldn't stop for them as well. Today, from June to September, Ann Franklin drives a fruit and produce route though eastern Oregon that would weary a UPS delivery driver.

In late summer she loads her van with 300 ears of Golden Jubilee corn her husband Ken has picked that morning, 250 pounds of sweet Roadside cantaloupe, 850 pounds of Bartlett pears, 250 pounds of vine-ripened tomatoes, 250 pounds of Redhaven peaches, 300 pounds of Elberta peaches, 250 pounds of Hale peaches, 30 pounds of Little Red nectarines, 120 pounds of Gravenstein apples, 75 pounds of green beans, a case of green peppers, a box of Satsuma plums, and a case of dryland Tilton apricots, the last of the season. "Either one of us or the other," Ann Franklin says, "the van or me, is going to have to get a girdle."

Ken and Ann Franklin now live on 10.9 acres of farmland down the Columbia River from The Dalles outside Hood River. The Franklins bought the place in 1978 when their six boys—three hers and three his—had pretty much gone their own ways. They run a little cattle, like many other pocket farmers in the area. Ken still puts in a full day at the nearby marina. But fruit is the big issue, mostly berries. In spring, when she's putting the thorny berries up on wires, Ann Franklin will go through seven pairs of gloves. Ken gets home from work and is already changing clothes by the time he hits the front door, headed for the bedroom. He'll move irrigation pipe or rototill new beds until it is dark, then come back to the house with the blood pressure of a young, relaxed man.

The Franklins grow marionberries, blueberries, tayberries, raspberries, boysenberries, and most recently, kotata berries, a delicious newcomer from the Oregon State University breeding station. It is a big, black, glossy berry, similar in many ways to the marion, though sweeter. "I like it because I can hold it a few days without refrigeration and it doesn't fall and get all weepy," Ann Franklin says, "and that's something you want for the fresh fruit market."

The Franklins grow peaches as well: Early Gold, Sunbright, Halehaven, Elberta, and Halberta. Ann swears by the Halehaven and replaces any tree with that peach. "They're solid," she says. "They don't mush up, and they have that Redhaven flavor, so that makes a good peach. It bruises—don't get me wrong. But when you can it, if it's got marks on it, it will come back to its natural form, just like it was fresh picked." Ann calls that "bounce back."

Ann Franklin's day begins sometime before 6. By 7 she's on the road in a white Chevy van that has seen a lot of wear and tear. The engine roars like a bulldozer. Inside the van the gentle odors of fruit take turns being prominent until the day is warm enough for the cantaloupe to become most apparent of all. The top of the dashboard is a landscape of road maps, old gas receipts, notebooks, scrap paper, and a carton of Kents. Ann is a serious smoker. She travels with a thermos of coffee and adds Cremora to her cup as she drives.

Ann heads in-country at Arlington, where the Columbia River is wide and flat and motionless in the morning. The town is hidden off the highway by sagebrush-covered, wind-rounded bluffs with exposed pockets of black lava. She parks the van in shade in the parking lot of the Pheasant Grill Drive-In, a roadside cafe she will return to at the end of the day for a maple-pecan ice cream cone. Ruby, the cook, is a big woman who moves slowly over to the open van door. She wears shorts, a polo shirt, and an apron, and Ann sells her cantaloupe. "I've got some nice Golden Jubilee corn picked this morning," Ann says, but Ruby answers that she's on a new diet and corn isn't part of it. Al, the Shell gas station owner, pulls up in a long car with his wife. He's looking for peaches. "There are only two of us," Al says, "so all we need is a half dozen. We just want 'em to eat." Al ends up buying cantaloupe and corn as well. Ann slams shut the van door and climbs into the driver's seat. She pauses to light a cigarette before starting the engine.

It is all uphill between Arlington and Condon, and then Condon to Fossil, from near sea level to 3,366 feet at Cummings Hill. Local high school students have no open rock faces or concrete bridge abutments to paint with their graffiti, so they use the two-lane highway in one long section out of Arlington. The messages are written to be read both driving uphill and coming back down.

The landscape takes on a visual counterpoint of juniper, sagebrush, and carefully scribed wheat fields. This is a long-settled piece of country, with grain elevators standing beside abandoned railroad track, and farm machinery lined up in careful rows next to weathered outbuildings, an open land with all the signs of people, but no people to be seen. Hay has been baled in some fields, bundled into giant shredded wheat biscuits in others. Where the wheat has been harvested, the golden brown stubble sticks up like a worn-out old brush that's lost too many bristles to be of much use. In some fields, circular irrigation rigs with electric motor-driven wheels pivot too slowly to be noticed by the passing eye. In other fields old Aeromotor windmills pump water for lazy cattle, the remnants of the high country ranching empires.

Ann Franklin understands farmers and their hard times and their instinct for the land. She has seen her own crops destroyed by weather, and she worries about this coming winter. The ducks and geese have been flocking up too early on the river, and Ann fears the worst. "Last year we got rain when we shouldn't have and it ruined the wheat, or they couldn't harvest. This year we got too much wheat with an early heat wave and the grain didn't mature. A lot of these farmers plowed their crops under. These people want my fruit, but they don't know where the next dollar is coming from. Same's true in town."

Ann Franklin leaves the highway for a smaller side road that takes her to Mikkalo, a general store and post office surrounded by black locust trees that date back to the turn of the century. The Mikkalo family has farmed all the nearby country for genera-tions. Some of the Mikkalo women had asked Ann if she wouldn't drive in to them rather than making them drive all the way to Condon, and Ann complied. "The people are so nice," she says ingenuously, "you can't turn them down. I could drop all my routes and just stay in The Dalles, but I like all the people where I go."

As Ann nears a farm house built close to the highway between Condon and Fossil, she explains that in summer, when the black Bing cherries are in, the farmer stands next to his mailbox waiting for her van to appear at the crest of the hills. "He knows about when I'll show up," Ann says, "and as soon as he sees me he starts waving this big red flag. Every week the cherries are in he buys a box. Twenty pounds. He's convinced his

wife that they are good for gout. I prefer the Rainier cherry myself. I think it's the up-and-coming cherry. The flavor's great. You can eat them, and you can bake them, and they hold up in a cool place with a wet gunnysack over them and they taste just-picked."

Fossil is the county seat of Wheeler County. Five-hundred-thirty people live there, a lot of them retired. The two garages seem to account for the majority of the business in town, though a sign in front of a house on the way into Fossil indicates that dew worms and night crawlers are for sale on the premises. Ann Franklin parks her van under a tall, old cottonwood tree, one among many planted long ago around the Fossil town park.

The senior citizen center is nearby, and men and women wander over after lunch to see what Ann has today.

Her stops on the route have all lasted between 15 and 30 minutes. But not Fossil. She spends the better part of the afternoon under the cottonwood, and she rarely has time to sit down for lunch. Cars continually drive up, some from 60 miles away. If the crowd gets too big, as often as not someone will jump into the van with Ann and help bag fruit, take orders, weigh up produce, and make change. Without Ann Franklin these people would have no fruit to put up, no berries for jam and jelly. Certainly not of the quality and variety that she supplies. The growing season is too short for them to do a lot of it themselves, and what the deer don't eat, the grasshoppers finish off. "I've been over after the 4th of July," Ann says, "and it was so cold it was raining and sleeting and there was snow in the grain in the fields."

The drive home is a straight shot in a near-empty van. Patches of rain look like steel wool hanging off in the distance. Ann looks windblown, her hair springing off in several directions. It has been a long, hot day, and the ice cream cone she buys when she gets down out of the high country and back onto the river at Arlington barely revives her for the last stretch home. "Ken" she says, "won't let me go out much past October. It gets rainy and the roads ice up. Condon can have icy fogs that last for weeks. It's just too dangerous. People'd like me to keep coming with the fall apples, but I only do the Transparent, Lodi, and winter Gravenstein. The rest are just too late."

Just past The Dalles the air changes. It is cooler, more moist, and feels close to home. The tall evergreens appear, and out on the Columbia Indian fishermen have set their nets for salmon the way they have done for countless centuries past. Fall is close.

``My little guy won a blue ribbon with his tayberry wine," Ann says with transparent pride. She is speaking of a longtime customer in Fossil who is either pushing 80 or has already gone over the edge. Whenever Ann shows up with a new fruit, the Red Bartlett pears, for example, he's the first to latch on. He recognized the kotata berry for its blue ribbon potential, but held off on jam in deference to kotata berry wine. It won't be ready until next year's county fair. "I was out until all hours picking him the last of those kotatas so he'd have enough for his wine," Ann Franklin says. "Ken had wanted them, too. But I just couldn't say no to that little guy. And Ken understood. Aren't too many men out there as understanding as my Ken."

Schuyler Ingle
Northwest Bounty

Pears

Bartlett: Both red and green varieties are sweet, soft, early pears, good for eating and canning. The reds are exceptionally beautiful. (Regions 4, 5, 7, 8, and 9)

Bennett: Similar to Bartlett, but better suited to West Coast climates, being resistant to scab. Developed in Whatcom County, Washington, around 1880.

Bosc: Russeted, thin-necked winter pear, with a spicy flavor. Best for cooking. (Regions 4 and 7)

Comice: Big, juicy, with a melting texture and a wonderful flavor. Red and green varieties; the green has a red blush. Needs a month of storage before it's ripe. Ripens in October and can keep until Christmas. (Regions 4, 5, 7, and 9)

Conference: A late-maturing French variety. Ready in October and keeps past Christmas.

d'Anjou: Winter pear, best for cooking. Green and red varieties. (Regions 4, 7, and 9)

Forelle: Small, sweet, winter pear. (Regions 7 and 9)

Rescue: Big, sweet, yellow pear with a reddish blush. Ripens in September and keeps until December.

Seckel: Small, reddish winter pear with a grainy texture and a sweet taste.

Asian Pears

Asian pears, unlike most European pears, are supposed to ripen on the tree. Flavorless ones were probably picked unripe, and time did not improve them. The season begins in late summer, and some varieties keep until spring. Flesh ranges from crunchy to tender, but they are never melting soft. (Regions 1, 2, 4, 5, 6, and 7)

Chojuro: Russet brown. Ripens in September and keeps well. It has a rather thick skin, which you may wish to peel, and a flavor that one grower describes as "real exotic. It almost tastes like perfume."

Hosui: Golden brown with a sweet, rich flavor; stores well.

Kosui: Yellow/russet fruit; tender flesh. Ripens in October.

Nijisseiki/Twentieth Century: The most popular variety in Japan. Yellow fruit, with thin skin and a crisp, sweet flavor.

Shinseiki/New Century: Ripens in August. Sweet, mellow flavor; keeps till January. Yellow fruit with white flesh.

BRAD'S SUMMER PUDDING

Chef Brad Patterson says that any combination of berries such as loganberries, tayberries, gooseberries, blueberries, and huckleberries will work in this recipe. Strawberries are not recommended.

1 pint blackberries
1 pint raspberries
1 pint boysenberries
1 pint fresh red or black currants
½ cup superfine sugar, or enough to sweeten fruit
1 pound loaf country white bread
⅓ cup Grand Marnier liqueur
Crème Anglaise or custard sauce (see note; optional)
Lightly whipped farm cream
1 teaspoon grated orange zest

Place berries and sugar in a medium-sized bowl and mix lightly. Set aside for 1 hour, or until berries have given off about ¾ cup juice.

Remove crusts from bread, then cut bread into 2-inch fingers. Line bottom and sides of 6 to 8 custard cups or a 2-quart soufflé dish with bread fingers, cutting slices to fit snugly. Reserve some bread for the top. Combine berry juice with Grand Marnier in a small bowl. Brush bread lining with berry juice until well covered.

Spoon berries into bread lining and cover with a bread "lid." Brush top with remaining berry juice, and cover with plastic wrap. Set a plate or tray on top of the cups or soufflé dish and place a weight on top so that the plate or tray fits snugly. Refrigerate 24 hours.

When ready to serve, remove plate and invert soufflé dish or individual cups onto a serving plate or plates. Nap pudding with Crème Anglaise, if desired, and serve with the whipped cream into which the grated orange zest has been folded.

Serves 6 or more.

Note: Crème Anglaise is a standard custard sauce. Consult a good, general cookbook for a recipe.

Gasperetti's Restaurant
Yakima, Washington

WARM SALAD DRESSING

Shallots, a member of the onion family, have a flavor somewhere between that of garlic and onion. They cook rapidly and are excellent with any meat, in sauces, soups, and salad dressings. Sauté them in butter and add to any vegetable. This unusual recipe for a dressing to be served with wilted greens was created by Gayla Guenther.

2 shallots
¼ cup olive oil
2 tablespoons balsamic or seasoned rice vinegar
Salt and pepper to taste

Slice shallots and sauté slowly in olive oil. Cook just until limp. Add vinegar and salt and pepper to taste.

Use as a dressing for wilted spinach or escarole. Garnish with feta cheese and black olives, if desired.

Makes about ½ cup.

Klickitat Creek Farm
Goldendale, Washington

KLICKITAT CREEK SCALLOPED POTATOES

This is a tried-and-true accompaniment to barbecued salmon, roast pork, or ham. If you have leftovers, warm them in a skillet with smoked ham and serve for breakfast. This dish also cooks nicely in a microwave.

6 to 8 potatoes
3 or 4 large shallots, sliced thin
2 tablespoons chopped fresh parsley
2 tablespoons flour
Salt and pepper to taste
1½ cups chicken broth
1½ to 2 cups grated Cheddar cheese

Preheat oven to 350°F.

Slice potatoes and shallots into thin rounds as you layer them in a 2-quart casserole dish. Layer potatoes, shallots, parsley, flour, salt, and pepper, making 3 layers. Pour chicken broth over layers. Cover and bake 30 to 45 minutes, until potatoes are tender.

Remove from oven and cover with grated cheese. Return potatoes to oven for 5 minutes, or until cheese melts. Sprinkle dish with coarsely ground pepper or cracked peppercorns.

Serves 8.

Klickitat Creek Farm
Goldendale, Washington

U-PICK FARMS AND ROADSIDE STANDS

U-Pick Guidelines: Call first, especially near the beginning and end of the season. Find out if your small children are welcome to help pick. Farms will supply picking containers, but you will need bags or boxes to transport your produce home. Pick carefully and conscientiously; a well-tended berry field or orchard represents years of knowledgeable labor. (Dogs should stay in the car.)

Harvests may vary greatly from year to year. A local chamber of commerce or county extension office can often supply up-to-date seasonal information. Also, many newspapers publish local farm maps in the late spring or summer.

HOOD RIVER COUNTY, OREGON

Ace-High Orchards ☆ **(503) 386-1974**
Samuel Asai
4600 Kenwood Drive, Hood River
Call ahead.

Pears (d'Anjou, Bartlett, Bosc, Comice), apples (Newtown Pippin, Red Delicious, and Golden Delicious), cherries.

Call for directions.

Apeasay Fabulous Fruit ☆ **(503) 386-6784**
North Cheatham
789 Highline Road, Hood River
Fall months: call for hours.

Certified organic specialty apples and pears.

Call for directions.

Columbia Gorge Organic Fruit Company
☆ **(503) 354-1066**
3610 Central Vale Road, Hood River
July–April: Monday–Saturday, 9am–4pm.

Organic ready-picked peaches, cherries, apples, pears. Canned and dried fruit as well.

Eight miles south of I-84 on Highway 35 (the Mount Hood Highway) to Central Vale Road.

Crippen Family Orchards ☆
(503) 386-3084
The Crippens
17~~50~~ ~~Road~~, Hood River [CLOSED]
Ye~~ar-r~~ound: Monday–Saturday, 9am–5pm.

Pears (d'Anjou, Bartlett, Bosc, Comice), apples (Newtown Pippin, Red Delicious, and Golden Delicious), cherries, peaches, berries, and other fruits and vegetables. U-pick or ready-picked.

Take exit 62 off I-84 onto Country Club Road.

Frisbie Orchards ☆ **(503) 386-6187**
Harold Frisbie
4000 Pheasant Drive, Hood River
July–October: daily, 8am–dark.

Apples, cherries, peaches, berries, and other fruits.

Five miles from I-84 on Pheasant Drive.

The Fruit Tree ☆ **(503) 386-6688**
4140 West Cliff Drive
Hood River, OR 97031
Year-round: daily, 9am–6pm.

Retail and mail-order outlet for Hood River fruit and other Oregon products.

Take exit 62 off I-84, turn west. Store is on right, next to the Columbia Gorge Hotel.

McClure Orchards ☆ **(503) 354-2034**
The McClures
2650 Wy'east Road, Hood River
July–October: daily, dawn–dusk.

Pears (d'Anjou, Bartlett, Bosc, Comice), apples (Newtown Pippin, Red Delicious, and Golden Delicious), cherries, peaches, and other fruits.

Between Hood River and Odell; take Highway 281 (Tucker Road) to Wy'east Road.

Moore Orchards ☆ (503) 386-4628
Allen Moore
Highway 35, Hood River
September–April: Monday–Friday, 8am–5pm;
Saturday, 8am–noon.

Pears (d'Anjou, Bartlett, Bosc) and apples.

From I-84 take exit 64, go south 6 miles on Highway 35.

Oates Orchards ☆ (503) 354-1782
Mike and Kathy Oates
4200 Chamberlin Drive, Hood River
October: daily, 8am–5pm.

Newton Pippin, Red Delicious, and Golden
Delicious apples.

Take Odell exit off Highway 35. Go north through Odell, turn left on Summit, right on Wy'East Drive, and left onto Chamberlin. Turn in by red barn.

Parks Orchards ☆ (503) 386-4852
Shirley Parks Nickelson
1901 Highway 35, Hood River
August–September: call for days open.

Bartlett and d'Anjou pears.

On Highway 35, 3 miles south of I-84.

Pheasant Valley Orchard ☆ (503) 386-2803
J. Scott Hagee
3890 Acre Drive, Hood River
August–September: Monday–Friday; call for hours.

Certified organic apples and pears.

Two miles from Hood River off Tucker Road on Acre Drive. Look for signs.

Rasmussen Farms ☆ (503) 386-4622 or (800) 548-2243
3020 Thomsen Road
Hood River, OR 97031
October–mid-November: daily, 9am–6pm.

"Pumpkin Funland" and other family activities.
Also U-pick pumpkins and apples from bins. Call
or write for gift-pack mailing list.

Take exit 64 off I-84. Go 6 miles south on Highway 35 and watch for the sign; call to arrange bus tours from Mount Hood.

River Bend Country Store ☆ (503) 386-8766
2363 Tucker Road,
Hood River, OR 97031
March–December: daily, 10am–5pm.

U-pick flowers, herbs, vegetables, and berries;
dried flowers and herbs, baked goods, specialty
foods, and ready-picked produce. Also sells organic fruit gift packs by mail.

Five miles south of Hood River; take Oak Street west to 13th Street and turn south. Follow the signs toward the town of Odell.

Sappington Orchard ☆ (503) 386-3357
Bill and Betty Sappington
3187 Highway 35, Hood River
Mid-August–April: daily, 10am–6pm.

Pears (d'Anjou, Bartlett, Bosc, Comice), apples
(Newtown Pippin, Red and Golden Delicious),
cherries, peaches, berries, other fruits, and cider.

Take exit 64 off I-84 in Hood River.

Stewart Farms ☆ (503) 354-1066 or (503) 386-6343
Ronald A. Stewart
3610 Central Vale Road, Hood River
July–March: Monday–Saturday, 8am–4pm; call
ahead.

Certified organic apples (Red and Golden Delicious, Empire, Granny Smith, Newtown Pippin),
cherries (Lambert, Van), pears (A-Ree-Rang,
Comice, Bartlett, d'Anjou, Hosui, Stark Crimson).

From I-84, take Mount Hood Highway and drive 8 miles. Turn right on Central Vale Road.

Bob Merten Berry Ranch ☆ (503) 352-6926
Bob Merten
5665 Lava Bed Drive, Parkdale
June–first frost: daily, 7am–dark.

Berries and sweet corn.

Take Baseline Drive one mile west of Parkdale to Lava Bed Drive.

Merz Orchards ☆ (503) 352-7565
Lewis and Janice Merz
8160 Clear Creek Road, Parkdale
Mid-September–mid-November: daily, 8am–dark.

D'Anjou, Bartlett, and Bosc pears, apples, cider, and lots of animals.

Take exit 64 (Hood River) off I-84. Go south 17 miles on Highway 35 into Parkdale and look for signs.

WASCO COUNTY, OREGON

Rasmussen Fruit and Flower ☆ (503) 298-5463
3000 W 6th Street, The Dalles
In season: daily, 9am–6pm.

Roadside stand.

Take exit 82 off I-84. Turn east on 6th Street.

Zion Farms ☆ (503) 296-8578
Gary and Lori Fischer
7661 Skyline Road, The Dalles
In season: Monday–Saturday, 8am–6pm.

Certified organic, U-pick and ready-picked.

Take The Dalles exit off I-84 and look for signs.

KLICKITAT COUNTY, WASHINGTON

Klickitat Creek Farm ☆ (509) 773-3895
Gayla Guenther
335 Snowberry Lane
Goldendale, WA 98620
Late August–January.

On-farm and mail-order sales of organic shallots and potatoes. Shallots are also available at Larry's Markets in the Seattle/Bellevue area.

Three miles north of Goldendale off Highway 97. Take Woodland Road east about 3 miles to Snowberry Lane.

Oak Ridge Organic Orchard ☆ (509) 493-3891
Dennis White
367 Oak Ridge Road, White Salmon
August–February: daily, daylight hours.

Certified organic pears and apples.

Take Highway 141 7 miles north of White Salmon to Husum, then go east 3 miles on Oak Ridge Road.

YAKIMA COUNTY, WASHINGTON

Granger Berry Patch ☀ (509) 854-1413
Ken and Sandi Fein
1731 Beam Road
Granger, WA 98932
June–September: U-pick and fresh produce; year-round: gourmet foods and beef; daily, 8am–7pm.

Standard and specialty berries, including huckleberries, blackcaps, tayberries, currants, gooseberries, and yellow and black raspberries. The whole-berry spreads, jams, jellies, and syrups are processed in small batches on the farm, and are also available by mail order. The spreads contain 80% berries and 20% honey; the syrups are 90% berries, 10% honey. The Feins are active promoters of regional agriculture, editing the Yakima Valley Farm Products guide and sponsoring seasonal festivals on their farm.

Take exit 58 off I-82, go east ½ mile, then turn left on Beam Road. Go 1½ miles; farm is on the east side of the road.

Schell Farms Bean and Produce ☀ (509) 865-4511 or -4348
Rich and Barb Schell
1611 Drainbank Road, Granger
Mid-June–October: Monday–Saturday, 8am–5pm; Sunday, 11am–3pm.

Variety of produce, including corn, peppers, and melons.

Five miles east of Toppenish on Highway 22. Or take the Highway 223 exit off I-82 and go south 3 miles to Highway 22. Turn right, go ¼ mile to Harris Road; stand is on the left.

Sky Ranch ☀ (509) 854-1866 or (206) 232-2716
Loren and Muriel Oliver Winterscheid
800 Nass Road on Cherry Hill, Granger
Mid-June–July 1.

Cherries—Bing and Van.

From I-82 take exit 58. Turn south on Highway 223 and drive 1½ miles to Emerald Road exit. Go east on Emerald Road for 2 miles, turn left on Cherry Hill Road to Nass Road. Look for signs.

Hollmeyer Farms ☀ (509) 894-4045
Jack Hollmeyer
1381 Hollmeyer, Mabton
April–July: daily, daylight hours; August–January: call ahead.

Certified organic asparagus, onions, carrots, and sweet corn.

Five miles west of Mabton or 14 miles east of Toppenish on Highway 22. Watch for Hollmeyer Road.

Thompson's Farm ☀ (509) 653-2589
John and Nancy Thompson
9535 Old Naches Highway, Naches
June–December: daily until October, Monday–Friday afterwards; sunup–sundown during harvest.

Family-owned orchard since 1898. Fresh cherries, apricots, peaches (many unusual varieties), pears, nectarines, prunes, plums, and apples. Cider, vinegars, honey, jams, and jellies. Orchard tours and fruit samples.

Northeast corner of Naches. From Highway 12, turn north onto Shaffer Avenue, between Precision Fruit and the old blue gas station. Driveway is located about ½ mile north, at intersection of Shaffer and the Old Naches Highway.

Johnson Family Farm ☀ (509) 837-8844
Gordon and Cherie Johnson
481 Price Road, Outlook
End of June–frost: daily, 9am–6pm.

A variety of fresh produce.

Take Outlook exit off I-82. Turn left onto Yakima Valley Highway; take second right and follow signs.

B & L Herb Farm ☀ (509) 786-3724
Bob and Lorne Gordon
Rundle Road, Prosser
April–July 4th: daily, 10am–5pm, or by chance or appointment.

Certified organic herb farm. Potted and fresh-cut herbs; dried herbs in summer, fall, and winter. Gourmet and unusual vegetables, herbal vinegars, potpourri, herbal tea, herb display garden.

From Yakima: Take Gap exit off I-82 and go right to North River Road. Go 3½ miles and turn left on Rundle Road; farm is on the left. From Tri-Cities:

Take Prosser exit off I-82 and go left past Cottage Court Market and Prosser Motel. Cross old concrete bridge over Yakima River and go left on North River Road. Go 3½ miles to Rundle Road and turn left; farm is on the left.

Chukar Cherries ✳ (509) 786-2055
Guy and Pamela Auld
306 Wine Country Road, Prosser
Year-round: daily, 10:30am–5pm.

Cherries and other regional specialties, dried cherries and berries, preserves, and sauces; also available at the Pike Place Market in Seattle and area supermarkets.

Take Gap Road exit off I-82 and head south toward Prosser. Located on the corner of the airport, 1 mile from the freeway.

Triple "R" Ranches ✳ (509) 973-2456
Albert L. Rapp
Rothrock Road, Prosser
Year-round: daylight hours.

Apricots, peaches, nectarines, pears, and plums.

Take Gap exit off I-82 and go north to Evans Road. Turn east and go about 4 miles to Rothrock Road; house is on the right.

Guerra's Produce ✳ (509) 837-8897
4800 Maple Grove, Sunnyside
In season: Monday–Saturday, 9am–6pm; Sunday, 10am–6pm.

Sweet and hot peppers, tomatoes, melons, cucumbers, and pinto beans.

Take exit 63 off I-82; turn right onto Yakima Valley Highway and then left on Maple Grove Road. Go north about 5 miles.

Hogue Farms ✳ (509) 837-4188
Gary and Margie Stonemetz, Gary Hogue, Mike Hogue
300 Warehouse Avenue, Sunnyside
Year-round: Monday–Friday, 9am–3pm in winter; 8am–5pm in summer.

Preserved asparagus, beans, sugar snap peas, and peppers; also available in supermarkets throughout the Northwest.

Take exit 63 off I-82.

Tucker Cellars Winery and Fruit Stand ✳ (509) 837-8701
Dean and Rose Tucker
70 Ray Road, Sunnyside
Year-round: daily, 8am–6pm in summer; 9am–4:30pm in winter.

Melvin and Vera Tucker operated one of Washington's first commercial wineries after the end of Prohibition. They made white port and muscatel under the Upland label. Their children, Dean and Rose, switched to sugar beets in the 1940s, and then back to wine grapes and produce in the late 1970s. Grandson Randy Tucker and his sister, Deanna, and brothers, Mike and John, now make wine, apple cider, and pickled vegetables, and sell farm produce at their Sunnyside stand.

Yakima Valley Highway at Ray Road.

Yakima Valley Cheese Company ✳ (509) 837-6005
105 S 1st Street
P.O. Box 814
Sunnyside, WA 98944
Year-round: Monday–Saturday, 9:30am–5pm.

Goudas, plain, herbed, and smoked; Edams, Double Cream, and other cheeses sold in loaves and wheels. This venture between dairymen and cheesemakers produces wonderfully fresh cheeses. Cheesemaking tours; call first for large groups. The sales room has gourmet products from a 70-mile radius. Mail-order catalog available.

Take exit 67 off I-82; go south on Midvale Road to Alexander Road and turn left. Second place on the right.

B. B. & R. Farm ✳ (509) 865-3088
5900 Ashee Road, Toppenish
June–November: daily.

All sorts of fruits and vegetables; seasonal U-pick peppers, tomatoes, okra, onions, garlic, and green beans.

On Highway 97, 2 miles north of Toppenish.

Boo 'n Doc's Deli Fruit and Produce ✳ (509) 865-5533
Judy and Jerry Boekholder
604 W 1st Avenue, Toppenish

April–October (produce); year-round (deli):
Monday–Saturday.

All sorts of produce and gift items made from Yakima Valley products. Soup, sandwiches, and salads at the deli.

In Toppenish at the corner of Elm and W 1st Avenue.

Gehlen Farms ✷ (509) 865-4046
Susan M. Gehlen
2311 E Branch Road, Toppenish
Mid-June–mid-September: daily, 7am–7pm; call ahead for availability.

A variety of produce, including corn (Jubilee, white, and Super Sweet) and tomatillos.

Take exit 50 off I-82 and head toward Toppenish. Farm is ½ mile after Yakima River; follow signs.

Badgley Ranch ✷ (509) 877-2043
Dave Badgley
73 W Parker Heights Road, Wapato
End of June–mid-September: daily.

Peaches, plums, nectarines, apricots, pears, apples, and cherries.

Take exit 40 off I-82, turn right at the stop sign and go 1.8 miles to Parker Heights Road. Turn left and watch for sign.

Belzer Orchards ✷ (509) 877-4359
Paul and Lois Belzer
620 E Parker Heights Road, Wapato
Mid-July–October: daily, 8am–7pm.

Cherries (U-pick and ready-picked), apricots, peaches, pears, prunes, and apples.

From I-82 take exit 44. Go north toward Donald and drive ⅓ mile to the end of the road. Turn left toward Yakima, take first paved road to the right (E Parker Heights Road). Cross over bridge and keep to the right; go ¾ mile.

Caribou Ranches, Inc. ✷ (509) 848-2277 or -2523
Dee, Sara, and Andy Schilperoort
7281 Progressive Road, Wapato
Year-round: 8am–4pm; call ahead to verify.

Asparagus and potatoes (Norkotah, Norland, and Yukon Gold).

Take Highway 97 exit off I-82, then take the Lateral A exit. Follow south 5 miles to the 4-way stop at Kiles Korner; continue south another 2 miles to Progressive Road. Turn right and follow spuds signs for 3¼ miles.

Donald Fruit and Mercantile ✷ (509) 877-3115
Paul and Amy McDonald
4461 Yakima Valley Highway, Wapato
June–December: Monday–Saturday, 9am–6pm; Sunday, 10am–6pm.

Fresh fruit and produce in season, Yakima Valley gift items, fresh cider, and peach sundaes. U-pick pumpkins in October. Picnic area.

Eleven miles southeast of Yakima, next to the Minimart in the town of Donald. Take exit 44 off I-82, turn left to Donald, and look for sign.

Five Star Ranch ✷ (509) 877-4456
Carl Schilperoort
Lateral A, Wapato
In season: Wednesday–Saturday, 10am–5pm; Sunday, noon–5pm.

Peaches, nectarines, and pears.

Take Highway 97 exit off I-82, and take Lateral A exit off Highway 97. Farm is ¼ mile south on Lateral A on west side of the road.

Husch Ranch ✷ (509) 877-3766 or -2657
Allen Husch
Lateral A and Lundberg Road, Wapato
Late July–November: daily, 8am–5pm.

Peaches (Roza, Golden Elberta), pears (Bartlett), Italian prunes, and apples (Criterion, Ryan Red). Mostly ready-picked, some U-pick peaches.

Take Highway 97 exit off I-82, then take Lateral A exit. Ranch is located on corner of Lateral A and Lundberg Road.

Inaba Produce Farms ✷ (509) 848-2982
8351 McDonald Road, Wapato
June–October: daily, 8am–5pm.

Mostly wholesale, but will sell some retail in quantity: zucchini, green beans, cucumbers, cabbage, sweet corn, bell peppers, tomatoes, onions, and watermelon.

One mile south of Harrah; ½ mile east on McDonald Road.

Krueger Pepper Gardens ☆
(509) 877-3677
Gayle and Patti Krueger
3491 Branch Road, Wapato
In season: Sunday–Thursday, dawn–dusk; Fridays until 3pm.

U-pick or on-farm sales of vegetables, fruit, onions, cilantro, 60 varieties of peppers, and 18 kinds of winter squash. After 40 years of magnificent peppers, Krueger's is on everyone's list of don't-miss places. Free recipe booklet. Bring your own containers. In Seattle, buy Krueger Peppers at El Mercado Latino in the Pike Place Market.

Take Highway 97 into Wapato. Turn west at Fort Restaurant, go ½ mile to Campbell Road and then 2½ miles to Knights Lane. Turn left; farm is at the end of the lane on Branch Road.

Malko Sunny Slope Ranch ☆
(509) 877-4903
Jerry Malko
730 Henderson Road, Wapato
Mid-June–August: call ahead for hours.

Cherries, apricots, peaches, nectarines, and plums.

Ten miles from Yakima; 3 miles from I-82.

Turcott Orchard ☆ (509) 877-2688
Willard and Roberta Turcott
801 Clark Road, Wapato
In season: daily, 8am–6pm; call ahead.

Cherries (mid-June through mid-July), peaches (early August through early September), nectarines, Bartlett pears (mid-August) and apples (late August through mid-October). U-pick or boxed. Call ahead for large orders.

Take exit 44 off I-82 and go north through Donald to Yakima Valley Highway. Turn right onto Sawyer, north onto Lombard Loop to Clark Road. Fourth house on left.

Johnson Orchards ☆ (509) 966-7479
or -0294
Roy and Eric Johnson
4906 Summitview Avenue, Yakima
Mid-June–mid-December: daily, 8am–5pm.

Cherries (Bing, Lambert, Rainier, Van), Bartlett pears, apples (Delicious, Rome, Winesap, Spartan).

Nine blocks west of 40th Avenue on Summitview Avenue in Yakima.

McFarlane Vineyards ☆ (509) 966-2626
Lee and Julie McFarlane
110 Wapatox Hills Lane
FAX: (509) 965-19
September-0   all ahead.

CLOSED

U-pick   apes and home winemaker services. Customers come for harvest weekends of picking, crushing, German meals, fresh grape juice, and samplings of last year's production of Riesling, Gewürztraminer, Cabernet Sauvignon and Pinot Chardonnay. They leave with carboys full of grape "must," ready for fermentation at home. A smaller harvest of frozen grapes is held in December for Ice Harvest wine and vine trimmings are available for wreaths. Call first for information and harvest schedules.

Take Gleed exit off Highway 12; vineyard is 5 miles west of Yakima.

Residential Fruit Stands ☆
(509) 575-5358
Yakima (see directions)
Late July–late October: daily, 9am–dusk.

All local produce delivered fresh daily.

Take exit 34 off I-82 and turn west. Go 2 miles to southwest corner of 3rd and Nob Hill.

Snokist Public Sales ☆ (509) 882-3131
or (509) 457-8444
614 Yakima Valley Highway, Grandview
10 W Mead, Yakima
Grandview: October–May: Monday–Friday, 8am–5pm; Saturday, 9am–1pm.
Yakima: year-round: Monday–Saturday, 9am–2pm.

Cooperatively owned source for apples (Delicious, Granny Smith, Criterion, Jonagold, Rome, Fuji), pears (d'Anjou, Bosc), honey (clover, alfalfa, fireweed, desert flower, huckleberry, blackberry, mint, and honeycomb), walnuts, and apple chips.

Grandview: From I-82 take exit 73. Turn left on Yakima Valley Highway, go 1 mile into town. Snokist is on the right side of the road.
Yakima: Take Nob Hill exit from I-82 and head west; take first left. Turn right onto Mead.

Willow Springs Farm ☆ (509) 966-6287
Tom and Barb Mohagen
2910 S 62nd Avenue, Yakima
Hours by appointment; call ahead.

On-farm sales of organically grown edible flowers, fresh herbs, salad greens, and carrots. One happy customer is Gasperetti's in Yakima, one of the best-known and best-loved restaurants in Eastern Washington.

Go south off of Ahtanum Road onto 62nd.

Albatross Farm ☆ (509) 829-5185
Paul and Janet Allison
901 Eagle Peak Road, Zillah
Mid-July–mid-September: daily, 7am–6pm; call for other times.

Cherries, apricots, peaches, nectarines, pears, and all manner of apples: Gala, Prime Gold, Red Rome, Golden Delicious, Red Delicious, Ginger Gold, Granny Smith, Fuji, Braeburn.

From I-82 take exit 54, turn north on Yakima Valley Highway to East Zillah Drive, turn right, go 2 miles, and turn left on Eagle Peak Road; farm is the second on the right.

Argo Apples ☆ (509) 829-5461
Dave and Margaret Argo
1880 N Granger Road, Zillah
Mid-September–mid-October: 6am–6pm.

Apples.

From I-82, take exit 54 to Divison Road, go east 2 miles, turn south on N Granger Road to the first house on the west side of the road.

RML Orchards, Inc. ☆ (509) 829-6313
2970 Gilbert Road, Zillah
June–September.

Cherries, apricots, peaches, nectarines, pears, apples.

Take exit 52 off I-82, go north on Cheyne for 3 miles, look for northwest corner of Cheyne and Gilbert roads.

FARMERS MARKETS

HOOD RIVER COUNTY, OREGON

Farmers in the Park, Hood River
Contact: Kay White, (503) 386-8766
June–October: Saturday, 9am–3pm.

Baked goods, produce, fruit.

In Jackson Park. Take first Hood River exit off I-84 to yellow blinking light. Turn right on 13th, go 4 blocks; market is on the right.

The story of the dry side of the Pacific Northwest is one of water: getting it, using it, and keeping it.

In spots, the natural land is so dry it hurts. Six inches of rainfall is a wet year around Pasco. About the only thing that grows in any abundance naturally is sagebrush. Starting in the north around Interstate 90, the sagebrush carpet sweeps across central Washington, through the river canyons that cut into the eastern Oregon highlands, and down into the Great Basin and Snake River country of eastern Oregon.

You can't farm it, graze livestock on it, or eat it, although Georgia O'Keeffe did try to season a Thanksgiving turkey with sagebrush when she first moved out West. It took her years to find humor in the situation. Even the resourceful Indians found only two main uses for sagebrush: weaving the bark or burning the whole plant.

The Indians first arrived here perhaps 12,000 years ago. When they moved down from the Okanogan ridges, they saw huge rock basins scoured and gouged, dry waterfalls hanging silently over sage-filled hollows, coulees empty of everything save wind.

An Ice Age had sent glaciers rasping southward perhaps a million years ago. One of these blocked what was then a major channel of the Columbia River in present-day Montana, creating the vast, primordial Lake Missoula. Gradually the weather warmed, and the ice dam groaned, then burst.

It must have been an awe-inspiring sight. A roaring wall of water 600 feet high cluttered with ice chunks as big as a house. The wind alone, pushed ahead by the mountain of water, would have knocked you down. A billion cubic feet per second spilled toward the Pacific. That's 30 times the combined flow of all the rivers in the world today.

The desolation the Indians saw had once been a rich valley. To the east above the floodline was the Palouse, an undulating sea of hills built from wind-blown soil called loess. To the south and west were the Horse Heaven Hills. The hills were covered in bunchgrass and big game, but they were still an unfriendly land to people who wouldn't have horses until about 1730. What lay beyond to the south was worse—the Blue and Wallowa mountains, cut only by deep, twisting river canyons, and then the arid Great Basin of eastern Oregon.

It was hardly an Eden, except for one thing: the Columbia. Salmon swam up the river by the millions. They literally filled streams, nudging those on the outside into death in the shallows. The Columbia and Snake River tribes ate about a pound of salmon a day per person, making them some of the greatest meat eaters the world has ever known. Lewis and Clark, when they encountered this abundance almost 200 years ago, became so sick of salmon that the expedition began bartering for dogs to eat.

The Indians were mobile, following a sensible and pleasing annual track between hunting camps, root-digging camps, and fishing camps. The fishing camps were also the trade centers, for the rivers were the major highways of the times.

These water routes also brought the first Europeans to the interior—
scouts for the great fur-trading empires. The traders were just passing
through. Their companies actively discouraged settlers, since more farms
meant fewer furs.

The first American settlers nosing west in the 1840s didn't want the inland
Northwest anyway. Their journey toward the Willamette Valley took them
through the region at its worst. Late summer meant poor grazing, dust, and

vicious heat. The missionaries who settled near Walla Walla in the 1830s
learned the fertility of the land, but their ignorance of the people they had
come to proselytize led to their own deaths and to the Indian wars that
followed.

Real settlement of eastern Washington and Oregon began in the 1860s, after the Indian wars. Miners swarming to the gold and silver fields in the Blue
and Wallowa mountains and to northern Idaho became the first real agricultural market the Northwest had outside of San Francisco. And many gold-
seekers soon recognized that on the average it was more profitable to feed a
miner than to be one. The Palouse began to fill up with wheat farmers, and

Walla Walla became the largest town in Washington Territory. By the 1880s, wheat fields also covered much of northeastern Oregon.

Into the Great Basin came ranchers who found under its broad horizons prime ingredients for raising beef—grazing, meager as it was, and an absence of farmers' fences. Men like Jack Renihan brought in Texas longhorns and men to tend them. These cowboys were the first Hispanics to settle in the Northwest.

The cattle barons built huge empires. It was said that Henry Miller could ride from the Kern River in California up through Nevada to the Malheur River in eastern Oregon without sleeping one night off his land.

The cattle system was simple: Buy, or hire someone to homestead, a few acres around water. If you controlled a necklace of watering holes, you controlled the land around them—much to the disappointment of sheep ranchers who came later. But the sheep did come, for the interior of Oregon was prime grazing land for flocks. The Basque herdsmen ranchers brought to the area also stayed, enriching the life of far eastern Oregon. Isolated railheads in towns like Shaniko helped set the world's price for wool in the 1880s.

The basic blueprint of dryland ranch life remains. Malheur County is a good example. Three-quarters of this huge county is publicly owned, and it is the seventh largest cow county in the nation. (Irrigated field crops—grain, potatoes, sugar beets, corn, and onions—cover much of the private acreage.) Sheepherding has gone out of favor, primarily because of the shortage of labor for this lonely work. But folks in Harney and Malheur counties still honor the culinary contributions of the Basques. While the Jordan Valley rodeo offers pit-cooked beef each May, the ladies of the Arock Grange ("just about 100 miles from anywhere," one says) put on special Basque dinners for civic groups. Several restaurants also continue to offer such delicacies as roasted leg of lamb, pigs' feet with pimiento, Dutch oven bread, and the essential Basque dish, *bacaloa*—salt cod cooked with tomatoes.

Like ranchers and sheepherders, wheat farmers in the inland Northwest mainly rely on water where it naturally lands and flows. Washington, Oregon, and Idaho account for about 85 percent of soft white wheat production in the United States. Used mainly in Asia for noodles and pastries, soft wheat is a prime export item for ports in Puget Sound and Portland. Yet, while dryland wheat farmers may be intimate with markets in Tokyo, Shanghai, and

Karachi, they still must rely on—and battle—water from the skies back home. The rain is usually barely enough, and what there is often comes in a soil-destroying rush. One key weapon in the battle for soil and water conservation is contour planting. A Palouse farmer will take one strip of a hill for winter wheat, planted in the fall to give it a head start. Another he plants in spring wheat. On still another ring he plants a rotation crop to provide some income, but more important, to break a cycle of wheat pests—peas, perhaps,

or sunflowers, garbanzos, or lentils. And some rings will be left fallow, set aside to collect moisture for next year.

In the spring, the result is impressive. It's also funny. Before you rises the largest green parfait in the world.

Perhaps the farmer has never stepped back far enough to see the humor in his work. But any dryland grower would appreciate it. When you depend on rain on the dry side of the Cascades, you have to be able to laugh. If you can't, you'll spend more time crying than farming.

For other growers, a sense of humor is less important than the skill to put water on the land. They're the irrigators. From the air over eastern Washington you can see huge irrigation circles laid upon land that once was blasted by the Spokane Floods. This is the work of farmers and the massive Columbia Basin Irrigation Project. Sagebrush land is now producing corn, mint, onions, irrigated wheat, alfalfa, asparagus, cherries, apples, peaches, Concord grapes, wine grapes, and millions upon millions of potatoes.

The Columbia Basin Irrigation Project, which spans much of central Washington, is the largest of the irrigation projects. Similar schemes produce harvests throughout the dry side of the Northwest. You'll find fine orchards and experimental popcorn crops in Oregon's Grant County, deep in the heart of mountainous mining country but fed by the John Day River. In the Walla Walla Valley there are the famous Walla Walla Sweet onions and the best shallots in the world. In Washington's Benton County, farmers are working with everything from baby's breath to basil.

Don't expect many mom-and-pop roadside stands in the dryland Northwest. Farming on the east side is big business, expensive business. It simply costs too much money and energy to get water for the crops. Yet talk to a farmer in August, ankle-deep in wheat stubble, with more dust on his John Deere cap than most west-siders will see in a year, and he'll talk about food for people: wheat, lentils, peas, fruit, beef.

And always he will talk about water.

Don McManman
Kennewick, Washington

WALLA WALLA SWEETS

Pasquale Sturno did something quite unusual for an Italian immigrant of 1875. He moved to Walla Walla.

Sturno was born in 1850 on an island off the coast of Naples, and like many of his countrymen, he saw in the United States a refuge from civil warfare and hunger. But unlike most, he stopped only briefly in New York City. His brethren were cutting new fields for truck gardens in the loam of Long Island and New Jersey, but Sturno had heard— it's not clear how—about the rich farmland around Walla Walla.

He took a train west and arrived, with 25 cents in his pocket, in a ragged community known best at the time for its disease-ridden wells, muddy streets, and itinerant harvest crews. He began growing vegetables.

His market was the wheat ranchers, harvest crews, town merchants, and most important, miners in the mountains to the east. They lived on salt pork and flour. Any kind of produce, if not worth its weight in gold, was at least paid for in gold. Most of it was carried by freight wagon and pack animals. This demanded sturdy products: potatoes, green beans, cabbage, and, of course, onions.

Sturno had a market, rich bottomland, and a strong back. He also had a promoter's instinct. He wrote home to the Old Country about the richness of the land and the money to be made.

The Italians who answered the call came poor but not empty-handed. They brought seeds for crops they had grown accustomed to in the Old Country—including an onion so mild it was commonly eaten raw. A Frenchman, Peter Pieri, probably grew the first Italian-style onion in the Walla Walla Valley, but the *paesani* were the ones who refined it, developing it into the Walla Walla Sweet we know today.

John Arbini worked on improving the imported onion stock throughout the 1920s, and with interpollination and carefully documented records, he came up with what he called the Yellow Globe.

The name didn't take. Miners, freight packers, and harvest crews had all relished the sweet onion. My grandfather, who worked at all three jobs as a young man in eastern Washington and in Idaho during the early years of the century, always marveled at the onion you could "eat like an apple." He and others who looked forward to midsummer days when the onions would first come in from the fields gave them a name that stuck—the Walla Walla Sweet.

Nick Taruscio's grandfather was fresh from Italy and farming in the Walla Walla Valley at about the time mine was mule-packing into the mining camps above Lewiston. Nick still farms in the shadow of the Blue Mountains—75 acres of asparagus, spinach, and beans, and only about 25 in Sweets. "I don't think I could afford to raise more."

He's not talking about the money, for if everything goes right, the Sweets are a lucrative crop. He's speaking of the price a farmer pays in headaches and occasional heartaches. It's a year-round gamble on weather, water, labor, and markets.

Seeds, about the size of a piece of freshly ground peppercorn, are planted in September after the fine topsoil has been prepared. Farmers want growth on the onions before winter, to give them a head start the following summer. They generally grow their own seed. This is important. The Walla Walla Sweet Onion Commission has established a precise geographical region in which genuine Sweets may be grown. It's much like an appellation for wines. Sweets, and seeds for Sweets, must come from the Walla Walla River watershed—consisting of only part of Walla Walla County and a sliver of northeastern Oregon around Milton-Freewater.

Now the worrying begins. If there's too much rain, the ground can freeze and push the tiny bulb upward, ripping off its roots. Too little rain, and the plant becomes desiccated before irrigation time in the spring. Too much wind from the north, too little blanketing snow, and the onion plant freeze-dries in place.

Come April, it's time to wage war on pests. Sweets actually have very little sugar. Their culinary allure arises from a relatively low amount of sulphur, about half that of regular onions. This lack of an eye-watering defense also makes them attractive to insects.

Growers start watering in the spring. It's a delicate balance. Too little water and you don't get the growth. Too much and you've got a wetneck, an onion so filled with moisture that it weeps when the leaves are cut off. Even a perfect Walla Walla Sweet will keep only about a month after harvest, but a wet one will implode within a few days.

Come June, when Walla Walla's summer is gearing up for its annual rampage, the tops of Sweet onions begin to nod over. No more irrigation. It's time to harden the plants for a harvest that will come within two weeks. Rain at this time can ruin a crop and usher in solemn conversations between farmer and banker.

No farmer growing onions under the auspices of the commission harvests without the approval of an inspector. The purpose is two-fold:

—To keep a steady but not overwhelming flow of onions to valley processors. Too many onions at one time would reduce quality.

—To keep poor onions off the market.

When conditions are right and the inspector has given the OK, farmers enter the field and mechanically lift the onions from the soil. It's at this time that the entire Walla Walla Valley is covered with the luscious but mild (as befitting the Sweet) aroma of onions. Post offices throughout the region are packed with the scent—the legacy of gift boxes being sent across the country.

The stoop labor begins after the onions have been allowed to dry in the fields for a few hours. First the workers move down the rows of fat globes and individually cut off each top. Then it's back to the beginning, and each onion is picked up individually.

"We put them in five-gallon buckets. That's the only way to protect them. They're just not very tough," Taruscio says.

But inspectors are. At the processing plants (only eight are certified to handle the genuine Sweet), each onion is inspected. Again, splits and wet-necks are culled out. If an onion is scarred more than one parchment skin deep, it goes to the dump.

The rest go the market, many sold in gift boxes in much the same way as Washington apples.

That's where the payoff is for farmers like Taruscio, his wife, Donita, and their two boys.

"We're trying to put a quality product out. That's where the profit is. If you don't have quality, you don't have much. How we grow the Sweets has improved, but the quality is just the same."

Call it savvy marketing, if you will. But there's probably something more. When Nick Taruscio's grandfather came from Italy almost 100 years ago, he brought his skill— and he brought seed.

Were seeds that contributed to the genetic stock of today's Walla Walla Sweets among them? No one knows.

But it's clear what Walla Walla thinks about the men and women who helped build the diverse agricultural industry in the valley. In a region where Lewis and Clark, Chief Joseph, and the pioneers of northern European stock who trudged across the continent are immortalized, Walla Walla is different. Outside the Walla Walla County Courthouse is a statue not to a builder of the Pacific Northwest but to another explorer, Christopher Columbus.

Don McManman

PISSALADIÈRE
ONION AND ANCHOVY PIZZA

Pissaladière is a dish served up by the bakers and street vendors of Nice, in Provence. It is made of bread dough spread with a mixture of onions that have been cooked almost to the melting point in olive oil, garnished with a lattice of anchovies, and dotted with black olives.

There are as many different versions of this dish as there are cooks who prepare it. Sometimes a few tomatoes are added to the onions, but this is a rather recent development. Use your favorite recipe for the dough or buy raw bread dough from your local bakery or frozen pizza dough from an Italian bakery.

The flavor of the onion is essential to this preparation. When Walla Walla Sweets are in the local markets, use these lovely, mild-flavored onions. Serve the Pissaladière as a first course with a Grignolino wine.

1 pound pizza or bread dough
¼ cup fruity olive oil
3 pounds Walla Walla Sweet onions, very thinly sliced
2 cloves garlic, finely chopped (optional)
3 or 4 sprigs fresh thyme, finely chopped
1 bay leaf
½ teaspoon salt
Freshly ground pepper
Scant ½ cup grated Parmesan cheese
2 cans (2 oz each) anchovy fillets, drained and separated
Imported black olives, pitted and cut in half

Let dough rise until doubled in bulk, then punch it down and knead it several times. Shape into a rectangle using your hands or a rolling pin, and press into a 17- by 12-inch greased rimmed baking sheet. Push the dough a bit higher than the sides and crimp it so that it forms a rim. Cover and let rise until doubled in bulk, about 1 hour.

While the dough is rising, heat the olive oil in a heavy 4-quart Dutch oven; add the onions, garlic, thyme, bay leaf, salt, and pepper. Cover and cook over moderate heat for 5 minutes.

Remove the cover, raise the heat to high, and cook until the juice released from the onions has evaporated, about 5 minutes. Cover once again, reduce heat, and simmer for about 1 hour, until the onions have almost melted into a purée. Taste for seasoning and set aside.

Preheat oven to 350°F.

When the dough in the baking pan has doubled in bulk, sprinkle the surface with the grated cheese and cover with the onion mixture (bay leaf and thyme sprigs removed), leaving a 1-inch border. Over this, make a lattice pattern with the anchovy fillets. (If you're not overly fond of the strong taste of anchovy, you might wish to soak the fillets in milk for about 10 minutes; this removes the too-salty flavor.) In each of the open spaces remaining, place half an olive.

Put the pan in the middle of the oven and bake for about 45 minutes. Serve slightly warm or at room temperature.

Serves 8 to 10.

Judie Geise
New Northwest Kitchen

RANCH LIFE

Certain literary types, refugees from the east or south, have now arrived in the Northwest to wax eloquent about the natives, as if they were Peter Mayle and this were the south of France. And they think we're provincial! Well, they don't know the half of it.

Farmers in particular exist in stereotype for most, fueled perhaps by Grant Wood's *American Gothic*, or maybe Willie Nelson and the AT&T commercials. My grandfather liked to refer to himself as a farmer, much the same way that Joe DiMaggio called himself a ballplayer. In his later years he really played up the farmer bit, talking like a cowboy, wearing patched jeans, and always driving a really beat-up old something, sometimes a pickup, sometimes a Lincoln. My grandmother wanted a Rolls—they could well afford it—but Grandsire (that's what we all called him) knew it wouldn't look good when he was out trading horses or selling cattle.

His good ol' boy act made it easy for him to deal with roustabouts and cattle buyers. In truth he was the well-educated scion of prosperous eastern Washington homesteaders who had, by the time of his birth in 1893, already accumulated several thousand acres of prime wheatland and sent sons off to Stanford and Johns Hopkins.

The Snyders of Adams County had arrived early, although when as a child I asked my great-grandfather if he came in a covered wagon he harrumphed, "No darlin', we came on the train." His tone of voice told me he and his parents and brothers had no intention of suffering the rigors of the trail. They felt destined to prevail, and they were content to wait and take the civilized route.

The Snyders believed they could work harder, longer, and smarter than the other homesteaders. History proved them correct. My great-grandmother harvested the first 130-acre wheat crop with her hand scythe. She also did all the cooking, trading her fresh-baked bread with the Palouse Indians for she knew not what, until they brought her a milk cow for her trouble. She never asked where the cow came from. Instead she started making butter in her "spare" time—salting it, putting it in crocks, and selling it. Meanwhile my great-grandfather and his sons were digging a 70-foot well, shovelful by shovelful. By the time I was old enough to notice, my grandfather had parlayed the family farms into a sprawling wheat and cattle empire headquartered on the Bar U Ranch near Washtucna.

I have a vivid memory of my grandmother at 70, sitting on her terrace overlooking an expanse of lawn, the creek, and a meadow full of box elders and Simmental bulls, reading Balzac aloud, in French, to my son, and slitting the pages with a sterling letter opener. Not your typical farmer's wife, and yet…

My granny could prepare two food items when she arrived on the ranch as a young bride fresh from the Tri Delt house at the University of Washington. She was raised in Spokane in the more genteel tradition of the last century; servants did everything and the cooks cooked. She ended up cooking three meals a day for 40 years for—oh— 10 to 50 people, depending on the time of year. What this meant in eastern Washington from 1920 until electricity came in 1941 was the wood stove. It also meant baking all the bread, churning the butter, smoking the bacon, stuffing the sausage, canning all the vegetables and fruits, and on and on with the seasons of the year, year in and year out.

So, in my family, cooking wasn't such a big deal. If you were female you planned all the meals, figured out the groceries, and prepared it all for however many wanted to eat. Enormous quantities of food, every day. This was a lot more fun after the advent of electricity. My grandmother told me it rejuvenated her entire approach. She was very fast in the kitchen. She wanted to spend her time doing other things. Oh, she was proud of her peach pie, but she was more interested in party politics and the vagaries of breeding peacocks. She would be highly amused that I have made my way in the world cooking, and also very pleased that those hours we spent together in the kitchen peeling, hulling, and chopping did not go for naught. After all, it was she who nixed my idea of taking Home Ec, telling me I should not waste my precious time on something I could learn at home, and while we are on the subject, forget learning to type too. She told me I should study French instead.

Christina Reid

BIRCH CREEK GOURMETS

In the foothills of the Blue Mountains outside of Milton-Freewater, Oregon, Terry Farley watches as an azure mist hugs the mountains beyond the family's 850-acre farm.

Farley is the third generation to live off the land, but it's taken innovative thinking and long, hard work to stay here. A few years ago, 78-year-old James R. Bailey was trying to decide what to do with the farm that he and his wife, Gladys, bought in 1936. His grandson Terry Farley gave him the answer.

"I've always wanted to farm, and I've been farming with him for about 13 years. We formed a partnership in 1985 and then two years later we started looking into the specialty food business to diversify our farm and get more out of the products we were raising," said 32-year-old Farley.

In 1988 Farley and his wife, Diane, began Birch Creek Gourmets Inc., a pickled vegetable business. In a turn-of-the-century schoolhouse that works as a licensed kitchen, office, and warehouse, the family processes vegetables fresh from the fields, using recipes Diane developed. Their products feature mild vinegar so that the true vegetable flavor comes through and whole, not ground, spices so that the flavor permeates gradually and thoroughly.

They started making pickled asparagus but have since expanded with Spiced Dilly Beans, Sweet Asparagus Medley, Pickled Carrots, and Pickled Onions. Their products are sold at all Oregon Nordstrom stores, Made in Oregon shops, and at Strohecker's in Portland.

Food critics love these farm-fresh pickled veggies: Birch Creek Pickled Carrots were finalists in the hors d'oeuvres category at the 1991 National Association for Specialty Food trade show in New York City. But getting recognition doesn't make the work any less strenuous. "It's a challenge," Terry said. "But I like having my own business. And I don't mind hard work." It's not uncommon for the family to work 16-hour days during the peak harvesting season. Once the crops are harvested, the high season begins for pickling vegetables. To help with the workload, the farm employs five people, including Terry's uncle, Ron Farley, and his wife, Marlene. About 50 percent of the asparagus crop and 20 percent of the green beans grown on the farm are pickled. The carrots and onions come from local farmers.

"It's extremely tough to make a living on the farm anymore," Terry said. "A farm has to be very diversified, and you have to keep a fine line on the financing."

In the early years, James and Gladys Bailey grew wheat and barley and harvested it with a team of horses. Without irrigation, they had to rely strictly on Mother Nature's kindness. But the land was good to them, and the couple raised three children here. As the farm gets passed on to the next generation, Terry is thankful that Diane and their two children can continue the family tradition. And Diane credits James Bailey's support for making it possible.

"Grandpa Bailey was willing to take a chance to better the future of our family and our place on the farm for the next 50 years," she said. "Because of his love and support and encouragement, we were able to go ahead and pursue this dream."

"And of course, Mother Nature is always your silent partner," said Terry. "You just have to hope for the best and do the best job you can."

NancyAnn Mayer

Birch Creek Gourmets
Terry and Diane Farley
Milton-Freewater, Oregon
(503) 938-7782

Birch Creek products are sold in stores nationwide, including The Bon and Nordstrom in Washington and the Made in Oregon stores in Oregon.

ASPARAGUS FRITTATA

1 tablespoon olive oil
1 clove garlic, cut into 4 thin slices
6 spears asparagus, trimmed and cut diagonally into
    ½-inch pieces
¼ cup diced red bell pepper
4 large eggs
2 tablespoons grated Cheddar cheese
2 tablespoons grated Monterey Jack cheese
Salt and pepper to taste
2 tablespoons grated Parmesan cheese
Sour cream and chives, for garnish

Preheat broiler. Heat oil over moderate heat in an 8- or 9-inch nonstick sauté pan. Add garlic and cook until light brown. Do not burn. Discard garlic, and add asparagus and peppers to the oil. Sauté for a minute or so.

Mix the eggs in a bowl with Cheddar, Monterey Jack, salt, and pepper. Beat fairly well with a fork. Add the egg mixture to the sautéed vegetables and stir around in the pan a little. Cook over moderate heat, lifting the edges with a rubber spatula to allow egg on top to run underneath. When nearly set, but still moist, loosen from pan with spatula and slide onto a lightly oiled ovenproof plate.

Sprinkle with Parmesan cheese and place under broiler until top is golden brown and frittata puffs up.

Serve topped with a little sour cream and chives, and with boiled red potatoes with dill butter on the side.

Makes 2 generous servings.

Patit Creek
Dayton, Washington

GROCERIES

In the roadless canyon of the Snake River, we moved our sheep camps and supplies by horse or mule. Much of the trail along the river was a rocky ledge—a wall on the left, and on the right a sheer drop to the deep green river hissing past below. I led a string of seven mules.

In blue-brown November dusk I arrived at the ranch, where I would pick up supplies. Old Henry, the caretaker and irrigator, was gathering squash from his garden into a wheelbarrow. He asked me if I would eat winter squash. You bet, I said. He had bushels of butternuts, acorns, and turquoise sweetmeat squashes. I took two of each, thinking of how I would halve the small butternuts, scoop out the seeds, and bake them with butter and brown sugar.

Both herders had dictated their grocery lists to me out in camp. In the supply pantry of the main house, I lit a lantern, put two sets of plywood pack boxes before me on the floor, and scanned the lists. Like most packers I took satisfaction in handling groceries.

In a Snake River sheep camp in 1979, coffee and tobacco, flour, sugar, and evaporated milk, and ham and bacon were still basic supplies. We lived in canvas tents and cooked our food in iron pans on small sheet-metal woodstoves. The herders were old men.

In one of John's boxes I placed a 25-pound sack of white flour. Every other day John would bake an 8- by 10-inch pan full of lovely light sourdough biscuits in his tiny oven, and they would rise clear above the pan all around. Mac got two cartons of the biscuit mix he preferred. A sack of sugar and a three-pound can of coffee would suffice each camp for the 10 to 14 days between supply trips.

Although we had fresh elk meat in both camps, the herders liked their ham and bacon. Each would get part of a dry-cured smoked ham and a half-side of bacon. These were hard to find any more, but the watery modern versions just wouldn't keep. We hung them in cloth sacks on the north side of a tree. If mold grew on them we'd scrape it off and rub them with vinegar.

Canned goods, corn and milk and peas and peaches, formed the foundation of a well-packed box. In the gaps I placed glass jars of pickles and jam, home-canned tomatoes from Henry's garden, and bottles of ketchup. I would lift each box several times in the course of filling it, concentrating on its heft. Each box of a set has to weigh the same in order to balance on a mule.

Potatoes and onions and the squash went on top of the cans. Cartons of eggs, wrapped in clean gunnysacks that I hoarded for such uses, were nestled in carefully prepared spaces near the tops of the boxes. The weekly mailboat from Lewiston had brought us two letters. I read mine, and put Mac's in a plastic bag on top of the eggs.

In the morning I caught and saddled my packstring and slung the loaded boxes on them. I cast canvas tarps over the loads and tied diamond hitches over the tarps. By the barn I packed up mule-loads of alfalfa pellets for our horses and mules, and salt for the sheep.

The trail led me upriver in frost-filled shadows. Where it crossed a side creek I stopped at a patch of wild peppery watercress. A herd of elk had eaten through it recently, but I picked a good bunch from the upper end. Mules like watercress too, and they crowded in the shallow water to graze.

The sunlight crept down toward the river trail, clearing frost from the blond grass as it came. High up, the ridgetops were white with snow. I turned to watch the packstring behind me. Back along the bobbing mass of ears, canvas, and Manila rope, all my loads were riding level.

I remembered an abandoned homestead where two apple trees were heavy with fruit. I'd take a mule with empty boxes and fill them with apples. We would have plenty for eating and baking pies in our little square pans, some to treat our horses and mules, and I could bring some to Henry on my next trip to the ranch.

Peter Donovan

HARVESTING THE WHEAT

Jim and Geraine Hansen have a room in their basement that's probably bigger than your living room. Inside, large tables await a crowd. A commercial kitchen—the kind you'd find in a small restaurant—stands cold in a side alcove. Empty chairs circle the tables, enough for 20 men and women to elbow up for chow. On the door, carved in wood, is a sign: "Harvest Room." The room isn't old or dusty but, in a way, it's lonely.

"We'd hire all these kids, college kids mostly. We'd house them, feed them, work them. But it was great. We had a good time, just like a fraternity. Boy, I really miss that," says Jim Hansen.

Hansen isn't talking about the old days of his Depression childhood. He's remembering a time, not so long ago, when his six children were young. Hansen farmed his own land and also hired out as a contract harvester. He still does both. What's different is the machinery.

"We used to have nine combines and six or seven trucks. I'd hire a mechanic just to keep everything going. We'd get a cook for the harvest. We had to put in that kitchen.

"Now we have two combines. My daughter Mary runs one and I run the other. My son Norman has the tractor and bankout wagon. He hauls to two semis, and they haul it down to a river port. That's all it takes, but we can cut as much wheat as we did twenty years ago."

For 68 years Jim Hansen has had the ideal window seat on changing agricultural technology, a wheat farm on Coppei Mountain near Waitsburg.

Hansen's grandfather, Robert Leid, bought 160 acres of land in 1889 from the Semple family for $2,500 in gold coin. Leid cleared the land with muscle—human and animal—and began to put his stamp on the place.

"He was a big, big Scotsman. He worked hard," says Hansen. "He expected people to work that way, and his horses. But he fed good. He'd dump five gallons of oats to each horse when they were working.

"You hear about the Scots, how they're supposed to be so cheap. I don't think he was cheap, just frugal."

Leid ended up with three separate farms, one for each of his children. Life was still relatively primitive on all three during the 1930s.

"We did have running water. He had a windmill and built a cistern to hold the water. But we had outside toilets."

For meals there was meat, potatoes, gravy, beans, and homemade bread—and even more of it during harvest time.

"I still remember those tremendous meals, my mother working straight through to feed the crew," Hansen says. "We just didn't have the equipment in those days, so that meant a lot of hard labor."

The crews, many of them Dust Bowl refugees, earned 35 cents an hour and paid 35 cents a meal. "They didn't have much money, so most of them would only have one meal a day at noon. But they'd come in and eat three meals' worth during that one."

Hansen attended what was then called Washington State College in Pullman, and he joined the Army during World War II. He came back to the shoulders of the Blue Mountains, married Geraine, and started looking around.

"When we first got married, I said, 'What do you want to do?' " said Geraine. "He wanted to be a farmer. 'Well,' I said, 'We'd better get started.' "

They started from scratch, leasing some eroded land in 1947. "I never inherited one acre. I bought every acre I own," Jim says. They now own about 2,300 acres, as well as renting the old Leid home place, which has remained in a family trust. At first it was much the same kind of farming that had been going on since part of Coppei Mountain was first cleared. The Hansens had a tractor, but they still tilled the land without fertilizer or chemicals.

"It was hard work. It seemed like we were always busy. I'm sure glad we're not doing it now," Geraine says.

It was a major battle simply to reclaim the gullied land. "I remember having to cross some ditches that were 25 feet deep. Huge things," Hansen said.

But the same rain that dug the ditches became an ally in fighting erosion. The Coppei area gets an average of about 25 inches of rain a year, nearly as much as Seattle. It allowed the Hansens to forego the traditional fallow periods, when the land is bare and most vulnerable to wind and water.

Hansen switched to a chisel plow, which disturbs the soil less than the moldboard plow, and he left the plant refuse from the previous year on the soil as mulch instead of burning it. "I don't have ditches any more," he says.

The relatively wet slopes of the Coppei also offered Hansen the chance to follow in the footsteps of his father and grandfather and do custom harvesting. The extra moisture means they harvest later than their neighbors. "We'd go out and help with harvest someplace else, and then come back here and take care of our own crop. Once it started, it just kept right on growing."

By the mid-1960s the Hansens had a fleet of trucks and a conga line of nine combines moving across the fields. They had the Harvest Room, full of tired—but happy—young people.

But technology has a way of turning on its past accomplishments, of gobbling up tradition. Two behemoths now do the work of nine combines. One wheat buggy has replaced a fleet of trucks. The big machines have removed the bone-numbing toil from farming, but they have also cut away some of the humanness.

"Those boys and girls we used to have—it was like a big family. I miss it."

Don McManman
Adapted from the Walla Walla Union-Bulletin Ag Review

THE WOOLLY RUMPUSES OF LA GRANDE

Herding sheep gives the mind some room to unwind. Nancy Dake knows this, for she and her husband, Ron, have spent many days—spring, summer, fall, and winter—herding a flock of sheep on foot, raising lamb for meat and sheep for wool. Tending sheep has even moved Nancy to write poetry.

Does the dust have a lasting soul and if so
Is that why it settles every chance it gets
On the skin of every inch I dare expose.

When Ron and Nancy Dake moved to Oregon from sunny San Diego in 1971, looking for a life close to the land, they slowly gravitated to the eastern half of the state. There they met up with old-time sheep ranchers like Jack Shumway, who provided a romantic link to the days when eastern Oregon was a power in the nation's sheep industry. It wasn't long before the Dakes were building a flock of their own.

Today the Dakes raise sheep near the town of La Grande, in the Grande Ronde Valley of northeastern Oregon. Their 200-acre ranch of bottomland pasture, with swayback barn and all, sits at 2,700 feet. The Blue Mountains rise to the west, the Wallowas to the east. "It's not a prime sheep ranching area, but that has advantages," says Nancy. "We have a monopoly of sorts."

The Dakes' operation, named Grande Ron Lamb (a play on words that Ron especially appreciates), has grown to 350 ewes. Making a living strictly as sheep ranchers is a challenge in the modern day, but the Dakes have learned to make the most of their relatively small flock. They focus on both wool and meat production and have learned some cost-saving tricks through the years—like wintering their flock near the town of Wallula, Washington, on the Columbia River, for example. "In the winter we put them on corn stubble, or what's left of other vegetable crops in the Columbia Basin," explains Nancy. "It saves on feed costs, and the sheep love it."

At other times of the year the Dakes's flock stays in La Grande, where the pasture diet consists primarily of clover and grass. The menu occasionally includes sage or potatoes, and Nancy says they would like to experiment with alfalfa, spinach, radishes, and silage (which is concentrated feed). "Sheep are picky eaters, but the idea is that you want good lambs to build your reputation," says Nancy. The idea is also to raise the best meat possible.

Ewes lamb in the spring, and six months later the lambs are ready to be sold for meat and pelts (in the United States there is not much of a market for mature sheep meat, or mutton). Strong ewes breed good lambs, and good lambs bring a higher price on the meat market. That is what's behind the fancy diets and loving attention the Dakes give their flock. The couple tend their sheep on foot because "it's healthy," Ron explains. They look for help from their three border collies and two sheep guard dogs.

The Dakes breed Polypay ewes with Suffolk rams in the fall. Breeding goes on for 30 days, so that the lambing period—starting in mid-March—is also 30 days. Each ewe/lamb pair gets an individual pen for about a day, moves to small groups for around 10 days, and then goes out to pasture with a group of about 100 head. The lambs are weaned and marketed in August.

The Dakes sell their lambs to buyers at auction yards or to a small group of producers. "The market is fairly small," Nancy notes, touching on a sore point with many sheep ranchers.

"Lamb is thought of as a gourmet specialty product in this country, but that gourmet price certainly doesn't come to the producer." said Nancy. "We've got to figure out a way to market directly to consumers."

The Dakes would like to head in that direction. Nancy is currently working to put together a list of other Oregon sheep ranchers who want a direct-market approach. In the meantime, the Dakes are busy enjoying their sheep-ranching.

Facing front do you remember her?
Turn around resembling a tide of woolly rumpus
Marching to the rhythm in their band.

Michael Page-English

Grande Ron Lamb
Nancy and Ron Dake
66105 Hunter Road, La Grande, Oregon
(503) 963-7812
Call to arrange a tour.

LAMB

Of all the animal flesh, furred or feathered, eaten by man, not alone for nourishment but also for purely gustatory reasons, lamb deserves to be placed at the head of the list. Whether the flesh of lamb is roasted or pan-fried in the skillet or made into a stew, the preferred flavoring agents, in addition to salt and pepper, are garlic, fresh rosemary, capers, parsley, lemon juice, olive oil, and dry vermouth. For a leg of lamb roast proceed thus: Remove the bone. In the resulting cavity, spread 2 tablespoons of the following all coarsely minced together: 3 cloves of garlic, a dozen capers, leaves of parsley and rosemary. Salt and pepper. Sprinkle over the whole a tablespoon of olive oil, the juice of half a lemon. Add a sacramental spray of dry vermouth. Enfold the bone in the cavity, tie the whole securely with heavy twine. Roast it medium-rare in a 350°F oven in a pan just large enough to contain it. Baste occasionally with its own juices enriched with a bit of vermouth. You are not likely to find this recipe in any of the cookbooks.

Nor the following, but have faith in Pellegrini: Place lamb shanks or ribs in an iron skillet in the oven preheated to 375°F. When about half done, drain out all the fat. Sprinkle with olive oil; add coarsely cut garlic, a few sprigs of rosemary, a squirt or two of lemon juice fired with a squirt of Tabasco. Salt and pepper to taste. Give the skillet a thoroughly professional shake, return it to the oven, and reduce the heat to 300°F. In a few minutes the ribs will be done. The shanks will require more time.

For lamb chops and steak: Mince finely garlic and rosemary. Put in a small bowl, add olive oil and lemon juice. Remove what fat you can from the chops, rub them with this mixture, salt and pepper to taste, and cook them in a skillet rubbed with butter. When about done, spray them lightly with vermouth.

For a fricassee or stew, cut neck bones and meat from the shoulder in small pieces. Dust them with flour flavored with salt, pepper, and curry powder. Using a heavy skillet, brown them in olive oil. Remove them with a slotted spoon onto a dish. In the same skillet, with no additional fat, sauté onion, celery, carrot, and potato, all coarsely chopped and in what quantity desired. To a cup of stock add a squirt of Tabasco, the juice of half a lemon, 2 tablespoons of tomato sauce, and a scant teaspoon of arrowroot for thickening. Stir well and pour over the sauté. The sauce should be dense but fluid. If too dense, add some vermouth. If too fluid, add more arrowroot. Return the meat to the skillet, mix thoroughly, clamp on the lid, and simmer over low heat for 5 or so minutes.

Angelo Pellegrini
Vintage Pellegrini

U-PICK FARMS AND ROADSIDE STANDS

U-Pick Guidelines: Call first, especially near the beginning and end of the season. Find out if your small children are welcome to help pick. Farms will supply picking containers, but you will need bags or boxes to transport your produce home. Pick carefully and conscientiously; a well-tended berry field or orchard represents years of knowledgeable labor. (Dogs should stay in the car.)

Harvests may vary greatly from year to year. A local chamber of commerce or county extension office can often supply up-to-date seasonal information. Also, many newspapers publish local farm maps in the late spring or summer.

MALHEUR COUNTY, OREGON

Terry Tallman ✱ **(503) 339-3785**
706 Mount Hood, Boardman
July–September: daily, 9am–6pm.
Melons, flowers, other produce.

From I-84 take exit 165. Go ¼ mile south on Laurel Lane, look for signs.

Ontario Produce ✱ **(503) 889-6485**
The Nagaki brothers
44 SE 9th Avenue, Ontario
August–March: Monday–Friday, 8am–5pm; Saturday, noon–1pm.

This packing operation sells mostly wholesale, but will retail onions and onion gift packs if you drop by.

Take exit 376 off I-84. Go west on Idaho Avenue, turn left onto Oregon Avenue, and go to the end of the street.

UMATILLA COUNTY, OREGON

Spring Creek of Paradox Farm ✱
(503) 278-0300
Larry Stevens
Adams
Call ahead for hours.

Certified organic cantaloupe, crenshaw, gallicum, and honeydew melons.

Call for directions.

Anastasio's ✱ **(503) 567-5389**
Tom Ikonomou
Hermiston
Call ahead for hours.

Organically grown melons, U-pick or ready-picked.

A couple of miles north of Hermiston; call for directions.

UNION COUNTY, OREGON

Don and Mary Calder ✱ **(503) 963-7906**
1301 O Avenue, La Grande
Call ahead for hours.

Winter squash, pickling cucumbers, green beans, raspberries, and cherries. They're waiting for a patent on a new breed of sweet cherry that's self-pollinating and great for cold climates.

On I-84 in La Grande.

Grande Ron Lamb ✱ **(503) 963-7812**
Nancy and Ron Dake
66105 Hunter Road, La Grande
Call to arrange a tour of their sheep farm.

Singletree Farm ✱ **(503) 562-5247**
Dan and Cindy Sharratt
309 W Fir, Union
Call ahead.

Organic produce includes potatoes, onions, beans, peas, beets, corn, berries, and apples.

Call for directions.

WALLOWA COUNTY, OREGON

Bade's Bee Farm, Inc ☆ (503) 938-5378
Danny P. Bade
Triangle Station Road, Milton-Freewater
Year-round: Monday–Friday, 10am–5pm; call for after-hours service.

Raw, pure honey, packaged at the farm. Customers can bring their own containers and fill from bulk tank.

Three miles west of Highway 11 on Umapine Highway; take Umapine Highway to Triangle Station Road.

Birch Creek Gourmets ☆ (503) 938-7782
Terry and Diana Farley
Milton-Freewater

Pickled vegetables, fresh from their fields, include asparagus, dilly beans, carrots, and onions. Birch Creek products are sold in stores nationwide, including The Bon in Washington and Nordstroms and the Made in Oregon Stores in Oregon.

Edwards Family Farm ☆ (503) 938-5933 or (509) 558-3896
Old Walla Walla Highway, Milton-Freewater
August–October: daily, daylight hours.

Vegetables, melons, apples, Bartlett pears, fresh cider.

On the Old Walla Walla Highway in Milton-Freewater between Ballou Street and Ferndale Road.

Grant's Orchard ☆ (503) 938-5826
Bill Grant
Sunnyside Road, Milton-Freewater
July–October: daily, daylight hours.

Apricots, prunes, Delicious apples.

Sunnyside Road, 3 miles west of Milton-Freewater drive-in theater.

Lefore Orchards ☆ (503) 938-4744
John Lefore
Old Milton-Freewater Highway, Milton-Freewater
In season: Sunday–Friday.

Apples and holiday gift boxes.

Roadside stand at the city limits on Old Milton-Freewater Highway. Boxed fruit available at orchard (call for directions).

Reese Orchards ☆ (503) 938-5018
James Reese
Umapine Highway, Milton-Freewater
In season: daily, daylight hours on weekends; call for weekday hours.

U-pick or boxed sweet and pie cherries, boxed apples; self-service cider sales—fresh October–January, frozen year-round.

Two miles west on Umapine Highway from new Walla Walla Highway.

Zerba Gardens and Produce Outlet ☆ (503) 938-6031
Cecil and Marilyn Zerba
New Walla Walla Highway, Milton-Freewater
In season: daily, all day.

Produce stand specializing in local crops and plants.

One mile north of Milton-Freewater at Highway 11 and Sunnyside Road.

ADAMS COUNTY, WASHINGTON

Jay Faix and Sons ☆ (509) 488-9585

850 S Highway 17, Othello
Mid-July until frost: call for availability.

Roadside stand with cantaloupe, seedless and regular watermelons, strawberries, blackberries, raspberries, sweet corn, and other produce. Also sells at Moses Lake Farmers Market.

Call for directions.

BENTON COUNTY, WASHINGTON

Perseus Gourmet Vinegars ☆ (509) 582-2434
Kay Roth and Penny Morgan
1426 E 3rd, #8, Kennewick
Year-round: Monday–Friday, 8am–4pm.

Herbal vinegars, including Sabroso (peppers and herbs) and Sageberry (sage, cranberry, and shallot); fruit vinegars (blueberry, peach-ginger, raspberry, and apple mint); balsamic vinegar; and olive oil (flavored and plain). Small retail shop at the warehouse, or available by mail at P.O. Box 6994, Kennewick, WA 99336.

Take Columbia Drive exit off Highway 395 and follow to Gum Street. Turn right on Gum toward Finley and bear left onto 3rd after road narrows.

COLUMBIA COUNTY, WASHINGTON

Mustard Bumper Crop Company ☆
(509) 382-4028
Chuck and Nancy Turner
406 South 2nd Street
Dayton, WA 99328

Mail-order source for mustard made from home-grown barley. This sweet-hot mustard, prepared from Nancy's grandmother's recipe, is said to in-hibit cholesterol and comes either prepared or dry—just add vinegar.

FRANKLIN COUNTY, WASHINGTON

Gray's Farms ☆ (509) 297-4305
820 Juniper Street,
Mesa, WA 99343

Mail-order source for five soups: asparagus, broccoli, cauliflower, country bean, and split pea.

WALLA WALLA COUNTY, WASHINGTON

Cavalli's Onion Acres ☆ (509) 520-1377
Ben Cavalli, Jr.
960 Wallula Road, Walla Walla
Mid-June–October: daily, all day. Call ahead for large orders.

Walla Walla Sweets (and cookbooks for them), winter onions, garlic, radishes, and spinach.

Roadside stand at northeast corner of Wallula and Campbell roads.

Gardeners Market ☆
(509) 525-7070 or (800) 553-5014
205 N 11th Avenue
Walla Walla, WA 99362

Year-round: Monday–Saturday, 9am–6pm; Sunday, noon–5pm.

A little store with fresh produce and Italian spe-cialties. The Walla Walla Gardeners Association—the market's parent organization—also sells the famous onions by mail in 10- and 20-pound boxes.

Behind Carroll Adams tractor dealership on Rose Street.

Robison Ranch ☆ (800) 525-3699
Walla Walla
In season: Monday–Friday, 7am–5pm.

The Robisons have been farming in the Walla Walla Valley since 1918. In addition to wheat and barley, they produce specialty lines of pickles: asparagus, Rainier cherries, green beans, pep-pers, Walla Walla Sweets, and shallots. Fresh shallots available for cooking or for seed.

Take 2nd Street exit off Highway 12 and turn north; stay right at the Y. Next sign is for Rees Avenue. Cross, go straight up the hill (you'll see a dead end sign), and the farm is at the top.

Stiller Farms ☆ (509) 525-5079
Ed and Marianne Stiller
Highway 12, Walla Walla
April–November: daily, daylight–dark.

Selling asparagus, tomatoes, and both winter and Walla Walla Sweet onions for 30 years.

On Highway 12, 7 miles west of Walla Walla. Look for big sign.

Gene Tom ☆ (509) 529-4934
Walla Walla
In season: daily, daylight hours; call ahead for availability and large orders.

Walla Walla Sweets, winter onions, Asian vegeta-bles. Minimum onion order is 25 pounds.

First place west of Highway 12 bypass, near Pendleton and Dell Avenue intersection.

WHITMAN COUNTY, WASHINGTON

WSU Creamery ☆ (509) 335-4014
Washington State University
Pullman, WA 99164

Year-round: Monday–Friday, 9:30am–4:30pm.

WSU's canning method allows their Cougar Gold (a full-bodied aged cheese) and Viking (milder, creamy) cheeses to be made without preservatives. The cheese is sold by mail; WSU Creamery cheeses, ice cream, and milkshakes are available at Ferdinands, a campus eatery. One of the last campus creameries around.

From Spokane, take Highway 195, turn off at Pullman exit. Follow signs to Stadium Way.

FARMERS MARKETS

UNION COUNTY, OREGON

Blue Mountain Producers Co-op, La Grande
Contact: Jenny Nicholson, (503) 963-8049
Mid-June–September: Saturday (weather permitting), 9am–1:30pm.

Featured crops are cherries, sweet corn and carrots, Mount Adams huckleberries, and "eleven different members of the onion family." The market has been going since 1980 and is a good place to meet growers.

Sunflower Book Store lawn, 1114 Washington Avenue.

MALHEUR COUNTY, OREGON

Cairo Farmers Market
Contact: Richard Bunn, (503) 889-5531
Year-round: Monday–Saturday, 8am–8pm; Sunday, 10am–5pm.

Local produce, including onions, potatoes, squash, beans, and fruit. Ready-picked.

At the Cairo Junction on Highway 201 between Ontario and Nyssa.

BENTON COUNTY, WASHINGTON

Kennewick Central Open Air Market
Contact: Randy Rutherford, (509) 582-7221
Mid-July–October: Saturday, 8am–noon.

Corner of Benton and Kennewick streets.

FRANKLIN COUNTY, WASHINGTON

Pasco Farmers Market
Contact: Jeanene Landby, (509) 545-0738
May–November: Wednesday and Saturday, 9am–sellout; Thursday, 4pm–sellout.

4th between Lewis and Columbia.

9

SOUTHERN OREGON

The coastal mountains of southern Oregon do more than provide craggy vistas. Blocking the cool air that moderates the climate of the Willamette Valley to the north, they bring hot summers and dry winters to the area around Grants Pass and Medford. The contrast between the thin coastal strip west of the Klamath Mountains and the inland valleys is dramatic.

Drive along the southern coast and you'll see fields of flowers. Most of the Easter lilies sold in the United States are grown here, along with azaleas and other nursery crops. Miles of sand dunes, and the strong winds that drive them, restrict the opportunities for agriculture, although the area around

Bandon supports both dairy farms and cranberry bogs.

The Coast Range itself is traversed by rivers that find their way through rugged canyons. Here and there the steep terrain gives way to a plateau, and in season you'll see rows of corn, tomato plants, and even crenshaw melons nurtured by the proprietors of wild-river fishing lodges.

Once you traverse the initial range of mountains, you come to the fertile western Oregon valleys that spelled "home" to the weary pioneers who journeyed to Oregon more than a century ago, traveling by covered wagon over the Oregon and Applegate trails. The valleys are still fertile today, home to

pear orchards, vineyards, gardens growing a myriad of vegetables, and small cottage industries producing everything from pesto to garlic greens to gourmet lettuce. Some foods, such as blackberries, grow so abundantly that they are treated as weeds.

Farther east the Cascade Range divides western Oregon from the eastern two-thirds of the state. The growing season is shorter at these higher elevations, but backyard gardens are still in evidence, as are wild crops such as huckleberries. Glacial runoff 150,000 years ago eroded the canyons of western Oregon that would later become the channels of such rivers as the Rogue and Umpqua. Violent volcanic activity also helped create the Cascade topography. Some 7,500 years ago, Mount Mazama blew its top, creating the body of water known today as Crater Lake. Southeast of Bend, the Newberry Crater is testament to eruptions 6,000 years ago and again as recently as 1,300 years ago. Great stretches of volcanic pumice, some of it more than 50 feet thick, create surreal landscapes where little can grow, but the weathered minerals from older eruptions contribute to the region's fine soil. Where there is water, the plateaus of south-central Oregon produce fine examples of the American classics—beef and potatoes.

The first residents of southwest Oregon were the Native Americans who originally had migrated across the Bering Strait from Mongolia about 11,000 years ago. They lived for centuries along the rivers and on the coast, thriving mainly on salmon and a cereal meal they made from acorns.

Then, in 1827, a Hudson's Bay Company trapper named Peter Skene Ogden made the circuit through what is now Bend, Klamath Falls, and Medford. The British controlled the Pacific Northwest at that time, and Ogden's mission was to so deplete southern Oregon rivers of beaver that American trappers coming north from California would think the territory worthless and turn back.

The ploy obviously didn't work. Settlers arrived from the East and from California, bringing livestock and seed and combined those resources with the abundant native foods. They settled the lowlands first, and by the 1880s families were searching out the fertile pockets along the upper Rogue River.

Today, the Rogue River Valley is the center of the region's food production, and Medford, the area's largest city, is the pear capital of this part of the world. Only the Hood River region grows more pears. Yellow-white blossoms cover acres of orchards in the spring, just in time for the annual Pear Blossom Festival.

Pears rank seventh in gross sales among Oregon agricultural commodities, according to the Oregon State University Extension Service, behind cattle, farm forestry, nursery crops, dairy, wheat, and potatoes. Medford is the home of Harry and David and of Pinnacle Fruit, two mail-order giants whose specialty is pears.

Pears are the big industry, but a myriad of other foods are grown in Jackson County. Rising Sun Farm, south of Ashland, produces pesto and flavored vinegars, while Foxtail Farms, near Shady Cove, has nurtured the tayberry,

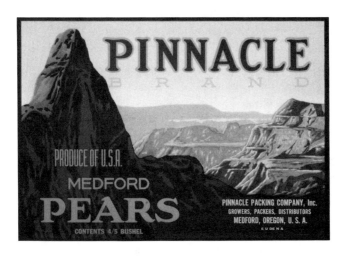

a cross between a blackberry and raspberry. Butte Creek Mill in Eagle Point, built in 1872, is a leading producer of gourmet flour from Jackson County grains.

A growing industry in both Jackson and Josephine counties is wine. Seven wineries bottle varietals in the two-county area. More than 50 vineyards raise wine grapes. Cabernet Sauvignon is a local specialty, as the grapes respond well to the area's hot summers.

In Josephine County, grains, tree fruits, and field crops are the leading harvests, although none are grown in great abundance. Grants Pass is the home of numerous cottage industries, producing garlic greens, soup mixes, and mustard. Windy River Farm has attracted regional attention as a grower and processor of herbs.

Coastal Curry County grows some small fruits and berries as well as backyard vegetables, but agricultural land is at a premium. Plots are tucked in here and there. Take a jet boat ride up the Rogue River and you'll see the cornfields at Lucas Lodge, a rare level spot in the otherwise steep canyon 32 miles upriver from the ocean. The lodge, built in 1916, serves meals to hundreds of boat passengers on summer days. Come mid-August, homegrown produce makes it to the table.

The sights, elevation, and crops change as you head east across the Cascades into Klamath and Lake counties. Rainfall decreases sharply. Douglas fir forests give way to ponderosa pine and sagebrush. The growing season becomes shorter due to the higher elevation of the terrain, much of it at 4,000 feet or above. Although the climate is more severe and the markets more distant, the land offers compensations to the farmers who understand it. Here ranching is the main enterprise.

"Oregon ranch country in early summer is unbelievably beautiful—no skies so blue, no sun so bright," wrote Dorothy Lawson McCall, remembering her introduction to central Oregon as a bride in 1911. "First-cutting alfalfa is just beginning to blossom, fence high and emerald green, with millions of butterflies fluttering over the purple buds. Great, thriving ranches sprawl on both sides of the road all the way into town." Later, one of McCall's sons, Tom, would bring his ranch-bred independence to bear as one of Oregon's most memorable and popular governors.

Cleve Twitchell
Medford, Oregon

MELONS

Melons and clouds don't mix. That's why most of the melons grown in the Pacific Northwest are nurtured in areas where the summer climate is sunny, hot, and dry, like the interior valleys of southwest Oregon.

Melons—cantaloupes, crenshaws, watermelons, and honeydews—all thrive on heat. "I've got to have the heat to get the flavor," says Willard Lucas of Lucas Lodge at Agness, on the lower Rogue River, about 32 miles inland from the Pacific Ocean.

"The hotter the better," agrees Mike Gallagher of Gallagher Family Farm near Grants Pass, who grows melons along with other produce and sells them at farmers markets. He sees a correlation between heat and the sweetness of the melon.

Lucas Lodge, founded in 1916, serves meals to thousands of jet boat travelers each summer. Along about the middle of August, the fare starts to include homegrown cantaloupes and crenshaws.

Lucas grows his melons on a half-acre patch near the river. He buys melon plants grown by a nursery in Grants Pass and gets them in the ground by early June.

"I've found it best to grow from plants; otherwise the blue jays, coons, and weather can be a problem," says Lucas. By July, daytime high temperatures often reach the 95° to 102° range, ideal melon-ripening weather. If it gets much hotter than 102°, watch out, says Lucas. The melons may suffer from sunburn.

Lucas picks melons each night to be served to guests the next day.

"A melon often will ripen overnight. It can be ripe one evening and overripe the next," he says. "A lot of it is picking at the right moment." He is fussy and rejects one melon in ten.

Lucas faces one problem that may be peculiar to his area. Both deer and bear are abundant in the vicinity, and they both love melons. The melon garden is fenced. That keeps the deer out but not the bear. If a bear gets in and eats a melon or two, he may then lie down on top of the plants, take a nap, and kill everything underneath his body.

Another bit of advice from Lucas on growing good melons: "Don't water them. Never touch them with water."

Gallagher agrees on that point and elaborates. Melon plants have deep roots and can get the water they need on their own. Watering a melon plant excessively cools it off, and the melons won't grow as fast. Watering may also cause the roots to stay closer to the surface, hindering the plant's ability to draw water from deeper underground.

Rogue Berries

The Ditsworth strawberries were of such fabulous quality that people still talk about them, 30 years after the last crop was harvested. Frank Ditsworth always denied that he ever insulted the virgin soil with commerical fertilizer, but Leo Hoag came upon him one day laying a thin streak of superphosphate along the rows. Embarrassed, Frank insisted that his young neighbor keep his secret. Even during the Depression, people drove many miles for the privilege of picking their own berries from the Ditsworth fields, but Frank never allowed them into the patch until the best of the crop had been gathered by his own pickers. On weekends in late June, as many as a hundred visitors lounged in their cars or in the shade of the great oaks, waiting for permission to "U-pick."

The season lasted about four weeks, from early June until just after the Fourth of July. During this time we toiled up and down the endless rows, dragging our carriers along and snipping the tough stems with stained fingernails. The sun burned our arms and backs. Strawberry picking is absorbing for a while, then tedious, and finally backbreaking. Growers usually close the fields in midafternoon because the mounting heat, strain, and monotony make the pickers careless....

At the time we worked for them, the Ditsworths paid their pickers 25 cents for a clean, full-weight, 12-cup crate. An average picker could fill a crate in an hour.

Wallace Ohrt
The Rogue I Remember

Gallagher, who has been growing melons for 20 years, plants them in mounds. He says the mounds hold in heat at night and encourage faster growth. If you must water the plants, do so around the mounds, he suggests.

Gallagher raises cantaloupes, watermelons, crenshaws, and honeydews, several varieties of each, figuring that if one doesn't do well in a particular year, another will. He develops his own plants from seeds in a greenhouse. He starts moving the young plants out into the garden in early May, letting them sit outside in their greenhouse box for a week or so first so that they gradually adjust to the colder temperature. He plants groups of crops every week for two months. In most years, melons planted in late May or early June catch up to the early-May crop, but once in a while a warm spring helps those early plantings earn him a head start at the market.

Growing seasons vary from 65 days for the smaller cantaloupes to 95 days for watermelons. And that means good-quality growing days, Gallagher finds. A few days of clouds or rain can put melon growth on hold. Gallagher and Lucas agree that the effort is worth it. A vine-ripened homegrown southwest Oregon melon, they say, is "just fantastic."

Cleve Twitchell

Gallagher Family Farm
Mike Gallagher
6968 New Hope Road, Grants Pass
(503) 479-5438
February–Thanksgiving: Monday–Friday and sometimes Saturday, 9am–6pm.
Take Highway 238 south out of Grants Pass for 2 miles. New Hope Road is on the right; farm is 3½ miles out.

ROAST DUCKLING WITH ROGUE VALLEY BARTLETT PEARS

Pears are one of the few fruits that ripen to perfection only after they have been harvested. Ripen pears at room temperature; they are ready to eat when they become slightly soft at the stem.

6 fresh Bartlett pears
1 tablespoon lemon juice
1 cup pear nectar, divided
6 tablespoons Oregon pear brandy, divided
2 ducklings (4½ pounds each)
½ cup sugar
½ cup white wine
½ cup pear or raspberry vinegar

2 cups brown stock or duck stock
2 tablespoons arrowroot
1 tablespoon lemon juice
1½ ounces Chambord liqueur

Peel and core pears. Arange in a saucepan and cover with water to which 1 tablespoon of lemon juice has been added. Poach in this mixture until tender, 5 to 9 minutes. Let cool in liquid. Drain. Cover pears with ½ cup of the nectar, 3 tablespoons of Oregon pear brandy, and water to cover, and cool 2 hours or overnight.

Preheat oven to 325°F.

Truss ducklings with kitchen twine, and prick the skin with the tip of a sharp knife to release fat. Place each duckling on its side in a roasting rack over a pan with 1 inch of water in the bottom. Cook for 45 minutes, then turn duckling to its other side and cook for 45 more minutes. Turn ducklings breast up and cook for approximately 1 hour longer until meat is tender and skin is crisp. Remove from oven and keep warm.

For the sauce, combine the sugar, white wine, vinegar, and ½ cup nectar in a heavy-bottomed saucepan. Bring to a boil over high heat, and reduce until liquid is a light syrup. Add brown stock and reduce liquid again by half. Mix arrowroot with a little cold water until a smooth paste forms. Stir into sauce along with lemon juice, Chambord, and remaining 3 tablespoons pear brandy. Bring to a boil and cook until thickened slightly. Strain, and serve to accompany carved ducklings. For garnish, cut poached pears to form fans around ducklings.

Serves 6.

Chateaulin Restaurant
Ashland, Oregon

WINDY RIVER FARM

Judy Weiner and her husband, Peter Liebes, enjoy gourmet cookery, but for a long time had trouble finding good herbs.

In 1980, they decided to grow their own.

The result is Windy River Farm, a 25-acre agricultural enterprise along the Rogue River, about 13 miles west of Grants Pass in southwestern Oregon. Here the Weiners grow herbs, vegetables, and fruits. They also produce herbal teas, herb vinegars, dried fruits and vegetables, and skin care products for market.

They wholesale their products, under the label Cottage Garden, to a few stores in nearby towns, but concentrate on direct sales to the consumer, through mail order, booths at local farmers markets, and a gift shop at the farm.

A key ingredient here is an emphasis on good health. "We are definitely involved with health. That's our theme," says Weiner. And the couple doesn't want to be stingy with their knowledge. They hold frequent tours and workshops designed to teach others how to grow healthy herbs and produce, and how to plant gardens that will "sustain them through the year."

Herbs are the main concern at Windy River Farm. Weiner says the problem with many supermarket herb stocks is that the herbs are grown in other countries, are dirty, and are sprayed with pesticides and then fumigated.

"A lot can be hidden in an herb jar," says Weiner. "It's really important to know where your food comes from." Windy River Farm was among the first Oregon farms to be certified by Oregon Tilth, an organic farming group whose guidelines include crop rotation as a means to enhance the natural nitrogen cycle and to promote high levels of biological activity in the soil. The Weiners achieve this by using compost and planting "green manure" cover crops such as an oat and pea mix or fava beans to enrich their soil.

Walk around through the demonstration gardens here and sniff the herb plants. The aromas are vibrant. And the dried herbs smell almost as pungent in the jar.

"People are overwhelmed by our aromas and flavors," Weiner says.

The farm uses a solar dryer. Weiner says the secret is to dry herbs at a low temperature and in low light. "Light is very destructive to herbs," she says.

While herbs like basil, oregano, mint, and thyme are bottled and sold singly, Windy River Farm produces nine different blends: English, French, Greek, Italian, Mexican, Riviera, Scandia, Sweet Spice, and Thai. These blends are called sprinkles.

The Thai sprinkle, for example, contains lemon basil, mint, garlic, chili, and peppers. In the Mexican sprinkle, you'll find oregano, tomatillo, tomato, onion, parsley, cayenne,

coriander, lovage, and bay. And in the Sweet Spice are orange balsam, thyme, sweet marjoram, spice basil, sage, and rosemary. The farm grows six different kinds of basil. Although some herb producers market one blend for poultry, another for fish, and still another for salad, Weiner advocates a different approach. "Season by the country, not the food," she advises. Thus, you can use the Cottage Garden Italian Sprinkle on spaghetti, veal parmesan, or antipasto salad.

Weiner passes along one culinary secret: Sprinkle herbs into food shortly before serving, not earlier in the cooking process. Why? With a few exceptions, such as bay, herbs lose their potency the longer you cook them.

As Windy River Farm continues to catch the attention of regional agricultural groups and the southern Oregon public, Weiner says, "It's really fun to turn people on to good food."

Cleve Twitchell

Windy River Farm
Peter Liebes and Judy Weiner
348 Hussey Lane, Grants Pass
(503) 476-8979
June–October: Tuesday–Thursday, call ahead.
Call for directions.

PURPLE POTATOES

"A potato is pretty much a potato," says Jim Baggenstos, a potato grower in Sherwood, Oregon, and potato consumers would more or less agree. What's more basic than a potato?

But in the aisles of supermarkets, at weekend farmers markets, and in the produce sections of natural food stores, Oregon and Washington potato customers are beginning to wonder. *Is* a potato a potato anymore? What about these purple potatoes, yellow potatoes, and red potatoes?

Slowly at first, and more frequently in recent years, specialty potatoes are making their way into grocery store bins throughout the Pacific Northwest. Consumer interest has been tweaked by these tuberous novelties, and produce managers are warming up to the idea of stocking a bin full of purple potatoes next to the bin of standard Russets.

Indeed, specialty potatoes may someday change the face of the giant potato industry of Oregon and Washington. But Yellow Finns aren't going to take over any time soon. For now, specialty potatoes are a very small and quiet revolution.

As one of just a handful of specialty potato growers in Oregon and Washington, Baggenstos is well aware of this. The Sherwood farmer has grown more fresh-market specialty potatoes—Yukon Gold, Red Norland, Desiree, All-Blue, LaSoda, Sangre—than anyone else in Oregon. But now he grows just 3 acres of All-Blues potatoes on a 300-acre farm.

Call the department of agriculture in either state, and you'll have a hard time finding out anything about specialty potatoes. "We don't keep stats on crops that small," says Patsy Chandler at Oregon's agricultural statistics office.

So think of specialty potatoes as a small but interesting crop. Baggenstos says he first got into specialty potatoes five years ago when he was reading a potato industry magazine. There was an article about All-Blue potatoes, a purple-skinned, purple-fleshed variety grown in the Pacific Northwest. It occurred to Baggenstos that he could expand his market with some experimentation.

"I called the local extension agent and tracked down a seed source for All-Blues," he said. "Then I researched the market to see how receptive it was. I grew about an acre the first year and I sold them all."

This encouraged him to grow more varieties and acres of specialty potatoes during ensuing seasons, with modest success, but Baggenstos says the specialty potato market is still peanuts compared to the overall potato market. "Growing specialty pota-toes doesn't always work out. You can plant them, but you better have a market for them. Most produce managers aren't willing to move these."

Scott Fenters, a potato farmer in Malin, Oregon, who specializes in seed potato sales, backs that up. "It's the kind of crop," he says, "that if everybody put in an acre or two you better make sure the pigs like them. It doesn't take much to flood the market."

At present that market is primarily in larger cities like San Francisco and Los Ange-les. "I'd say 80 percent of my crop goes there," Baggenstos says. But he also sells to supermarkets in both Oregon and Washington, and interest is slowly growing. Farmers in Washington are finding a good market for Yellow Finns, a yellow-fleshed potato of good baking and boiling quality. Yukon Gold, another yellow-fleshed potato, is gaining ground in Oregon. Red potatoes have almost shed the "specialty" tag in both states, and pur-ple potatoes are no longer a shocking item.

Baggenstos says that from the farmer's point of view, growing these less-common varieties is no different than growing a white Russet. And he notes that specialty pota-toes have enabled him to make it in seasons when the price for common potatoes was low. "The All-Blues have done really well, and I've had good luck with the other specialty varieties. It's allowed me to diversify."

Michael Page-English

Jim Baggenstos
16520 SW Beef Bend Road
Sherwood, OR 97140
(503) 649-9258
Wholesales specialty potatoes to local grocery stores, including Safeway, Thriftway, and Fred Meyer.

Sources for specialty seed potatoes (for growing in the garden) and eating potatoes:

Cheyne Brothers
Depot Road, Malin
(503) 723-2028
All-Blue and other specialty varieties sold as tubers, by mail (P.O. Box 49, Malin, OR 97632) and to anyone who stops by.
In the middle of Malin.

Nichols Garden Nursery
1190 North Pacific Highway
Albany, OR 97321-4598
(503) 928-9280
Mail-order seed tubers for Yellow Finn, Yukon Gold, and Bintje. Retail store also has herbs and seeds.
At the north end of town.

CRAWFISH

I have always been very partial to crawfish, yet it would be hard to champion its flavor against the different, though equally exquisite, savors of fresh Dungeness crab, side-stripe shrimp, or gooseneck barnacles, because all of these delectable crustaceans make unique taste statements. But the meat of fresh Pacific Northwest crawfish is far superior to that of the lobsters flown in from Maine or the Canadian maritime provinces. Lobsters, like other crustaceans, begin to die as soon as they are removed from their native habitat and, while they may still be somewhat alive when you buy them from your fishmonger, they will have lost much of their tastiness. Crawfish on the other hand, are available fresh from our lakes and rivers, and they keep well in freshwater tanks.

In recent years, numerous attempts have been made on the West Coast to come up with a successful method of aquaculture for growing lobster. I wish the experimenters would concentrate on crawfish instead. These not only taste better and have a better meat texture but they are small enough to make cooking and serving fairly easy. I have eaten fresh crawfish for at least a couple of decades now, but I have never yet bought any. I have always caught my own. In recent years, I have had good luck on Lake Whatcom, near Bellingham, Washington, using shrimp traps baited with fish heads, but I have most often caught crawfish with my bare hands. I still fondly remember one of my greatest crawdad hauls—and it happened some 15 years ago.

I had stopped at a small meadow on the banks of southern Oregon's meandering Applegate River. The place looked as though it had once been a homestead or ranch. The buildings were gone, but here and there a crumbling foundation or a hewn stone poked through the brambles and blooming fruit trees mingled with the buckbrush and oaks of the abutting hillside. I had spent the night in the shelter of several large weeping willows which grew near the shore, watching their long branches trail in the sluggish stream. The morning fog rose from the upstream cataracts and veiled the Siskiyous, reminding me of a painting by the emperor Kao-tsung. Walking to my car for my sketchbook, I repeated several lines from a Su Shih poem *(translation by Irving Y. Lo)*:

> *The fisherman wakes.*
> *At noon on the spring river;*
> *Fallen blossoms, flying catkins intrude into his dream.*
> *Sobered up from wine and still drunk, drunk and yet sober—*
> *He laughs at the human world, both past and present.*

I felt entrapped in an enchantment. Returning to the river, I noticed a slight commotion in the foliage of a Hind's willow and saw something I had not expected to see this side of the tropics. Several feet off the ground, a slender green snake was gliding through the branches of gray willows and brown dogwoods. I tried to follow, but the snake (it turned out to be a yellow-bellied racer when I looked it up later in a reptile guide) easily outdistanced me. Reaching the end of the thicket at the weeping willow grove, the snake dropped onto the trunk of an old red willow and vanished. I searched the surrounding grasses and hedges to get another look at it, but to no avail. The racer had flushed a small aquatic garter snake from its hiding place under the bank, and I watched this snake for a while as it stemmed the current with its writhing body, head erect like a periscope. After it had reached the further shore, I looked into the water and beheld—breakfast.

A large grandfather crawdad sat on the bottom of the stream, only a foot and a half beneath me. I stepped back carefully, trying not to alarm him, got a bucket from my car, and filled it a quarter full of river water. Then I stretched out on the bank and carefully put my hand into the water above the unsuspecting crawfish. Snatch! I had him! His large claws bent backwards, trying to nip me, but I held him firmly at the junction of tail and carapace, just out of reach of his pincers, and dropped him into the bucket. This crawfish must have occupied a favored spot under the bank (with little birds and other food dropping down from the willow?) for, no sooner was I back in place than another crawfish walked out of the weeds to occupy the newly abandoned gravel patch. Grab! Then two more, fighting each other. They didn't even disengage as I put them in the pail. This was too good to be true, I thought, as crawfish after crawfish joined his buddies in my bucket. I seemed to be going right down the pecking order among local crawdads, but the crustaceans weren't getting any smaller. My arm numbed from the cold water, and I did not even notice I was bleeding until I saw little curls of red flow downstream. Had a crawdad pinched me? My arm was too numb to tell. The blood really seemed to bring out the critters and numb or not, I kept snatching them until my bucket was overflowing. Here was not just breakfast, but lunch and dinner as well.

I killed about two dozen of the crawfish by twisting off their tails (this separates the spinal cord), then dropped the tails and the large claws into a bowl of white wine and left them to marinate as I built a small fire in a ring of fieldstones. While the coffee water heated up on the fire, I cut myself a few slices of French bread, scooped the coral from the carapaces, and spread it onto the slices. It was delicious. When the coffee was done and the wood had burned down into white coals, I set my small portable grill onto the rock, pulled the crawfish tails and claws from the marinade, and arranged them on the barbecue. After they had warmed up, I threw a handful of Oregon myrtle and cut-leaved sage leaves onto the fire. The short flare-up sealed in the juices and the myrtle and sage flavored the crawfish nicely. A touch of salt and pepper and the crawfish were done.

I ate about half of the claws and tails hot for breakfast and the others cold for lunch. I changed the water in the bucket a couple of times to make sure the live crawfish would have enough oxygen, and wedged the pail behind my seat before I drove off. Later that day, I had crawfish and mussel stew for dinner as I camped on a protected beach near Bandon.

I have always made sure to have a ready supply of crawfish on hand, but not until several years after the Applegate bounty did I once again encounter that many crawfish in one place (outside a trap, that is). Crawfish are common in lakes and streams in Oregon, Washington, and north into British Columbia, but they seem to do best in moderately warm waters. I have consistently caught more crawfish in Oregon than in Washington, and I have found the crawfish south of the Columbia River larger and tastier. But I may be splitting hairs: All Pacific Northwest crawfish are delicious, wherever they are found, and, best of all, they can be prepared in a variety of ways.

John Doerper
Eating Well: A Guide to Foods of the Pacific Northwest

CRAWFISH IN APPLE CIDER

This recipe calls for a dry cider made from tart apples. You may have trouble using the sweet ciders sold in our stores—unless you have a sweet tooth—but you should have no difficulty finding a nice, tart cider at a roadside stand or at a farmers market. Serve with mashed potatoes, crisp-cooked vegetables, and a chilled, dry Sauvignon Blanc or Semillon or, if you have used sweet cider, with a sweet Reisling.

1½ pounds *cooked,* peeled crawfish tails (preferably all
    the same size)
3 tablespoons unsalted butter
2 tablespoons shallots, finely chopped
    2 tablespoons concentrated dry cider (see note)
¾ cup whipping cream
Salt and freshly ground black pepper to taste

To cook crawfish tails, drop into boiling salted water until the tails turn opaque. Remove immediately.

Rinse cooked crawfish tails under cold running water, remove vein running down the back, and pat dry.

Melt butter in a heavy skillet and add tails and shallots. Add concentrated cider and stir. Remove tails with slotted spoon. Keep warm.

Add cream to skillet and cook over high heat for 1 minute. Add salt and pepper to taste. Return crawfish tails to skillet and cook just to heat through.

Serves 4 to 6.

Note: To make concentrated cider, boil down 1 cup of dry cider until you have 2 tablespoons of concentrate. If you like a stronger flavor, boil down 2 cups.

John Doerper
The Eating Well Cookbook

U-PICK FARMS AND ROADSIDE STANDS

U-Pick Guidelines: Call first, especially near the beginning and end of the season. Find out if your small children are welcome to help pick. Farms will supply picking containers, but you will need bags or boxes to transport your produce home. Pick carefully and conscientiously; a well-tended berry field or orchard represents years of knowledgeable labor. (Dogs should stay in the car.)

Harvests may vary greatly from year to year. A local chamber of commerce or county extension office can often supply up-to-date seasonal information. Also, many newspapers publish local farm maps in the late spring or summer.

CURRY COUNTY, OREGON

Thunder Rock Farm ☆ **(503) 247-7408**
Ronald Warden
36044 Highway 101 N, Gold Beach
Call ahead for hours and availability.

Certified organic—specialty produce, herbs, edible flowers, and warm-weather crops, including avocados and oranges.

Twelve miles north of Gold Beach at milepost 315.

Elephant Rock Farm/Sisters Natural Grocery ☆ **(503) 332-3640**
Melvin Sutton, Debbie Lohry, and Liz Vahradian
832 Oregon Street, Port Orford
Year-round: Monday, Wednesday, Thursday, and Friday, 11am–5pm.

Organic produce from Elephant Rock Farm in Sixes and other local producers. Rice, grains, herbs, and other natural foods.

On Highway 101 in Port Orford, kitty-corner from the theater.

JACKSON COUNTY, OREGON

Rogue River Valley Creamery ☆ **(503) 664-2233**
Thomas Vella
311 N Front, Central Point
Year-round: Monday–Friday, 9am–5pm.

The creamery, under the same ownership since 1935, makes Cheddar, jack, and blue cheeses (the only blue, they claim, west of the Mississippi)

and butter. Rogue Gold Dairy, the packagers in Grants Pass, have a retail store which also features raw milk and curds (also known as "squeak cheese").

Take exit 32 off I-5 (the Central Point exit). Turn right on Front Street. Rogue Gold Dairy is located at 234 SW Fifth Street in Grants Pass (Josephine County); (503) 476-7786.

Green Ridge Farm ☆ **(503) 855-1650**
Monica and Markus Ray
12310 Ramsey Road, Gold Hill
April–November for produce, all year for specialty candies.

Call to order organic vegetables (leeks, spinach, broccoli, cauliflower), fruit, nuts, and hand-dipped truffles. Pick order up at the Grants Pass Grower's Market.

Sackett Farm ☆ **(503) 855-9366**
Dannette and Glen Sackett
1776 Rogue River High~~~~~~~~ld Hill
May–November: d~~~~~~~~am–6pm.

Organic p~~~~~~~including U-pick asparagus,
cuc~~~~~~and greens. Apples, pears, melons,
honey, and more. A good-sized 160-acre farm.

At exit 45A off I-5.

CLOSED

Harry and David ☆ **(503) 776-2277**
2836 S Pacific Highway, Medford
Year-round: daily, 9am–6pm.

This big operation, in business since 1934, has a continually expanding line of gourmet foods, kitchen wares, and flowers, but is still primarily known for seasonal fruit (especially apples and pears), including the famous "Fruit of the Month" club. The specialty food lineup features chocolates, fruit spreads, baked goods, smoked salmon, nuts, and cheeses.

One mile south of Medford on Highway 99; you can't miss it. Mail order also available from 2518 S Pacific Highway/P.O. Box 712, Medford, OR 97501. They also operate a second retail store in Troutdale: the Columbia Gorge Factory Store, NW 257th Avenue, Suite 506, Troutdale; (503) 666-6550.

Oakcroft Farm ☆ (503) 779-2495
John and Laurie Shonerd
2775 Mel-Lowe Lane, Medford
Mid-July–September: call ahead; bring containers.

Certified organic basil, eggplant, garlic, peppers, strawberries, summer squash, tomatoes, and corn—U-pick.

Take Highway 99 to South Stage Road. Go 3 miles on South Stage, turn left on Griffin Creek, and go 2 miles to Mel-Lowe Lane.

Pinnacle Orchards ☆
(800) 448-9604 or (503) 772-6271 for catalog
441 S Fir Street
Medford, OR 97501
April–January: Monday–Friday (sometimes Saturday), 9am–5pm.

Mail-order source for pears, especially red and green Comices, since 1937. An extensive catalog includes other Oregon products. Their store, The Pantry (also at 441 S Fir), is an outlet for Tillamook ice cream and other local goods.

Near 10th and Fir.

Rolling Hills Farm ☆ (503) 773-2361
Dave and Sherry Belzberg
2931 W Griffin Creek Road, Medford
Mid-July–mid-October: daily, 8am–5pm.

Certified organic peaches, tomatoes, and other produce.

Take Barnett exit off I-5. Go left on Riverside toward Medford, turn right on South Stage Road, left on Griffin Road, and right on W Griffin Creek Road. Farm is on the left.

JOSEPHINE COUNTY, OREGON

The Upper Crust ☆ (503) 474-5091
Linda D'Amato
Grants Pass

Pies made with local fruit, organic when available. Available at the Grants Pass Growers market from spring through fall, and at the Farmers Market in Phoenix year-round. Call for custom orders.

Gallagher Family Farm ☆ (503) 479-5438
Mike Gallagher
6968 New Hope Road, Grants Pass
February–Thanksgiving: Monday–Friday and sometimes Saturday, 9am–6pm.

Melons in several varieties, including cantaloupes, watermelons, crenshaws, and honeydews, and 150 varieties of produce—garlic, peppers (hot and sweet), apples (15 varieties), pears (7 varieties), walnuts, berries, grapes (8 varieties), bedding plants, and all sorts of vegetables.

Take Highway 238 (Williams Highway) south out of Grants Pass for 2 miles. New Hope Road is on the right; farm is 3½ miles out.

Windy River Farm ☆ (503) 476-8979
Peter Liebes and Judy Weiner
348 Hussey Lane, Grants Pass
June–October: Tuesday–Thursday, call ahead.

Certified organic herbs, seasonings, teas, dried vegetables and fruits, soup blends, herb honey, herbed quick-bread mixes, and salves. Sells at the Grants Pass Growers Market.

Call for directions.

Middleton Farm ☆ (503) 592-3160
James Middleton
Eight Dollar Road, Kerby
Mid-June–November.

Certified organic produce, U-pick or call ahead for ready-picked.

On Highway 199 between Grants Pass and Crescent City in Illinois Valley, 22 miles southwest of Grants Pass on Redwood Highway; turn onto Eight Dollar Road and go ¼ mile.

Merlin of the Rogue Valley ✫
(503) 474-5090
Wayne and Helen Brad
P.O. Box 1340 Merlin, OR 97532

Gourmet garlic products include a potent garlic powder ("the potentest on the market," according to Wayne), garlic greens, tipsy garlic (a sort of garlic pickle marinated in vinegar, water, and vermouth), garlic jelly, jalapeño and garlic jelly, and whole garlic in season (July–December). The Brads are proud of the fact that they sell their products down in Gilroy, California, the garlic capital of the world. The products are all natural, made from herbs grown on their farm and Oregon-grown garlic ("We like to help the local economy," explains Helen). There are no on-farm sales, but products are available in shops all over Washington and Oregon, including The Herbfarm in Fall City, Washington; Made in Oregon stores throughout Oregon; Inside Passage in Bellingham, Washington; The Little Shop in Leavenworth, Washington; and LeFore's Honey of a Gift in Milton-Freewater, Oregon. Call Helen to find a store in your area. Also available by mail, and sometimes at the Grants Pass Growers Market.

High Hoe Produce ✫ **(503) 846-6676**
Chi and Michelle Scherer
1785 Caves Camp Road, Williams
In season: daily; call ahead for hours.

Certified organic garlic, melons, onions, winter squash, greens, and potatoes.

From I-5 take Highway 238 near Grants Pass going toward Provolt. Before Provolt, follow signs for Williams. Take Cedar Flat Road 3 miles past the town center and turn left on Caves Camp Road.

Southern Oregon Organics ✫
(503) 846-7173
Alan Venet
1130 Tetherow Road, Williams
April–August: call ahead for hours.

Certified organic cucumbers, herbs, onions, squash, and bedding plants. Organic seeds available as well; culinary herbs available year-round.

Take Williams Highway off Highway 238 to the town of Williams. Look for the Williams General Store at the corner of Williams Highway and Tetherow Road.

Williams Creek Farms ✫ **(503) 846-6481**
Randy Carey, Jr.
18843 Williams Highway, Williams
In season: call ahead.

Specializes in organically grown produce: some root crops, golden and red raspberries, lettuce and other greens, 6 kinds of apples, and 4 kinds of pears.

One mile toward Provolt from Williams General Store.

KLAMATH COUNTY, OREGON

Clifford Family Farm ✫ **(503) 884-2288**
Daniel and Donna Clifford
9059 Highway 66, Klamath Falls
August–October: Monday–Friday, 1pm–6pm.

Certified organic produce, including herbs and Asian vegetables. Ready-picked.

Off Highway 66 in Klamath Falls.

Cheyne Brothers ✫ **(503) 723-2028**
Depot Road, Malin

All-Blue and other specialty potato varieties sold as tubers, by mail (P.O. Box 49, Malin, OR 97632) and to anyone who stops by.

In the middle of Malin.

FARMERS MARKETS

JACKSON COUNTY, OREGON

Ashland Market
Contact: Joyce Schillen, (503) 855-1326
Mid-April–mid-November: Tuesday,
8:30am–1:30pm.

This is the Ashland branch of the Medford
Growers and Crafters Association Market.

Water Street under the Lithia Way overpass.

Medford Market
Contact: Joyce Schillen, (503) 855-1326
Mid-April–October: Thursday (weather permitting),
8:30am–1pm.

From the Medford Growers and Crafters Association. Fruit, produce, and herbs (especially sun-lov-
ing varieties suited to the region's Mediterranean
climate).

Next to Sears at the Medford Shopping Center.

Medford Ranch Market
Contact: (503) 779-5596
Year-round: daily.

*4998 Crater Lake Highway, at the intersection of
Crater Lake Highway and Vilas Road.*

Medford Saturday Market
Contact: Joyce Schillen (503) 855-1326
July–October: Saturday 8:30am–1:30pm.

At Miles Field on Highway 99.

JOSEPHINE COUNTY, OREGON

Grants Pass Growers Market
Contact: Marty Fate, (503) 476-5375
Easter–Thanksgiving: Saturday, 9am–1pm.

*At the corner of 4th and F streets behind the
post office.*

APPENDIXES

NORTHWEST FOOD FESTIVALS

JANUARY

★ Medford, OR: **A Taste of Ashland**, end of January/early February. Winter wine, food, and arts festival including winemakers' dinners, seminars, gourmet food and wine tasting. An afternoon of wine and song features an opera luncheon and wine auction; outdoors there's cross-country skiing and ice sculpture contests, (503) 482-3486.

FEBRUARY

★ LaConner, WA: **Smelt Derby**, first Saturday in February. Everyone invited to fish for the biggest and smallest smelt from the public docks, (206) 466-4778.

★ Roseburg, OR: **Greatest of the Grape**, first Saturday in February. The fairgrounds are magically transformed when 20 wineries bring their finest, accompanied by food prepared expressly for particular vintages by area restaurants. Douglas County Fairgrounds, (503) 673-7901.

★ Newport, OR **Seafood and Wine Festival**, last full weekend in February. Lots of food and wine vendors offering their wares for tasting and buying. The culinary competition, wine competition, and wine dinner are all held during the preceding weeks. Newport Marina at South Beach, (503) 265-6638.

MARCH

★ Coupeville, WA: **Penn Cove Mussel Festival**, early March. This festival of the black-and-blue bivalve takes place at the Captain Whidbey Inn and includes mussel eating and recipe contests, cooking demos, tours of the cove (you can see the mussel rafts), and a dinner with mussels in every course, (800) 366-4097.

★ Roseburg, OR: **Spring Fair**, mid- to late March. Douglas County Fairgrounds, (503) 440-4505.

APRIL

★ Westport, WA: **Crab Races and Crab Feed**, mid-April. A crab dinner follows the day's festivities. Held at the dock area in Westport, (206) 268-9422 or (800) 345-6223.

★ Salem, OR: **AG Fest**, mid-April. Family festival includes food booths and exhibits. State fairgrounds, (503) 378-3247.

☆ Yakima Valley, WA: **Spring Barrel Tasting**, late April. Valley vintners open their wineries to the public. Taste wine from the barrel—some vintages are two or three years from maturity. At wineries all over the valley, (509) 248-2021.

MAY

☆ Toppenish, WA: **Central Washington Jr. Livestock Show**, early May. Toppenish Rodeo Grounds, (509) 865-5313.

☆ Lacey, WA: **Northwest MicroFest**, mid-May. Foods and microbrews of the Pacific Northwest at St. Martin's Pavilion, (206) 491-4141.

☆ Woodinville, WA: **Spring Wine Fair**, mid-May. New releases make their debut. Columbia Winery, (206) 488-2776.

☆ Yacolt, WA: **Pomeroy House Annual Herb Festival**, third weekend in May. Plants for sale, crafts, and food, (206) 686-3537.

☆ Bandon, OR: **Wine and Seafood Festival**, late May. Booths and displays; specialties from Bandon's chefs and restaurant owners; Oregon wines. In City Park, 11th Street between Highway 101 and the beach, (503) 347-2779.

☆ South Bend, WA: **Oyster Stampede**, last weekend in May. Tours of the town's processing plant (this is the self-proclaimed Oyster Capital of the World; you'll know you're there by the enormous heaps of bleached white oyster shells that line the road), oyster eating and shucking contests, oyster dredge races, and pearl prizes, (206) 875-5231.

JUNE

☆ Lebanon, OR: **Strawberry Festival**, first weekend in June. Oregon's second oldest "continually running" festival. Includes food booths and world's largest shortcake as well as non-food activities. Call for directions, (503) 258-4444.

☆ Lynden, WA: **Farmers Day Parade and Plow Match**, early June. This farm day stars draught horses and plows, and includes an antique show and rides for kids, (206) 354-5995.

☆ The Dalles, OR: **Mid-Columbia Jr. Livestock Show**, early June. Animal exhibits. 404 W Second St, (503) 298-1016.

☆ Toppenish, WA: **Annual Food Fair**, early June. Pioneer Park, (509) 865-3262.

☆ Ocean Park, WA: **Annual Garlic Festival**, mid-June. Garlic eating and peeling contests, crafts and food (some, naturally, bearing the signature pungency), (206) 642-2400 or (800) 451-2542.

★ Hillsboro, OR: **Pacific International Livestock Exposition**, mid-June (another held in October). Exhibits, rodeo, and food booths. Washington County Fairgrounds #39, (503) 257-7881.

★ Wilsonville, OR: **Annual Strawberry Festival at Meridian Church of Christ**, mid-June. Ham and potato dinner followed by, of course, strawberry shortcake. Contact: Rev. Linda Mines Elliott, (503) 682-0339.

★ Sunnyside, WA: **Cheese Festival**, the Saturday before Father's Day. Display of Washington cheeses and other local specialty foods, including smoked salmon and pickled vegetables. Entertainment features cowboy poetry and Indian dancers from the Yakima Nation. In Sunnyside's Central Park, (509) 839-7678.

★ Ferndale, WA: **Antique Farm Fair**, Father's Day weekend. Hovander Homestead Park, (206) 384-3042.

★ Fall City, WA: **Microbrewery Festival**, Father's Day weekend. Fifteen microbreweries bring their wares for tasting; the Herbfarm provides the eggplant sandwiches, herb-pot salad, and other choice morsels. The Herbfarm, (206) 784-2222.

★ Burlington, WA: **Berry Dairy Days**, mid–late June. Includes Dairy Open House, strawberry shortcake, and non-food activities. Various locations around Burlington, (206) 755-9382 or -9593.

JULY

★ Yachats, OR: **Smelt Fry**, early July. Buffet, entertainment, and old-time fiddling, (503) 547-3530.

★ Walla Walla, WA: **Sweet Onion Festival**, mid-July. Games utilizing the famous onion include the onion shot put, onion golf, onion carving, and onion cooking. Fort Walla Walla, (509) 525-0850.

★ Vashon Island, WA: **Strawberry Festival**, mid-July, (206) 463-6217.

★ Seattle, WA: **Ballard's Seafoodfest**, late July. Fifteen to twenty vendors selling all manner of offerings from the sea, from blackened salmon to seafood kebabs. The lutefisk-eating contest is only for the brave, (206) 784-9705.

AUGUST

★ Mossyrock, WA: **Mossyrock Blueberry Festival**, first Sunday in August. Public dinner with blueberry muffins and desserts. Mossyrock Grange Hall, (206) 983-3295.

★ Tualatin, OR: **Crawfish Festival**, second Saturday in August. A pancake breakfast and parade are followed by a dog show, crawfish- and watermelon-eating contests (separately). Tualatin Community Park, (503) 692-0780.

★ Prosser, WA: **Prosser Wine and Food Fair**, second weekend in August. Wines and gourmet foods. At the school stadium, (509) 786-3177.

★ Cave Junction, OR: **Wild Blackberry Festival**, second weekend in August. Lots of non-food events, but there are food booths and a pie-eating contest. Main Street, (503) 592-2507.

★ Pasco, WA: **Pasco Good Life Festival and Barnburner**, mid-August. Ag tours, food booths with local foods. Pasco Memorial Park, (509) 547-9755.

★ Nehalem, OR: **Nehalem Bay Blackberry Festival**, late August, (503) 368-5100.

★ Monroe, WA: **Evergreen State Fair**, late August–early September, (206) 794-7832.

★ Salem, OR: **Oregon State Fair**, late August–early September. 2330 N Marine Dr, (503) 378-3247.

★ Springfield, OR: **Springfield Filbert Festival**, late August–early September. Food booths, filbert (hazelnut) products, bake-off. Island Park, (503) 726-3703.

SEPTEMBER

★ Westport, WA: **Annual Westport Seafood Festival**, the Saturday of Labor Day weekend. A seafood dinner buffet includes oysters and several other kinds of fish. Westport Maritime Museum, (206) 268-9422 or (800) 345-6223.

★ Welches, OR: **Mt. Hood Huckleberry Festival**, Labor Day weekend. Native American huckleberry ceremony, wild berry bake-off, etc. Fifteen miles east of Sandy on Highway 26, (503) 622-4994 or -4798 or -3280.

★ Bremerton, WA: **Blackberry Fest**, the Sunday of Labor Day weekend. Ethnic food fair, crafts, and blackberry bake-off. On the boardwalk, (206) 377-3041.

★ Seattle, WA: **Tilth Organic Harvest Fair**, September. Twenty-nine farms attend what used to be called the "Organic Bite of Seattle," with organic produce, garden workshops, and composting demonstrations. Upscale organic food vendors provide snacks and food to take home. At the Good Shepherd Center, (206) 633-0451.

★ Pasco, WA: **Pasco Autumn Festival**, early September. Downtown Pasco, (509) 547-9755.

★ Oakland, OR: **Umpqua Valley Wine, Art, Jazz Festival**, early September. Downtown Oakland, (503) 672-2648.

★ Vancouver, WA: **Vancouver Sausage Fest**, first weekend after Labor Day. A full dinner includes sausage, sauerkraut, and potatoes. Sausage food booths, as well as a carnival, dance, and music, St. Joseph Parish, 6500 Highland Dr, (206) 696-4407.

★ Quincy, WA: **Farmer-Consumer Awareness Day**, second weekend in September. Guided tours of local operations, fresh farm produce, exhibits, tractor pull, (509) 787-2140.

★ Pullman, WA: **National Lentil Festival**, mid-September. Pullman grows 98 percent of the nation's lentils. Celebrate this fact on Lentil Lane, an avenue of fifteen booths, all serving different lentil recipes. Microbrew tasting also, (509) 334-3565.

⭐ Bandon, OR: **Cranberry Festival**, mid-September. Cranberry food Fair, cranberry memorabilia, local cheese tasting. Various locations around Bandon, (503) 347-4659.

⭐ Canby, OR: **Grape Stomping Festival**, third week in September. Live German music (the musicians are flown in from the motherland for the occasion), German sausage and sauerkraut; sign up for grape-stomping. St. Josef's Winery, (503) 651-3190.

⭐ Harrisburg, OR: **Annual Harrisburg Harvest and South Valley Tractor Pull**, third Saturday in September, (503) 998-6154.

⭐ Ellensburg, WA: **Annual Threshing Bee and Antique Equipment Show**, third weekend in September. Threshing and exhibits. The day's grain is ground, cleaned, and made into baked goods. Olmstead Place State Park, (509) 962-2222.

⭐ Mt. Angel, OR: **OktoberFest**, mid–late September. This Bavarian theme festival features beer and wine gardens as well as 52 food booths, (503) 845-9440.

⭐ Willamette Valley Vineyards, OR: **Harvest Festival**, mid–late September. Grape-stomp competition, wine tasting, and tours, (503) 588-9463.

⭐ Deming, WA: **Mt. Baker Grapestomp Competition**, late September. Lots of local food to sample and buy, including jam, cheese, and gourmet chocolates. No carnival-type food here, but the Lummi tribe makes smoked salmon. The vineyards are open, and the grapes get stomped. Mt. Baker Vineyards, (206) 592-2300.

⭐ Portland, OR: **Wintering-In**, late September. Annual harvest festival at 1857 farm. Games, arts and crafts, and cider-pressing, (503) 222-1741 ext. 71.

⭐ St. Helens, OR: **Harvest Festival**, late September. Small flea market and food booths, (503) 397-4231.

OCTOBER

⭐ Westport, WA: **Special Westport Basin Salmon Season**, early October through early November. From the docks at the Westport Boat Basin, fish for salmon as they return to the site of their rearing pens, (206) 268-9422 or (800) 345-6223.

⭐ Tacoma, WA: **Scandinavian Days**, early October. Celebrate Scandinavian culture through food, crafts, music, and cooking demonstrations. Puyallup Fair Grounds, (206) 627-2836.

⭐ Vancouver, WA: **Old Apple Tree Festival**, early October. Family-oriented festival includes apple pressing, apple pie, caramel apples, and other apple products. Sample other food, crafts, hayrides, and see the Northwest's oldest living apple tree. Old Apple Tree Park, (206) 693-1313.

⭐ Central Point, OR: **Rogue Valley Harvest Fair and Wine Fest**, early October. This festival highlights agriculture, agricultural products, seasonal produce, and commercial exhibits. Upscale food booths and a wine judging spice up the atmosphere. Jackson County Fairgrounds, (503) 776-7237.

☆ Shelton, WA: **West Coast Oyster Shucking Championship and Seafood Festival**, first full weekend in October. Informational exhibits, all manner of oyster dishes to sample, other food. Mason County Fairgrounds, (206) 426-2021.

☆ Molalla, OR: **Apple Festival**, second Saturday in October. A mostly-crafts festival accompanied by apple pie and homemade ice cream. At the Dibble House, (503) 829-6941.

☆ Steilacoom, WA: **Steilacoom Apple Squeeze**, the closest Sunday to Columbus Day weekend. Bring your apples to be pressed free in one of the 20 presses (some motorized, some hand-cranked); three gallons' worth of apples are squeezed for free. Sample apple pie with ice cream or cinnamon sauce, apple butter on hot bread, and hot cider. There's cider for sale in case you forgot your apples. On Lafayette Street in downtown Steilacoom, (206) 584-4133.

☆ Anderson Island, WA: **Anderson Island Historical Society Apple Squeeze**, mid-October. Apple juice making is accompanied by spiced cider and potluck meals; call ahead to see about transportation from the ferry, (206) 884-4905.

☆ Ilwaco, WA: **Cranberry Festival**, mid-October. Food booths featuring cranberry products, cranberry bog tours, cranberry fudge. Non-cranberry activities include music, crafts, and quilting, (206) 642-2400 or (800) 451-2542.

☆ Chelan, WA: **World Federation Pumpkin Weigh-Off**, mid-October. Pumpkins weighing 600 pounds, squash, and other specimens from all over the state, (509) 687-3534.

☆ Merrill, OR: **Merrill Potato Festival**, mid-October. This two day event begins with a coronation and banquet, and continues with a free barbeque and agricultural events. Exhibits display local produce and other foods. Nancy Kandra, (503) 798-5640.

☆ Hood River, OR: **Hood River Harvest Fest**, third weekend in October. Fresh produce, lots of food, and crafts, (503) 386-2000 or (800) 366-3530.

☆ Ferndale, WA: **Great Pumpkin Growing Contest**, late October. Prizes for the biggest, smallest, and scariest pumpkins; pumpkin carving contests; cider and cookies for munching. This annual event has created a sister-city in Miyoshimura, Japan, whose citizens were inspired to create their own contest with pumpkin seeds sent from Ferndale. Boys and Girls Club, (206) 384-3042.

NOVEMBER

☆ Pasco, WA: **Tri-Cities Northwest Wine Festival**, first or second weekend in November. Meals by local chefs, wine contests, and sampling. At the Red Lion Inn, (509) 375-3399.

☆ Tacoma, WA: **Tacoma Wine Festival**, November. Thirty to forty vineyards from Oregon, Washington, and Idaho show up for this festival for wine sampling accompanied by gourmet regional foods. (206) 566-5257.

☆ Location to be announced: **Annual Beekeeper Show**, mid-November. This educational Washington/Oregon show features speakers, commercial displays, and concentrates on the agricultural side of beekeeping. A honey-tasting contest is a potential activity. Call for next year's location: (503) 864-2138.

PRODUCE AVAILABILITY CHART

Produce	Jan	Feb	Mar	Apr	May	Jun	July	Aug	Sept	Oct	Nov	Dec
Apples (fresh picked)							☆	☆	☆	☆	☆	☆
Apricots							☆	☆				
Arugula							☆	☆	☆			
Asparagus				☆	☆							
Basil						☆	☆	☆	☆	☆		
Beans, green							☆	☆	☆	☆		
Beets						☆	☆	☆	☆	☆	☆	☆
Blackberries							☆	☆	☆			
Blueberries							☆	☆	☆			
Bok choy						☆	☆	☆	☆	☆	☆	
Boysenberries							☆	☆	☆			
Broccoli						☆	☆	☆	☆	☆	☆	
Brussels sprouts									☆	☆	☆	
Cabbage, Chinese							☆	☆	☆	☆		
Cabbage, green							☆	☆	☆	☆	☆	☆
Cabbage, red							☆	☆	☆	☆	☆	
Cabbage, Savoy							☆	☆	☆	☆		
Carrots			☆	☆	☆	☆	☆	☆	☆	☆	☆	☆
Cauliflower	☆	☆	☆				☆	☆	☆	☆	☆	☆
Celery								☆	☆	☆	☆	
Chard									☆	☆		
Cherries (pie)						☆	☆					
Cherries (sweet)					☆	☆						
Chile peppers									☆	☆		
Collard greens							☆	☆	☆	☆	☆	

Produce	Jan	Feb	Mar	Apr	May	Jun	July	Aug	Sept	Oct	Nov	Dec
Corn							☆	☆	☆	☆		
Cucumbers, pickling							☆	☆	☆			
Cucumbers, slicing								☆	☆			
Currants						☆	☆	☆	☆			
Daikon								☆	☆	☆	☆	☆
Dill							☆	☆	☆			
Eggplant								☆	☆			
Garlic							☆	☆	☆	☆	☆	☆
Gooseberries							☆	☆	☆	☆		
Gourds, ornamental									☆	☆	☆	
Grapes									☆	☆		
Herbs				☆	☆	☆	☆	☆	☆	☆		
Honey	☆	☆	☆	☆	☆	☆	☆	☆	☆	☆	☆	☆
Kale									☆	☆	☆	
Kohlrabi							☆	☆	☆	☆	☆	☆
Leeks	☆	☆	☆						☆	☆	☆	☆
Lettuce, head					☆	☆	☆	☆	☆	☆	☆	
Lettuce, leaf				☆	☆	☆	☆	☆	☆	☆		
Loganberries							☆	☆				
Marionberries							☆	☆				
Melon, bitter							☆	☆				
Melons							☆	☆	☆			
Mint					☆	☆	☆					
Mizuna				☆	☆	☆						
Mushrooms, wild									☆	☆		
Mustard greens					☆	☆	☆	☆	☆	☆	☆	
Nectarines							☆	☆	☆			
Nuts								☆	☆	☆	☆	
Onions, green				☆	☆	☆	☆	☆	☆	☆	☆	

Produce	Jan	Feb	Mar	Apr	May	Jun	July	Aug	Sept	Oct	Nov	Dec
Onions, Walla Walla							☆	☆	☆			
Onions, yellow							☆	☆	☆	☆	☆	☆
Parsley							☆	☆	☆			
Peaches							☆	☆	☆			
Pears								☆	☆	☆	☆	
Peas, green					☆	☆	☆					
Peas, snow					☆	☆						
Peppers							☆	☆	☆	☆	☆	
Potatoes, Finnish								☆	☆	☆	☆	☆
Potatoes, German									☆	☆	☆	☆
Potatoes, red									☆	☆	☆	☆
Pumpkins									☆	☆	☆	
Quince										☆		
Radishes				☆	☆	☆	☆					
Raspberries						☆	☆	☆	☆	☆		
Rhubarb			☆	☆	☆							
Rutabaga									☆	☆	☆	☆
Shallots								☆	☆	☆	☆	☆
Spinach			☆	☆	☆	☆	☆	☆	☆			
Squash, summer						☆	☆	☆	☆			
Squash, winter								☆	☆	☆	☆	☆
Strawberries					☆	☆	☆					
Tomatoes						☆	☆	☆	☆			
Turnips						☆	☆	☆	☆	☆	☆	☆
Watercress					☆	☆	☆	☆	☆			
Zucchini						☆	☆	☆	☆			

WINERIES

REGION 1
NORTHWEST WASHINGTON
AND THE SAN JUAN ISLANDS

McCrea Cellars
12707 18th Street SE, Lake Stevens, WA
(206) 334-5248
By appointment only.

Cabernet Sauvignon.

Call for directions.

Mount Baker Vineyards
4298 Mount Baker Highway, Deming, WA
(206) 592-2300
April–December: Wednesday–Sunday,
11am–5pm.
January–March: Saturday–Sunday, 11am–5pm.

Chardonnay, Pinot Noir, Gewürztraminer, Madeline Angevine, Müller-Thurgau.

Take the Mount Baker Highway east from I-5.

Quilceda Creek Vintners
5226 Machias Road, Snohomish, WA
(206) 568-2389
By appointment only.

Cabernet Sauvignon.

From I-5, go east on Highway 2 just north of Everett to Highway 9. Go north on Highway 9 to Bunk Foss Road (52nd Street SE) and head east. At Machias Road go north.

Whidbeys
Wonn Road, Greenbank, WA
(206) 678-7700
Year-round: daily, 10am–4:30pm.

Loganberry liqueur, port, and other fruit wines.

Off Highway 525 on Whidbey Island.

REGION 2
PUGET SOUND AND SEATTLE

Andrew Will Cellars
1450 Elliott Avenue W, Seattle, WA
(206) 282-4086
By appointment.

Cabernet and Merlot

Take Elliott Avenue north from downtown Seattle toward the Ballard Bridge.

Bainbridge Island Winery
682 State Highway 305 NE, Winslow, WA
(206) 842-9463
Year-round: Wednesday–Sunday, noon–5pm.

Müller-Thurgau, Siegerrebe, Madeleine Angevine.

From Winslow, go north on Highway 305.

Cavatappi Winery
9702 NE 120th Place, Kirkland, WA
(206) 823-6533
By appointment only.

Sauvignon Blanc, Cabernet Sauvignon, and Nebbiolo. The adjacent Cafe Juanita, owned by winemaker Peter Dow, serves fine northern Italian food.

From Highway 405, take NE 116th Street, which turns into Juanita Drive, to 97th Avenue. Go north on 97th to 120th Place and turn right.

Chateau Ste. Michelle
One Stimson Lane, Woodinville, WA
(206) 488 1133
Year-round: daily, 10am–4:30pm (summer to 6pm).

Wines from the Grandview facility and others (see listing under Region 7).

Off Highway 202 in Woodinville.

Columbia Winery
14030 NE 145th, Woodinville, WA
(206) 488-2776
Year-round: daily, 10am–5pm.

Off Highway 202 in Woodinville.

E. B. Foote Winery
9354 4th Avenue S, Seattle, WA
(206) 763-9928
Year-round: Tuesday and Thursday, 6:30pm to 9:30pm; Saturday, 9:30am to 3:30pm.

Chardonnay, Gewürztraminer, Riesling, and some late-harvest wines.

From Highway 99, exit to S 96th Street and go north on 4th Avenue S.

Facelli Winery
16120 Woodinville-Redmond Road, Woodinville, WA
(206) 488-1020
Year-round: Friday–Saturday, noon–4pm, and by appointment.

Merlot and some white varietals.

On Highway 202 in Woodinville, in the K and S Business Park.

French Creek Cellars
17721 132nd Avenue NE, Woodinville, WA
(206) 486-1900
Year-round: daily, noon–5pm.

Chardonnay, Riesling (some late-harvest styles), Cabernet, Merlot, and Lemberger.

From I-405 go east on Highway 522 to 132nd Avenue NE. On 132nd, head south to the winery.

Hedges Cellars
1105 12th Avenue NW, Issaquah, WA
(206) 391-6056
Year-round: Thursday–Saturday, noon–6pm.

Cabernet and Merlot blends.

One block off Gilman Boulevard on 12th Avenue NW, behind Safeway.

Johnson Creek Winery
19248 Johnson Creek Road SE, Tenino, WA
(206) 264-2100
By appointment.

From I-5, take exit 88 east to Highway 12, and follow it 7 miles to Highway 507. Continue east 5 miles to Johnson Creek Road and go south to the winery.

Manfred Vierthaler Winery
17136 Highway 410 E, Sumner, WA
(206) 863-1633
Year-round: daily, noon–6pm.

Cream Sherry, Port, Cabernet Sauvignon, Gewürztraminer, late-harvest Rieslings. Winemaker Vierthaler also runs the Roofgarden Restaurant, serving traditional German cuisine.

From I-5, take Highway 410 east to the winery.

Paul Thomas Winery
1717 136th Place NE, Bellevue, WA
(206) 747-1008
Year-round: Friday–Saturday, noon–5pm.

Fruit wines from local cherries, pears, rhubarb, as well as Chardonnay, Cabernet Sauvignon, Riesling, Chenin Blanc, Sauvignon Blanc, and Muscat.

From Highway 520, take the 124th Avenue NE/Northup exit to Northup Way and head east to 136th Place NE.

Rich Passage Winery
7869 NE Day Road W, Building A, Bainbridge Island, WA
(206) 842-8199
By appointment.

Pinot Noir, Chardonnay, Fumé Blanc.

Five miles north of Winslow on Highway 5; go west (left) on Day Road 2 blocks.

Silver Lake Winery
17616 15th Avenue SE, Bothell, WA
(206) 485-2437
Year-round: Monday–Friday, noon–5pm.

Riesling (dry and ice wine), Sauvignon Blanc, Chardonnay, Cabernet, and Merlot.

From I-5 take the 164th Street exit and go right on 164th. Continue east to the intersection of 164th and the Bothell-Everett Highway; go south one mile, past the Per Business Park, and turn left at the end of the park onto 15th. Make a left into the park; the winery is the back building.

Wines are also available in the Country Village Tasting Room, 4 miles south on the Bothell-Everett Highway.

Snoqualmie Winery
1000 Winery Road, Snoqualmie, WA
(206) 392-4000
Year-round: daily, 10am–4:30pm.

Take exit 27 off I-90 and follow the signs.

Vashon Winery
12629 SW Cemetary Road, Vashon Island, WA
(206) 463-9092 or -2990

A tasting room for their Cabernet, Semillon and Chardonnay is in the planning stages.

REGION 3
THE OLYMPIC PENINSULA

Hoodsport Winery
N 23501 Highway 101, Hoodsport, WA
(206) 877-9894
Year-round: daily, 10am–6pm.

Reds, whites, and fruit wines.

On Highway 101 in Hoodsport.

Lost Mountain Winery
730 Lost Mountain Road, Sequim, WA
(206) 683-5229
By appointment only, except for the annual 'open winery' the last week of June and first week of July.

From Highway 101 go south on Taylor Cutoff Road (just west of the Dungeness River) to Lost Mountain Road.

Neuharth Winery
148 Still Road, Sequim, WA
(206) 683-9652
Mid-May–September: daily, 9:30am–5:30pm.
October–Mid-May: Wednesday–Sunday, noon–5pm.

Chardonnay, Riesling, Cabernet, and Merlot.

Go south off Highway 101 on Still Road ¼ mile to the winery.

REGION 4
NORTHERN OREGON AND
SOUTHWEST WASHINGTON

Adams Vineyard Winery
1922 NW Pettygrove Street, Portland, OR
(503) 294-0606
By appointment only.

Pinot Noir and Chardonnay.

2.6 miles northwest of Newberg, at NW 19th and Pettygrove.

Adelsheim Vineyard
22150 NE Quarter Mile Lane, Newberg, OR
(503) 538-3652
Call for visiting dates.

Pinot Noir, Chardonnay, Pinot Gris, Riesling, Merlot.

No tasting room, but wines are available at the Elk Cove Tasting Room in Dundee.

Amity Vineyards
18150 Amity Vineyards Road SE, Amity, OR
(503) 835-2362
June–November: daily, noon–5pm.
December, February–May: Saturday–Sunday, noon–5pm.

Pinot Noir, White Riesling, Chardonnay, Gamay Noir, Gewürztraminer, Oregon Blush.

From Highway 99W at Amity go east on Rice Lane. Wines are also available at the Oregon Tasting Room in the Lawrence Gallery, 9 miles southwest of McMinnville on Highway 18, (503) 843-3787.

Argyle (The Dundee Wine Company)
691 Highway 99W, Dundee, OR
(503) 538-8520
Spring: daily, 11am–4:30pm or by appointment.

Sparkling wines.

On Highway 99W just west of Dundee.

Arterberry Winery
905-907 E 10th Avenue, McMinnville, OR
(503) 244-0695 or (503) 472-1587
May–December: daily, noon–5pm.

Chardonnay, White Riesling, Sauvignon Blanc, Gewürztraminer, and sparkling wines.

From Highway 99W in McMinnville, go south on Lafayette Avenue at the West Valley Farmers Co-op, then go west on 10th.

Autumn Wind Vineyard

15225 N Valley Road, Gaston, OR
(503) 538-6931
April–November: Saturday–Sunday, noon–5pm.

Take Highway 240 exit off Highway 99W to Ribbon Ridge Road. Go north 8 miles, then west on N Valley Road.

Chateau Benoit Winery

6580 NE Mineral Spings Road, Carlton, OR
(503) 864-2991
Year-round: daily, 10am–5pm.

Brut sparkling wine, Sauvignon Blanc, Müller-Thurgau, Pinot Noir, Chardonnay, Riesling, Merlot.

From Highway 99W go north at Lafayette on Mineral Springs Road; it's 1½ miles to the winery. Wines also available at the Chateau Benoit Wine and Food Center, Quality Factory Village, Lincoln City, (503) 996-3981.

Cooper Mountain Vineyards

9480 SW Grabhorn Road, Beaverton, OR
(503) 649-0027
Call ahead.

Pinot Noir, Chardonnay, Pinot Gris grown for local wineries as well as their own wines.

On Grabhorn Road, off Highway 208.

Edgefield Winery

2126 SW Halsey Street, Troutdale, OR
(503) 665-2992
Year-round: daily, 11am–9pm.

Pinot Noir Nouveau, Riesling, Chardonnay, Pinot Gris, Cabernet, Merlot.

Take the Wood Village exit off I-84 to Halsey.

Elk Cove Vineyards

27751 NW Olson Road, Gaston, OR
(503) 985-7760
Year-round: daily, 11am–5pm.

Pinot Noir, Riesling (dry style and ice wine), Chardonnay, Pinot Gris, Gewürztraminer, Cabernet Sauvignon, late-harvest Riesling.

From Portland, take Highway 8 to Forest Grove, then go south on Highway 47 to Olson Road. Wines are also available at Dundee Wine Cellar, 575 SW Highway 99, Dundee, (503) 538-0911, and Hood River Wine Tasting Room, 1108 E Marina Way, Hood River, (503) 386-9466.

The Eyrie Vineyards

E 10th Street, McMinnville, OR
(503) 472-6315
Thanksgiving weekend and by appointment.

Pinot Noir, Chardonnay, Pinot Gris, Muscat Ottonel, and Pinot Meunier.

From Highway 99W go south on Lafayette Avenue from the West Valley Farmers Co-op in McMinnville to E 10th Street.

Hidden Springs Winery

9360 SE Eola Hills Road, Amity, OR
(503) 835-2782
March–November: Saturday–Sunday, noon–5pm.

Pinot Noir, Chardonnay, Pacific Sunset, and White Riesling (dry, reserve, and dessert style).

From Highway 99W at Amity, take Amity Road east to Old Bethel Road; Eola Hills Road runs east off Old Bethel.

Knudsen Erath Winery

Worden Hill Road, Dundee, OR
(503) 538-3318
Mid-May–mid-October: daily, 10:30am–5:30pm.
Mid-October–mid-May: daily, 11am–5pm.

Chardonnay, Cabernet Sauvignon, Gewürztraminer, Pinot Noir, and White Riesling.

From Highway 99W at Dundee, go northwest on 9th Street, which becomes Worden Hill Road.

Kramer Vineyards

26830 NW Olson Road, Gaston, OR
(503) 662-4545
April–December: Friday–Sunday, noon–5pm.

Pinot Noir, Chardonnay, Riesling, Pinot Gris, Gewürztraminer, Müller-Thurgau, and berry wines.

From Forest Grove go south on Highway 47 to Olson Road.

Lange Winery
18380 NE Buena Vista, Dundee, OR
(503) 538-6476
January–April: Saturday–Sunday, 11am–5pm or by appointment.
May–December: daily, 11am–5pm (to 6pm in summer).
Pinot Noir, Chardonnay, Pinot Gris.

From Highway 99W at Dundee take 9th Street/Worden Hill Road to Fairview Road. Fairview becomes Buena Vista.

Laurel Ridge Winery
David Hill Road, Forest Grove, OR
(503) 359-5436
February–December: daily, noon–5pm or by appointment.
Pinot Noir, Gewürztraminer, Semillon, Sylvaner, and Rielsing.

Take Highway 8 through Forest Grove to David Hill Road. Wines also available at the Laurel Ridge Oregon Tasting Room, 2210 N Main Street, Tillamook, (503) 842-7744.

Marquam Hill Vineyards
35803 S Highway 213, Mollala, OR
(503) 829-6677
June–mid-September: daily, noon–6pm.
October–December, February–May: Saturday–Sunday, noon–6pm.
January: by appointment only.
Pinot Noir, Chardonnay, Riesling, Gewürztraminer, Müller-Thurgau.

Eighteen miles south of Oregon City and 7½ miles north of Silverton on Highway 213 near Marquam.

Montinore Vineyards
Dilley Road, Forest Grove, OR
(503) 359-5012
May–October: daily, noon–5pm.
November–April: Saturday–Sunday, noon–5pm.
Pinot Noir, Chardonnay, White Riesling, Pinot

Gris, Pinot Meunier, Müller-Thurgau, Gewürztraminer, Sauvignon Blanc, Chenin Blanc.

Take Highway 47 to Dilley Road, 2½ miles south of Forest Grove.

Oak Knoll Winery
29700 SW Burkhalter Road, Hillsboro, OR
(503) 648-8198
Year-round: Wednesday–Friday, Sunday, noon–5pm; Saturday, 11am–5pm; Monday–Tuesday, by appointment.
Chardonnay, Pinot Noir, Riesling, Gewürztraminer, Cabernet Sauvignon, dessert wines.

From Hillsboro take Highway 219 south to Burkhalter Road. Wines also available at Shipwreck Cellars, 3524 SW Highway 101, Lincoln City, (503) 996-3221.

Ponzi Vineyards
14665 SW Winery Lane, Beaverton, OR
(503) 628-1227
February–December: Saturday–Sunday, noon–5pm; wine sales also available Monday–Friday, 9am–4pm.
Pinot Noir, Pinot Gris, Chardonnay, White Riesling.

From Beaverton, take Highway 217 south to Highway 210, then go west 4½ miles to Vandermost Road which leads to Winery Road.

Rex Hill Vineyards
30835 N Highway 99W, Newberg, OR
(503) 538-0666
April–December: daily, 11am–5pm.
February–March: Friday–Sunday, 11am–5pm.
Pinot Noir, Chardonnay, Pinot Gris, White Riesling.

On Highway 99W, 5½ miles from Tigard and 1.4 miles from Newberg.

St. Josef's Wine Cellars
28836 S Barlow Road, Canby, OR
(503) 651-3190
May–October: daily, 11am–5pm.
November–April: Saturday–Sunday, 11am–5pm.

From I-5, take Woodburn exit to Highway 221. Go east on 221 to Barlow Road.

Salishan Vineyards
35011 N Fork Road, La Center, WA
(206) 263-2713
May–December: Saturday–Sunday, 1pm–5pm.

Pinot Noir, Chardonnay, Cabernet Sauvignon, Chenin Blanc, Riesling.

One mile north of La Center—take Aspen Road.

Shafer Vineyard Cellars
Forest Grove, OR
(503) 357-6604
June–September: daily, noon–5pm.
October–May: Saturday–Sunday, noon–5pm.

Chardonnay, White Riesling, Pinot Noir, Pinot Noir Blanc, Gewürztraminer, and Sauvignon Blanc.

Off Highway 8, 4½ miles west of Forest Grove.

Sokol Blosser Winery
500 Sokol Blosser Lane, Dundee, OR
(503) 864-2282
May–October: daily, 10:30am–5:30pm.
November–April: daily, 11am–5pm.

Chardonnay, Pinot Noir, White Riesling, Gewürz-traminer, Müller-Thurgau.

Just west of Dundee off Highway 99W; go north on Sokol Blosser Lane.

Tualatin Vineyards
Forest Grove, OR
(503) 357-5005
February–December: Monday–Friday, 10am–4pm; Saturday–Sunday, noon–5pm.

White Riesling, Gewürztraminer, Chardonnay, Pinot Noir.

Thirty minutes west of Portland on the way to the Oregon Coast. Follow the blue signs west on Highway 26, then Highway 6.

Veritas Vineyard
31190 NE Veritas Lane, Newberg, OR
(503) 538-1470
June–October: daily, 11am–5pm.
November–mid-December, March–May:
Friday–Sunday, 11am–5pm.

Pinot Noir, Chardonnay, Riesling, Pinot Gris, Müller-Thurgau.

Twenty miles west of Portland; take Highway 99W to Corral Creek Road. Veritas Lane is off Coral Creek.

Yamhill Valley Vineyards
16250 Oldsville Road, McMinnville, OR
(503) 843-3100
May–Thanksgiving: daily, 11am–5pm.
March–April: Saturday–Sunday, 11am–5pm.

Pinot Noir, Chardonnay, Riesling, Pinot Gris.

From Highway 99W take Highway 18 west ½ mile to Oldsville Road.

REGION 5
THE WILLAMETTE VALLEY AND
CENTRAL OREGON COAST

Airlie Winery
15305 Dunn Forest Road, Monmouth, OR
(503) 838-6013
March–December: Saturday–Sunday, noon–5pm.

Pinot Noir, Chardonnay, Marechal Foch, Müller-Thurgau, Riesling, Gewürztraminer, and late-harvest Gewürztraminer.

From Highway 99W just north of Corvallis, take Airlie Road west to the town of Airlie and head south to Dunn Forest Road.

Alpine Vineyards
25904 Green Peak Road, Alpine, OR
(503) 424-5851
Mid-June–mid-September: daily, noon–5pm.
Mid-September–December, February–mid-June: Saturday–Sunday, noon–5pm.

Chardonnay, Pinot Noir, Riesling, Gewürztraminer, Cabernet Sauvignon, and White Cabernet.

From Highway 99W just north of Monroe, go east on Alpine Road 5½ miles to Green Peak Road.

Bellfountain Cellars
25041 Llewllyn Road, Corvallis, OR
(503) 929-3162
April–November: Saturday–Sunday, 11am–6pm; the rest of the year by appointment.

Pinot, Cabernet, Chardonnay, Sauvignon Blanc, dry Riesling, and Gewürztraminer.

Take the Corvallis exit from either I-5 or Highway 99W and continue east on Highway 20. At Philomath, go south on Fern Road, then west on Llewllyn Road.

Bethel Heights Vineyard

6060 Bethel Heights Road NW, Salem, OR
(503) 581-2262
March–December: Tuesday–Sunday, 11am–5pm.

Estate-bottled Pinot Noir, Chardonnay, Chenin Blanc, Riesling, Gewürztraminer, and limited Cabernet Sauvignon.

From Highway 99W go east on Zena Road just south of Amity; after 3.3 miles go north on Bethel Heights Road NW.

Broadley Vineyards

265 S 5th, Monroe, OR
(503) 847-5934
Year-round: Tuesday–Sunday, 11am–5pm.

Pinot Noir.

On the banks of the Long Tom River on Highway 99W in Monroe.

Callahan Ridge Winery

340 Busenbark Lane, Roseburg, OR
(503) 673-7901
April–October: daily, 11:30–5pm.

Three miles west of Roseburg; take Garden Valley, then Melrose Road to Busenbark Lane.

Ellendale Winery

Highway 99W at Rickreall Road, Rickreall, OR
(503) 623-6835 or -5617
April–October: daily, 10am–6pm.
November–March: Monday–Saturday, 10am–6pm; Sunday, noon–5pm.

"Crystal Mist" sparkling wine, Pinot Noir, Chardonnay, White Riesling, Gewürztraminer, and Cabernet Franc; Mead (wine from honey), Niagara (a grape native to America), and "Wooly Booger" (a blend of berries and cherries).

The winery is on Highway 99W at Rickreall Road, 10 miles west of Salem. The vineyards are 3 miles west of Dallas.

Eola Hills Wine Cellar

501 S Pacific Highway, Rickreall, OR
(503) 623-2405
June–December: daily, noon–6pm.

Estate-bottled Chardonnay, Pinot Noir, Sauvignon Blanc, Chenin Blanc, and Cabernet Sauvignon.

On Highway 99W just south of Rickreall Road.

Flynn Vineyards

2200 W Pacific Highway, Rickreall, OR
(503) 623-8683
April–September: Tuesday–Sunday, noon–5pm.
October–December, February–May: Saturday–Sunday, noon–5pm and by appointment.

Pinot Noir, Chardonnay, Pinot Noir Blanc, Brut, and Blanc de Blanc.

On Highway 99W, 2 miles north of Highway 22.

Forgeron Vineyard

89697 Sheffler Road, Elmira, OR
(503) 935-1117 or -3530
June–September: daily, noon–5pm.
October–December, February–May: Saturday–Sunday, noon–5pm.

Pinot Noir, Cabernet Sauvignon, Chardonnay, White Riesling, Pinot Gris.

Take Highway 126 exit off I-5 and go west to Territorial Road. Go north on Territorial to Warthern, then west to Sheffler.

Girardet Wine Cellars

895 Reston Road, Roseburg, OR
(503) 679-7252
May–September: daily, noon–5pm.
October–mid-December, February–April: Saturday, noon–5pm.

Riesling, Chardonnay, Sauvignon Blanc, Pinot Noir, Cabernet Sauvignon.

Take I-5 to Highway 42, and Highway 42 west to Reston Road.

Henry Estate Winery

687 Hubbard Creek Road, Umpqua, OR
(503) 459-5120 or -3614
Year-round: daily, 11am–5pm.

Gewürztraminer, Chardonnay, Pinot Noir, Pinot Noir Blanc, Cabernet Sauvingon, Riesling.

*Take the Sutherlin exit off I-5 and go west to
Umpqua on Highway 9. Highway 9 becomes
Hubbard Creek Road.*

Hillcrest Vineyard
240 Vineyard Lane, Roseburg, OR
(503) 673-3709
Year-round: daily, 11am–5pm.

Cabernet Sauvignon and late-harvest Riesling.

*From Roseburg, take Garden Valley Boulevard
west to Melrose Road; where Melrose curves
south, look for Doerner Road. From Doerner,
go north on Elgarose Road, which leads to Vineyard Lane.*

Hinman Vineyards
27012 Briggs Hill Road, Eugene, OR
(503) 345-1945
Year-round (except from Christmas Eve to New
Year's Day): daily, noon–5pm.

*From I-5 take Highway 126 west through Eugene
to Bertlesen Road. Go 5 miles to the Lorane
Highway, then go west on Lorane Highway 2½
miles to Briggs Hill Road. The vineyards are 3½
miles down Briggs Hill Road.*

Honeywood Winery
1350 Hines Street SE, Salem, OR
(503) 362-4111 or (800) 726-4101
Year-round: Monday–Friday, 9am–5pm; Saturday,
10am–5pm; Sunday 1pm–5pm.

Pinot Noir, Riesling, Chardonnay, Muscat, fruit
and specialty wines.

*On Hines Street in Salem, off Mission Street. Also
have a tasting room at the Seaside Town Center
in Seaside.*

Lookingglass Winery
6561 Lookingglass Road, Roseburg, OR
(503) 679-8198
June–August: daily, noon–5pm.

Pinot Noir and Cabernet Sauvignon under the
Rizza Cellars label.

*From I-5 take exit 124 to Lookingglass Road.
Take Lookingglass Road west to Cinbar Drive;
winery is on the left.*

Mirassou Winery Inc/Pellier
6785 Spring Valley Road NW, Salem, OR
(503) 371-3001
March–September: Wednesday–Sunday,
11am–5pm.
October–November: Saturday–Sunday,
11am–5pm.

*Nine miles northwest of Salem. Take Bethel
Road east 7 miles from Highway 99W to Spring
Valley Road.*

Oregon Cellars Winery
92989 Templeton Road, Cheshire, OR
(503) 998-1786
June–September (except Labor Day weekend):
Saturday–Sunday, noon–5pm.

Sparkling wines under the Northern Silk label;
Pinot Noir and Chardonnay under the Rainsong
label.

*Take I-5 or Highway 99W to the Belt Line and go
north to Highway 36. Take Highway 36 west
through Cheshire to Goldson Road. Templeton
Road is off Goldson.*

St. Innocent Winery
2701 22nd Street SE, Salem, OR
(503) 378-1526
By appointment and on Memorial and
Thanksgiving day weekends.

Pinot Noir, Chardonnay, and sparkling wine.

On 22nd Street, off McGilchrist Street.

Schwarzenberg Vineyards
11975 Smithfield Road, Dallas, OR
(503) 623-6420
Year-round: Tuesday–Sunday, 11am–5pm.

Chardonnay.

*Take Smithfield Road off Highway 99W for 3½
miles or Highway 22 for 2½ miles.*

Secret House Vineyards Winery
88324 Vineyard Lane, Veneta, OR
(503) 935-3774
May–September: Tuesday–Saturday, noon–6pm.
October–April (except for the last week or so of
the year): Wednesday–Sunday, noon–5pm.

Pinot Noir, Riesling, Chardonnay.

Between Eugene and Florence, 2.4 miles west of Veneta on Highway 126.

Serendipity Cellars Winery
15275 Dunn Forest Road, Monmouth, OR
(503) 838-4284
May–October: Wednesday–Monday, noon–6pm, or by appointment.
November–April: Saturday–Sunday, noon–6pm, or by appointment.

Müller-Thurgau, Chenin Blanc, Chardonnay, Cabernet Sauvignon, Zinfandel, and Marechal Foch.

From Highway 99W (between Monmouth and Corvallis) go west on Airlie Road for 6 miles. At the town of Airlie, go south on Maxfield Creek Road to Dunn Forest Road.

Silver Falls Winery
4972 Cascade Highway SE, Sublimity, OR
(503) 769-9463
June–September: daily, noon–5pm.
October–December, March–May: Saturday–Sunday, noon–5pm, or by appointment.

On the Cascade Highway between Silverton and Stayton; 7 miles from Silver Falls State Park.

Springhill Cellars
2920 NW Scenic Drive, Albany, OR
(503) 928-1009
April–October: Saturday–Sunday, 1pm–5pm.

Pinot Noir, Chardonnay, Riesling.

From Highway 99E at Albany go north on N Albany Road, west on Gibson Hill Road, and north on Scenic Drive.

Tyee Wine Cellars
26335 Greenberry Road, Corvallis, OR
(503) 753-8754
May–October: Saturday–Sunday, noon–5pm.
Thanksgiving Day weekend: Friday–Sunday, noon–5pm.
November–April: by appointment.

Take Highway 99W 7 miles south of Corvallis to the Greenberry Store. Go west 2.3 miles on Greenberry Road.

Willamette Valley Vineyards
8800 Enchanted Way, Turner, OR
(503) 588-9463 or (800) 344-9463
Year-round: daily, 11am–6pm.

Pinot Noir, Chardonnay, Riesling.

Take exit 248 (Sunnyside/Turner) off I-5 and go south of Salem to Enchanted Way, past the Enchanted Forest.

Witness Tree Vineyards
7111 Spring Valley Road NW, Salem, OR
(503) 585-7874
March–December: Saturday–Sunday, noon–5pm.

Chardonnay, Pinot Noir.

Take Highway 22 exit off I-5 and go west to Wallace Road. Go 5.8 miles north to Zena Road, then west to Spring Valley Road.

REGION 6
NORTHERN WASHINGTON

Arbor Crest Cellars
N 4705 Fruithill Road, Spokane, WA
(509) 927-9463
Year-round: daily, noon–5pm

Take I-90 east of downtown Spokane, and cross the Spokane River on Argonne to Upriver Drive; look for signs.

Latah Creek Wine Cellars
E 13030 Indiana Avenue, Spokane, WA
(509) 926-0164
Year-round: Monday–Saturday, 10am–5pm; Sunday, noon–5pm (closes at 4pm during the winter).

Chenin Blanc, Chardonnay, Semillon, Merlot, Cabernet Sauvignon, and a special strawberry and herb Maywine.

From I-90, take Pines Road north to Indiana Avenue.

Livingstone Wines
E 14 Mission, Spokane, WA
(509) 328-5069
Year-round: daily, noon–5pm.

Riesling, Chardonnay, Sauvignon Blanc.

At Mission and Division.

Mountain Dome Winery
Rt. 2, Box 199M, Spokane, WA
(509) 928-2788
By appointment

A cuvée of Pinot Noir and Chardonnay. No tours or tastings at this time.

Call for directions.

Wenatchee Valley Vintners
1111 VanSickle Avenue S, East Wenatchee, WA
(509) 884-8235
Year-round: Saturday–Sunday, noon–6pm.

Chardonnay, Riesling, Gewürztraminer, Sauvignon Blanc, and Merlot.

From Highway 2/97, continue southwest on Highway 28 to Grant Road in Wenatchee. Go east on Grant to Union, south on Union to 10th, and east on 10th to VanSickle.

White Heron Cellars
101 Washington Way N, George, WA
(509) 785-5521
June–September: Wednesday–Sunday,
11am–5pm.
October–May: call ahead.

A dry Riesling ("bone dry"), Pinot Noir, and Chantepierre (a blend of Cabernet and Merlot).

In downtown George.

Worden's Washington Winery
7217 W 45th Avenue, Spokane, WA
(509) 455-7835

Chardonnay, Cabernet, Merlot, Chenin Blanc, Riesling, Gewürztraminer, and others.

From I-90, take exit 276 (5 miles west of Spokane) and follow it south to Thorpe Road. Take a right at Thorpe and follow the road around to the winery.

REGION 7
THE YAKIMA VALLEY AND
NORTH-CENTRAL OREGON

Bonair Winery
500 S Bonair Road, Zillah, WA
(509) 829-6027
Year-round: Thursday–Sunday, 10am–5pm.

Chardonnay, Riesling, Cabernet Sauvignon.

From I-82, take exit 52 to Zillah and take either 5th (which becomes Roza north of Highway 12) or Cheyne to Highland Drive and go east to Bonair Road. Go south on Bonair to the winery.

Charles Hooper Family Winery
196 Spring Creek Road, Husum, WA
(509) 493-2324
April–October: Saturday–Sunday and most weekdays, 11am–6pm.

From Highway 14, go north at Bingen on Highway 141 to Husum. At Husum, turn west on North Fork Spring Creek Road.

Chateau Ste. Michelle
205 W 5th Street, Grandview, WA
(509) 882-3928
Year-round: daily, 10am–4:30pm.

Cabernet Sauvignon, Merlot, among others.

From I-82, take the Highway 12 exit south to Avenue B. Continue south on B to W 5th Street and turn east.

Coventry Vale
Wilgus and Evans Roads, Grandview, WA
(509) 882-4100
By appointment only.

Champagne and others.

From I-82 take exit 75 north to County Line Road, and go east at McCreadie Road. At Wilgus Road go north to Evans Road; winery is on the corner.

Covey Run Vintners
1500 Vintage Road, Zillah, WA
(509) 829-6235
Year-round: Monday–Saturday, 10am–5pm;
Sunday, noon–5pm.

Cabernet, Merlot.

From I-82, take exit 52 to 5th (which becomes Roza north of Highway 12), and go north to Highland Drive. Go east on Highland to Vintage Road and continue north to the winery.

Eaton Hill Winery
530 Gurley Road, Granger, WA
(509) 854-2220
Call for hours.

Riesling, Semillon.

From I-82, take exit 58 to Highway 12 and go north to Gurley Road.

Hood River Vineyards
4693 Westwood Drive, Hood River, WA
(503) 386-3772
March–December: daily, 10am–5pm.

Chardonnay, Pinot Noir, Cabernet Sauvignon, White Riesling, Gewürztraminer, Zinfandel, raspberry and pear wines.

East of Portland off I-84.

Horizon's Edge Winery
4530 E Zillah Drive, Zillah, WA
(509) 829-6401
Year-round: daily, 10am–5pm.

From I-82, take exit 58 north to Highway 12. Go west on Highway 12 to Gurley Road, and go east briefly on Gurley to Thacker. Go north on Thacker to E Zillah Drive.

Hyatt Vineyards
2020 Gilbert Road, Zillah, WA
(509) 829-6333
Year-round: Friday–Sunday, 11am–5pm or by appointment.

Chardonnay, Riesling, Sauvignon Blanc, Merlot.

From I-82, take Cheyne Road to Highland Drive and continue north to Gilbert Road.

Mont Elise Vineyards
315 W Steuben, Bingen, WA
(509) 493-3001
Year-round: daily, noon–5pm.

On Highway 14 in Bingen.

Portteus Winery
5201 Highland Drive, Zillah, WA
(509) 829-6970
Call for hours.

Chardonnay and others.

From I-82 take exit 52 to 5th (which becomes Roza north of Highway 12), and head north to Highland Drive. Go east to the winery.

Staton Hills Winery
71 Gangl Road, Wapato, WA
(509) 877-2112
Year-round: Tuesday–Sunday, 11am–5pm.

From I-82 take exit 40 east to Gangl Road.

Stewart Vineyards
1711 Cherry Hill Road, Granger, WA
(509) 854-1882
Year-round: Monday–Saturday, 10am–5pm; Sunday, noon–5pm.

From I-82, take exit 58 to Highway 223 and head south to Cherry Hill Road.

Thurston Wolfe
27 N Front Street, Yakima, WA
(509) 452-0335 or (509) 965-5642
February–December: Wednesday–Friday, 11am–5:30pm; Saturday, 11am–6pm; Sunday, noon–5pm.

Dessert wines, as well as some unique table wines, such as Lemberger.

Take exit 33 off I-82 to Yakima Avenue. Head west to Front Street and go north one block.

Tucker Cellars
Ray Road, Sunnyside, WA
(509) 837-8701
Year-round: daily, 9am–4:30pm (to 6pm in summer).

Chardonnay, Cabernet Sauvignon, Riesling, Muscat, and others. Fresh fruit and vegetables also available.

From I-82 take Highway 12 exit and go west to Ray Road.

Washington Hills Cellars
111 E Lincoln Avenue, Sunnyside, WA
(509) 839-9463
Year-round: daily, call for hours.

Washington Hills' wines used to be produced by Cascade Estates, but they are now producing their own quality wines—12 varietals and Apex, their premium label.

Take exit 67 off I-82 and go north ½ mile to Lincoln Avenue.

Zillah Oakes Winery
1500 Vintage Road, Zillah, WA
(509) 829-6990
Year-round: Monday–Saturday, 10am–5pm; Sunday, noon–5pm.

Chardonnay, Riesling, Muscat, Maywine, and Zillah Blushed.

From I-82, take exit 52 and go north to the winery.

REGION 8
THE GREAT BASIN

Badger Mountain Vineyards
110 Jurupa, Kennewick, WA
(509) 627-4986

Chardonnay, Cabernet Franc, Riesling. No tasting room.

Barnard Griffin Winery
1707 W 8th Place, Kennewick, WA
(509) 586-6987

The winery isn't open to the public, but their oak-aged wines are available throughout the Northwest.

Biscuit Ridge Winery
Biscuit Ridge Road, Dixie, WA
(509) 529-4986
Year-round: daily, 10am–5:30pm.

Gewürtztraminer, Pinot Noir.

From Highway 12 in Dixie, go south to the winery.

Blackwood Canyon Vintners
Sunset Road, Benton City, WA
(509) 588-6249
Year-round: Saturday–Sunday, 10am–6pm and by appointment.

Chardonnay, Semillon, late-harvest Rieslings.

From I-82, take exit 96 to Highway 224; from 224 turn north onto Sunset Road.

Bookwalter Winery
2708 N Commercial Avenue, Pasco, WA
(509) 547-8571
Year-round: daily, 10am–5pm.

Riesling, Chenin Blanc, Chardonnay, Muscat, Champagne, late-harvest White Riesling, and Cabernet Sauvignon.

From I-182, take Highway 395 north to Hillsboro Road and go south on Commercial.

Chateau Gallant
1355 Gallant Road S, Pasco, WA
(509) 545-9570
Year-round: daily, 2pm–4pm, or by appointment.
Just off I-182 near Burbank.

Chinook Wines
Wine Country Road, Prosser, WA
(509) 786-2725
February–December: Friday–Sunday, noon–5pm or by appointment.

Chardonnay, Sauvignon Blanc, and Merlot.

From I-82 take exit 82 onto Wine Country Road and go east to Wittkopf Road.

Columbia Crest Winery
Highway 221, Paterson, WA
(509) 875-2061
Year-round: daily, 10am–4:30pm.

One mile north of Patterson; take Highway 221 to Columbia Crest Lane.

Gordon Brothers Cellars
531 Levey Road, Pasco, WA
(509) 547-6624
Summer: Saturday–Sunday, 11am–5pm or by appointment.

Chardonnay, Johannisberg Riesling, Sauvignon Blanc, Cabernet

From I-182, take the Kahlotus Highway northeast to Levey Road.

Hinzerling Vineyards
1520 Sheridan Avenue, Prosser, WA
(509) 786-2163
Year-round: daily, 10am–5pm.

Chardonnay, Riesling, Gewürztraminer.

Just north of downtown Prosser, on Sheridan.

The Hogue Cellars
Wine Country Road, Prosser, WA
(509) 786-4557
Year-round: daily, 10am–5pm.

Cabernet Sauvignon, Merlot, and others.

From I-82, take exit 82 to Wine Country Road and go east.

Kiona Vineyards
Sunset Road, Benton City, WA
(509) 588-6716
Year-round: daily, noon–5pm.

Chardonnay, Cabernet, Riesling, and Lemberger, among others.

From I-82 take exit 96 to Highway 224, and go east to Sunset Road.

L'Ecole No. 41
41 Lowden School Road, Lowden, WA
(509) 525-0940
Call for hours.

Chenin Blanc (Walla Voila!) and others.

East of Lowden on Highway 12; take Lowden School Road north.

Leonetti Cellar
1321 School Avenue, Walla Walla, WA
(509) 525-1428
By appointment only, except for the annual open house the weekend after Labor Day.

Cabernet Sauvignon and Merlot.

From Highway 12, go south on Wilbur to Pleasant Street. Go east to School Avenue and go south again.

Oakwood Cellars
Demoss Road, Benton City, WA
(509) 588-5332
Year-round: Wednesday–Friday, 6pm–8pm; Saturday–Sunday, noon–6pm.

Riesling, Chardonnay, Merlot, Cabernet Sauvignon, Rosé.

From I-82, take exit 96 to Highway 224 and go east to DeMoss Road.

Patrick and Paul Vineyards
1554 School Avenue, Walla Walla, WA
(509) 522-1127
Call for appointment.

Cabernet Franc, Cabernet Franc Blanc, Concord dessert wine.

From Highway 12, go south on Wilbur to Alder and east on Alder to School. Head south on School Avenue to the winery.

Pontin del Roza Winery
Hinzerling Road, Prosser, WA
(509) 786-4449
Year-round: daily, 10am–5pm.

Chenin Blanc, Riesling, Chardonnay, Cabernet Sauvignon, among others.

Take exit 80 off I-82 and head north on Gap Road to Johnson or Kingtull Road. Go east on either of these to Hinzerling Road and head north.

Preston Wine Cellars
502 E Vineyard Drive, Pasco, WA
(509) 545-1990
Year-round: daily, 10am–5:30pm.

Take I-182 to Highway 395 just east of Pasco and head north to Vineyard Drive.

Quarry Lake Winery
2520 N Commercial Avenue, Pasco, WA
(509) 547-7307
Year-round: Thursday–Sunday, noon–5pm.

Chardonnay, Riesling, Cabernet Sauvignon, Merlot.

Take I-182 to Highway 395 just east of Pasco and head north to Hillsboro Road. Go east on Hillsboro to Commercial and head south.

Seth Ryan Winery
Sunset Road, Benton City, WA
(509) 588-6780
By appointment only.

Chardonnay, Riesling, Gewürztraminer.

From I-82, take exit 96 to Highway 224; from 224 turn north onto Sunset Road.

Seven Hills Winery

235 E Broadway, Milton-Freewater, OR
(503) 938-7710
By appointment and for special events.

Merlot, Sauvignon Blanc, Cabernet Sauvignon.

From I-84 at Pendleton go north on Highway 11 30 miles to the winery.

Tagaris Winery

1625 W "A" Street, Suite E, Pasco, WA
(509) 547-3590

Chardonnay, Fumé Blanc, Chenin Blanc, Riesling. No tasting room at this time.

On the corner of 17th and A streets.

Waterbrook Winery

McDonald Road, Lowden, WA
(509) 522-1918
Year-round: Wednesday–Saturday, noon–4pm.

Chardonnay, Sauvignon Blanc, Merlot, Cabernet Sauvignon.

From Highway 12 between Pasco and Walla Walla, head south on McDonald Road.

Woodward Canyon Winery

Highway 12, Lowden, WA
(509) 525-4129
Year-round: daily, noon–4pm.

Cabernet Sauvignon and Chardonnay.

Ten miles west of Walla Walla on Highway 12.

Yakima River Winery

N River Road, Prosser, WA
(509) 786-2805
Year-round: daily, 10am–5pm (to 6pm in summer).

Cabernet Sauvignon, Merlot, Pinot Noir, Fumé Blanc, Riesling, and late-harvest wines.

From I-82, take exit 80 and head south on 6th Street to N River Road. Head west to the winery.

REGION 9
SOUTHERN OREGON

Ashland Vineyards

2775 E Main Street, Ashland, OR
(503) 488-0088
April–December: Tuesday–Sunday, 11am–5pm.
February–March: Saturday–Sunday, 11am–5pm.

Cabernet Sauvignon, Merlot, Chardonnay, Sauvignon Blanc, and Müller-Thurgau.

Take exit 14 off I-5 and head north.

Bridgeview Vineyards

4210 Holland Loop Road, Cave Junction, OR
(503) 592-4688
November–April: daily, 11am–4pm.

Pinot Noir, Chardonnay, Riesling, Gewürztraminer, Pinot Gris, Müller-Thurgau, and "Inspiration," an Oregon table wine.

From I-5, take Highway 199 exit. At Cave Junction go east to Holland Loop Road. Wines also available at The Oregon Wine Barrel, 24310 Redwood Highway, Kerby, (503) 592-4698.

Foris Vineyards Winery

654 Kendall Road, Cave Junction, OR
(503) 592-3752
Year-round: daily, noon–5pm.

Pinot Noir, Chardonnay, Gewürztraminer, and early Muscat.

From I-5, take Highway 199 southwest to Cave Junction, then go east on Highway 46 to Holland Loop Road; Holland Loop Road leads to Kendall Road.

Weisinger's of Ashland

3150 Siskiyou Boulevard, Ashland, OR
(503) 488-5989
April–September: Tuesday–Saturday, 11am–6pm; Sunday, 12:30pm–6pm.
October–December, March: Friday–Saturday, 11am–5pm; Sunday, 12:30pm–5pm.
January–February: by appointment.

Cabernet Blanc, Cabernet Sauvignon, Chardonnay, Gewürztraminer, and Mescolare (a blend).

Exit 11 off I-5.

CONTRIBUTING WRITERS

Angela Allen is the food editor for the *Vancouver Columbian.* She lives in Portland, Oregon.

John Bonica runs his own advertising business in Winthrop, Washington. He lives in the Methow Valley.

John Doerper is the food editor for *Pacific Northwest* magazine and has written extensively about Northwest food and farms. He lives in Bellingham, Washington.

Peter Donovan is a writer and editor. He recently moved from Seattle to Enterprise, Oregon.

Eunice Farmilant is a certified organic grower in Olympia, Washington. She is the author of two natural foods cookbooks and also works as a freelance photo editor.

Sue Frause is a features columnist for the *South Whidbey Record.* She lives in Langley, Washington, on Whidbey Island, and raises chickens, turkeys, and cows on three acres.

Gloria Bledsoe Goodman retired recently after 23 years with the Salem, Oregon, *Statesman-Journal.* She is working on her third book.

Hazel Heckman is the sage of Anderson Island and author of *Island in the Sound* and *Island Year.*

Kathy Hogan wrote the "Kitchen Critic," a weekly column for the *Grays Harbor Post,* during World War II.

Margaret Hollenbach is a writer. She recently moved from the San Juan Islands to attend film school in Vancouver, British Columbia.

Schuyler Ingle writes on food for the *Seattle Weekly.* His most recent project is *Vintage Pellegrini,* a collection of essays by Angelo Pellegrini, which he edited. He lives in Seattle.

Mauny Kaseburg is president of a Seattle food and wine public relations and consulting firm. She has developed regional menus for local restaurants and is a food commentator for public radio.

Ann Katzenbach is a teacher, travel writer, and photographer. She lives in Port Townsend, Washington.

Grant McConnell was Professor Emeritus at the University of California at Santa Cruz. Born in Portland, he lived for a number of years in Stehekin, Washington.

Julie McFarlane runs a vineyard for home winemakers in Yakima, Washington.

Don McManman is assistant city editor at the *TriCity Herald* in Kennewick, Washington.

Marnie McPhee is a writer and organic agriculture activist. She lives in Portland, Oregon.

James Mayer is a reporter for the Portland *Oregonian.*

NancyAnn Mayer writes for the "Food Day" section of the Portland *Oregonian.*

Lane Morgan raises beef, poultry, and vegetables in Sumas, Washington. She is the author of *Winter Harvest Cookbook.* She teaches journalism at Western Washington University and often writes about regional food and agriculture.

Michael Page-English lives in Eugene, Oregon. He is a reporter for the Creswell, Oregon, *Chronicle* and a former English instructor at the University of Oregon.

Angelo Pellegrini immigrated to Washington State in 1913. He was Professor Emeritus at the University of Washington and the author of award-winning books on food, wine, and the good life. He died in 1991.

Christina Reid is the owner of Christina's on Orcas Island.

Braiden Rex-Johnson is the author of *Pike Place Market Cookbook.* She lives in Seattle, Washington.

Robert Steelquist works for the Puget Sound Water Quality Authority. He has written several books on Northwest natural history and geology.

Alice Sullivan is coordinator for the Colville Farmers Market. She and her husband have sold their orchard and now concentrate on a half-acre garden in Kettle Falls, Washington. She is active in Citizens for a Clean Columbia, an environmental group.

Cleve Twitchell edits the "Life" and "Tempo" sections of the Medford, Oregon, *Mail Tribune.* He has been writing about food and travel for 30 years.

CREDITS

TEXT

"Curried Red Lentil and Tomato Soup" from *Northwest Palate: Seasons of Great Cooking* by Susan Bradley. Copyright ©1991 by Susan Bradley. Reprinted by permission of Addison-Wesley.

"Crawfish in Apple Cider" from *Eating Well Cookbook* by John Doerper. Copyright ©1984 by John Doerper. Reprinted by permission of the author.

"Pleasant Valley Cheese" and "Crawfish" from *Eating Well: A Guide to Foods of the Pacific Northwest* by John Doerper. Copyright ©1984 by John Doerper. Reprinted by permission of the author.

"Pissaladière Onion and Anchovy Pizza" from *Judie Geise's New Northwest Kitchen* by Judie Geise. Copyright ©1987 by Judie Geise. Reprinted by permission of Madrona Publishing.

"Blueberry-Raspberry Upside-Down Cake" from *Dungeness Crabs and Blueberry Cobblers* by Janie Hibler. Copyright ©1991 by Janie Hibler. Reprinted by permission of Alfred A. Knopf, Inc.

"Catching, Cleaning, Cooking Salmon" from *The Kitchen Critic: Cohassett Beach War Correspondent* by Kathy Hogan. Copyright ©1991 by Klancy de Nevers and Lucy Hart. Reprinted by permission of Klancy de Nevers and Lucy Hart.

"Hood River Fruit Lady" from *Northwest Bounty: The Extraordinary Foods and Wonderful Cooking of the Pacific Northwest* by Schuyler Ingle and Sharon Kramis. Copyright ©1988 by Schuyler Ingle and Sharon Kramis. Reprinted by permission of Simon & Schuster, Inc.

"Japanese Geoduck Soup" first appeared in *The Seattle Times.* Copyright ©1985 by Susan Hermann Loomis. Reprinted by permission of the author.

"Rhubarb Barbecue Sauce" first appeared in *Seattle Weekly.* Copyright ©1987 by Ann Lovejoy. Reprinted by permission of *Seattle Weekly.*

"Pot Roast with Hazelnut Barley" from *Winter Harvest Cookbook: How to Select and Prepare Fresh Seasonal Produce All Winter Long* by Lane Morgan. Copyright ©1990 by Lane Morgan. Reprinted by permission of Sasquatch Books.

"The Magic of Mushrooms," "Lamb," and "Seeing and Eating the Artichoke" from *Vintage Pellegrini: The Collected Wisdom of an American Buongustaio* by Angelo Pellegrini. Copyright ©1991 by Angelo Pellegrini. Reprinted by permission of Sasquatch Books.

"When to Visit the Market" and "Produce Availability Chart" from *Pike Place Market Cookbook: Recipes, Anecdotes, and Personalities from Seattle's Renowned Public Market* by Braiden Rex-Johnson. Copyright ©1992 by Braiden Rex-Johnson. Reprinted by permission of Sasquatch Books.

PHOTOGRAPHS

Front and back cover: Barbara F. Gundle and Gregory J. Lawler/Small Planet Photography, Portland, Oregon

3   Nick Gunderson, *Seattle Weekly*
4   Kim Zumwalt, *Seattle Weekly*
16 Mike Urban, *Seattle Weekly*
35 Lisa Stone, *Seattle Weekly*
40 Spencer Johnson
43 Kim Zumwalt, *Seattle Weekly*
52 Kim Zumwalt, *Seattle Weekly*
70 Nick Gunderson, *Seattle Weekly*
77 Nick Gunderson, *Seattle Weekly*
84 Special Collections, University of Washington Libraries, negative #UW5785
90 *Seattle Weekly*
94 Asahel Curtis, Special Collections, University of Washington Libraries, negative #19971
99 Ron Holden, *Seattle Weekly*
103 Kim Zumwalt, *Seattle Weekly*
114 Spencer Johnson
133 Nick Gunderson, *Seattle Weekly*
135 Lisa Stone, *Seattle Weekly*
141 Don Wallen, *Seattle Weekly*
160 Nick Gunderson, *Seattle Weekly*
164 Kim Zumwalt, *Seattle Weekly*
171 Gregory J. Lawler/Small Planet Photography
172 Barbara F. Gundle/Small Planet Photography
175 Scott Spiker, courtesy of USA Dry Pea and Lentil Council
197 Don Wallen, *Seattle Weekly*
201 Barbara F. Gundle/Small Planet Photography
205 Lisa Stone, *Seattle Weekly*
210 Alex Orth, courtesy of Merz Orchards, Parkdale, Oregon
219 Gregory J. Lawler/Small Planet Photography
221 Nick Gunderson, *Seattle Weekly*
238 Nick Gunderson, *Seattle Weekly*
246 Courtesy of the Oregon Department of Agriculture
255 Spencer Johnson

INDEX

THE GOOD FOOD GUIDE REPORT FORM

Every effort has been made to list all of the producers of fresh regional foods in Washington and Oregon. Some farms asked not to be listed because they sell everything they raise to their regular customers and cannot handle additional sales at this time. But we may have missed one of your favorites. Please let us know about your preferred farmer, fish outlet, cheesemaker, farmers market, etc.

_____

_____

_____

_____

_____

_____

(Include addresses and phone numbers if possible.)

Please print your name and address so that we can inform you of updates to this book:

Name:_____

Address:_____

_____

Send to:
Good Food Guide
c/o Sasquatch Books
1931 Second Avenue
Seattle, WA 98101

Did you enjoy this book?

Sasquatch Books publishes books and guides related to the Pacific Northwest. Our books are available at bookstores and other retail outlets throughout the region. Here is a partial list of our current cookbooks, gardening titles, and guidebooks:

COOKBOOKS AND FOOD LITERATURE

Breakfast in Bed
The Best B&B Recipes from Northern California, Oregon, Washington, and British Columbia
Carol Frieberg

Eight Items or Less Cookbook
Fine Food in a Hurry
Ann Lovejoy

The Good Food Guide to Washington and Oregon
Discover the Finest, Freshest Foods Grown and Harvested in the Northwest
Edited by Lane Morgan

Pike Place Market Cookbook
Recipes, Anecdotes, and Personalities from Seattle's Renowned Public Market
Braiden Rex-Johnson

Seasonal Favorites from The Herbfarm
A Giftbook Collection
Ron Zimmerman and Jerry Traunfeld

The Territorial Seed Company Garden Cookbook
Homegrown Recipes for Every Season
Edited by Lane Morgan

Vintage Pellegrini
The Collected Wisdom of an American Buongustaio
Angelo Pellegrini, edited by Schuyler Ingle

Winter Harvest Cookbook
How to Select and Prepare Fresh Seasonal Produce All Winter Long
Lane Morgan

GARDENING

The Border in Bloom
A Northwest Garden Through the Seasons
Ann Lovejoy

Gardening Under Cover
A Northwest Guide to Solar Greenhouses, Cold Frames, and Cloches
William Head

Growing Vegetables West of the Cascades
Steve Solomon's Complete Guide to Natural Gardening
Steve Solomon, 3rd edition

Three Years in Bloom
A Garden-Keeper's Journal
Introduction by Ann Lovejoy

Trees of Seattle
The Complete Tree-finder's Guide to the City's 740 Varieties
Arthur Lee Jacobson

Winter Gardening in the Maritime Northwest
Cool Season Crops for the Year-Round Gardener
Binda Colebrook, 3rd edition

The Year in Bloom
Gardening for All Seasons in the Pacific Northwest
Ann Lovejoy

TRAVEL

Back Roads of Washington
74 Trips on Washington's Scenic Byways
Earl Thollander

Northwest Cheap Sleeps
Mountain Motels, Island Cabins, Ski Bunks, Beach Cottages, and Hundreds of Penny-pinching Travel Ideas for the Adventurous Road-tripper
Stephanie Irving

Northwest Best Places
Restaurants, Lodgings, and Touring in Oregon, Washington, and British Columbia
David Brewster and Stephanie Irving

Portland Best Places
A Discriminating Guide to Portland's Restaurants, Lodgings, Shopping, Nightlife, Arts, Sights, Outings, and Annual Events
Stephanie Irving

Seattle Best Places
The Most Discriminating Guide to Seattle's Restaurants, Shops, Hotels, Nightlife, Sights, Outings, and Annual Events
David Brewster and Stephanie Irving

Seattle Cheap Eats
300 Terrific Bargain Eateries
Kathryn Robinson and Stephanie Irving

Sasquatch books are available at bookstores throughout the Pacific Northwest. To receive a Sasquatch Books catalog, or to inquire about ordering our books by phone or mail, please contact us at the address below.

SASQUATCH BOOKS
1931 Second Avenue • Seattle, WA 98101 • (206) 441-5555